Praise for the first edition:
"A Practitioner's Guide to Asset Allocation"

"Asset allocation is the most important yet challenging decision faced by every investor. By masterfully bridging theory and practice, Kinlaw, Kritzman, and Turkington have produced a modern guide to the topic that will be useful to practitioners and scholars alike."

—**Robin Greenwood**, George Gund Professor
of Finance and Banking, Harvard Business School

"*A Practitioner's Guide to Asset Allocation* is an exceptionally comprehensive treatise on the subject, as can be seen from just a sampling of the chapter headings— Fallacies (of which there are many), Time Diversification (not as easy as it may seem), Factors (points out some issues with this current hot trend), Illiquidity (what does it really cost), Risks (not just *at*-horizon, but also *within*- and *beyond*-horizon), and perhaps most important of all, Regime Shifts. This book has a lot to say, and a page-by-page read may be a bit much for the typical 'Practitioner,' but the authors provide a very readable chapter of Takeaways that should perhaps be the first point of entry. But even these more compact Takeaways are full of fresh insights into this truly important topic that is all too often given too short a shrift."

—**Martin L. Leibowitz, PhD,**
Vice Chairman – Research, Morgan Stanley

"Kinlaw, Kritzman, and Turkington have a long history of discovering and very clearly describing surprising and useful investment results. This book continues that tradition by correcting several common myths about asset allocation and presenting the latest thinking about this fundamental issue. All investors who practice asset allocation for a living will benefit from reading this."

—**Ronald N. Kahn,** Global Head
of Scientific Equity Research, BlackRock

"One of the best books ever written on applied research for asset allocation. This outstanding effort provides the missing link between academic research and practice. With remarkable clarity, the authors explain how to put risk at the center of portfolio construction. Speaking from experience advising some of the largest pools of assets in the world, they bring the practice and science of risk-based investing to a whole new level, and challenge conventional wisdom along the way. Everyone involved in asset allocation should read this book, including CIOs, quants, non-quants, academics, consultants, portfolio managers, advisors, individual investors, and plan sponsors. It will become a reference for the next wave of innovation in our industry. Bravo!"

—**Sébastien Page, CFA,** Head of Asset Allocation, T. Rowe Price; author, *Beyond Diversification: What Every Investor Needs to Know About Asset Allocation*

"Everything you ever wanted and need to know about asset allocation but were afraid to ask, written by three accomplished practitioners who put their money where their mouths are."

—**Andrew W. Lo,** Charles E. and
Susan T. Harris Professor, MIT Sloan School of Management

Asset Allocation

From Theory to Practice and Beyond

WILLIAM KINLAW
MARK KRITZMAN
DAVID TURKINGTON

WILEY

Published by John Wiley & Sons, Inc., Hoboken, New Jersey.
Published simultaneously in Canada.

For general information on our other products and services or for technical support, please contact our Customer Care Department within the United States at (800) 762-2974, outside the United States at (317) 572-3993, or fax (317) 572-4002.

Wiley publishes in a variety of print and electronic formats and by print-on-demand. Some material included with standard print versions of this book may not be included in e-books or in print-on-demand. If this book refers to media such as a CD or DVD that is not included in the version you purchased, you may download this material at http://booksupport.wiley.com. For more information about Wiley products, visit www.wiley.com.

Library of Congress Cataloging-in-Publication Data is Available:

9781119817710 (hardback)
9781119817734 (epdf)
9781119817727 (epub)

Cover design: Wiley
Cover Image: © Kentoh/Getty Images
SKY10027664_062121

Contents

CHAPTER 25
Statistical and Theoretical Concepts   **272**

Foreword to the First Edition

A Practitioner's Guide to Asset Allocation by William Kinlaw, Mark Kritzman, and David Turkington speaks to the "forgotten man" of our field: he or she who interacts with the client and delivers professional investment advice. They are the foot soldiers of our field. Our field has an abundance of articles by academics trying to persuade other academics as to how practitioners should advise clients; articles written by academics for "quantitative" practitioners, who are actually academics, usually employed by large institutional investors, either as window dressing, or to build systems to replace "nonquantitative" academics; textbooks trying to educate students as to how they too can write academic articles – enough of them to achieve tenure – on how practitioners should practice; and, now and then, books written by academics for practitioners on "what every academic knows and I'll try to explain to you." But there are remarkably few well-written books or articles, by learned scholars, for practitioners, without calculus, on controversial topics of practical importance, on which the scholar has published strong views.

The Kinlaw, Kritzman, and Turkington "Guide" fills this void. Specifically, among its 16 chapters for practitioners (plus an "Addendum" with chapters on statistical concepts and a glossary of terms) is a discussion of why it is *not* true that the Markowitz optimization procedure maximizes rather than minimizes risk for given return, and why the investment practitioner's clients would *not* be better served by the practitioner recommending an equal weighted portfolio rather than going through the demanding modern portfolio theory (MPT) process.

This guide should be of interest to practitioners; scholars who seek to develop or evaluate techniques that can be of practical value in practitioners' hands; academics who would like to create, explore, or evaluate, empirically or theoretically, relationships that can guide the development of such techniques; investors (especially institutional investors) who must evaluate alternative current or potential advisors; and broadly read non-finance readers who enjoy a good intellectual fight.

Harry Markowitz,
Nobel Prize Recipient, 1990, Economic Sciences;
President, Harry Markowitz Company

Preface

Harry Markowitz published his landmark article on portfolio selection more than 60 years ago. This groundbreaking theory empowered generations of academics and practitioners to pursue asset allocation with rigor. Many have made great strides to extend and enhance the application of portfolio theory. And yet, despite all this progress, few would argue that allocating assets effectively is an easy task today. As in many areas of scientific development, progress has been uneven. It has been punctuated with instances of misleading research, which has contributed to the stubborn persistence of certain fallacies about asset allocation. In addition, new markets, technologies, and economic realities continue to present opportunities as well as challenges. Our goal in writing this book is twofold: to describe several important innovations that address key challenges to asset allocation and to dispel certain fallacies about asset allocation.

This book contains the 16 chapters from our 2017 book *A Practitioner's Guide to Asset Allocation*, plus 8 additional chapters on topics that have come into sharp focus in recent years. The core tenets of asset allocation do not change over time, but new themes emerge. Designing portfolios and strategies to hedge against downside loss is an important theme today. We include new chapters on the divergence of long-run risk from short-term risk (Chapter 5), the asymmetry of correlations during market gains and losses (Chapter 6), the need for more dynamic asset allocation (Chapter 10), and how to forecast the correlation between stocks and bonds (Chapter 14). Another hot topic is factor investing. We add a new chapter on asset allocation and factor investing, including a way to get the best of both worlds (Chapter 16). As a third theme, we have noticed that many investors benefit from qualitative judgment and debate but struggle to marry these techniques with quantitative analysis. We include new models for forecasting (Chapter 13) and scenario analysis (Chapter 23) that can improve the rigor and effectiveness of traditional quantitative techniques while offering easy interpretation to complement judgment and debate. We also expand our discussion of illiquid alternative assets to address specific challenges associated with measuring the true risk exposure of private equity (Chapter 11). The topics and methodologies introduced in other chapters remain as relevant today as they were in 2017.

We have made two enhancements to this edition to help readers navigate the content more efficiently. First, there are a number of common threads in this book that link the chapters, both new and old, together. To highlight these linkages, we now include references to related topics at the end of each chapter so that readers can explore their particular interests efficiently. Second, we now begin the book with a summary of key takeaways from each of the chapters. Readers can peruse these takeaways and then decide which chapters are of particular interest. Of course, we hope that readers will find all the chapters interesting.

We divide the rest of the book into four sections. Section I covers the fundamentals of asset allocation, including a discussion of the attributes that qualify a group of securities as an asset class, as well as a detailed description of the conventional application of mean-variance analysis to asset allocation. In describing the conventional approach to asset allocation, we include an illustrative example that serves as a base case, which we use to demonstrate the impact of the innovations we describe in subsequent chapters.

Section II presents certain fallacies about asset allocation, which we attempt to dispel either by logic or with evidence. These fallacies include the notion that asset allocation determines more than 90% of investment performance, that time diversifies risk, that risk parameters are stable across return intervals, that correlations are symmetric, that optimization is hyper-sensitive to estimation error, that factors provide greater diversification than assets and are more effective at reducing noise, that equally weighted portfolios perform more reliably out-of-sample than optimized portfolios, that policy portfolios matter, and that the volatility of private equity is greater than that of public equity due to private equity's higher leverage.

Section III describes several innovations that address key challenges to asset allocation. We present an alternative optimization procedure to address the challenge that some investors have complex preferences and returns may not be elliptically distributed. We introduce a new forecasting technique that exploits information about the relevance of historical observations. We apply advances in quantitative methods to forecast the stock–bond correlation. We show how to overcome inefficiencies that result from constraints by augmenting the optimization objective function to incorporate absolute and relative goals simultaneously. We describe how to integrate asset allocation with factor investing. We demonstrate how to use shadow assets and liabilities to unify liquidity with expected return and risk. And we address the challenge of currency risk by presenting a cost/benefit analysis of several linear and nonlinear currency-hedging strategies.

We show how to reduce estimation error in covariances by introducing a nonparametric procedure for incorporating the relative stability of covariances directly into the asset allocation process. We address the challenge of choosing between leverage and concentration to raise expected return by relaxing the simplifying assumptions that support the theoretical arguments. We describe a dynamic programming algorithm as well as a quadratic heuristic to determine a portfolio's optimal rebalancing schedule. We address the challenge of regime shifts with several innovations, including stability-adjusted optimization, blended covariances, and regime indicators. We introduce a mathematically rigorous and empirically driven approach for carrying out scenario analysis. Finally, we show how to evaluate alternative asset mixes by assessing exposure to loss throughout the investment horizon based on regime-dependent risk.

Section IV provides supplementary material, including an expanded chapter on relevant statistical and theoretical concepts as well as a comprehensive glossary of terms.

This book is not an all-inclusive treatment of asset allocation. There are certainly some innovations that are not known to us, and there are other topics that we do not cover because they are well described elsewhere. The topics that we choose to write about are ones that we believe to be especially important, yet not well known nor understood. We hope that readers will benefit from our efforts to convey this material, and we sincerely welcome feedback, be it favorable or not.

Some of the ideas in this book originally appeared in journal articles that we coauthored with past and current colleagues. We would like to acknowledge the contributions of Nelson Aruda, Alain Bergeron, Wei Chen, George Chow, David Chua, Paula Cocoma, Eric Jacquier, Ding Li, Kenneth Lowry, Simon Myrgren, Sébastien Page, Baykan Pamir, Grace (Tiantian) Qiu, Don Rich, and Gleb Sivitsky. And we would like to express special gratitude to Megan Czasonis, who coauthored many of the articles that underpin much of this book's content and who has contributed importantly to shaping our views and understanding of asset allocation.

In addition, we have benefited enormously from the wisdom and valuable guidance, both directly and indirectly, from a host of friends and scholars, including Peter Bernstein, Stephen Brown, John Campbell, Edwin Elton, Frank Fabozzi, Gifford Fong, Martin Gruber, Martin Leibowitz, Andrew Lo, Harry Markowitz, Robert C. Merton, Krishna Ramaswamy, Stephen Ross, Paul A. Samuelson, William Sharpe, and Jack Treynor. Obviously, we accept sole responsibility for any errors.

Finally, we would like to thank our wives, Michelle Kinlaw, Abigail Turkington, and Elizabeth Gorman, for their support of this project as well as their support in more important ways.

William Kinlaw
Mark Kritzman
David Turkington

Key Takeaways

Chapter 1: What Is an Asset Class?

- The composition of an asset class should be stable.

- The components of an asset class should be directly investable.

- The components of an asset class should be similar to each other.

- An asset class should be dissimilar from other asset classes in the portfolio as well as combinations of other asset classes.

- The addition of an asset class to a portfolio should raise its expected utility.

- An asset class should not require selection skill to identify managers within the asset class.

- An asset class should have the capacity to absorb a meaningful fraction of a portfolio cost-effectively.

Chapter 2: Fundamentals of Asset Allocation

- A portfolio's expected return is the weighted average of the expected returns of the asset classes within it.

- Expected return is measured as the arithmetic average, not the geometric average.

- A portfolio's risk is measured as the variance of returns or its square root, the standard deviation.

- Portfolio risk must account for how asset classes co-vary with one another.

- Portfolio risk is less than the weighted average of the variances or standard deviations of the asset classes within it.

- Diversification cannot eliminate portfolio variance entirely. It can only reduce it to the average covariance of the asset classes within it.

- The efficient frontier comprises portfolios that offer the highest expected return for a given level of risk.

- The optimal portfolio balances an investor's goal to increase wealth with the investor's aversion to risk.

- Mean-variance analysis is an optimization process that identifies efficient portfolios. It is remarkably robust. For a given time horizon or assuming returns are expressed in continuous units, it delivers the correct result if returns are approximately elliptically distributed, which holds for return distributions that are not skewed, have stable correlations, and comprise asset classes with relatively uniform kurtosis, or if investor preferences are well described by mean and variance.

Chapter 3: The Importance of Asset Allocation

- It is commonly assumed that asset allocation explains more than 90% of investment performance.

- This belief is based on flawed analysis by Brinson, Hood, and Beebower.

- The analysis is flawed because it implicitly assumes that the default portfolio is not invested; it thereby fails to distinguish between the risk driven by asset allocation decisions and the risk driven by the fundamental decision to invest in the first place.

- Also, this study, as well as many others, analyzes actual investment choices rather than investment opportunity. By analyzing actual investment choices, these analyses confound the natural importance of an investment activity with an investor's choice to emphasize that activity.

- Bootstrap simulation of the potential range of outcomes associated with asset allocation and security selection reveals that security selection has as much or more potential to affect investment performance as asset allocation does.

- It does not necessarily follow, though, that investors should devote more resources to security selection than asset allocation, because, as argued by Paul Samuelson, it is easier to be successful at asset allocation than security selection.

- Asset allocation is very important, but not for the reasons put forth by Brinson, Hood, and Beebower.

Chapter 4: Time Diversification

- It is widely assumed that investing over long horizons is less risky than investing over short horizons, because the likelihood of loss is lower over long horizons.

- Paul A. Samuelson showed that time does not diversify risk because, though the probability of loss decreases with time, the magnitude of potential losses increases with time.

- It is also true that the probability of loss *within* an investment horizon never decreases with time.

- Finally, the cost of a protective put option increases with time to expiration. Therefore, because it costs more to insure against losses over longer periods than shorter periods, it follows that risk does not diminish with time.

Chapter 5: Divergence

- Investors commonly assume that standard deviations of asset returns scale with the square root of time and that correlations of returns between assets are invariant to the return interval from which they are estimated.

- Both beliefs rest on the same underlying assumption that returns are serially independent from one period to the next.

- However, this assumption is empirically false; standard deviations and correlations of longer-interval returns diverge substantially from the standard deviations and correlations estimated from shorter-interval returns.

- Investors usually attribute this divergence to non-normality of the returns, but instead it is usually driven by nonzero lagged autocorrelations and cross-correlations.

- The divergence of high- and low-frequency estimates of standard deviations and correlations has important implications for portfolio construction, performance measurement, and risk management.

Chapter 6: Correlation Asymmetry

- Investors mistakenly believe that diversification is unconditionally beneficial because they implicitly assume that correlations are symmetric.

- The evidence shows, however, that correlations differ significantly depending on the size and direction of returns.

- Investors should seek diversification when their portfolios' main growth component is performing poorly and unification when their portfolios' main growth component is performing well.

- Unfortunately, most asset class pairs exhibit unfavorable correlation profiles characterized by unification on the downside, when it is not wanted, and diversification on the upside, when it is not needed.

- Investors can employ full-scale optimization, which is introduced in Chapter 12, to construct portfolios that account implicitly for asymmetric correlations.

Chapter 7: Error Maximization

- Some investors believe that optimization is hypersensitive to estimation error because, by construction, optimization overweights asset classes for which expected return is overestimated and risk is underestimated, and it underweights asset classes for which the opposite is true.

- We argue that optimization is not hypersensitive to estimation error for reasonably constrained portfolios.

- If asset classes are close substitutes for each other, it is true that their weights are likely to change substantially given small input errors, but because they are close substitutes, the correct and incorrect portfolios will have similar expected returns and risk.

- If asset classes are dissimilar from each other, small input errors will not cause significant changes to the correct allocations; thus, again the correct and incorrect portfolios will have similar expected returns and risk.

- Nevertheless, estimation error is an important challenge to optimization, and investors would be well served to explore ameliorative measures such as Bayesian shrinkage, resampling, and the use of stability-adjusted return distributions.

Chapter 8: Factors

- Some investors believe that factors offer greater potential for diversification than asset classes because they appear less correlated than asset classes.

- Factors appear less correlated only because the portfolio of assets designed to mimic them includes short positions.

- Given the same constraints and the same investable universe, it is mathematically impossible to regroup assets into factors and produce a better efficient frontier.

- Some investors also believe that consolidating a large group of securities into a few factors reduces noise more effectively than consolidating them into a few asset classes.

- Consolidation reduces noise around means, but no more so by using factors than by using asset classes.

- Consolidation does not reduce noise around covariances.

- Our results challenge the notion that investors should use factors as portfolio building blocks.

- Nevertheless, factors can be useful for other reasons. Factor analysis can help investors understand and manage risk, harvest risk premiums, and enhance returns for investors who are skilled at predicting factor behavior. But we should weigh these potential benefits of factor investing against the incremental noise and trading costs associated with factor replication.

Chapter 9: 1/N

- It has been argued that equally weighted portfolios perform better out of sample than optimized portfolios.

- The evidence for this result is misleading because it relies on extrapolation of historical means from short samples to estimate expected return. In some samples, the historical means for riskier assets are lower than the historical means for less risky assets, implying, contrary to reason, that investors are occasionally risk seeking.

- Optimization with plausible estimates of expected return reliably performs better than equal weighting.

- Also, equal weighting limits the investor to a single portfolio, regardless of the investor's risk tolerance, whereas optimization offers a wide array of investment choices.

Chapter 10: Policy Portfolios

- Investors seek to grow wealth and avoid large drawdowns along the way, but these goals conflict with each other.

- A policy portfolio, which prescribes a fixed allocation to a set of asset classes, is intended to balance these conflicting goals.
- However, a policy portfolio is just a means to an end.

- Investors do not care about a specific asset mix, but rather the return distribution they expect it to generate.

■ Unfortunately, a fixed-weight portfolio delivers a highly unstable return distribution that often conflicts with an investor's risk preference.

■ It is preferable to implement a flexible investment policy that delivers a relatively stable return distribution than a rigid policy portfolio that delivers an unstable return distribution.

Chapter 11: The Private Equity Leverage Myth

■ The standard deviation of observed private equity returns is unrealistically low compared to the standard deviation of public equity returns.

■ This apparent low volatility is caused by valuing private equity based on appraisals that are anchored to prior period valuations, which has the effect of smoothing returns.

■ When private equity volatility is estimated from longer-interval returns, which offsets the smoothing effect, private equity volatility is about the same as public equity volatility.

■ Many investors believe that private equity volatility should be much higher than public equity volatility because private equity is more highly levered than public equity.

■ However, not only is there no discernible relationship between leverage and private equity volatility, it does not exist in the public market either.

■ Leverage does not appear to affect private equity volatility because private equity managers tend to invest in companies whose underlying business activities are inherently less risky, which cancels out the leverage effect.

■ The volatility estimated from longer-interval private equity returns is the correct approximation of volatility because it approximates the actual distribution of outcomes realized by private equity investors over longer horizons.

Chapter 12: Necessary Conditions for Mean-Variance Analysis

■ It is a widely held view that the validity of mean-variance analysis requires that investors have quadratic utility and that returns are normally distributed. This view is incorrect.

■ For a given time horizon or assuming returns are expressed in continuous units, mean-variance analysis is precisely equivalent to expected utility maximization if returns are elliptically distributed, of which the normal distribution is a more restrictive special case, or (not "and") if investors have quadratic utility.

- For practical purposes, mean-variance analysis is an excellent approximation to expected utility maximization if returns are approximately elliptically distributed or investor preferences can be well described by mean and variance.

- For intuitive insight into an elliptical distribution, consider a scatter plot of the returns of two asset classes. If the returns are evenly distributed along the boundaries of concentric ellipses that are centered on the average of the return pairs, the distribution is elliptical. This is usually true if the distribution is symmetric, kurtosis is relatively uniform across asset classes, and the correlation of returns is reasonably stable across subsamples.

- For a given elliptical distribution, the relative likelihood of any multivariate return can be determined using only mean and variance.

- Levy and Markowitz have shown using Taylor series approximations that power utility functions, which are always upward sloping, can be well approximated across a wide range of returns using just mean and variance.

- In rare circumstances, in which returns are not elliptical and investors have preferences that cannot be approximated by mean and variance, it may be preferable to employ full-scale optimization to identify the optimal portfolio.

- Full-scale optimization is a numerical process that evaluates a large number of portfolios to identify the optimal portfolio, given a utility function and return sample. For example, full-scale optimization can accommodate a kinked utility function to reflect an investor's strong aversion to losses that exceed a chosen threshold.

Chapter 13: Forecasting

- Asset allocation requires investors to forecast expected returns, standard deviations, and correlations whose values vary over time.

- Long-run averages are poor forecasts because they fail to capture this time variation.

- But extrapolating from a short sample of recent history is ineffective because it introduces noise and assumes a level of persistence that does not reliably occur.

- As an alternative, investors often regress these asset class variables on economic variables to derive forecasts, but this approach may not help because additional variables contribute noise along with information.

- The investor's challenge is to maximize the information content and minimize the noise, thereby generating the most reliable predictions.

- The prediction from a linear regression equation can be equivalently expressed as a weighted average of the past values of the dependent variable in which the weights are the relevance of the past observations of the independent variables.

- Within this context, relevance has a precise mathematical meaning. It is the sum of statistical similarity and informativeness.

- Statistical similarity equals the negative of the Mahalanobis distance of the past values for the independent variables from their current values, and informativeness equals the Mahalanobis distance of the past values of the independent variables from their average values. In other words, prior periods that are more like the current period but different from the historical average are more relevant than those that are not.

- Investors may be able to improve the reliability of their forecasts by filtering historical observations for their relevance and using this mathematical equivalence to produce new forecasts.

Chapter 14: The Stock–Bond Correlation

- Investors rely on the stock–bond correlation to construct optimal portfolios and to assess risk.

- Investors should care less about how stocks and bonds co-move from month to month as they do about their co-movement over the duration of their investment horizon.

- The most common approach to estimating the longer-term correlation of stocks and bonds is to extrapolate the correlation of monthly returns over a prior period. This approach is decidedly unreliable, because the autocorrelations and lagged cross-correlations of stock and bond returns are nonzero.

- As an alternative, investors may consider estimating the stock–bond correlation from longer-horizon returns, but this approach is unreliable because the stock–bond correlation varies over time.

- To address these problems, this chapter introduces the notion of a single-period correlation that measures the extent to which stock and bond returns move synchronously or drift apart over the course of the investment horizon.

- In addition, this chapter introduces several fundamental variables to predict the longer-horizon stock–bond correlation, some of which are expressed as paths rather than as single-period average values.

- This chapter also describes how to filter historical observations for their historical relevance, as discussed more fully in Chapter 13.

- Together, these innovations significantly improve the reliability of the forecast of the stock–bond correlation.

Chapter 15: Constraints

- Investors constrain their allocation to certain asset classes because they do not want to perform poorly when other investors perform well.

- Constraints are inefficient because, of necessity, they are arbitrary.

- Investors can derive more efficient portfolios by expanding the optimization objective function to include aversion to tracking error as well as aversion to absolute risk.

- Mean-variance-tracking error optimization produces an efficient surface in the dimensions of expected return, standard deviation, and tracking error.

- This approach usually delivers a portfolio that is more efficient in three dimensions than the portfolio that is produced by constrained mean-variance analysis.

Chapter 16: Asset Allocation Versus Factor Investing

- Some investors prefer to construct portfolios from asset classes because asset classes are readily observable and directly investable.

- Other investors prefer to allocate to factors because they believe asset classes are defined arbitrarily and do not capture the fundamental determinants of performance as directly as factors do. Also, some factors carry risk premiums that are not directly available from asset classes.

- Investors can have it both ways by continuing to invest in asset classes but augmenting the Markowitz objective function to include a term that penalizes deviation from a desired factor profile.

Chapter 17: Illiquidity

- Investors rely on liquidity to implement tactical asset allocation decisions, to rebalance a portfolio, and to meet demands for cash, among other uses.

- To account for the impact of liquidity, investors should attach a shadow asset to the liquid asset classes in a portfolio that enable them to use liquidity to increase a portfolio's expected utility, and they should attach a shadow liability to illiquid asset classes in a portfolio that prevent them from preserving a portfolio's expected utility.

- These shadow allocations allow investors to address illiquidity within a single unified framework of expected return and risk.

Chapter 18: Currency Risk

- Investors may improve portfolio efficiency by optimally hedging a portfolio's currency exposure.

- Linear hedging strategies use forward or futures contracts to offset currency exposure. They hedge both upside returns and downside returns. They are called linear hedging strategies because the portfolio's returns are a linear function of the hedged currencies' returns.

- Investors can reduce risk more effectively by allowing currency-specific hedging, cross-hedging, and overhedging. These strategies retain exposure to currencies that diversify the portfolio and reduce exposure to currencies that do not.

- Nonlinear hedging strategies use put options to protect a portfolio from downside returns arising from currency exposure while allowing it to benefit from upside currency returns. They are called nonlinear hedging strategies because the portfolio's returns are a nonlinear function of the hedged currencies' returns.

- Nonlinear hedging strategies are more expensive than linear hedging strategies because they preserve the upside potential of currencies.

- A basket option is an option on a portfolio of currencies and therefore provides protection against a collective decline in currencies.

- A portfolio of options offers protection against a decline in any of a portfolio's currencies.

- A basket option is less expensive than a portfolio of options because it offers less protection.

Chapter 19: Estimation Error

- When investors estimate asset class covariances from historical returns, they face three types of estimation error: small-sample error, independent-sample error, and interval error.

- Small-sample error arises because the investor's investment horizon is typically shorter than the historical sample from which covariances are estimated.

- Independent-sample error arises because the investor's investment horizon is independent of history.

- Interval error arises because investors estimate covariances from higher-frequency returns than the return frequency they care about. If returns have nonzero autocorrelations, the standard deviation does not scale with the square root of time. If returns have nonzero autocorrelations or nonzero lagged cross-correlations, correlation is not invariant to the return interval used to measure it.

- Common approaches to controlling estimation error, such as Bayesian shrinkage and resampling, make portfolios less sensitive to estimation error.

- A new approach, called stability-adjusted optimization, assumes that some covariances are reliably more stable than other covariances. It delivers portfolios that rely more on relatively stable covariances and less on relatively unstable covariances.

Chapter 20: Leverage Versus Concentration

- Theory shows that it is more efficient to raise a portfolio's expected return by employing leverage rather than concentrating the portfolio in higher-expected-return asset classes.

- The assumptions that support this theoretical result do not always hold in practice.

- If we collectively allow for asymmetric preferences, nonelliptical returns, and realistic borrowing costs, it may be more efficient to raise expected return by concentrating a portfolio in higher-expected-return asset classes than by using leverage.

- However, if we also assume that an investor has even a modest amount of skill in predicting asset class returns, then leverage is better than concentration even in the presence of asymmetric preferences, nonelliptical distributions, and realistic borrowing costs.

Chapter 21: Rebalancing

- Investors typically rebalance a portfolio whose weights have drifted away from its optimal targets based on the passage of time or distance from the optimal targets.

- Investors should approach rebalancing more rigorously by recognizing that the decision to rebalance or not affects the choices the investor will face in the future.

- Dynamic programming can be used to determine an optimal rebalancing schedule that explicitly balances the cost of transacting with the cost of holding a suboptimal portfolio.

- Unfortunately, dynamic programming can only be applied to portfolios with a few asset classes because it suffers from the curse of dimensionality.

- For portfolios with more than just a few asset classes, investors should use a quadratic heuristic developed by Harry Markowitz and Erik van Dijk, which easily accommodates several hundred assets.

Chapter 22: Regime Shifts

- Rather than characterizing returns as coming from a single, stable regime, it might be more realistic to assume they are generated by disparate regimes such as a calm regime and a turbulent regime.

- Investors may wish to build portfolios that are more resilient to turbulent regimes by employing stability-adjusted optimization, which relies more on relatively stable covariances than on unstable covariances, or by blending the covariances from calm and turbulent subsamples in a way that places greater emphasis on covariances that prevailed during turbulent regimes.

- These approaches produce static portfolios, which still display unstable risk profiles.

- Investors may instead prefer to manage a portfolio's asset mix dynamically, by switching to defensive asset classes during turbulent periods and to aggressive asset classes during calm periods.

- It has been shown that hidden Markov models are effective at distinguishing between calm and turbulent regimes by accounting for the level, volatility, and persistence of the regime characteristics.

Chapter 23: Scenario Analysis

- Scenario analysis requires investors to define prospective economic scenarios, assign probabilities to them, translate the scenarios into expected asset class returns, and identify the most suitable portfolio given all these inputs.

- The greatest challenge to scenario analysis is determining each scenario's probability.

- We can estimate a scenario's probability by measuring its statistical similarity to current economic conditions or normal economic conditions using a statistic called the Mahalanobis distance.

- This framework also allows us to identify the smallest changes in the scenario descriptions that would be required to equate the empirical probabilities with our subjective views.

- We can further enhance scenario analysis by describing scenarios as paths rather than as single-period average outcomes.

Chapter 24: Stress Testing

- Investors typically evaluate exposure to loss based on a portfolio's full-sample distribution of returns at the end of their investment horizon.

- However, investors care about what happens throughout their investment horizon and not just at its conclusion.

- They also recognize that losses are more common when markets are turbulent than when they are calm.

- First passage time probabilities enable investors to estimate probability of loss and value at risk throughout their investment horizon.

- The Mahalanobis distance allows investors to distinguish between calm and turbulent markets.

- Investors can assess risk more realistically by applying first passage time probabilities to the returns that prevailed during turbulent subsamples.

CHAPTER 1

What Is an Asset Class?

Investors have access to a vast array of assets with which to form portfolios, ranging from individual securities to broadly diversified funds. The first order of business is to organize this massive opportunity set into a manageable set of choices. If investors stratify their opportunity set at too granular a level, they will struggle to process the mass of information required to make informed decisions. If, instead, they stratify their opportunity set at a level that is too coarse, they will be unable to diversify risk efficiently. Asset classes serve to balance this trade-off between unwieldy granularity and inefficient aggregation.

In light of this trade-off and other considerations, we propose the following definition of an asset class.

> *An asset class is a stable aggregation of investable units that is internally homogeneous and externally heterogeneous, that when added to a portfolio raises its expected utility without requiring selection skill, and which can be accessed cost-effectively in size.*

This definition captures seven essential characteristics of an asset class. Let us consider each one in detail.

STABLE AGGREGATION

The composition of an asset class should be relatively stable. Otherwise, ascertaining its appropriate composition would require continual monitoring and analysis, and maintaining the appropriate composition would necessitate frequent rebalancing. Both efforts could be prohibitively expensive.

Asset classes whose constituents are weighted according to their relative capitalizations are stable, because when their prices change, their relative capitalizations change proportionately. By contrast, a proposed asset class whose constituents are weighted according to attributes that shift through time, such as momentum, value, or size, may not have a sufficiently stable composition to qualify as an asset class. Sufficiency, of course, is an empirical issue. Momentum is less stable than value, which is less stable than size. Therefore, a group of momentum stocks would likely fail to qualify as an asset class, while stocks within a certain capitalization range might warrant status as an asset class. Value stocks reside somewhere near the center of the stability spectrum and may or may not qualify as an asset class.

Investable

The underlying components of an asset class should be directly investable. If they are not directly investable, such as economic variables, then the investor would need to identify a set of replicating securities that tracks the economic variable. Replication poses two challenges. First, in addition to the uncertainty surrounding the out-of-sample behavior of the economic variable itself, the investor is exposed to the uncertainty of the mapping coefficients that define the association between the economic variable and the replicating securities. Second, because the optimal composition of the replicating securities changes through time, the investor is exposed to additional rebalancing costs.

INTERNALLY HOMOGENEOUS

The components within an asset class should be similar to each other. If they are not, the investor imposes an implicit constraint that two or more distinct groupings within the proposed asset class must be held according to their weights within the asset class. There is nothing to ensure that the weights of distinct groupings within a larger group are efficient. If the proposed asset class is disaggregated into distinct groupings, the investor is free to weight them for maximum efficiency.

Consider, for example, global equities. Domestic equities may behave very differently from foreign equities, and developed market foreign equities may behave differently from emerging market equities. Investors may be able to form a more efficient portfolio by disentangling these equity markets and weighting them based on their respective contributions to a portfolio's expected utility, as opposed to fixing their weights as they appear in a broad global index. Not only might the optimal weights of these components shift relative to each other, but the optimal allocation to equities as a whole might shift up or down relative to the allocation that would occur if they were treated as a unified asset class.

EXTERNALLY HETEROGENEOUS

Each asset class should be sufficiently dissimilar from the other asset classes in a portfolio as well as linear combinations of other asset classes. If the asset classes are too similar to each other, their redundancy will force the investor to expend unnecessary resources analyzing their expected return and risk properties and searching for the most effective way to invest in them.

In Chapter 2, we build portfolios from seven asset classes: US equities, foreign developed market equities, emerging market equities, Treasury bonds, corporate bonds, commodities, and cash equivalents. We considered including intermediate-term bonds as well. However, the lowest possible tracking error of a portfolio composed of these asset classes with intermediate-term bonds is only 1.1%. Intermediate-term bonds are, therefore, redundant. The lowest possible tracking error with commodities, by contrast, is 19.5%; hence, we include commodities in our menu of asset classes. Although there is no generically correct tracking error threshold to determine sufficient independence, within the context of a particular group of potential asset classes the answer is usually apparent.

EXPECTED UTILITY

The addition of an asset class to a portfolio should raise the portfolio's expected utility. This could occur in two ways. First, inclusion of the asset class could increase the portfolio's expected return. Second, its inclusion could lower the portfolio's risk, either because its own risk is low or because it has low correlations with other asset classes in the portfolio.

The expected return and risk properties of an asset class should not be judged only according to their average values across a range of market regimes. A particular asset class such as commodities, for example, might have a relatively low expected return and high risk on average across shifting market regimes, but during periods of high financial turbulence could provide exceptional diversification against financial assets. Given a utility function that exhibits extreme aversion to large losses, which typically occur during periods of financial turbulence, commodities could indeed raise a portfolio's expected utility despite having unexceptional expected return and risk properties on average.

It might occur to you that in order to raise a portfolio's expected utility, an asset class must be externally heterogeneous. This is true. It does not follow, however, that all externally heterogeneous asset classes raise expected utility. An asset class could be externally heterogeneous, but its expected return may be too low or its risk too high to raise a portfolio's expected utility. Therefore, we could have omitted the criterion of external heterogeneity because it is subsumed within the notion of expected utility. Nevertheless, we think it is helpful to address the notion of external heterogeneity explicitly.

SELECTION SKILL

An asset class should not require an asset allocator to be skillful in identifying superior investment managers in order to raise a portfolio's expected utility. An asset class should raise expected utility even if the asset allocator randomly selects investment managers within the asset class or accesses the asset class passively. Not all investors have selection skill, but this limitation should not disqualify them from engaging in asset allocation.

Think about private equity funds, which are actively managed. Early research concluded that only top-quartile private equity funds earned a premium over public equity funds.[1] If this were to be the case going forward, private equity would not qualify as an asset class, because it is doubtful that the average asset allocator could reliably identify top-quartile funds prospectively, much less gain access to them. More recent research, however, shows that private equity funds, on average from 1997 through 2014, outperformed public equity funds by more than 5% annually net of fees.[2] If we expect this level of performance to persist, private equity would qualify as an asset class, because an asset allocator who is unskilled at manager selection could randomly select a group of private equity funds and expect to increase a portfolio's utility.

COST-EFFECTIVE ACCESS

Investors should be able to commit a meaningful fraction of their portfolios to an asset class without paying excessive transaction costs or substantially impairing a portfolio's liquidity. If it is unusually costly to invest in an asset class, the after-cost improvement to expected utility may be insufficient to warrant inclusion of the asset class. And if the addition of the asset class substantially impairs the portfolio's liquidity, it could become too expensive to maintain the portfolio's optimal weights or to meet cash demands, which again would adversely affect expected utility.

Collectibles such as art, rare books, stamps, and wine may qualify as asset classes for private investors whose wealth is limited to millions of dollars and who do not have liquidity constraints, but for institutional investors such as endowment funds, foundations, pension funds, and sovereign wealth funds, these collectibles have inadequate capacity to absorb a meaningful component of the portfolio. This distinction reveals that the defining characteristics of an asset class may vary, not in kind, but in degree depending on an investor's circumstances.

POTENTIAL ASSET CLASSES

We believe the following asset classes satisfy the criteria we proposed, at least in principle, though this list is far from exhaustive.

Cash equivalents	Foreign developed market equities
Commodities	Foreign emerging market equities
Domestic corporate bonds	Foreign real estate
Domestic equities	Infrastructure
Domestic real estate	Private equity
Domestic Treasury bonds	Timber
Foreign bonds	Treasury Inflation Protected Securities (TIPS)

The following groupings are often considered asset classes, but in our judgment fail to qualify for the reasons specified. Obviously, this list is not exhaustive. We chose these groupings as illustrative examples.

Art	Not accessible in size
Global equities	Not internally homogeneous
Hedge funds	Not internally homogeneous and require selection skill
High-yield bonds	Not externally heterogeneous
Inflation	Not directly investable
Intermediate-term bonds	Not externally heterogeneous
Managed futures accounts	Not internally homogeneous and require selection skill
Momentum stocks	Unstable composition

Let's focus on hedge funds for a moment, since many investors treat this category as an asset class. Most hedge funds invest across a variety of asset classes; thus, they are not internally homogeneous. Moreover, they comprise actively managed variants of other asset classes, so they are not externally heterogeneous. Finally, it is unlikely that a random selection of hedge funds will improve a portfolio's expected utility. Rather than treating hedge funds as an asset class, investors should think of them as a management style. The decision to allocate to hedge funds, therefore, should be a second-order decision. After determining the optimal allocation to asset classes, investors should next consider whether it is best to access the asset classes by investing in passively managed vehicles, active separately managed accounts, mutual funds, limited partnerships, or hedge funds.

In the next chapter, we describe the conventional approach to determining the optimal allocation to asset classes.

REFERENCES

Kaplan, S. and Schoar, A. 2005. "Private Equity Performance: Returns, Persistence and Capital Flows," *Journal of Finance*, Vol. 60, No. 4.
Kinlaw, W., Kritzman, M., and Mao, J. 2015. "The Components of Private Equity Performance," *Journal of Alternative Investments*, Vol. 18, No. 2 (Fall).

NOTES

1. See Kaplan and Schoar (2005).
2. See Kinlaw, Kritzman, and Mao (2015).

CHAPTER 2

Fundamentals of Asset Allocation

THE FOUNDATION: PORTFOLIO THEORY

E-V Maxim

Asset allocation is one of the most important and difficult challenges investors face, but thanks to Harry Markowitz, we have an elegant and widely accepted theory to guide us. In his classic article, "Portfolio Selection," Markowitz reasoned that investors should not choose portfolios that maximize expected return, because this criterion by itself ignores the principle of diversification.[1] He proposed that investors should instead consider variances of return, along with expected returns, and choose portfolios that offer the highest expected return for a given level of variance. Markowitz called this rule the E-V maxim.

Expected Return

Markowitz showed that a portfolio's expected return is simply the weighted average of the expected returns of its component asset classes. A portfolio's variance is a more complicated concept, however. It depends on more than just the variances of the component asset classes.

Risk

The variance of an individual asset class is a measure of the dispersion of its returns. It is calculated by squaring the difference between each return in a series and the mean return for the series, and then averaging these squared differences. The square root of the variance (the standard deviation) is usually used in practice because it measures dispersion in the same units in which the underlying return is measured.

   Variance provides a reasonable gauge of the risk of an asset class, but the average of the variances of two asset classes will not necessarily give a good indication of the risk of a portfolio comprising these two asset classes. The portfolio's risk also depends on the extent to which the two asset classes move together – that is, the extent to which their prices react in like fashion to new information.

To quantify co-movement among security returns, Markowitz applied the statistical concept of covariance. The covariance between two asset classes equals the standard deviation of the first times the standard deviation of the second times the correlation between the two.

The correlation, in this context, measures the association between the returns of two asset classes. It ranges in value from 1 to –1. If the returns of one asset class are higher than its average return when the returns of another asset class are higher than its average return, for example, the correlation coefficient will be positive, somewhere between 0 and 1. Alternatively, if the returns of one asset class are lower than its average return when the returns of another asset class are higher than its average return, then the correlation will be negative.

The correlation, by itself, is an inadequate measure of covariance because it measures only the direction and degree of association between the returns of the asset classes. It does not account for the magnitude of variability in the returns of each asset class. Covariance captures magnitude by multiplying the correlation by the standard deviations of the returns of the asset classes.

Consider, for example, the covariance of an asset class with itself. Obviously, the correlation in this case equals 1. The covariance of an asset class with itself thus equals the standard deviation of its returns squared, which is its variance.

Finally, portfolio variance also depends on the weightings of its constituent asset classes – the proportion of a portfolio's wealth invested in each asset class. The variance of a portfolio consisting of two asset classes equals the variance of the first asset class times its weighting squared plus the variance of the second asset class times its weighting squared plus twice the covariance between the asset classes times the weighting of each asset class. The standard deviation of this portfolio equals the square root of the variance.

From this formulation of portfolio risk, Markowitz was able to offer two key insights. First, unless the asset classes in a portfolio are perfectly inversely correlated (that is, have a correlation of –1), it is not possible to eliminate portfolio risk entirely through diversification. If a portfolio is divided equally among its component asset classes, for example, as the number of asset classes in the portfolio increases, the portfolio's variance will tend not toward zero but, rather, toward the average covariance of the component asset classes.

Second, unless all the asset classes in a portfolio are perfectly positively correlated with each other (a correlation of 1), a portfolio's standard deviation will always be less than the weighted average standard deviation of its component asset classes. Consider, for example, a portfolio consisting of two asset classes, both of which have expected returns of 10% and standard deviations of 20% and which are uncorrelated with each other. If we allocate the portfolio equally between these two asset classes, the portfolio's expected return will equal 10%, while its standard deviation will equal 14.1%. The portfolio offers a reduction in risk of nearly 30% relative to investment in either of the two asset classes separately. Moreover, this risk reduction is achieved without sacrificing any expected return.

Efficient Frontier

Markowitz also demonstrated that, for given levels of risk, we can identify particular combinations of asset classes that maximize expected return. He deemed these portfolios "efficient" and referred to a continuum of such portfolios in dimensions of expected return and standard deviation as *the efficient frontier*. According to Markowitz's E-V maxim, investors should choose portfolios located along the efficient frontier. It is almost always the case that there exists some portfolio on the efficient frontier that offers a higher expected return and less risk than the least risky of its component asset classes (assuming the least risky asset class is not completely risk free). However, the portfolio with the highest expected return will always be allocated entirely to the asset class with the highest expected return (assuming no leverage).

The Optimal Portfolio

Though all the portfolios along the efficient frontier are efficient, only one portfolio is most suitable for a particular investor. This portfolio is called the optimal portfolio. The theoretical approach for identifying the optimal portfolio is to specify how many units of expected return an investor is willing to give up to reduce the portfolio's risk by one unit. If, for example, the investor is willing to give up two units of expected return to lower portfolio variance (the squared value of the standard deviation) by one unit, his risk aversion would equal 2. The investor would then draw a line with a slope of 2 and find the point of tangency of this line with the efficient frontier (with risk defined as variance rather than standard deviation). The portfolio located at this point of tangency is theoretically optimal because its risk/return trade-off matches the investor's preference for balancing risk and return.

PRACTICAL IMPLEMENTATION

There are four steps to the practical implementation of portfolio theory. We must first identify eligible asset classes. Second, we need to estimate their expected returns, standard deviations, and correlations. Third, we must isolate the subset of efficient portfolios that offer the highest expected returns for different levels of risk. And fourth, we need to select the specific portfolio that balances our desire to increase wealth with our aversion to losses.

Before we describe these steps in detail, it may be useful to review two conditions upon which the application of portfolio theory depends.

Required Conditions

For a given time horizon or assuming returns are expressed in continuous units, it is a remarkably robust portfolio formation process, assuming that at least one of two conditions prevails: either investor preferences toward return and risk can be well described by just mean and variance, or returns are approximately elliptically distributed.

The objective function for mean-variance analysis is a quadratic function, which many investors find problematic because it implies that at a particular level of wealth investors would prefer less wealth to more wealth. Of course, such a preference is not plausible, but as shown by Levy and Markowitz (1979),[2] mean and variance can be used to approximate a variety of plausible utility functions across a wide range of returns reasonably well. If this condition is satisfied, it does not matter how returns are distributed, because investors care only about mean and variance.

If this condition is not satisfied, however, mean-variance analysis requires returns to be approximately elliptically distributed. The normal distribution is a special case of an elliptical distribution, which is itself a special case of a symmetric distribution. A normal distribution has skewness equal to zero, and its tails conform to a kurtosis level of three.[3] An elliptical distribution, in two dimensions (two asset classes), describes a scatter plot of returns in which the return pairs are evenly distributed along the boundaries of ellipses that are centered on the mean observation of the scatter plot.[4] It therefore has skewness of zero just like a normal distribution, but it may have non-normal kurtosis. The same is true for symmetric distributions more generally, though they also allow for return pairs in a two-dimensional scatter plot to be unevenly distributed along the boundaries of ellipses that are centered on the mean observation of the scatter plot, as long as they are distributed symmetrically. A symmetric distribution that comprises subsamples with substantially different correlations would not be elliptical, for example. The practical meaning of these distinctions is that mean-variance analysis, irrespective of investor preferences, is well suited to return distributions that are not skewed, have correlations that are reasonably stable across subsamples, and have relatively uniform kurtosis across asset classes, but may include a higher number of extreme observations than a normal distribution.

Asset Classes

In Chapter 1, we introduced seven characteristics that define an asset class:[5]

1. The composition of an asset class should be stable.
2. The components of an asset class should be directly investable.
3. The components of an asset class should be similar to each other.
4. An asset class should be dissimilar from other asset classes in the portfolio as well as combinations of the other asset classes.
5. The addition of an asset class to a portfolio should raise its expected utility.
6. An asset class should not require selection skill to identify managers within the asset class.
7. An asset class should have capacity to absorb a meaningful fraction of a portfolio cost-effectively.

For illustrative purposes we begin by considering the following seven asset classes in our asset allocation analysis: domestic equities, foreign developed market equities, emerging market equities, Treasury bonds, US corporate bonds, commodities, and cash equivalents.[6]

Estimating Expected Returns

Before we estimate expected returns, we must decide which definition of expected return we have in mind. If we base our estimate of expected return on historical results, we might assume that the geometric average best represents the expected return. After all, it measures the rate of growth that occurred historically or what should happen prospectively with even odds of a better or worse result. However, it does not measure what we should expect to happen on average over many repetitions; the arithmetic average gives this value. But there is a more practical reason for choosing the arithmetic average instead of the geometric average as our estimate of expected return. The average of the geometric returns of the asset classes within a portfolio does not equal the geometric return of the portfolio, but the average of the arithmetic returns does indeed equal the portfolio's arithmetic return. Because we wish to express the portfolio's return as the weighted average of the returns of the component asset classes, we are forced to define expected return as the arithmetic average.[7] Of course, we are not interested in the arithmetic average of past returns unless we believe that history will repeat itself precisely. We are interested in the arithmetic average of prospective returns.

To estimate expected returns, we start by assuming that markets are fairly priced; therefore, expected returns represent fair compensation for the degree of risk each asset class contributes to a broadly diversified market portfolio. These returns are called equilibrium returns, and we estimate them by first calculating the beta of each asset class with respect to a broad market portfolio. This calculation implicitly reflects the historical standard deviations and correlations of the assets. Next, we estimate the expected return for the market portfolio and the risk-free return. We calculate the equilibrium return of each asset class as the risk-free return plus the product of its beta and the excess return of the market portfolio. Moreover, we can easily adjust the expected return of each asset class to accord with our views about departures from fair value. Suppose we estimate the market's expected return to equal 7.5% and the risk-free return to equal 3.5%. Given these estimates, together with estimates of beta based on monthly returns from January 1976 through December 2015, we derive the equilibrium returns shown in Table 2.1.

TABLE 2.1   Expected Returns

Asset Classes	Equilibrium Returns (%)	Views (%)	Confidence (%)	Expected Returns (%)
US Equities	8.8			8.8
Foreign Developed Market Equities	9.5			9.5
Emerging Market Equities	11.4			11.4
Treasury Bonds	4.1			4.1
US Corporate Bonds	4.9			4.9
Commodities	5.4	7.0	50.0	6.2
Cash Equivalents	3.5			3.5

Assumes 3.5% risk-free return and 4.0% market risk premium.

This approach is straightforward to implement in practice, even with more nuanced assumptions. The current risk-free return is readily observable. There are a variety of methods for estimating the expected return of a diversified market portfolio. For example, we might adjust the historical risk premium to accord with current risk levels and add this adjusted risk premium to the current risk-free return. We may expect some asset classes to produce returns that differ from those that would occur if markets were in equilibrium and perfectly integrated, especially if they are not typically arbitraged against other asset classes. Suppose we expect commodities to return 7.0% and we assign as much confidence to this view as we do to the equilibrium return. We can blend the equilibrium estimate with our view to derive expected return. The final column of Table 2.1 shows the expected returns for each of the asset classes in our analysis.

Estimating Standard Deviations and Correlations

We also need to estimate the standard deviations of the asset classes as well as the correlations between each pair of asset classes. We estimate these values, shown in Table 2.2, from the monthly returns for the period beginning in January 1976 and ending in December 2015.

TABLE 2.2 Standard Deviations and Correlations

Asset Classes	Standard Deviations (%)	Correlations a	b	c	d	e	f
a US Equities	16.6						
b Foreign Developed Market Equities	18.6	0.66					
c Emerging Market Equities	26.6	0.63	0.68				
d Treasury Bonds	5.7	0.10	0.03	−0.02			
e US Corporate Bonds	7.3	0.31	0.24	0.22	0.86		
f Commodities	20.6	0.16	0.29	0.27	−0.07	0.02	
g Cash Equivalents	1.1	0.02	0.02	0.03	0.18	0.09	0.06

Efficient Portfolios

With this information, we use optimization to combine asset classes efficiently, so that for a given level of expected return the efficiently combined asset classes offer the lowest level of risk, measured as the standard deviation.

A continuum of these portfolios plotted in dimensions of expected return and standard deviation is called the efficient frontier, as we discussed earlier.

There are a variety of methods for identifying portfolios that reside along the efficient frontier. We next describe two methods and illustrate them with a hypothetical portfolio that consists of just two asset classes: stocks and bonds.

Matrix Inversion

To begin, we define a portfolio's expected return and risk.

As noted earlier, the expected return of a portfolio is simply the weighted average of the assets' expected returns. Equation 2.1 shows expected return for a portfolio consisting of only stocks and bonds:

$$\mu_p = w_s \mu_s + w_b \mu_b \tag{2.1}$$

In Equation 2.1, μ_p equals the portfolio's expected return, μ_s equals the expected return of stocks, μ_b equals the expected return of bonds, w_s equals the percentage of the portfolio allocated to stocks, and w_b equals the percentage allocated to bonds.

As noted earlier, portfolio risk is a little trickier. It is defined as volatility, and it is measured by the standard deviation or variance (the standard deviation squared) around the portfolio's expected return. To compute a portfolio's variance, we must consider not only the variance of the asset class returns, but also the extent to which they covary. The variance of a portfolio of stocks and bonds is computed as follows:

$$\sigma_p^2 = w_s^2 \sigma_s^2 + w_b^2 \sigma_b^2 + 2 w_s w_b \rho \sigma_s \sigma_b \tag{2.2}$$

Here σ_p^2 equals portfolio variance, σ_s equals the standard deviation of stocks, σ_b equals the standard deviation of bonds, and ρ equals the correlation between stocks and bonds.

Our objective is to minimize portfolio risk subject to two constraints. Our first constraint is that the weighted average of the stock and bond returns must equal the expected return for the portfolio. We are also faced with a second constraint: we must allocate our entire portfolio to some combination of stocks and bonds. Therefore, the fraction we allocate to stocks plus the fraction we allocate to bonds must equal 1.

We combine our objective and constraints to form the following objective function:

$$f(w) = \left[w_s^2 \sigma_s^2 + w_b^2 \sigma_b^2 + 2w_s w_b \rho \sigma_s \sigma_b \right] + \lambda_1 \left[w_s \mu_s + w_b \mu_b - \mu_p \right]$$
$$+ \lambda_2 \left[w_s + w_b - 1 \right] \tag{2.3}$$

The first term of Equation 2.3 up to the third plus sign equals portfolio variance, the quantity to be minimized. The next two terms that are multiplied by λ represent the two constraints. The first constraint ensures that the weighted average of the stock and bond returns equals the portfolio's expected return. The Greek letter lambda (λ) is called a Lagrange multiplier. It is a variable introduced to facilitate optimization when we face constraints, and it does not easily lend itself to economic interpretation. The second constraint guarantees that the portfolio is fully invested. Again, lambda serves to facilitate a solution.

Our objective function has four unknown values: (i) the percentage of the portfolio to be allocated to stocks, (ii) the percentage to be allocated to bonds, (iii) the Lagrange multiplier for the first constraint, and (iv) the Lagrange multiplier for the second constraint. To minimize portfolio risk given our constraints, we must take the partial derivative of the objective function with respect to each asset weight and with respect to each Lagrange multiplier and set it equal to zero, as shown below:

$$\frac{\partial f(w)}{\partial w_s} = 2w_s \sigma_s^2 + 2w_b \rho \sigma_s \sigma_b + \lambda_1 \mu_s + \lambda_2 = 0 \tag{2.4}$$

$$\frac{\partial f(w)}{\partial w_b} = 2w_b \sigma_b^2 + 2w_s \rho \sigma_s \sigma_b + \lambda_1 \mu_b + \lambda_2 = 0 \tag{2.5}$$

$$\frac{\partial f(w)}{\partial \lambda_1} = w_s \mu_s + w_b \mu_b - \mu_p = 0 \tag{2.6}$$

$$\frac{\partial f(w)}{\partial \lambda_2} = w_s + w_b - 1 = 0 \tag{2.7}$$

Given assumptions for expected return, standard deviation, and correlation (which we specify later), we wish to find the values of w_s and w_b associated with different values of μ_p, the portfolio's expected return. The values for λ_1 and λ_2 are merely mathematical by-products of the solution.

Next, we express Equations 2.4, 2.5, 2.6, and 2.7 in matrix notation, as follows:

$$
\begin{bmatrix}
2\sigma_s^2 & 2\rho\sigma_s\sigma_b & \mu_s & 1 \\
2\rho\sigma_s\sigma_b & 2\sigma_b^2 & \mu_b & 1 \\
\mu_s & \mu_b & 0 & 0 \\
1 & 1 & 0 & 0
\end{bmatrix}
\cdot
\begin{bmatrix}
w_s \\
w_b \\
\lambda_1 \\
\lambda_2
\end{bmatrix}
=
\begin{bmatrix}
0 \\
0 \\
\mu_p \\
1
\end{bmatrix}
\tag{2.8}
$$

We next substitute estimates of expected return, standard deviation, and correlation for domestic equities and Treasury bonds shown earlier in Tables 2.1 and 2.2.

With these assumptions, we rewrite the coefficient matrix as follows:

$$
\begin{bmatrix}
0.08 & 0.02 & 0.12 & 1.00 \\
0.02 & 0.02 & 0.08 & 1.00 \\
0.12 & 0.08 & 0.00 & 0.00 \\
1.00 & 1.00 & 0.00 & 0.00
\end{bmatrix}
$$

Its inverse equals:

$$
\begin{bmatrix}
0 & 0 & 25 & -2 \\
0 & 0 & -25 & 3 \\
25 & -25 & -37.5 & 3 \\
-2 & 3 & 3 & -0.26
\end{bmatrix}
$$

Because the constant vector includes a variable for the portfolio's expected return, we obtain a vector of formulas rather than values when we multiply the inverse matrix by the vector of constants, as follows:

$$
\begin{bmatrix}
w_s \\
w_b \\
\lambda_1 \\
\lambda_2
\end{bmatrix}
=
\begin{bmatrix}
25\mu_p - 2 \\
-25\mu_p + 3 \\
-37.5\mu_p + 3 \\
3\mu_p - 0.26
\end{bmatrix}
\tag{2.9}
$$

We are interested only in the first two formulas. The first formula yields the percentage to be invested in stocks in order to minimize risk when we substitute a value for the portfolio's expected return. The second formula yields the percentage to be invested in bonds. Table 2.3 shows the allocations to stocks and bonds that minimize risk for portfolio expected returns ranging from 9% to 12%.

TABLE 2.3   Optimal Allocation to Stocks and Bonds

Target Portfolio Return	9%	10%	11%	12%
Stock Allocation	25%	50%	75%	100%
Bond Allocation	75%	50%	25%	0%

THE SHARPE ALGORITHM

In 1987, William Sharpe published an algorithm for portfolio optimization that has the dual virtues of accommodating many real-world complexities while appealing to our intuition.[8] We begin by defining an objective function that we wish to maximize:

$$E(U) = \mu_p - \lambda_{RA}\sigma_p^2 \tag{2.10}$$

In Equation 2.8, $E(U)$ equals expected utility, μ_p equals portfolio expected return, λ_{RA} equals risk aversion, and σ_p^2 equals portfolio variance.

Utility is a measure of well-being or satisfaction, whereas risk aversion measures how many units of expected return we are willing to sacrifice in order to reduce risk (variance) by one unit. (Chapter 25 includes more detail about utility and risk aversion.) By maximizing this objective function, we maximize expected return minus a quantity representing our aversion to risk times risk (as measured by variance).

Again, assume we have a portfolio consisting of stocks and bonds. Substituting the equations for portfolio expected return and variance (Equations 2.1 and 2.2), we rewrite the objective function as follows:

$$E(U) = w_s\mu_s + w_b\mu_b - \lambda_{RA}\left(w_s^2\sigma_s^2 + w_b^2\sigma_b^2 + 2w_sw_b\rho\sigma_s\sigma_b\right) \tag{2.11}$$

This objective function measures the expected utility or satisfaction we derive from a combination of expected return and risk, given our attitude toward risk. Its partial derivative with respect to each asset weight, shown in Equations 2.12 and 2.13, represents the marginal utility of each asset class:

$$\frac{\partial E(U)}{\partial w_s} = \mu_s - \lambda_{RA}\left(2w_s\sigma_s^2 + 2w_b\rho\sigma_s\sigma_b\right) = 0 \tag{2.12}$$

$$\frac{\partial E(U)}{\partial w_b} = \mu_b - \lambda_{RA}\left(2w_b\sigma_b^2 + 2w_s\rho\sigma_s\sigma_b\right) = 0 \qquad (2.13)$$

These marginal utilities measure how much we increase or decrease expected utility, starting from our current asset mix, by increasing our exposure to each asset class. A negative marginal utility indicates that we improve expected utility by reducing exposure to that asset class, whereas a positive marginal utility indicates that we should raise the exposure to that asset class in order to improve expected utility.

Let us retain our earlier assumptions about the expected returns and standard deviations of stocks and bonds and their correlation. Further, let us assume our portfolio is currently allocated 60% to stocks and 40% to bonds, and that our aversion toward risk equals 2. A risk aversion of 2 means that we are willing to reduce expected return by two units in order to lower variance by one unit.

If we substitute these values into Equations 2.12 and 2.13, we find that we improve our expected utility by 0.008 units if we increase our exposure to stocks by 1%, and that we improve our expected utility by 0.04 units if we increase our exposure to bonds by 1%. Both marginal utilities are positive. However, we can only allocate 100% of the portfolio. We should therefore increase our exposure to the asset class with the higher marginal utility by 1% and reduce by the same amount our exposure to the asset class with the lower marginal utility. In this way, we ensure that we are always 100% invested.

Having switched our allocations in line with the relative magnitudes of the marginal utilities, we recompute the marginal utilities given our new allocation of 59% stocks and 41% bonds. Again, bonds have a higher marginal utility than stocks; hence, we shift again from stocks to bonds. If we proceed in this fashion, we find when our portfolio is allocated 1/3 to stocks and 2/3 to bonds, the marginal utilities are exactly equal to each other. At this point, we cannot improve expected utility any further by changing the allocation between stocks and bonds. We have maximized our objective function.

By varying the values we assign to λ, we identify mixes of stocks and bonds for many levels of risk aversion, thus enabling us to construct the entire efficient frontier of stocks and bonds. Figure 2.1 shows the efficient frontier based on the expected returns, standard deviations, and correlations shown in Tables 2.1 and 2.2. All the portfolios along the efficient frontier offer a higher level of expected return for the same level of risk than the portfolios residing below the efficient frontier.

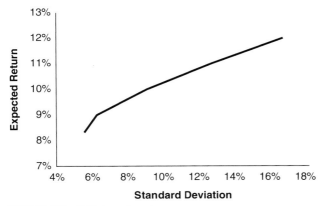

FIGURE 2.1   Efficient frontier.

Now let us consider the efficient frontier that is composed of the six asset classes specified in Tables 2.1 and 2.2. In particular, let us now focus on three efficient portfolios that lie along this efficient frontier: one for a conservative investor, one for an investor with moderate risk aversion, and one for an aggressive investor. Table 2.4 shows the three efficient portfolios.

TABLE 2.4   Conservative, Moderate, and Aggressive Efficient Portfolios

Asset Classes	Conservative (%)	Moderate (%)	Aggressive (%)
US Equities	15.9	25.5	36.8
Foreign Developed Market Equities	14.5	23.2	34.5
Emerging Market Equities	5.6	9.1	15.8
Treasury Bonds	15.5	14.3	0.0
US Corporate Bonds	11.4	22.0	8.9
Commodities	4.0	5.9	4.0
Cash Equivalents	33.2	0.0	0.0
Expected Return	6.0	7.5	9.0
Standard Deviation	6.8	10.8	15.2

The composition of these portfolios should not be surprising. The conservative portfolio has nearly a 1/3 allocation to cash equivalents.

The moderate portfolio is well diversified and not unlike many institutional portfolios. The aggressive portfolio, by contrast, has more than an

86% allocation to US and foreign equities. It should be comforting to note that we did not impose any constraints in the optimization process to arrive at these portfolios. The process of employing an equilibrium perspective for estimating expected returns yields nicely behaved results.

The Optimal Portfolio

The final step is to select the portfolio that best suits our aversion to risk, which we call the optimal portfolio. As we discussed earlier in this chapter, the theoretical approach to identifying the optimal portfolio is to specify how many units of expected return we are willing to give up to reduce our portfolio's risk by one unit. We would then draw a line with a slope equal to our risk aversion and find the point of tangency of this line with the efficient frontier. The portfolio located at this point of tangency is theoretically optimal because its risk/return trade-off matches our preference for balancing risk and return.

In practice, however, we do not know intuitively how many units of expected return we are willing to sacrifice in order to lower variance by one unit. Therefore, we need to translate combinations of expected return and risk into metrics that are more intuitive. Because continuous returns are approximately normally distributed,[9] we can easily estimate the probability that a portfolio with a particular expected return and standard deviation will experience a specific loss over a particular horizon. Alternatively, we can estimate the largest loss a portfolio might experience given a particular level of confidence. We call this measure value at risk. We can also rely on the assumption that continuous returns are normally distributed to estimate the likelihood that a portfolio will grow to a chosen value at some future date. Table 2.5 shows the likelihood of loss over a five-year investment horizon for the three efficient portfolios, as well as value at risk measured at a 1% significance level, which means we are 99% confident that the portfolio value will not fall by more than this amount.

TABLE 2.5   Exposure to Loss

Risk statistics for end of five years

	Conservative (%)	Moderate (%)	Aggressive (%)
Probability of Loss (return below 0%)	2.5	6.7	10.8
1% Value at Risk	5.1	17.0	28.7

If exposure to loss were our only consideration, we would choose the conservative portfolio, but by doing so we forgo upside opportunity. One way to assess the upside potential of these portfolios is to estimate the distribution of future wealth associated with investment in each of them.

Table 2.6 shows the probable terminal wealth as a multiple of initial wealth at varying confidence levels 15 years from now. For example, there is only a 5% chance that our nominal wealth would grow to less than 1.4 times initial wealth in 15 years, assuming we invest in the moderate portfolio. And there is a 5% chance $(1 - 0.95)$ that our wealth could grow to a value as high as 5.2 times initial wealth.

TABLE 2.6 Distribution of Wealth 15 Years Forward (as a Multiple of Initial Investment)

Terminal wealth, multiple, end of 15 years

Confidence Level (%)	Conservative	Moderate	Aggressive
1	1.3	1.1	0.9
5	1.5	1.4	1.3
10	1.7	1.7	1.6
25	2.0	2.1	2.2
50	2.3	2.7	3.2
75	2.7	3.6	4.5
90	3.2	4.5	6.3
95	3.5	5.2	7.6
99	4.1	6.8	11.0

These estimates of future wealth ignore any contributions or disbursements that may be added to or subtracted from the portfolios. To estimate future wealth taking cash flows into account, we would need to simulate the portfolios' performance between all cash flows throughout our investment horizon.

By mapping the portfolios' expected returns and standard deviations onto estimates of exposure to loss and the distribution of future wealth, we should have a clear idea of the merits and limitations of each portfolio. It is important to keep in mind, though, that there is no universally optimal portfolio; it is specific to each investor. If our focus is to avoid losses, the conservative portfolio might be optimal. If, instead, we believe that we can endure significant losses along the way in exchange for greater opportunity to grow wealth, then we might choose the aggressive portfolio. If our goal is to limit exposure to loss, yet still maintain a reasonable opportunity to grow wealth, then perhaps the moderate portfolio would suit us best.

Asset allocation is a complex process, yet one we should not ignore. Our intent in this chapter is to present the theoretical foundation of asset allocation as well as to discuss the practical implementation of this theory at its most basic level. In subsequent chapters, we describe various refinements to the basic approach described here. But before we move on to these refinements, we discuss some fallacies about asset allocation and do our best to dispel them.

REFERENCES

Levy, H. and Markowitz, H. 1979. "Approximating Expected Utility by a Function of Mean and Variance," *American Economic Review*, Vol. 69, No. 3 (June).

Markowitz, H. 1952. "Portfolio Selection," *Journal of Finance*, Vol. 7, No. 1 (March).

Sharpe, W. 1987. "An Algorithm for Portfolio Improvement," *Advances in Mathematical Programming and Financial Planning, Vol. 1.* Greenwich, CT: JAI Press Inc.

NOTES

1. Markowitz (1952).
2. Levy and Markowitz (1979).
3. Kurtosis refers to the peakedness of a distribution. Kurtosis greater than 3 indicates that extreme returns are more likely than what one would expect from a normal distribution. Returns that are independent and identically distributed are likely to be normal.
4. This concept applies as well to any number of asset classes, but it is easier to visualize with only two asset classes.
5. See Chapter 1 for a detailed discussion of these characteristics.
6. Our empirical analysis is meant for illustration, and we do not intend to offer conclusions about any specific portfolio, investment universe, or data set. We calibrate models and assumptions using reasonable market proxies such as the S&P 500 for US equities; MSCI World ex USA and MSCI emerging markets for foreign and emerging market equities; Bloomberg Barclays aggregate US Treasury and corporate bond indexes; Bloomberg commodities index; and the risk-free rate from Kenneth French's data website.
7. For those who care deeply about maximizing the portfolio's geometric mean, the arithmetic approach may still offer a reasonable approximation that can be tested for efficacy and compared to optimization with other more complex numerical procedures.
8. See Sharpe (1987). Sharpe's algorithm can easily be adapted to accommodate transaction costs and allocation constraints.

9. A continuous return equals the natural logarithm of 1 plus the discrete return. It is the return that if compounded continuously would give the discrete return. Continuous returns that are independent and identically distributed are normally distributed. It is therefore common practice to convert discrete returns, which are lognormally distributed owing to the effect of compounding, to continuous returns in order to estimate probabilities. We then convert the continuous return back to a discrete return by raising the base of the natural logarithm to the power of 1 plus the continuous return and subtracting 1.

CHAPTER 3

The Importance of Asset Allocation

FALLACY: ASSET ALLOCATION DETERMINES MORE THAN 90% OF PERFORMANCE

No doubt, asset allocation is important, even critical to investment success. Otherwise, why would we bother to write this book? Nevertheless, most investors, as well as academics, have a much inflated perception of the value of asset allocation compared to security selection.

THE DETERMINANTS OF PORTFOLIO PERFORMANCE

This misperception can be traced to an influential article published in the *Financial Analysts Journal* in 1986 called "The Determinants of Portfolio Performance."[1] The authors, Gary Brinson, Randolph Hood, and Gilbert Beebower, analyzed the performance of 91 large corporate pension plans during the 10-year period from 1974 to 1983 in an effort to attribute their performance to three investment choices: asset allocation policy, timing, and security selection.

They defined the asset allocation policy return as the return of the long-term asset mix invested in passive asset class benchmarks. They then measured the return associated with deviations from the policy mix assuming investment in passive benchmarks, and they attributed this component of return to timing. Finally, they measured the return associated with deviations from the passive benchmarks within each asset class and attributed this component of return to security selection. For each of the 91 funds, they regressed total return through time on these respective components of return. These regressions revealed that asset allocation policy, on average across the 91 funds, accounted for 93.6% of total return variation through time and in no case less than 75.5%.

Fundamental Flaw

This methodology is flawed because it presents no notion of a normal or a default asset mix. Their analysis implicitly assumes that the pension plans' funds would otherwise be uninvested, perhaps contained in a very large coffee can. Because the authors failed to net out an average or typical asset mix, most of the variation in performance that they attributed to asset allocation policy arose not from the choice of a portfolio's asset mix but, instead, from merely the decision to invest. The authors simply demonstrated that we incur risk when we invest in risky assets.

A Practical View on Importance

To illustrate our point, consider a portfolio that consists of 75% technology stocks and 25% US bonds. From 2006 to 2013, what percentage of this portfolio's return variation is explained by asset allocation?

We begin by obtaining monthly historical returns for the actual portfolio. Next, we split the returns into two parts. The first part equals the monthly returns of a portfolio that holds 75% in a broad stock market index and 25% in US bonds. It mimics the asset allocation but ignores security selection. The second part equals the monthly returns of the actual portfolio – which contains a large concentrated position in technology stocks – in excess of the returns of the first part. It reflects the incremental return associated with security selection.

This separation allows us to decompose the portfolio's monthly return variation into its two component parts. We do so by calculating the fractional contribution to total variance (FCTV), as follows:

$$FCTV = \frac{\Sigma 1}{1'\Sigma 1} \tag{3.1}$$

In Equation 3.1, Σ is the covariance matrix of return components, 1 is a column vector of ones, and ' denotes the matrix transpose. The sum of FCTV across components always equals one (as can be seen from Equation 3.1, where the numerator will equal the denominator after pre-multiplying by 1').

In this example, the asset allocation component appears to explain 73% of the total return variation, dwarfing the 27% explained by security selection. This conclusion mirrors the logic of Brinson, Hood, and Beebower. Intuitively, it seems surprising that such a dramatic security selection tilt carries so little relative importance. In fact, this approach incorrectly implies that asset allocation is more important than security selection because it considers all market volatility to be the result of an asset allocation decision.

Now, let us propose a different perspective. In the absence of any skill, effort, or careful consideration, investors can still default to a broadly diversified portfolio such as 60/40 stocks and bonds. The default might represent, for example, the average allocation across a pool of similar investors. The returns of this default asset mix reflect the decision to invest. They do not reflect an asset allocation decision for the simple reason that it was chosen without any care or consideration at all.

The relevant question for investors is: how much impact can I have on return outcomes by deviating from the default asset allocation, as opposed to deviating from the default security selection? The answer to this question helps to allocate scarce time and attention across competing investment activities. Figure 3.1 shows that when we account for the return variation explained by the default asset mix, our conclusion is reversed. Only 16% of the return variation is due to asset allocation, which means it is less important than security selection in this example. More than half of the portfolio's variation in returns comes from the mere decision to invest.

FIGURE 3.1 Fractional contribution to total variance.

Reductio ad Absurdum

To stress our point even further, it is possible to construct a simple yet extreme example of the Brinson, Hood, and Beebower methodology that leads to an obvious contradiction. Kritzman (2006) describes an imaginary world with two stocks and two bonds.[2] The first stock always produces the same return as the first bond, and the second stock always produces the same return as the second bond. Thus, stocks and bonds as asset classes always have identical returns, which means that the weights assigned to stocks versus bonds have no impact. In other words, asset allocation is completely irrelevant to returns. Security selection does matter, though. Suppose that the second stock and second bond have returns that are always twice as large as those of the first stock and first bond. The punch line is that an investor who allocates entirely to the second stock and second bond will earn twice the return of an investor who allocates to the first stock and first bond, but both of their returns will be 100% correlated to their asset allocation benchmarks (equivalent to an R-squared of 100% in a regression of returns). The methodology proposed by Brinson, Hood, and Beebower would conclude that asset allocation explains 100% of performance variation across the two investors, but we know the opposite to be true: asset allocation is irrelevant in this example.

THE BEHAVIORAL BIAS OF POSITIVE ECONOMICS

The Brinson, Hood, and Beebower methodology has another feature that limits its ability to separate the relative importance of various investment activities, which is also common to other methodologies that address this question. Most studies analyze the actual performance of funds.[4] In this sense, they are positive, as opposed to normative; they rely on actual returns that reflect some combination of the relative importance of alternative investment choices as well as the behavior of investors; that is, the extent to which investors choose to engage in various investment activities.

For example, some investors choose to invest in actively managed funds with high tracking error relative to the norm, but choose an asset mix that is close to the norm, such as the average asset mix of a relevant universe. Other investors choose actively managed funds with low tracking error relative to the norm, but choose an asset mix that is substantially different from the normal asset mix. In the former case, security selection will be seen to be more important than it is normally thought to be, whereas asset allocation will be seen to be less important than it is typically construed to be. In the latter case, the opposite will be true. But these conclusions could be misleading, because they may reflect as much or more about the investors' choices to emphasize asset allocation over security selection than the potential impact asset allocation and security selection have on portfolio performance.

To separate the intrinsic importance of an investment choice from an investor's decision to emphasize that choice, we need to measure the potential for an investment choice to cause dispersion in wealth. Dispersion is important to investors who believe they are skillful because it enables them to increase wealth beyond what they could expect to achieve by passive investment or from average performance. Dispersion is also important to investors who are unlucky because it exposes them to losses that might arise as a consequence of bad luck.[3] As beneficial as it is for skillful investors to focus on activities that cause dispersion, it is equally important for unlucky investors to avoid activities that cause dispersion.

Determining Relative Importance Analytically

It is simple to measure the relative importance of asset allocation and security selection analytically if we limit our investment universe to two asset classes, each of which contains two securities. We simply measure the potential for dispersion as the tracking error between two investments that differ either by asset class composition or by security composition. We should expect security selection to cause greater dispersion than asset allocation because individual securities are more volatile than the asset classes that comprise them unless the securities move in perfect unison. Therefore, if we argue that asset allocation causes greater dispersion, we necessarily believe that high correlations among individual securities offset their relatively high individual volatilities.

Consider two asset classes that contain two securities each. Asset class A includes securities A1 and A2, while asset class B includes B1 and B2. We measure the relative volatility and hence the importance of security selection within asset class A as shown:

$$\xi_{A1,A2} = \sqrt{\sigma_{A1}^2 + \sigma_{A2}^2 - 2\rho\sigma_{A1}\sigma_{A2}} \qquad (3.2)$$

In Equation 3.2, $\xi_{A1,A2}$ equals the relative volatility between A1 and A2, σ_{A1} equals the standard deviation of A1, σ_{A2} equals the standard deviation of A2, and ρ is the correlation between A1 and A2. The same equation is used to calculate the relative volatility between securities B1 and B2.

We measure the importance of choosing between asset class A and asset class B the same way, but first we must calculate the standard deviation of each asset class. If we assume the individual securities are weighted equally within each asset class, the standard deviation of asset class A equals

$$\sigma_A = \sqrt{0.5^2\sigma_{A1}^2 + 0.5^2\sigma_{A2}^2 + 2\rho(0.5)\sigma_{A1}(0.5)\sigma_{A2}} \qquad (3.3)$$

Here, σ_A equals the standard deviation of asset class A, σ_{A1} equals the standard deviation of A1, σ_{A2} equals the standard deviation of A2, and ρ is the correlation between A1 and A2.

We repeat the same calculation to derive the standard deviation of asset class B.

The relative volatility between asset class A and asset class B equals

$$\xi_{A,B} = \sqrt{\sigma_A^2 + \sigma_B^2 - 2\rho\sigma_A\sigma_B} \qquad (3.4)$$

TABLE 3.1 Standard Deviation, Correlation, and Relative Volatility

	Standard Deviation (%)	Correlation (%)	Relative Volatility (%)
A1	10.0		
A2	10.0	0.0	14.1
B1	10.0		
B2	10.0	0.0	14.1
A	7.1		
B	7.1	0.0	10.0

	Standard Deviation (%)	Correlation (%)	Relative Volatility (%)
A1	10.0		
A2	10.0	50.0	10.0
B1	10.0		
B2	10.0	50.0	10.0
A	8.7		
B	8.7	50.0	8.7

	Standard Deviation (%)	Correlation (%)	Relative Volatility (%)
A1	10.0		
A2	10.0	50.0	10.0
B1	10.0		
B2	10.0	50.0	10.0
A	8.7		
B	8.7	33.3	10.0

	Standard Deviation (%)	Correlation (%)	Relative Volatility (%)
A1	10.0		
A2	10.0	50.0	10.0
B1	10.0		
B2	10.0	50.0	10.0
A	8.7		
B	8.7	25.0	10.6

In Equation 3.3, $\xi_{A,B}$ equals the relative volatility between A and B, σ_A equals the standard deviation of A, σ_B equals the standard deviation of B, and ρ is the correlation between A and B.

Suppose the four securities are uncorrelated with each other. Then security selection would be more important than asset allocation because the asset classes would be less risky than the average risk of the securities they comprise, which results in less relative volatility between the asset classes than between the securities within each asset class. Moreover, as more securities are added, the asset class standard deviations decline further, which in turn further reduces the relative volatility between the asset classes. If, for example, security returns are uncorrelated and the securities are equally weighted, then the asset class standard deviation diminishes with the square root of the number of securities included. It is only when the correlation between asset classes A and B is substantially less than the correlation between the individual securities within the asset classes that the relative volatility between asset classes is greater than the relative volatility between securities. These relationships are illustrated in Table 3.1.

The upper left panel shows that relative volatility between asset classes is less than relative volatility between securities when they are all uncorrelated with one another. The upper right panel shows the same result when they all are equally correlated with one another. The lower left panel shows the asset class and security correlations that lead to convergence between relative volatilities. Finally, the lower right panel provides an example in which the relative volatility between asset classes is higher than it is between securities.

Determining Relative Importance by Simulation

The associations between standard deviation, correlation, and relative volatility are easy to illustrate when we consider only two asset classes each divided equally between only two securities. These associations become less clear when we consider several asset classes weighted differently among hundreds of securities with a wide range of volatilities and correlations. Under these real-world conditions, it is easier to resolve the question of relative importance by a simulation procedure known as bootstrapping.

Unlike Monte Carlo simulation, which draws random observations from a prespecified distribution, bootstrapping simulation draws random observations with replacement from empirical samples. Specifically, we generate thousands of random portfolios from a large universe of securities that vary only because of asset allocation or security selection. This allows us to observe the distribution of available returns associated with each investment decision as opposed to studying the actual performance of managed funds, which reflects the biases of their investors. Kritzman and Page (2002) conducted such an analysis for investment markets in five countries: Australia, Germany, Japan, the United Kingdom, and the United States based on returns from 1988 to 2001. They showed that the dispersion around average performance arising from security selection was substantially greater than the dispersion arising from asset allocation in every country, and it was particularly large in the United States because the United States has a larger number of individual securities.[5]

L'Her and Plante (2006) refined the Kritzman and Page methodology to account for the relative capitalization of securities, and they also included a broader set of asset classes. Their analysis showed asset allocation and security selection to be approximately equally important – still a far different result from the conclusion of Brinson, Hood, and Beebower.

THE SAMUELSON DICTUM

We hope we have convinced you that asset allocation does not determine 94% of performance, and that contrary to this assumption, security selection has equal, if not greater, potential to affect the distribution of returns. Does it follow, therefore, that investors should focus more effort on security selection than asset allocation? Not at all. Paul A. Samuelson put forth the argument that investment markets are microefficient and macroinefficient, which implies that investors are more likely to succeed by engaging in asset allocation than in security selection. He argued that if an individual security is mispriced, a smart investor will notice and trade to exploit the mispricing, and by doing so will correct the mispricing. Therefore, opportunities to exploit the mispricing of individual securities are fleeting. However, if an aggregation of individual securities, such as an asset class, is mispriced, a smart investor will detect the mispricing and trade to exploit the mispricing. But one smart investor, or even several, would not have the scale to revalue an entire asset class. The mispricing of an asset class will likely persist until an exogenous shock jolts many investors, smart or not, to act in concert and thereby revalue the asset class. Thus, asset class mispricing endures sufficiently long to allow investors to profit from it.[6]

THE BOTTOM LINE

The notion that asset allocation is more important than security selection is based on a flawed analysis that failed to account for what an investor would do as an alternative to investing in the current portfolio. Also, many studies show asset allocation to be more important than security selection because they conflate investment choice with investment opportunity. If we correct for these two flaws, we find that security selection is at least as important, if not more important, than asset allocation. It does not follow, though, that investors should devote more resources to security selection than asset allocation, because, as argued by Paul Samuelson, it is easier to be successful at asset allocation than security selection. The bottom line is that asset allocation is very important, but not for the reasons put forth by Brinson, Hood, and Beebower.

RELATED TOPICS

- Chapter 22 shows how investors can exploit the macroinefficiency of markets to enhance returns by anticipating regime shifts.

REFERENCES

Brinson, G. P. and Hood, R. 2006. "Determinants of Portfolio Performance – 20 Years Later: Authors' Responses," *Financial Analysts Journal*, Vol. 62, No. 1 (January/February).

Brinson, G. P., Hood, L. R., and Beebower, G. L. 1986. "Determinants of Portfolio Performance," *Financial Analysts Journal*, Vol. 42, No. 4 (July/August).

Ibbotson, R. G. and Kaplan, P. D. 2000. "Does Asset Allocation Policy Explain 40, 90, or 100 Percent of Performance?" *Financial Analysts Journal*, Vol. 56, No. 1 (January/February).

Kritzman, M. 2006. "Determinants of Portfolio Performance – 20 Years Later: A Comment," *Financial Analysts Journal*, Vol. 62, No. 1 (January/February).

Kritzman, M. and Page, S. 2002. "Asset Allocation versus Security Selection: Evidence from Global Markets," *Journal of Asset Management*, Vol. 3, No. 3 (December).

L'Her, J. F. and Plante, J. F. 2006. "The Relative Importance of Asset Allocation and Security Selection," *Journal of Portfolio Management*, Vol. 33, No. 1 (Fall).

Samuelson, P. A. 1998. "Summing Up on Business Cycles: Opening Address," in *Beyond Shocks: What Causes Business Cycles*, edited by J. C. Fuhrer and S. Schuh. Boston: Federal Reserve Bank of Boston.

NOTES

1. See Brinson, Hood, and Beebower (1986).
2. This argument first appeared as a letter to the editor in the *Financial Analysts Journal* in July/August 2006. Gary Brinson and Randolph Hood responded to this critique in the same issue. See Kritzman (2006) and Brinson and Hood (2006).
3. We have yet to meet a manager who claims to be lucky nor one who claims to be unskillful.
4. See Ibbotson and Kaplan (2000).
5. See Kritzman and Page (2002).
6. See Samuelson (1998).

CHAPTER 4

Time Diversification

FALLACY: TIME DIVERSIFIES RISK

Most investors are willing to allocate a larger fraction of their portfolio to risky assets if they have many years to invest than they would, given a short investment horizon, because they believe time diversifies risk. Paul A. Samuelson famously showed that investors should not increase their exposure to risky assets as their investment horizon expands, with his landmark article "Risk and Uncertainty: A Fallacy of Large Numbers."[1]

SAMUELSON'S BET

Samuelson was inspired by a conversation he had with an MIT colleague. He offered his colleague a chance to win $200 or lose $100 with better than even odds. His colleague rejected the bet, arguing that he could not afford to lose $100. But his colleague put forth a counterproposal in which they would enter into 100 such bets. He reasoned that the law of large numbers would ensure his success. Investors use the same logic to support the conventional wisdom that it is safer to invest in risky assets over long horizons than short horizons. The conventional wisdom follows from the observation that over long horizons, above-average returns tend to offset below-average returns. In his article, Samuelson showed that this logic is a misuse of the law of large numbers.

TIME, VOLATILITY, AND PROBABILITY OF LOSS

The following analysis might convince you that time does indeed diversify risk. Consider an investment that has an annualized continuous return of 10% and an annualized standard deviation of continuous returns equal to 20%. Table 4.1 shows the annualized standard deviation in continuous units and the probability of loss, as a function of the investment horizon.

TABLE 4.1 Time, Volatility, and Probability of Loss

Investment Horizon (years)	Annualized Continuous Standard Deviation (%)	Probability of Loss (<0%) on Average over Horizon (%)
1	20.0	30.9
5	8.9	13.2
10	6.3	5.7
20	4.5	1.3

These results reveal that if investors think of risk as annualized standard deviation or as the probability of loss at the conclusion of their investment horizon, then risk declines with time. Samuelson, however, based his argument on expected utility.

TIME AND EXPECTED UTILITY

According to Samuelson, the willingness of an investor to take more risk with longer horizons depends on the investor's utility function. A utility function is simply a formula that maps varying amounts of wealth onto one's perception of his or her well-being. (We provide more details of this notion in Chapter 25.)

Samuelson showed that investors should not conclude that it is safer to allocate more of their wealth to risky assets over longer horizons if the following conditions hold and their intent is to maximize expected utility:

1. Investors have constant relative risk aversion, which means they maintain the same percentage exposure to risky assets regardless of changes in their wealth.
2. Investment returns are independent and identically distributed, which means they follow a random walk.
3. Future wealth depends only on investment results and not on work effort or consumption habits.

The notion of utility was introduced by the famous mathematician, Daniel Bernoulli in 1738.[2] Bernoulli asserted that for the typical investor utility is equal to the logarithm of wealth. A log-wealth utility function is one of a family of utility functions for which each additional increment of wealth is worth less to the investor than the previous increment. In other words, a given increment of wealth means more to a poor person than it will mean to a wealthy person. By the same token, reductions in wealth grow in importance as they mount up. Economists assume that most investors have utility functions that roughly resemble the shape depicted in Figure 4.1.

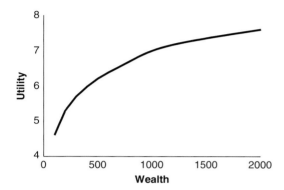

FIGURE 4.1 Log-wealth utility function.

Bernoulli also showed that for a particular utility function, we can identity a certain outcome that conveys the same amount of utility as a risky investment. This certain outcome is called a certainty equivalent. Consider, for example, a risky investment that has a 50% chance of a 1/3 gain and a 50% chance of a 1/4 loss. A $100 investment would have an equal chance of growing to $133.33 or falling to $75.00. An investor whose utility function is equal to the logarithm of wealth would derive 4.6052 units of utility from such an investment, which we calculate as $[0.5 \times \ln(\$133.33) + 0.5 \times \ln(\$75)]$. It turns out that the natural logarithm of $100 also equals 4.6052, which means that $100 is the certainty equivalent of this risky investment, because they both deliver the same amount of utility.

We can use the notion of a certainty equivalent to demonstrate Samuelson's argument that time does not diversify risk. Table 4.2 shows how the expected wealth of this $100 risky investment, which has an even chance of a 1/3 gain or a 1/4 loss, grows over three investment periods. It also shows how expected utility evolves through time.

Although expected wealth grows from $100 to $104.17 over one period, then to $108.51 over two periods, and finally to $113.03 over three periods, expected utility remains constant at 4.6052. Expected utility remains constant regardless of the duration of the investment horizon, assuming that

TABLE 4.2 Expected Wealth and Expected Utility

	Initial Wealth	1st Period Distribution	2nd Period Distribution	3rd Period Distribution
				237.04 × .125
			177.78 × .25	
				133.33 × .125
		133.33 × .50		
				133.33 × .125
			100.00 × .25	
				75.00 × .125
	100.00			
				133.33 × .125
			100.00 × .25	
				75.00 × .125
		75.00 × .50		
				75.00 × .125
			56.25 × .25	
				42.19 × .125
Expected wealth	100.00	104.17	108.51	113.03
Expected utility	4.6052	4.6052	4.6052	4.6052

investment returns are independent from period to period and investors have utility functions that display constant relative risk aversion. Power utility functions, of which the log-wealth utility function is a special case, satisfy this criterion. The fact that expected utility remains unchanged across different horizons shows that investors with constant relative risk aversion do not have a preference to accept more risk over longer horizons than shorter horizons. They are indifferent to the length of the investment horizon.

There is a simple economic rationale for Samuelson's argument. Although time diminishes the probability of a loss, it increases the magnitude of a potential loss in such a way that they are exactly offsetting. It might be easier to see this trade-off cross-sectionally. Instead of considering a sequence of years over which we invest, image investing $100 in 10 risky investments that have an equal chance of a 1/3 gain or a 1/4 loss, but whose outcomes are independent of each other. Although the likelihood of losing money on average is much lower than the likelihood of losing money on any of the individual investments, the amount that can be lost is 10 times as great. In Samuelson's argument, each year is an independent outcome that increases the amount one can lose.

Suppose that investment returns do not change randomly. Instead, they mean-revert, which means that an above-average return is more likely to be followed by a below-average return than by another above-average return. It would still be the case that a log-wealth investor would maintain the same risk exposure across different investment horizons. However, an investor who is more risk averse than a log-wealth investor will indeed choose to reduce risk over longer horizons, whereas an investor who is less risk averse than a log-wealth investor will prefer to increase risk over longer horizons. If, instead, returns mean-avert, which means they trend, the opposite would be true.

WITHIN-HORIZON RISK

Samuelson's utility-based result implicitly assumes that investors only consider outcomes at the end of their investment horizon. It is possible to refute time diversification without appealing to utility theory. If investors care about exposure to loss throughout their investment horizon, then time diversification fails based merely on the probability of loss. The likelihood of a within-horizon loss rises with time even as the likelihood of a terminal loss diminishes.

By using a statistic called the first passage time probability, we measure the probability of loss within an investment horizon.[3] It is equal to

$$\mathrm{Pr}_W = N\left[\frac{\ln(1+L) - \mu T}{\sigma\sqrt{T}}\right] + N\left[\frac{\ln(1+L) + \mu T}{\sigma\sqrt{T}}\right](1+L)^{\frac{2\mu}{\sigma^2}} \qquad (4.1)$$

In Equation 4.1, $N[\ ]$ equals the cumulative normal distribution function, ln equals the natural logarithm, L equals cumulative percentage loss in periodic units, μ equals the annualized expected return in continuous units, T equals the number of years in the investment horizon, and σ equals the annualized standard deviation of continuous returns. (See Chapter 24 for more details about the first passage time probability.)

The within-horizon probability of loss increases sharply as we begin to lengthen the horizon until it eventually levels off, but it never diminishes with time. Table 4.3 shows the likelihood that an investment with an annualized continuous return of 10% and an annualized standard deviation of continuous returns equal to 20% will breach a threshold that is 90% of its initial value within investment horizons ranging from three months to 100 years.

TABLE 4.3   Probability of a Within-Horizon 10% Loss

Investment Horizon (years)	Probability of −10%
0.25	22.1%
1	44.1%
5	56.7%
10	58.4%
20	59.0%
100	59.1%

A PREFERENCE-FREE CONTRADICTION TO TIME DIVERSIFICATION

We can also use options pricing theory to refute the notion of time diversification.[4] Investors often use put options to protect the value of their portfolios. The cost of a put option (as well as a call option) increases with the length of time to expiration. Because it is more expensive to insure a portfolio over longer horizons than over shorter horizons, it must therefore be the case that risk increases with time, contrary to the notion of time diversification.

       Option values are invariant to investor preferences. They depend, instead, on the notion that investors cannot profit from riskless arbitrage. Thus, unlike Samuelson's utility-based argument or the within-horizon probability-of-loss argument, options pricing theory provides a preference-free contradiction to time diversification.

THE BOTTOM LINE

It is perfectly reasonable for investors to accept more risk when they are young than old, not because investing is less risky over longer horizons, but instead because young investors have more time than old investors to recover from potential losses by working harder or consuming less. It remains the case, however, that risk does not diminish with time if returns fluctuate randomly and investors prefer to preserve the same percentage of exposure to risk regardless of their wealth.[5]

RELATED TOPICS

- Chapter 2 introduces utility theory and shows how it relates to mean-variance optimization and the efficient frontier.
- Chapter 5 debunks another fallacy related to investing over long horizons: the notion that the standard deviation scales with the square root of time and that correlations estimated from long intervals will equal those measured from short intervals.
- Chapter 24 shows how investors can stress test portfolios using within-horizon exposure to loss and continuous value at risk, which are based on first passage probabilities.

REFERENCES

Bernoulli, D. 1954. "Exposition of a New Theory on the Measurement of Risk," [translation from 1738 version], *Econometrica*, Vol. 22, No. 1 (January).

Bodie, Z. 1995. "On the Risk of Stocks in the Long Run." *Financial Analysts Journal*, Vol. 51, No. 3 (May–June).

Campbell, J. and Viceira, L. 2002. *Strategic Asset Allocation*, Oxford University Press.

Kritzman, M. and Rich, D. 2002. "The Mismeasurement of Risk," *Financial Analysts Journal*, Vol. 58, No. 3 (May/June).

Ross, S. 1999. "Adding Risks: Samuelson's Fallacy of Large Numbers Revisited," *Journal of Financial and Quantitative Analysis*, Vol. 34, No. 3 (September)

Samuelson, P. A. 1963. "Risk and Uncertainty: A Fallacy of Large Numbers," *Scientia*, 98 (April/May).

NOTES

1. See Samuelson (1963).
2. See Bernoulli (1954).
3. See Kritzman and Rich (2002).
4. See Bodie (1995).
5. Our analysis in this chapter is somewhat cursory. Interested readers should consult the broader literature to understand the complexities of this topic. In particular, Ross (1999) describes features of a utility function that satisfy the "eventual acceptance property," which is the notion that for a given finite number of bets there is a partial sum of them that is acceptable even though the bets individually are unacceptable. And Campbell and Viceira (2005) present a comprehensive analysis of multiperiod asset allocation.

CHAPTER 5

Divergence

FALLACY: VOLATILITY SCALES WITH THE SQUARE ROOT OF TIME, AND CORRELATION IS CONSTANT ACROSS RETURN INTERVALS

Investors commonly, and sometimes unknowingly, assume that the standard deviation of asset returns scales with the square root of time. They also make the analogous assumption that correlations are invariant to the return frequency from which they are estimated. Both beliefs rest on the same underlying assumption that returns are serially independent from one period to the next. This assumption is ubiquitous. It is hard-coded into risk and optimization platforms throughout the industry. Many institutions rely on it to determine their strategic asset mix. It is even embedded in the Global Investment Performance Standards (GIPS) to which most investment managers adhere when reporting results to their clients. Unfortunately, it is often incorrect.

We suspect that most sophisticated investors are aware that this assumption does not always hold but presume its impact is negligible. The evidence suggests otherwise. Major asset classes such as private equity and fixed income exhibit significant nonzero autocorrelation. Moreover, pairs of assets such as US and emerging market equities exhibit divergence between short- and long-interval correlations. In this chapter, we present an empirical analysis of this phenomenon across a range of asset classes and investment vehicles. We introduce a measure to quantify the degree of divergence as well as a methodology to account for it when constructing portfolios, estimating risk, or measuring performance.

EXCESS DISPERSION

Over the 24-year period starting in January 1990 and ending in December 2013, US and emerging market equities had remarkably similar annualized returns of 9.5% and 9.3%, respectively. Furthermore, the correlation of their monthly returns was 70%, and the annualized tracking error between the two was only 4.9%. Yet, the returns of these two seemingly correlated asset classes diverged sharply during some periods. During the three years ending in 2007, emerging market equities outperformed US equities by 121%. By contrast, during the three years ending in 2013, emerging markets underperformed by 62%. How can we reconcile divergences of this magnitude with such high correlation and low tracking error during the same period?

To answer this question, we introduce a new term. We define excess dispersion as the fraction of the empirical distribution of triennial returns that falls outside the one-standard-deviation tails of the distribution that is implied by estimation from monthly returns. Figure 5.1 shows the distribution of triennial relative returns between US and emerging market equities that is extrapolated from the monthly observations, if both assets' returns are serially independent and identically distributed. It also shows the distribution of actual triennial returns that occurred during this period.

■ Actual triennial returns　　——— Monthly TE tri-annualized

FIGURE 5.1 Excess dispersion of US and emerging markets relative returns (January 1990–December 2013).

In this example, we observe positive excess dispersion in both the right and left tails of the distribution: the frequency of actual triennial outcomes is significantly larger than the distribution extrapolated from monthly observations would imply. The overall excess dispersion is 27.6%. One may be tempted to conclude that these fat tails are driven by skewness or excess kurtosis in one or both return series. As we will later demonstrate, this is rarely the cause. In fact, in the case of US and emerging market equities, the effect of non-normality is counterintuitive: it serves to decrease, not increase, excess dispersion. In this and other instances, excess dispersion is instead driven by lagged autocorrelations and cross-correlations within and between the returns of the two asset classes. These effects have profound implications for parameter estimation. In this case, the correlation of the two assets' monthly returns is 70%, whereas the correlation of their triennial returns over the same period is merely 10%!

It is important not to confuse the type of error driven by excess dispersion, which we refer to as interval error, with traditional estimation error. Estimation error occurs when we extrapolate parameters from one sample to forecast the values that will prevail in another sample. It often arises in financial analysis when we use historical data to forecast the future. It is well documented, and investors can employ a range of techniques to address it. Interval error is different, and arises when we extrapolate parameters derived from higher-frequency observations to estimate lower-frequency parameters within the same sample. The excess dispersion we report in this chapter is a function of interval error, not estimation error. For more on the taxonomy of errors that arise in forecasting and how to address them, see Chapter 19.

Figure 5.1 captures concisely the fallacy that is the focus of this chapter: estimates of correlation and standard deviation extrapolated from shorter intervals provide good guidance for estimating the distribution of longer-interval returns. This fallacy has several practical implications which we will now explore.

THE EVIDENCE

The excess dispersion that we observe in the case of US and emerging market equities is not unique. Table 5.1 reports data for the five asset class pairs that exhibit the greatest magnitude of excess dispersion over the period from 1990 through 2013. For this analysis, we again focus on the dispersion between extrapolated monthly and actual triennial outcomes. We choose these frequencies because investors often employ monthly data to estimate parameters like volatility and correlation for purposes of asset allocation, whereas their actual investment horizons are often three years or longer. However, one could measure excess dispersion for any choice of a shorter and a longer interval such as daily and monthly intervals or weekly and annual intervals.

TABLE 5.1 Attribution of Excess Dispersion of Triennial Relative Returns

		Excess Dispersion						Correlation		Statistical Test	
		IID (%)	Non-normality (%)	Auto-correlation (%)	Lagged Cross-Correlation (%)	Auto-correlation and Cross-Correlation (%)	Actual (%)	Monthly Correlation	Triennial Correlation	Variance Ratio	Variance Ratio Test Statistic
US Domestic Assets											
Hedge Funds	Private Equity	0.0	0.7	24.8	5.3	26.8	26.2	0.79	0.72	3.60	4.01
Real Estate	Government Bonds	0.0	−0.8	20.3	4.3	22.9	22.7	−0.02	−0.23	3.13	3.28
Large Cap Equity	Government Bonds	0.0	−0.4	9.7	1.4	10.8	14.5	−0.06	−0.18	1.63	1.21
Corporate Bonds	Government Bonds	0.0	−1.9	−13.4	7.0	−4.6	−12.0	0.68	0.48	0.93	−0.13
Energy Stocks	Utilities Stocks	0.0	−0.5	−9.0	−18.7	−25.7	−26.6	0.58	0.84	0.29	−1.38
International Assets											
US Equities	Emerging Equities	0.0	−0.9	−2.7	20.6	21.7	27.6	0.70	0.10	2.72	3.32
Canadian Equities	US Equities	0.0	0.3	−1.2	14.8	15.1	24.4	0.78	0.55	1.74	1.43
Global Portfolio in USD	USD/AUD	0.0	0.2	−3.0	19.7	17.3	22.4	0.59	−0.01	2.17	2.26
USD/GBP	USD/JPY	0.0	−0.2	−1.5	13.2	11.1	11.0	0.19	−0.42	1.51	0.99
German Equities	UK Equities	0.0	0.4	−4.2	−11.8	−17.9	−19.1	0.77	0.88	0.40	−1.16

January 1990–December 2013

The sixth column in Table 5.1, labeled "Actual," reports the observed excess dispersion associated with each asset pair. The columns to the left provide an attribution of excess dispersion:

- The column labeled "IID" shows that there is no excess dispersion between the implied distribution and the empirical distribution if both assets' returns are serially independent and identically distributed and follow a normal distribution.
- The column labeled "non-normality" shows the excess dispersion attributable to the fact that the monthly returns are not perfectly normally distributed. We generate these results by bootstrapping the monthly returns, which preserves the higher moments but removes any time series properties.
- The column labeled "autocorrelation" shows the excess dispersion arising because the returns of one or both assets are autocorrelated.
- The column labeled "cross-correlation" shows the excess dispersion attributable to nonzero cross-correlations between the pair of assets at one or more lags.
- The column labeled "autocorrelation and cross-correlation" shows the excess dispersion arising from the combination of autocorrelations and lagged cross-correlations.
- The next two columns report for comparison the correlation of monthly relative returns and the correlation of triennial relative returns.
- The column labeled "variance ratio" shows the variance of triennial relative returns divided by the variance of monthly relative returns, normalized by dividing by 36. A variance ratio equal to 1.0 implies that the assets' relative returns are serially independent. The final column shows the significance of the variance ratio.

We can draw several conclusions from Table 5.1. First, there is persuasive evidence that excess dispersion affects major asset classes such as US equity, private equity, and government bonds. Second, in each instance, this excess dispersion is driven predominantly by lagged autocorrelations and cross-correlations rather than by non-normality in the monthly returns. Third, correlations can vary dramatically depending on the return intervals over which they are estimated. In some cases, such as with energy and utility stocks, the triennial correlation is significantly stronger than the monthly correlation. In others, such as with US and emerging market equities, the triennial correlation is significantly weaker.

THE INTUITION

The empirical evidence is conclusive: excess dispersion is widespread among major asset classes. What is the cause? The economic intuition varies depending on the assets in question. However, there are at least two plausible reasons to expect long-term volatility and correlations to differ from what we observe in the short term.

First, different types of information are disseminated into the market at different frequencies. For many tradable assets, changes in the discount rate (readily observable at high frequency) dominate shorter-term fluctuations in price, whereas changes in cash flows (such as earnings data, which are released quarterly) dominate longer-term price movements. A simple experiment lends credence to this hypothesis. We regress the cross section of 10 US equity sector returns on the cross section of changes in earnings over the same period. We also regress the same sector returns on the cross section of changes in beta during the same periods. We use beta as a proxy for sector discount rates with the intuition that investors demand higher returns from sectors that have greater systematic risk. Figure 5.2 shows the median R-squared for these cross-sectional regressions. It reveals rather starkly that high-frequency returns are more strongly related to changes in discount rates than to changes in earnings, whereas the opposite is true for relatively low-frequency returns.

Other studies also corroborate this hypothesis. Poterba and Summers (1998) suggest that time-varying required returns and "slowly decaying price fads" might explain strong serial correlation in US stock returns. Gilbert, Hrdlicka, Kalodimos, and Siegel (2013) find that the CAPM beta of

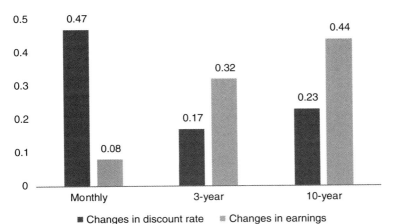

FIGURE 5.2 Median R-squared from cross-sectional regression of sector returns.

stocks is a more dominant factor at low frequencies than high frequencies. Ang, Goyal, and Illmanen (2014) document multi-month momentum and multi-year mean reversion for a variety of asset classes in institutional portfolios. And, we find that income-oriented assets such as bonds are also subject to autocorrelation in their total returns due to the recurring coupon payments.

Non-tradable assets are subject to excess dispersion for a different reason. Privately held asset classes have no market price; instead, their values are based on appraisals. Because appraisals have a backward-looking component linked to comparable sales, akin to a moving average, they introduce persistent autocorrelation to the returns of private assets. For more on this issue and its implications, see Chapters 11 and 17.

THE MATH

We now present the mathematics that relates high-frequency estimation of mean, standard deviation, and correlation to their low-frequency values. We assume throughout this section that the instantaneous rates of return for all assets are normally distributed with stationary means and variances.

We first define the discrete return of an asset X over the holding period $t-1$ to t as the percentage change in the price of X:

$$r_t = \frac{P_t}{P_{t-1}} - 1 \tag{5.1}$$

The cumulative multi-period return equals the cumulative product of the quantity one plus the single-period returns, minus one. We define the continuously compounded return X as the logarithm of the quantity one plus the discrete return. For ease of notation going forward, we denote the continuously compounded return of asset X with a lowercase x:

$$x_t = \ln\left(\frac{P_t}{P_{t-1}}\right) = \ln(1 + r_t) \tag{5.2}$$

The cumulative multi-period continuous return equals the cumulative sum of single-period continuous returns. The standard deviation of the cumulative continuous returns of x over q periods, $x_t + \ldots + x_{t+q-1}$, is given by

$$\sigma\left(x_t + \ldots + x_{t+q-1}\right) = \sigma_x \sqrt{q + 2\sum_{k=1}^{q-1}(q-k)\rho_{x_t, x_{1+k}}} \tag{5.3}$$

where σ_x is the standard deviation of x measured over single-period intervals. Note that if the lagged autocorrelations of x all equal zero, the standard deviation of x will scale with the square root of the horizon, q. However, to the extent that the lagged autocorrelations differ from zero, extrapolating the single-period standard deviation this way to the longer-horizon standard deviation may provide a poor estimate of the actual longer-horizon standard deviation.[1]

Now we introduce a second asset, Y, whose continuously compounded rate of return over the period $t-1$ to t is denoted y_t. The correlation between the cumulative returns of x and the cumulative returns of y over q periods, is given by

$$
\rho\left(x_t + \ldots + x_{t+q-1}, y_t + \ldots + y_{t+q-1}\right)
$$

$$
= \frac{q\rho_{x_t,y_t} + \sum_{k=1}^{q-1}(q-k)\left(\rho_{x_{t+k},y_t} + \rho_{x_t,y_{t+k}}\right)}{\sqrt{q + 2\sum_{k=1}^{q-1}(q-k)\rho_{x_t,x_{t+k}}}\sqrt{q + 2\sum_{k=1}^{q-1}(q-k)\rho_{y_t,y_{t+k}}}} \tag{5.4}
$$

The numerator equals the covariance of the assets taking lagged correlations into account, whereas the denominator equals the product of the assets' standard deviations as described by Equation 5.3. This equation allows us to assume values for the autocorrelations of x and y, as well as the lagged cross-correlations between x and y, in order to compute the correlations and standard deviations that these parameters imply over longer horizons. Although choices for autocorrelation do not uniquely determine cross-correlations, it is important to note that choices for some of the lags impose bounds on the possible values for other lags.[2]

We can now use the long-horizon standard deviations of x and y, together with their correlation, to compute the expected standard deviation of their relative performance after q periods, which we define as the tracking error between x and y:

$$
TE(x,y) = \sqrt{\sigma_x^2 + \sigma_y^2 - 2\rho\sigma_x\sigma_y} \tag{5.5}
$$

These results for long horizons are expressed in units of continuously compounded growth. For optimization, we are required to convert the mean and standard deviation of each asset into discrete units.[3]

The mathematical relationships described above enable us to make several general observations about excess dispersion:

- More positive autocorrelation increases the standard deviation of an asset, which increases excess dispersion. In contrast, more negative autocorrelation decreases excess dispersion.
- More positive lagged cross-correlation decreases excess dispersion. In contrast, more negative lagged cross-correlation increases excess dispersion.
- Shorter lags have a larger impact on excess dispersion than longer lags. The intuition for this is that shorter lags have more opportunity than longer lags to exert their influence within a given time horizon.
- Equal-size positive and negative lagged correlations do not necessarily change excess dispersion by the same amount.
- Changes in the assets' growth rates do not affect excess dispersion.
- If there are no lagged effects, changes in the investment horizon do not affect excess dispersion; it will equal zero for all horizons. If there are nonzero lagged effects, however, changes in the investment horizon do have an impact on excess dispersion.

A hypothetical game can provide some intuition for these dynamics. Imagine that two players are standing next to each other at one end of an athletic field. Each player is issued a stack of cards that instruct him or her to move either one step to the right or to the left. Before drawing each card, the players are also required to take one step forward. As they traverse the field, the two players will find that the distance between them diverges and converges due to their cumulative rightward and leftward movements.

If the cards are organized randomly and there is no relationship between the two decks, we can use straightforward statistics or simulations to forecast the distribution of distances between the players when they reach the far end of the field. Imagine instead that the players' cards are organized nonrandomly such that the left and right cards are grouped together. In this scenario, the players will experience "streaks" of moving in the same direction over successive turns. As a result, they will at times find themselves farther apart than they did when the cards were organized randomly. This illustrates the impact of positive lagged autocorrelation, which serves to increase excess dispersion.

Next, imagine that player 2's cards are organized to have a lagged relationship with player 1's cards. If player 1 draws a left card on one turn, then player 2 is likely to draw a left card on the following turn. In this scenario, we observe that player 2 is continually "catching up" to player 1 with a one-turn lag, and as a result, the two players will tend to stay closer together on the field. This is an example of positive lagged cross-correlation, which serves to reduce excess dispersion.

Finally, imagine a similar lagged relationship between the two players' cards, but in this case, the relationship is negative. When player 1 moves to the left, player 2 is likely to move to the right on the following turn. In this scenario, the distance between the two players will tend to expand over time as their divergences accumulate. This is an example of negative lagged cross-correlation, which serves to increase excess dispersion.

This game, which we admit is not particularly exciting, illustrates how lagged autocorrelations and cross-correlations exhibited in shorter intervals can accumulate and result in more – or less – dispersion over longer intervals. If we assume incorrectly that the cards are organized randomly, both within each deck and between the decks, we will make poor forecasts of the distribution of distances between the players.

IMPLICATIONS

The divergence between high- and low- frequency estimation has several practical implications for investors, which we will now explore. We begin by estimating the monthly and triennial parameters for each asset class in our prototypical portfolio. The top panel of Table 5.2 shows the asset class standard deviations and correlations derived from monthly data, whereas the bottom panel shows the same values derived from triennial data.

Table 5.2 reveals that, as discussed previously, the correlation between US and emerging market equities is significantly lower when measured at triennial intervals. Moreover, the correlation between emerging market equities and commodities nearly doubles and the correlation between emerging market equities and Treasury bonds rises from –2% to +24%. The standard deviations are not directly comparable owing to their different periodicities, but we observe ordinal changes. Commodities have higher volatility than foreign developed market equities at a monthly frequency, but the opposite is true at a triennial frequency. We will now discuss practical implications of these disparities for risk measurement, asset allocation, and performance measurement.

Risk Measurement

Imagine that an investor has an overweight position in emerging market equities and a corresponding underweight position in US equities relative to a particular benchmark. The investor wishes to estimate the likelihood that his or her portfolio will underperform that benchmark over a three-year period. This likelihood is a function of the asset classes' expected returns and covariances as well as the three-year time horizon. It will depend critically on the correlation between US equities and emerging market equities.

TABLE 5.2   Monthly and Triennial Standard Deviations and Correlations

Monthly Returns	Standard Deviations (%)	Correlations					
		a	b	c	d	e	f
a US Equities	4.3						
b Foreign Dev. Mkt. Equities	4.9	0.66					
c Emerging Market Equities	6.6	0.68	0.68				
d Treasury Bonds	1.5	0.10	0.03	−0.02			
e US Corporate Bonds	2.0	0.31	0.24	0.22	0.86		
f Commodities	5.6	0.16	0.29	0.27	−0.07	0.02	
g Cash Equivalents	0.3	0.02	0.02	0.03	0.18	0.09	0.06

Triennial Returns	Standard Deviations (%)	Correlations					
		a	b	c	d	e	f
a US Equities	28.4						
b Foreign Dev. Mkt. Equities	36.1	0.60					
c Emerging Market Equities	41.2	0.15	0.66				
d Treasury Bonds	11.0	0.20	0.12	0.24			
e US Corporate Bonds	14.2	0.30	0.16	0.23	0.86		
f Commodities	34.8	0.11	0.31	0.50	0.05	0.02	
g Cash Equivalents	9.5	0.27	0.24	0.31	0.60	0.25	0.33

(January 1988–December 2015)

If we assume this correlation is high, we are implicitly assuming that these two assets classes are close substitutes and that the short position will be an effective hedge for the long position. In this case, the two assets' returns are unlikely to diverge, and the risk of underperformance will be relatively low. On the other hand, if we assume that the correlation between the assets is low, we are implicitly assuming a higher likelihood that their returns will diverge. This will result in a much higher risk of underperformance.

In this case, the monthly correlation of 68% is more than four times as large as the triennial correlation of 15%. If our hypothetical investor estimates the three-year risk of loss using the monthly correlation, he or she will significantly underestimate the true risk of loss over a three-year period. In our 2014 paper, we present a simple example where exposure to longer-term underperformance is almost twice as large as an investor would have expected from monthly returns. Yet, many institutional investors compute their exposure to loss in precisely this manner.

Portfolio Construction

It is also common practice for investors with long horizons to extrapolate parameters estimated from shorter-interval data to construct portfolios. If investors care only about performance over short horizons or within long horizons, they could construct portfolios that reflect aversion to risk based on the covariances of monthly returns. Alternatively, if they are concerned only with performance at the conclusion of long horizons, they could estimate the covariance matrix from long-horizon returns, such as three years. Or, as is the most likely case, if they care about performance over both short and long horizons, they could include separate estimates of risk: one based on a covariance matrix of monthly returns and another based on a covariance matrix of triennial returns. It is straightforward to augment the standard Markowitz (1952) optimization framework to include additional terms for aversion to long-horizon risk and long-horizon variance:[4]

$$E(U) = \mu - \lambda_H \sigma_H^2 - \lambda_L \sigma_L^2 \tag{5.6}$$

In Equation 5.6, E(U) is expected utility, μ equals portfolio expected return, λ_H is aversion to risk estimated from high-frequency returns, σ_H^2 is portfolio variance based on high-frequency returns, λ_L is aversion to low-frequency risk, and σ_L^2 is portfolio variance based on low-frequency returns. It is also possible to preserve the original Markowitz format by blending the two covariance matrices in accordance with one's relative aversion to high- and low-frequency risk.

If we solve for the portfolio weights that maximize Equation 5.6 while holding λ_L constant and incrementally increasing λ_H, we produce a continuum of portfolios that comprise the iso-expected return curve shown in Figure 5.3. The portfolios along this curve all have the same expected return, but they have different combinations of monthly and triennial tracking error. For each portfolio along the curve, that portfolio offers the lowest achievable level of monthly tracking error for a given level of triennial tracking error and vice versa.

We construct this curve by first deriving a set of implied returns from the monthly covariance matrix. We then solve for the optimal weights using Equation 5.6, but we initially assume no aversion to triennial risk. This first optimization gives us the extreme upper-left portfolio on the curve, portfolio P1, which has the lowest monthly tracking error. We then progressively increase aversion to triennial risk, while holding expected return constant,

FIGURE 5.3 Stylized iso-expected return curve balancing short- and long-horizon tracking error.

which moves us down and to the right along the curve, to portfolio P2, which offers a balance between monthly and triennial tracking error. Portfolio P3 represents the optimal portfolio for an investor who is concerned only with triennial tracking error and not with monthly tracking error. This curve represents the available choices to an investor who cares about aversion to both short-term and long-term losses.

In our 2014 paper, we found that an investor would need to incur turnover of more than 45% to trade from portfolio P1 to portfolio P3. Put differently, if an investor who is concerned with risk over triennial periods constructed his or her portfolio using monthly parameters, the portfolio would be misallocated by more than 45% relative to the optimal portfolio. Figure 5.3 shows that it is possible to construct portfolios that simultaneously optimize high- and low-frequency risk in a manner that is consistent with an investor's relative aversion to these two measures of risk.

Performance Measurement

Investors have long relied on historical risk-adjusted returns to evaluate the performance of active portfolio managers. The Sharpe ratio is expressed as the portfolio's annualized return in excess of the risk-free rate divided by the annualized standard deviation of returns. The information ratio, its analogue for relative performance, equals the portfolio's annualized return in excess of a benchmark divided by the annualized standard deviation of excess returns. In both cases, the denominator is annualized. Investors typically estimate the standard deviation from monthly returns and then multiply this quantity by the square root of 12. In some cases, they are required to annualize in this manner if they wish to comply with industry standards. The CFA Institute includes the following statement in its GIPS Handbook:

> *To annualize the three-year annualized [sic] ex post standard deviation calculated using monthly returns, the result of the standard deviation (S) formula above must be multiplied by the square root of 12.*

We disagree with this approach. The assumption that returns are independent does not always hold, and we have shown how this fact can complicate portfolio construction and risk measurement. In our 2015 paper, we showed that it can also affect performance measurement for hedge funds, mutual funds, and risk parity strategies.

To estimate the impact of this effect on hedge funds, we examined the CISDM/Morningstar database of 569 hedge funds that reported performance between January 2000 and December 2013. We computed two Sharpe ratios for each fund: one where the numerator and denominator are estimated from monthly intervals and another where they are estimated from triennial intervals within the same period. We did not annualize either figure. We then ranked the hedge funds by the two Sharpe ratios such that we had one ranking based on triennial outcomes and another ranking based on monthly outcomes. Of course, the ranking of the numerators (the return) is identical across the two lists. But the ranking of the denominators (the standard deviation) changes depending on lagged autocorrelations.

We found that 27% of hedge fund Sharpe ratios switch quartiles when we move from monthly intervals to triennial intervals to compute standard deviation. The impact was greatest for global macro and US equity long-short funds, of which 47% and 35%, respectively, changed quartiles. One hedge fund, Equity Income Partners, LP, managed by Envision Capital, moved from the top quartile to the bottom quartile! Were we to annualize (or tri-annualize) Sharpe ratios using the "square root of t" rule, the levels of the ratios would change, but the rankings would not. These results therefore offer compelling evidence that this method of annualization can distort performance evaluation for longer-investment horizons.

We performed an analogous experiment for a database of mutual funds. Although the results are not as dramatic as with hedge funds, we still found that 18% of mutual funds change quartile when we measure their information ratios using triennial outcomes rather than monthly outcomes. Counterintuitively, the distortion is most pronounced for US large cap funds, where 22% change quartile with high statistical significance.

Finally, we assessed the impact of these effects on the performance of risk parity strategies. Investors who follow this once-popular investment strategy construct their portfolios such that each asset within the portfolio contributes equally to total portfolio risk. This requires that portfolio weights be proportional to the inverse of the assets' standard deviations.

Specifically, we compared the performance of US equities, US fixed income, a 60/40 portfolio, and a risk parity portfolio from January 1929 through December 2010. The 60/40 portfolio was rebalanced monthly. To construct the risk parity portfolio, we followed the same approach described in Asness, Frazzini, and Pedersen (2012). When we used annualized monthly returns, the risk parity portfolio dominates. The Sharpe ratio of the risk parity portfolio was 0.43 compared to 0.36 for the 60/40 portfolio. However, when we estimate Sharpe ratios using 10-year intervals, we arrive at a different conclusion. In this case, the Sharpe ratio of the risk parity strategy is merely 0.16, whereas that of the 60/40 portfolio is 0.23.

These results imply that the returns of the risk parity strategy are subject to positive lagged autocorrelation. This strategy exhibited the largest increase in annualized volatility when the interval length was increased. As a result, the risk of the strategy over longer horizons is significantly greater than one would assume by extrapolating shorter-interval risk estimates.

Proponents of risk parity argue that the strategy outperforms because the security market line has a slope less than 1, which means that high-beta asset classes deliver relatively low returns compared to low-beta asset classes. They point to leverage aversion as the likely cause of this flatness; that is, investors who require higher levels of return are more likely to assume the risk associated with unlevered equities than to invest in a lower-risk portfolio and lever it up to hit their required return. Indeed, the security market line of stocks and bonds is relatively flat when estimated from their monthly returns. It has a slope of 0.59. This is not the case, however, when we estimate the security market line from 10-year returns. Its slope approaches 1, which implies that bonds do not deliver a higher risk-adjusted return than stocks do when measured over longer intervals.

This finding is not unique to these two specific asset classes or this time period. We found similar results for a risk parity strategy encompassing a broader sample of assets, including corporate bonds and commodities, over a more recent time period. These results call into question arguments that risk parity strategies offer higher risk-adjusted returns than a 60/40 mix or a broader asset mix over long investment horizons.

THE BOTTOM LINE

Analysts and investors often find that realized correlations and standard deviations differ from their estimates. In some cases, they assume correctly that these differences are due to estimation error; that is, they arise because the parameter estimates were derived from a different sample. Our results suggest there is another culprit that is often overlooked. It is common practice to estimate standard deviations and correlations from shorter intervals and extrapolate these values to forecast what will prevail over longer intervals. Yet, even within the same sample, parameters estimated from short intervals do not always align with the longer-interval realizations. Investors may be tempted to attribute this divergence to non-normality in the returns, but our results suggest that interval error, driven by nonzero lagged autocorrelations and cross-correlations, is more often to blame.

In this chapter, we introduced excess dispersion, a new metric to capture the degree of interval error in the absolute returns of an asset or the relative returns between two assets. We defined it as the fraction of the realized distribution of triennial returns that falls outside the one-standard-deviation tails of the distribution that is implied by estimation from monthly returns. Empirical results confirm that excess dispersion is prevalent among major asset class pairs. We presented the mathematics of excess dispersion and showed how investors can extrapolate correctly from shorter to longer intervals in the presence of nonzero lagged autocorrelations and cross-correlations.

Most important, we discussed practical implications for investors as they relate to risk measurement, portfolio construction, and performance measurement in the presence of these time series properties. We recommend that investors account for the impact of interval error when estimating exposure to loss over long investment horizons, either by estimating parameters over longer intervals or testing directly for the presence of lagged autocorrelations or cross-correlations. We showed how to construct portfolios that strike an optimal balance between short- and long-interval risk and correlation properties. And, we showed how performance measures such as the Sharpe and information ratio can distort the quartile rankings of investment managers when evaluated over longer horizons.

RELATED TOPICS

- Chapter 15 introduces multi-goal optimization as a means to control for two distinct risks in a single utility function.
- Chapter 17 shows how to de-smooth the returns of private asset classes to adjust for their autocorrelation.
- Chapter 19 shows how to form portfolios that account for covariance instability and thereby address traditional estimation error.

REFERENCES

Ang, A., Goyal, A., and Illmanen, A. 2014. "Asset Allocation and Bad Habits," Working Paper (April).

Asness, C., Frazzini, A., and Pedersen, L. 2012. "Leverage Aversion and Risk Parity," *Financial Analysts Journal*, Vol. 68, No. 1 (January/ February).

Gilbert, T., Hrdlicka, C., Kalodimos, J., and Siegel, S. 2014. "Daily Data Is Bad for Beta: Opacity and Frequency-Dependent Betas," *Review of Asset Pricing Studies*, Vol. 4, No. 1.

Kinlaw, W., Kritzman, M., and Turkington, D. 2014. "The Divergence of High- and Low-Frequency Estimation: Causes and Consequences," *The Journal of Portfolio Management*, Special 40th Anniversary Issue, Vol. 40, No. 5.

Kinlaw, W., Kritzman, M., and Turkington, D. 2015. "The Divergence of High- and Low-Frequency Estimation: Implications for Performance Measurement," *The Journal of Portfolio Management*, Vol. 41, No. 3.

Kritzman, M. and Turkington, D. 2021. "History, Shocks and Drifts: A New Approach to Portfolio Formation," *MIT Working Paper* (March).

Lo, A. W. and MacKinlay, A. C. 1988. "Stock Market Prices Do Not Follow Random Walks: Evidence from a Simple Specification Test," *Review of Financial Studies*, Vol. 1, No. 1.

Markowitz, H. 1952. "Portfolio Selection," *Journal of Finance*, Vol. 7, No. 1 (March).

Poterba, J. M. and Summers, L. H. 1988. "Mean Reversion in Stock Prices: Evidence and Implications," *Journal of Financial Economics*, Vol. 22, No. 1 (October).

NOTES

1. This issue was highlighted by Lo and MacKinlay (1988), who introduced a variance ratio test to evaluate whether asset returns follow a random walk.
2. See Kinlaw, Kritzman, and Turkington (2014, 2015) for details.
3. To convert the mean into discrete units, we use the formula $\mu_d + e^{\mu_c + \sigma_c^2/2} - 1$. To convert the standard deviation into discrete units we use the formula

$\sigma_d = \sqrt{e^{2\mu_c + \sigma_c^2}\left(e^{\sigma_c^2} - 1\right)}$. In these equations, μ_d and σ_d are the mean and standard deviation of cumulative discrete returns, and μ_c and σ_c are the mean and standard deviation of cumulative continuous returns. Similarly, we compute the correlation between the cumulative discrete returns in terms of the means, standard deviations, and correlation ρ_c of cumulative continuous returns:

$$\rho_d = \frac{e^{\rho_c \sigma_{x,c} \sigma_{y,c}} - 1}{\sqrt{\left(e^{\sigma_{x,c}^2} - 1\right)}\sqrt{\left(e^{\sigma_{y,c}^2} - 1\right)}}.$$

4. Augmenting the utility function to account for two covariance matrices over different horizons addresses this challenge in the context of mean-variance analysis. Though the procedure is slightly more complex, it is also possible to address the challenge of multiple horizons in a more general and flexible setting. Kritzman and Turkington (2021) show how to create mixed-frequency return samples that are properly balanced for use with full-scale optimization (described in Chapter 12). This approach can accommodate different preferences for short-horizon versus long-horizon outcomes, and it accounts for the full complexity of an empirical sample of returns.

CHAPTER 6

Correlation Asymmetry

FALLACY: DIVERSIFICATION IS SYMMETRIC

That investors should diversify their portfolios is a core principle of modern finance. The correlation coefficient, the parameter that quantifies the degree to which two assets tend to offset – or diversify – one another, took on new significance in 1952 when Harry Markowitz published his landmark article "Portfolio Selection." Markowitz formalized the role of diversification in portfolio risk when he showed how to construct optimal portfolios given the expected returns, standard deviations, and correlations of their component assets. Nearly 70 years after it was introduced, the mean-variance paradigm has proved surprisingly robust. However, it makes two implicit assumptions about diversification that warrant careful consideration. Because it relies on a single parameter to approximate the way each pair of assets covary, mean-variance analysis assumes that correlations are symmetric on the upside and downside. Moreover, when we maximize the quadratic utility function that takes this single parameter as an input, we also assume that diversification is desirable on the upside as well as the downside.[1] The first assumption is occasionally correct, but the second assumption never is.

Diversification is most helpful to investors when the major engine of growth in the portfolio, typically domestic equities, performs poorly. They derive benefit from assets whose returns offset this poor performance. When the growth engine is performing well, they would actually prefer unification, which is the opposite of diversification. In this sense, the ideal complement to domestic equities would be an asset that is correlated positively when domestic equities are performing well and negatively when they are not. An adage, which has been attributed both to Mark Twain and Robert Frost, defines a banker as "a fellow who lends you his umbrella when the sun is shining but wants it back the minute it begins to rain."[2] Diversification often behaves like a banker if this characterization is to be believed.

In this chapter, we review the mathematics of correlation asymmetry and show how to distinguish true correlation asymmetry from the illusory correlation shifts that arise as an artifact of how the data are partitioned. We then present an empirical study of correlation asymmetry for the assets classes considered in this book. Finally, we show how investors can employ full-scale optimization to construct portfolios that exploit correlation asymmetry, thereby increasing correlation within the portfolio on the upside, where it is beneficial, and reducing correlation on the downside, where it is not.

CORRELATION MATHEMATICS

Market participants often remark that "correlations go to one" when the markets are in turmoil. But such differences do not necessarily indicate that the bivariate return distribution is non-normal or that returns are generated by more than one distribution. Correlation changes arise naturally as an artifact of how the full sample is partitioned, even if the underlying distribution is normal. We must account for these effects to detect correlation asymmetry properly.

Longin and Solnik (2001) introduce the notion of exceedance correlation, which they define as the correlation between two assets when the returns of both assets are either above or below a given threshold. For example, they might estimate the exceedance correlation for US and foreign equities from the subsample of returns where both asset classes suffer losses of 10% or more. Chua, Kritzman, and Page (2009) apply the same approach to a variety of asset pairs and find pervasive evidence of undesirable correlation asymmetry. However, this double-conditioning approach suffers from a fundamental flaw. It misses important instances of diversification because it ignores outcomes where, in this example, US equities perform poorly but foreign equities perform well. We propose instead that investors measure what matters: the degree to which a given asset diversifies the main growth engine when it underperforms. By applying the threshold to one asset only, rather than to both assets, we can better understand the diversification potential of the second asset.

Figure 6.1 presents a simple illustration of this point. We use Monte Carlo simulation to generate 500 returns for assets X and Y that conform to a bivariate normal distribution with identical means equal to zero, standard deviations equal to 20%, and a correlation of 0.50. Imagine that asset X is the main growth driver in the portfolio and that we have selected asset Y to diversify it. When asset X is performing well, we would prefer that asset Y follow suit. These outcomes reflect desirable upside unification and are associated with the upper-right quadrant of Figure 6.1. On the other hand, when asset X is suffering losses, we would prefer that asset Y decouple from asset X to offset those losses. These outcomes reflect desirable downside decoupling of asset Y and are associated with the upper-left quadrant of Figure 6.1. These are the periods where asset Y successfully diversifies asset X. Finally, the lower-left quadrant of Figure 6.1 is associated with very unpleasant outcomes where asset X underperforms and asset Y fails to diversify it.

FIGURE 6.1   Return observations for two assets.

Figure 6.2 presents a comparison of the single- and double-conditioning approaches for the bivariate normal distribution specified above. The left panel shows the subsample where both assets' returns are below the threshold; this is the approach taken by Longin and Solnik (2001); Chua, Kritzman, and Page (2009); Ang and Chen (2002), and others. We submit that investors should instead estimate downside correlations from the subsample of returns shown in the right panel, where the return of asset X is below a particular threshold, regardless of the return of asset Y.

The single conditioning approach introduces additional complexity because we are now able to estimate two downside correlation coefficients for each pair of assets, one conditioned on the returns of each asset. This doubles the number of correlation coefficients we must potentially consider. But it is reasonable for investors to focus their attention on a few of the

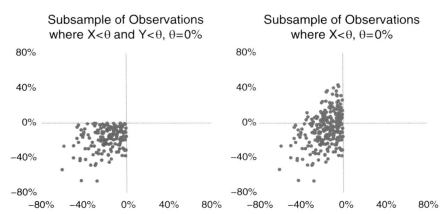

FIGURE 6.2 Subsamples of returns for assets X and Y where one or both assets underperform.

portfolio's main growth engines, the assets that contribute the largest share of portfolio risk, as the conditioning assets.

The upside and downside correlations between assets X and Y, conditioned on the returns of asset X, are given by Equation 6.1:

$$\rho(\theta) = \begin{cases} corr(x,y|x > \theta) \, if \, \theta > 0 \\ corr(x,y|x < \theta) \, if \, \theta < 0 \end{cases} \quad (6.1)$$

where ρ is the upside or downside correlation, x and y are observed returns for assets X and Y, and θ is the threshold applied to the returns of asset X. In practice, we express θ in units of standard deviation above or below the mean of asset X. So, if we set θ equal to +1.0, we would evaluate the top portion of Equation 6.1 and estimate correlation for all observations where the return of asset X is one standard deviation or more above its mean. If we set θ equal to −1.5, we would evaluate the bottom portion of Equation 6.1, which focuses on the subsample of returns where asset X is 1.5 standard deviations or more below its mean. In the unique case where θ equals zero, we evaluate both equations to estimate an upside correlation (where returns are above the mean) and a downside correlation (where returns are below the mean). Because the bivariate normal distribution is symmetric, the expected upside and downside correlations will be identical in this instance and for any instance where the thresholds have the same absolute value.

There are two ways to estimate conditional correlations for the bivariate normal distribution. The first is to employ Monte Carlo simulation and then estimate correlations from a partitioned sample. The second is to use the closed-form solution derived by Baykan Pamir, which is given by Equation 6.2:

$$Corr(x,y|x < \theta) = \frac{Cov(x,y|x < \theta)}{\sqrt{Var(x|x < \theta)Var(y|x < \theta)}} \tag{6.2A}$$

$$= \rho \frac{Var(x|x < \theta)}{\sqrt{Var(x|x < \theta)Var(y|x < \theta)}} \tag{6.2B}$$

$$= \rho \sqrt{\frac{Var(x|x < \theta)}{Var(y|x < \theta)}} \tag{6.2C}$$

$$= \rho \sqrt{\frac{\Phi(\theta) - \dfrac{\theta}{\sqrt{2\pi}}e^{-\frac{\theta^2}{2}} - \dfrac{1}{2\pi\,\Phi(\theta)}e^{-\theta^2}}{\Phi(\theta) - \dfrac{\rho^2\theta}{\sqrt{2\pi}}e^{-\frac{\theta^2}{2}} - \dfrac{\rho^2}{2\pi\,\Phi(\theta)}e^{-\theta^2}}} \tag{6.2D}$$

where x and y are the returns of assets X and Y, respectively; θ is the threshold applied to the returns of asset X; and $\Phi(\cdot)$ is the cumulative density of a truncated bivariate normal distribution. For the full proof, see Czasonis, Kritzman, Pamir, and Turkington (2021).

For the results presented in this chapter, we employ the Monte Carlo approach. Given Equation 6.1 and setting θ equal to zero, the upside and downside correlation associated with the bivariate distribution defined above is 0.33 as opposed to 0.50 for the full sample. If we modify Equation 6.1 to apply the threshold to both assets' returns, the upside and downside correlation is 0.27. Were these estimates derived from real data rather than simulated data, we might be tempted to conclude that diversification increases on the downside for this pair of assets. But this interpretation would be incorrect. These differences are an artifact of conditional correlation math and do not indicate any change in the relationship between the two assets in the tails.

Figure 6.3 shows how the expected upside and downside correlation varies as a function of the threshold value, θ, for US and foreign developed

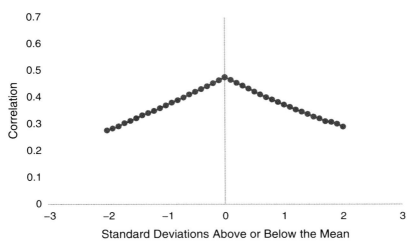

FIGURE 6.3 Expected upside and downside correlations for US and foreign developed equities as a function of threshold value, assuming a bivariate normal distribution (conditioned on US equities).

equities, which have a full-sample correlation of 0.66.[3] When we estimate upside and downside correlations from empirical data, we must compare them to these expected values. Only if we observe material differences between the empirical and expected correlation profiles can we conclude that the observed correlation asymmetry is a symptom either of a non-normal bivariate distribution or multiple distributions. It is in these instances that investors should account for correlation asymmetry when they construct portfolios or estimate downside risk exposure. Figure 6.4 shows the empirical correlation profile for US equities and foreign developed equities overlaid on the expected profile from Figure 6.3.

Figure 6.4 reveals that the empirical downside correlation is higher than the downside correlation implied by the bivariate normal distribution. In the right tail, we observe the opposite effect. This correlation profile represents downside unification and upside diversification and is therefore undesirable. Figure 6.5 shows a more desirable correlation profile. In this case, Treasury bonds diversify US equities on the downside but offer some unification on the upside.

In the next section, we present a comprehensive empirical analysis of correlation asymmetry among the asset classes considered in this book. To do so efficiently, we introduce a summary metric to capture the degree of

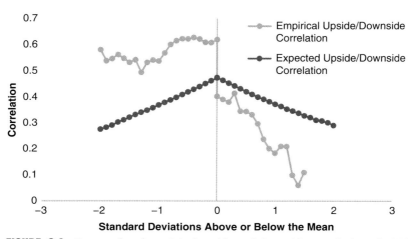

FIGURE 6.4 Expected and empirical upside and downside correlations for US and foreign developed equities as a function of threshold value (conditioned on US equities).

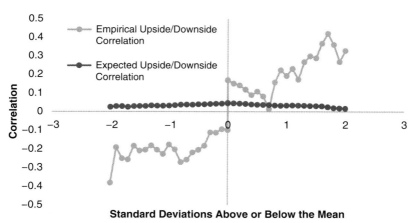

FIGURE 6.5 Expected and empirical upside and downside correlations for US equities and Treasury bonds as a function of threshold value (conditioned on US equities).

correlation asymmetry for each asset pair. The metric we choose is the average difference between the empirical and expected downside correlations across threshold values for down markets less the analogous quantity for up markets. We calculate these average differences for up and down markets as given by Equation 6.3:

$$
\mu_{dn} = \frac{1}{n} \sum_{i=1}^{n} \left[\rho_{emp}\left(\theta_i\right) - \rho_{\exp}\left(\theta_i\right) \right], \ \ for \ i < 0
$$

$$
\mu_{up} = \frac{1}{n} \sum_{i=1}^{n} \left[\rho_{emp}\left(\theta_i\right) - \rho_{\exp}\left(\theta_i\right) \right], \ \ for \ i > 0
$$

(6.3)

The terms μ_{dn} and μ_{up} are the average differences for up and down markets, respectively; $\rho_{emp}\left(\theta_i\right)$ is the empirical upside or downside correlation at threshold θ_i; and $\rho_{\exp}\left(\theta_i\right)$ is the corresponding expected upside or downside correlation for a bivariate normal distribution. For both up and down markets, we iterate through n thresholds equally spaced by intervals of 0.1 standard deviations. We stop iterating when there are less than 30 observations above or below the threshold. We then take the difference between the upside and downside averages given by Equation 6.3 ($\mu_{dn} - \mu_{up}$) to arrive at a summary metric for correlation asymmetry. Positive values for this metric indicate the presence of net undesirable downside unification or upside diversification. Negative values indicate desirable downside decoupling or upside unification. For US and foreign developed equities, this average difference is equal to 0.32, reflecting an unfavorable correlation profile.

CORRELATION ASYMMETRY BETWEEN ASSET CLASSES

Research has shown that most asset universes offer less diversification during down markets than up markets, including country equity markets, global industries, individual stocks, hedge funds and international bonds.[4] The relationship between stocks and bonds represents an exception to this pattern. Kritzman, Lowry, and Van Royen (2001) find that the stock-bond correlation within countries actually decreases during periods of market turbulence. In this section, we build on this finding to analyze the pervasiveness of correlation asymmetry across asset classes. To capture correlation asymmetry for each asset pair, we report the summary metric ($\mu_{dn} - \mu_{up}$) as given by Equation 6.3. Figure 6.6 shows the 10 asset class pairs with the most undesirable net downside unification as well as the five with the most desirable net downside decoupling.[5]

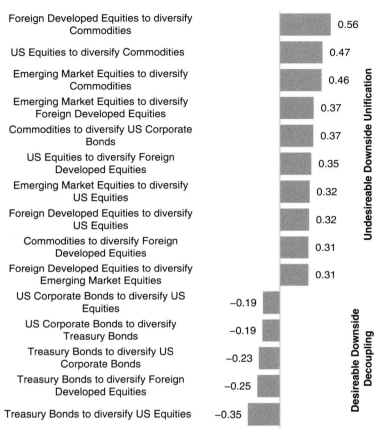

FIGURE 6.6 Asset class pairs with most desirable and undesirable correlation profiles (conditioned on returns of the second asset class).

It is evident from Figure 6.6 that both emerging market equities and foreign developed equities exhibit correlation asymmetry with US equities that is undesirable. There is also evidence that Treasury bonds offer a desirable correlation profile when paired with US equities, US corporate bonds, and foreign developed equities.

IMPLICATIONS FOR PORTFOLIO CONSTRUCTION

Having demonstrated that correlation asymmetry is prevalent among major asset classes, we now turn to the practical question of what investors should do about it. There are two ways to account for correlation asymmetry in portfolio management. Investors can

1. reallocate their portfolios dynamically in anticipation of regime shifts, increasing their exposure to safe-haven assets that offer downside diversification when they expect conditions to deteriorate, or
2. place greater weight on downside correlations when setting policy weights, thereby constructing a static portfolio that is more resilient to downturns.

Investors who pursue the first approach must monitor market conditions and predict which correlations are most likely to prevail in the future. For more on regime-switching models, see Chapter 22. On the other hand, investors who pursue the second approach seek to prepare rather than predict. They build portfolios as one might design a house on the seashore: for routine use during balmy conditions but sufficiently resilient to weather a hurricane if one should strike. This approach requires that the designer strike an optimal balance between resilience to storms and utility during fair weather conditions. A windowless, concrete bunker would provide maximum protection but would not be particularly appealing on a sunny day. We propose that investors strike the analogous balance when constructing portfolios.

There are several ways investors can construct portfolios that account for correlation asymmetry. One way is to perform mean-variance analysis using only the downside, rather than full-sample correlations. However, this approach would be optimal only during extreme conditions. Another way would be to blend the full-sample correlations with the downside correlations, but this leaves the critical choice of the blending ratio. Furthermore, in a portfolio with more than two assets, both methods require that the investor select a subset of the assets on whose returns the correlations will be conditioned.

We propose instead that investors use full-scale optimization to construct portfolios that account implicitly for asymmetric correlations as well as other peculiarities of the multivariate return distribution. Full-scale optimization, which we introduce in Chapter 12, identifies the optimal portfolio for any return distribution and any specification of investor preferences. Whereas, for a given time horizon or assuming returns are expressed in continuous units, mean-variance analysis yields an approximation of the in-sample solution if the return distribution is elliptical and investors have preferences that can be described by mean and variance, full-scale optimization yields the true optimal portfolio for a given return sample. Rather than relying on parameters like means and covariances to approximate the distribution, full-scale optimization relies on numerical search algorithms to solve for the weights that maximize the given utility function precisely. To demonstrate how this technique accounts for correlation asymmetries, we employ a kinked utility function like the one introduced in Chapter 12. This utility function is given by Equation 6.4:

$$U_{kinked}(R) = \begin{cases} \ln(1+R), for\, r \geq k \\ \ln(1+R) - \omega(k-R), for\, r < k \end{cases} \tag{6.4}$$

The term $U_{kinked}(R)$ denotes utility, R is the return of the portfolio, k is the location of the kink, and ω is the slope of the linear utility function below the link. With this utility function, investor satisfaction drops precipitously when returns fall below the kink. When returns are above the kink, investor satisfaction conforms to a log-wealth utility function. This utility function expresses strong aversion to large losses.

To determine whether full-scale optimization addresses correlation asymmetry effectively, we need a way to measure the degree of correlation asymmetry in a portfolio and whether it is of the desirable or undesirable variety. For this purpose we define the metric ξ in Equation 6.5:

$$\xi = \sum_{i=1}^{n}\sum_{j=1}^{n} w_i w_j \left(\mu_{i,j}^{dn} - \mu_{i,j}^{up} \right) \tag{6.5}$$

where n is the number of assets, w_i is the weight of asset i in the portfolio, w_j is the weight of asset j in the portfolio, and $\left(\mu_{i,j}^{dn} - \mu_{i,j}^{up} \right)$ is the correlation asymmetry summary metric for assets i and j given by Equation 6.3, conditioned on asset i. Larger values of ξ indicate that the portfolio has excess downside correlation, which is undesirable. Of course, investors do not derive utility by reducing correlation asymmetry; they derive utility by growing wealth. Full-scale optimization does not maximize desirable correlation asymmetry directly, but as we will demonstrate, utility is well served by pairing assets that unify on the upside and diversify on the downside. Mean-variance analysis cannot account for these kinds of asymmetries because it implicitly assumes that correlations are symmetric.

Table 6.1 shows a full-scale optimal portfolio (derived using the kinked utility function given by Equation 6.4 with a k value of –25%) and a corresponding mean-variance optimal portfolio with the same expected return.[6] It also shows the degree of undesirable correlation asymmetry for each portfolio.

Table 6.1 reveals that, as we would expect, the mean-variance optimal portfolio has a lower standard deviation than the full-scale optimal portfolio. However, the mean-variance portfolio suffers a larger average loss when its returns fall below –25%. The full-scale portfolio is able to achieve this reduction in downside exposure by reducing undesirable correlation

TABLE 6.1 Correlation Asymmetry of Mean-Variance and Full-Scale Optimal
Portfolios

	Expected Return (%)	Standard Deviation (%)	Full-Scale Optimal Portfolio (%)	Mean-Variance Optimal Portfolio (%)
US Equities	7.5	14.1	64.3	42.3
Foreign Developed Equities	7.8	16.4	9.7	16.6
Emerging Market Equities	8.5	22.4	4.1	10.0
Treasury Bonds	4.9	4.4	21.5	12.4
US Corporate Bonds	5.3	4.9	0.0	10.8
Commodities	6.5	20.4	0.5	7.8
Expected Return			7.0	7.0
Standard Deviation			10.9	10.6
Likelihood of Loss > 25%			0.2	0.2
Average Loss > 25%			27	30
Correlation Asymmetry (ξ)			4	15

asymmetry that is "invisible" to the mean-variance utility function. The
changes in weights are intuitive. The full-scale optimal portfolio has larger
allocations to US equities and Treasury bonds, the pair with the most desirable correlation asymmetry profile during the sample period. It holds almost
no allocation to commodities or corporate bonds, the pair with the least
desirable correlation asymmetry profile during the sample period.

THE BOTTOM LINE

In this chapter, we debunked the fallacy that diversification is always beneficial to investors and that correlations are symmetric on the upside and
downside. Although diversification is desirable on the downside, investors
would prefer that all assets rise in concert and should seek unification on the
upside. When measuring conditional correlations, it is important to adjust
for the correlation changes that arise naturally as an artifact of correlation math. To detect correlation asymmetry properly, we must (i) condition
returns on a single asset of interest rather than both assets and (ii) compare the empirical upside and downside correlations to the values we would
expect if returns emanated from a single, bivariate normal distribution.
Unfortunately, when we make these adjustments, we conclude that most
pairs of asset classes exhibit unfavorable correlation profiles. Diversification

often disappears on the downside when it is most needed. And, like an unwieldy umbrella on a sunny day, it is often present on the upside when it imparts no benefit. Finally, we showed how investors can use full-scale optimization to construct portfolios that account explicitly for asymmetric correlation profiles and other non-normal features of the distribution to maximize expected utility.

RELATED TOPICS

- Chapter 12 shows how to construct portfolios using full-scale optimization, which accounts for asymmetric correlations in addition to non-normal distributions of individual asset returns.

REFERENCES

Ang, A. and Chen, J. 2002. "Asymmetric Correlations of Equity Portfolios," *Journal of Financial Economics*, Vol. 63, No. 3, 443–494.

Chua, D., Kritzman, M., and Page, S. 2009. "The Myth of Diversification," *The Journal of Portfolio Management*, Vol. 36, No. 1 (Fall).

Czasonis, M., Kritzman, M., Pamir, B., and Turkington, D. 2021. "The Role of Crypto Currencies in Institutional Portfolios," *SSRN Working Paper*.

Kinlaw, W., Kritzman, M., Page, S., and Turkington, D. 2021. "The Myth of Diversification Reconsidered," *SSRN Working Paper*, forthcoming in the Journal of Portfolio Management.

Kritzman, M., Lowry, K., and Van Royen, A. 2001. "Risk, Regimes, and Overconfidence," *The Journal of Derivatives*, Vol. 8, No. 3 (Spring).

Longin, F. and Solnik, B. 2001. "Extreme Correlation of International Equity Markets," *The Journal of Finance*, Vol. 56, No. 2 (April).

Markowitz, H. 1952. "Portfolio Selection," *The Journal of Finance*, Vol. 7, No. 1 (March).

NOTES

1. For an overview of mean-variance optimization, see Chapter 2.
2. For more on this quote, see https://quoteinvestigator.com/2011/04/07/banker-umbrella/.
3. We estimate these upside and downside correlations using a Monte Carlo simulation with 10 million observations. We could also estimate them using the closed-form solution given in Czasonis et al. (2021).
4. For a summary of the literature on this subject, see Kinlaw, Kritzman, Page, and Turkington (2021).

5. We exclude cash from this analysis because its low expected return and standard deviation render its diversification properties less relevant. We estimate the empirical and expected correlation profile for each asset pair in the same manner as in Figures 6.4 and 6.5. We estimate the empirical correlation profile using data starting in January 1976 and ending in December 2019, except for emerging market equities, which start in January 1988. Emerging market equities values are estimated pairwise over this time period with each other asset class. We estimate only values for thresholds where at least 30 observations are available above or below the threshold. We then average across all thresholds to estimate the excess upside and downside correlation.

6. Because returns data for emerging market equities are not available until January 1988, and we cannot rely on backfilled returns to estimate correlation asymmetries, we use a shorter historical sample for this analysis than elsewhere in this book. We also use different expected returns and standard deviations. Expected returns are illustrative views. Standard deviations are annualized and estimated from monthly data over the period January 1988 through December 2019. We solve for the mean-variance optimal portfolio using these inputs as well as correlations estimated over the same period as standard deviations. We solve for the full-scale optimal portfolio using a nonlinear search function to maximize the kinked utility function given by Equation 6.4. For k and ω we select values of -25%, and 100, respectively, although the results are robust to reasonable variation in these parameters. We constrain expected return to equal 7% in both optimizations. We apply the full-scale algorithm to a simulated sample consisting of 1,000 years of return observations for each asset class. We construct each year in this sample by drawing 12 monthly multivariate return observations at random, with replacement, from the empirical sample (1988–2019). We then re-mean the 1,000 year sample to reflect our expected returns. Likelihood of loss is the frequency of portfolio returns falling below the k value of -25% in the 1,000-year simulated sample. Average loss is the average portfolio return for the subsample of portfolio returns that fall below this threshold. Correlation asymmetry reflects the weighted average summary metric, as given by Equation 6.5, for each portfolio. Correlation asymmetries are calculated over the period 1988–2019.

CHAPTER 7

Error Maximization

FALLACY: OPTIMIZED PORTFOLIOS ARE HYPERSENSITIVE TO INPUT ERRORS

Mean-variance analysis requires investors to estimate expected returns, standard deviations, and correlations, whose future realizations will vary from their estimated values. The process of optimization, by construction, will over-allocate to asset classes for which expected returns are overestimated and for which standard deviations and correlations are underestimated, and it will under-allocate to asset classes for which the opposite occurs. Moreover, the effect of estimation error is not diversified away as more asset classes are added; it usually becomes worse.

The effect of this problem is twofold: the weights of the efficient portfolios are misstated and their expected returns and risk are incorrect. The question arises, therefore, as to the seriousness of this problem. Are optimizers so sensitive to errors as to be of little or no value, or are critics of optimization overstating this problem? We believe the latter is true. In most cases, and for applications to asset allocation, optimization is reasonably robust to estimation error.[1]

THE INTUITIVE ARGUMENT

The intuition underlying our argument is straightforward. Consider optimization among asset classes that have similar expected returns and risk. Errors in the estimates of these values may substantially misstate efficient allocations. Despite these misallocations, however, the return distributions of the correct and incorrect portfolios will be quite similar. In this setting, we assume that portfolio weights are constrained to disallow leverage, which is typically the case. And even if we assume reasonable amounts of leverage, our result would typically still hold.

Now consider optimization among asset classes that have dissimilar expected returns and risk. Errors in these estimates will have little impact on efficient allocations; hence, again the return distributions of the correct and incorrect portfolios will not differ much. The following examples illustrate these points.

THE EMPIRICAL ARGUMENT

Country Allocation

Let us first consider an application of mean-variance analysis to the developed equity markets of France, Germany, and the United Kingdom. Table 7.1 shows estimates of the expected returns, standard deviations, and correlations. The expected returns are those that would occur if these assets were fairly valued given their historical covariances with the world equity market measured over the period from January 1976 through December 2015, which is to say that these returns are proportional to their historical betas. The standard deviations and correlations are calculated from the same historical sample.

Notice that these asset classes are close substitutes for each other given these assumptions about return and risk. The spread between the highest and lowest expected return is only 50 basis points, and there is little dispersion across the standard deviations and correlations.

Now suppose we wish to identify the optimal mix of these country equity markets, but we misestimate the expected returns. Specifically, we overestimate the expected returns of France and the United Kingdom by 1.0%, and we underestimate the expected return of Germany by 1.0%. We assume that we estimate the standard deviations and correlations correctly. Table 7.2 shows these misestimated expected returns.

Next, we solve for the optimal portfolio that targets a 7.5% expected return using the correct expected returns, and we do the same for the incorrect expected returns. Table 7.3 shows that these errors significantly distort

TABLE 7.1 Country Expected Returns, Standard Deviations, and Correlations

	Expected Returns (%)	Standard Deviations (%)	Correlations	
			France	Germany
France	7.8	25.3		
Germany	7.6	25.0	0.75	
United Kingdom	7.3	21.5	0.66	0.60

TABLE 7.2   Misestimated Country Expected Returns

	Correct Expected Returns (%)	Errors (%)	Expected Returns with Errors (%)
France	7.8	+1	8.8
Germany	7.6	−1	6.6
United Kingdom	7.3	+1	8.3

TABLE 7.3   Distortion in Optimal Country Weights

	Correct Weights (%)	Incorrect Weights (%)	Misallocation (%)
France	25.5	−5.7	−31.2
Germany	23.8	44.9	21.1
United Kingdom	50.7	60.8	10.1
Total Misallocation			62.4

the optimal portfolio when we apply mean-variance analysis. In total, more than 62% of the portfolio is misallocated.

This example shows that small errors in our estimates of expected returns substantially distort a portfolio's optimal weights, suggesting that optimizers are indeed hypersensitive to input errors. But is such a conclusion warranted? Although the portfolio resulting from the misestimated means is substantially misallocated, the return distribution of the perceived optimal portfolio is similar to that of the true optimal portfolio. Table 7.4, which shows each portfolio's exposure to loss, illustrates this point.

The misallocated portfolio has a 39% likelihood of experiencing a loss over a one-year horizon, whereas the truly optimal portfolio has a 38.7% chance of losing money during a single year. In other words, a massive 60% misallocation translates into a mere 0.3% increase in exposure to loss.

TABLE 7.4   Exposure to Loss for Correct and Incorrect Country Weights

	Correct Weights (%)	Incorrect Weights (%)
Probability of Loss	38.7	39.0
1% Value at Risk	−32.1	−32.3

The same is true if we consider exposure to loss as value at risk, which gives the worst outcome for a given probability. Over a one-year horizon, the worst outcome for the truly optimal portfolio given a 1% probability of occurrence is a loss of 32.1%, which increases to only 32.3% if we misallocate the portfolio by more than 60%.

The bottom line is that if asset classes have similar return distributions, small errors in their estimated means will lead to large errors in the composition of the perceived optimal portfolio. This sensitivity of the weights to errors in the means occurs because the assets are close substitutes for one another. But because they are close substitutes, the misallocations have comparatively little impact on the portfolio's return distribution. In other words, although a portfolio's weights may be hypersensitive to input errors, the risk profile of the incorrect portfolio is very similar to that of the truly optimal portfolio.

Asset Allocation

Now let us explore a situation in which the asset classes are less similar to each other. Table 7.5 shows the expected returns, standard deviations, and correlations for three asset classes: US equities, Treasury bonds, and commodities. The standard deviations and correlations are estimated from monthly returns beginning in January 1976 and ending in December 2015. The expected returns are the same returns we used for our base case example in Chapter 2. For the sake of this experiment, we assume these inputs are the true values that will prevail in the future.

Notice that the spread in expected returns is 4.7% compared to 50 basis points for the country allocation example. Moreover, the standard deviations and correlations are quite dissimilar compared to those of the country equity indexes.

As before, suppose we wish to allocate our portfolio optimally across these asset classes targeting a 7.5% expected return, but we overestimate

TABLE 7.5 Asset Class Expected Returns, Standard Deviations, and Correlations

			Correlations	
	Expected Returns (%)	Standard Deviations (%)	US Equities (%)	Treasury Bonds (%)
US Equities	8.8	16.6		
Treasury Bonds	4.1	5.7	0.10	
Commodities	6.2	20.6	0.16	−0.07

TABLE 7.6   Misestimated Asset Class Expected Returns

	Correct Expected Returns (%)	Errors (%)	Expected Returns with Errors (%)
US Equities	8.8	+1	9.8
Treasury Bonds	4.1	−1	3.1
Commodities	6.2	+1	7.2

TABLE 7.7   Distortion in Optimal Asset Class Weights

	Correct Weights (%)	Incorrect Weights (%)	Misallocation (%)
US Equities	66.7	55.0	−11.7
Treasury Bonds	19.8	27.0	7.2
Commodities	13.5	18.0	4.5
Total Misallocation			23.5

the expected returns of US equities and commodities by 1.0% and underestimate the expected return of Treasury bonds by 1.0%.[2] Table 7.6 shows these incorrect assumptions.

Table 7.7 reveals that, unlike the previous example, small errors in the estimates of expected returns result in relatively small misallocations. We would incur only 23.5% of turnover in order to shift the portfolio from the incorrect weights to the correct weights compared to nearly three times as much for countries.

Table 7.8 compares exposure to loss for the truly optimal asset class portfolio with exposure to loss for the misallocated asset class portfolio. It reveals that the differences again are relatively minor, but this time because the misallocation is within reason.

TABLE 7.8   Exposure to Loss for Correct and Incorrect Asset Class Weights

	Correct Weights (%)	Incorrect Weights (%)
Probability of Loss	27.5	26.1
1% Value at Risk	−17.5	−15.3

THE ANALYTICAL ARGUMENT

We now address the sensitivity of optimized portfolios to changes in the expected return using explicit mathematical formulas. Specifically, we compute the partial derivative (rate of change) of optimal weights with respect to a change in any of the asset classes' expected returns. We also compute the partial derivative of the optimal portfolio's standard deviation with respect to these changes in expected returns.

We start by expressing the optimal weights as a function of means, covariances, and risk aversion, for an unconstrained portfolio. These optimal weights are given by the following formula, where λ is a risk aversion parameter, Σ is the covariance matrix, and μ is a vector of expected returns:

$$w = \frac{1}{\lambda}\Sigma^{-1}\mu \qquad (7.1)$$

However, this optimization setup is problematic in a practical context. This formula implies that investors will increase exposure to asset classes with higher expected returns and thereby increase total risk, even employing leverage if necessary. In practice, the opposite reaction is more likely. Though investors will allocate too much to asset classes whose expected returns have been erroneously inflated, they will have an overly optimistic view of the expected return and, if they target a particular return or risk level, they will substitute safer and therefore lower-return asset classes elsewhere in their portfolio. This behavior is consistent with two simple constraints: portfolio weights sum to one, and the investor targets a specific expected return. Fortunately, it is possible to derive a formula for these optimal weights in terms of the expected returns, covariances, and a target expected return, μ_T:

$$w = z \cdot \left[\left(\mu_{unc} - \mu_T s_{unc}\right)\Sigma^{-1}\mathbf{1} + \left(\mu_T s_{min} - \mu_{min}\right)\Sigma^{-1}\mu\right] \qquad (7.2)$$

Interestingly, this solution is based on a weighted average of two portfolios: $\Sigma^{-1}\mu$ which is proportional to the unconstrained solution we described previously, and $\Sigma^{-1}\mathbf{1}$ which is proportional to the minimum-variance portfolio (because when all expected returns are equal to the same positive constant, optimization equates to risk minimization). The coefficients that blend these two portfolios are based on the means and the sum of weights associated with the two portfolios, and the weights are normalized by a factor which we call z. These quantities are defined as follows:

$$s_{min} = \mathbf{1}'\Sigma^{-1}\mathbf{1} \qquad (7.3)$$

$$\mu_{min} = s_{unc} = 1'\Sigma^{-1}\mu \tag{7.4}$$

$$\mu_{unc} = \mu'\Sigma^{-1}\mu \tag{7.5}$$

$$z = \frac{1}{\mu_{unc}s_{min} - \mu_{min}s_{unc}} \tag{7.6}$$

The optimal portfolio's variance is equal to

$$\sigma^2 = w'\Sigma w \tag{7.7}$$

$$\sigma^2 = z \cdot \left[s_{min}\mu_T^2 - 2\mu_{min}\mu_T + \mu_{unc} \right] \tag{7.8}$$

Using standard calculus and matrix algebra rules, we take the partial derivative of the weights with respect to changes in expected returns. Because the weights are a vector, the partial derivative of it with respect to another vector (expected returns) produces a matrix in which each column describes the amount each weight changes given a one-unit change in each of the expected returns. The expression below is long, but we will soon be able to compare it directly to the derivative of the standard deviation:

$$\frac{\partial w}{\partial \mu} = z \cdot \Sigma^{-1} \left[2\mu 1' - \mu_T 11' - 1\mu' \right] \Sigma^{-1} \tag{7.9}$$

$$+ \frac{\partial z}{\partial \mu} \cdot \left[\mu_{unc} 1' + s_{min}\mu_T\mu' - \mu_{min}\mu_T 1' - \mu_{min}\mu' \right] \Sigma^{-1}$$

$$+ z \cdot \left(s_{min}\mu_T - \mu_{min} \right) \Sigma^{-1}$$

For reasons that will become clear soon, we leave $\dfrac{\partial z}{\partial \mu}$ expressed as such in the derivative, but note that it is equal to

$$\frac{\partial z}{\partial \mu} = 2z^2 \cdot \left[s_{unc}\Sigma^{-1}1 - s_{min}\Sigma^{-1}\mu \right] \tag{7.10}$$

We express the derivative of portfolio variance with respect to changes in expected returns in a similar fashion. In this case, variance is a single number, so its derivative is a column vector of sensitivities to changes in each expected return:

$$\frac{\partial \sigma^2}{\partial \mu} = z \cdot \Sigma^{-1} \left[2\mu - 2\mu_T 1 \right] \tag{7.11}$$

$$+ \frac{\partial z}{\partial \mu} \cdot \left[\mu_{unc} + s_{min} \mu_T^2 - 2\mu_{min} \mu_T \right]$$

The derivative of weights is in intuitive units, because changes in weights occur against a backdrop of a set of weights that sum to one. For variance, though, it is hard to say whether a change is large or small when the size of the variance itself differs across portfolios. We make two adjustments to this equation for variance in order to facilitate our interpretation of risk sensitivity. First, we recast the derivative in terms of the standard deviation, which is the square root of variance. And second, we divide by the standard deviation of the original portfolio to put the size of each change in context. After these two changes, we have the following relationships:

$$\frac{1}{\sigma} \frac{\partial \sigma}{\partial \mu} = \frac{1}{\sigma} \frac{\partial}{\partial \mu} \left(\sqrt{\sigma^2} \right) = \frac{1}{2\sigma^2} \frac{\partial \sigma^2}{\partial \mu} \tag{7.12}$$

$$\frac{1}{\sigma} \frac{\partial \sigma}{\partial \mu} = \frac{1}{2} z \cdot \Sigma^{-1} \left[2\mu - 2\mu_T 1 \right] \frac{1}{\sigma^2} \tag{7.13}$$

$$+ \frac{1}{2} \frac{\partial z}{\partial \mu} \cdot \left[\mu_{unc} + s_{min} \mu_T^2 - 2\mu_{min} \mu_T \right] \frac{1}{\sigma^2}$$

As with any derivative, these sensitivities are linear approximations, which hold quite closely for small changes in expected returns but are less accurate for larger changes. We confirm the level of accuracy by introducing small perturbations in expected returns and by recomputing portfolio weights from Equation 7.2, which are predicted by the derivatives in Equations 7.9 and 7.13. It is precisely the small changes we are concerned with in evaluating stability, so we can derive a good amount of intuition from these relationships.

A visual comparison of Equations 7.9 and 7.13 suggests that weight sensitivity and standard deviation sensitivity have some similarities. The first term (on the first line) in each formula involves z, Σ^{-1}, and a similar expression inside the brackets. Whereas the weight formula is multiplied by the inverse covariance matrix at the end, the standard deviation formula is multiplied by $\frac{1}{\sigma^2}$, which is the inverse variance of the entire portfolio. Importantly, the term in the standard deviation formula is divided by 2 compared to the weight formula. This suggests that, on average, this component of standard deviation is less sensitive than the analogous component of optimal weights. The next terms (on the second lines of the formulas) are also similar. They both involve $\frac{\partial z}{\partial \mu}$ and a related expression inside the brackets. Once again, they are multiplied at the end by the inverse covariance matrix and inverse portfolio variance, respectively, and the standard deviation formula is divided by 2. The weight formula also has a third expression, for which the standard deviation formula has no parallel. It is, in fact, this component that leads to most of the instability in weights. It is a scalar multiple of the inverse covariance matrix, and the inverse covariance matrix is the quantity that "blows up" when assets are highly correlated. (Think of the covariance matrix as describing risk, and the inverse covariance matrix as describing how to neutralize this risk. When two assets are highly correlated, we neutralize their risk by taking massive long positions in one and massive short positions in the other.)

To quantify these differences, we apply these formulas to our portfolio example from Chapter 2. We ignore cash equivalents because their risk is close to zero; instead, we focus on the remaining six asset classes. We set the target return equal to 7.5%. The moderate portfolio does not hold any cash equivalents, so with these assumptions, Equation 7.2 yields the same moderate portfolio as we have shown previously. Table 7.9 shows the sensitivity of each optimal weight (in the columns) to a one percentage point increase in the expected return of each asset individually (in the rows). For example, the expected return of US equities increases from 8.8% to 9.8%. Table 7.10 shows the sensitivity of the optimal portfolio's standard deviation. We observe the following. Weights are not very sensitive to expected return errors in an asset class such as commodities, which is relatively dissimilar from other asset classes. And because the weights do not change by much, neither does the portfolio's standard deviation. On the other hand, when the change in the expected return is applied to an asset class such as Treasury bonds, which is a close substitute for US corporate bonds, the weights change by around 200%. This is of little consequence, though; the assets are indeed close substitutes with similar risk properties; hence, the risk of the total portfolio remains stable.

TABLE 7.9   Sensitivity of Weights to Changes in Expected Return

	Weight Sensitivity					
	US Equities (%)	Foreign Equities (%)	Emerging Market Equities (%)	Treasury Bonds (%)	US Corporate Bonds (%)	Commodities (%)
Sensitivity of Weights to 1% Increase in Expected Return						
US Equities	19	–11	–6	18	–21	1
Foreign Developed Market Equities	–11	17	–7	16	–13	–2
Emerging Market Equities	–6	–7	9	17	–13	–1
Treasury Bonds	7	6	14	191	–212	–7
US Corporate Bonds	–17	–9	–12	–200	235	2
Commodities	0	–3	–1	–5	1	7

TABLE 7.10   Sensitivity of Portfolio Standard Deviation to Changes in Expected Return

	Original Standard Deviation (%)	New Standard Deviation (%)	Percentage Change in Risk (%)
Sensitivity of Standard Deviation to 1% Increase in Expected Return			
US Equities	10.8	10.1	–6.5
Foreign Developed Market Equities	10.8	10.2	–5.9
Emerging Market Equities	10.8	10.6	–2.3
Treasury Bonds	10.8	10.4	–3.6
US Corporate Bonds	10.8	10.2	–5.6
Commodities	10.8	10.7	–1.5

THE BOTTOM LINE

The bottom line is that mean-variance analysis is not typically hypersensitive to estimation error. It only appears to be hypersensitive when asset classes are close substitutes for each other, because the optimal weights may shift significantly in response to input errors. But the incorrect portfolio will have a similar return distribution as the correct portfolio; thus, variation in weights may not be overly problematic.

Nevertheless, there are some situations in which estimation error poses a significant challenge to investors. Fortunately, we have procedures to address this challenge. Some investors resort to Bayesian shrinkage, which blends individual estimates of the expected return and risk with a prior belief such as the cross-sectional mean of the estimates or the estimate associated with the minimum-risk portfolio. Investors also rely on a technique called resampling in which they generate many efficient frontiers from a distribution of inputs and then average the weights of the portfolios with a given risk level to arrive at the optimal portfolio.[3] Both of these techniques are designed to make a portfolio less sensitive to estimation error. An alternative approach, called stability-adjusted optimization, addresses estimation error in a very different way. It makes portfolios more sensitive to estimation error, but in a constructive way. This approach measures the relative stability of covariances and incorporates this information as a distinct component of risk in the portfolio formation process. It increases dependency on asset classes with relatively stable covariances and reduces dependency on asset classes with relatively unstable covariances. In Chapter 19 we discuss stability-adjusted optimization in detail.

RELATED TOPICS

- Chapter 2 describes the foundations of mean-variance analysis in detail.
- Chapter 19 shows how to quantify estimation error and construct stability-adjusted portfolios.

REFERENCES

Kritzman, M. 2006. "Are Optimizers Error Maximizers?" The Journal of Portfolio Management, Vol. 3, No. 4 (Summer).
Michaud, R. O. and Michaud, R. O. 2008. *Efficient Asset Management: A Practical Guide to Stock Portfolio Optimization and Asset Allocation (2nd ed.)*, Oxford University Press, Inc.

NOTES

1. For more on this subject, see Kritzman (2006).
2. We assume a risk aversion of 1.0 in this example.
3. See Michaud and Michaud (2001) for more details about resampling.

CHAPTER 8

Factors

FALLACY: FACTORS OFFER SUPERIOR DIVERSIFICATION AND NOISE REDUCTION

In this chapter, we address two common fallacies about factors. The first fallacy is the notion that portfolios composed of factors are better diversified, and therefore more efficient, than portfolios composed of asset classes. This claim might seem plausible because correlations among factors tend to be lower than correlations among asset classes. But this comparison is specious, as we soon demonstrate.

The second fallacy is the notion that investors reduce noise more effectively by consolidating securities into factors as opposed to asset classes. In fact, we show the opposite to be true; factors are noisier than asset classes, which we explain and illustrate later on.

WHAT IS A FACTOR?

First, let us distinguish between factors and asset classes. They must be different, otherwise the premise of factor investing would be redundant. Perhaps the most important characteristics that distinguish asset classes from factors are that asset classes have stable composition and are directly investable. (See Chapter 1 for more about the characteristics of asset classes.) Factors, by contrast, are labels that reflect exposure to a source of risk and are not directly investable. Moreover, the composition of the collection of assets designed to replicate them is unstable. Investors must periodically rebalance the replicating assets.

The term *factor* is used in a variety of ways, including:

- A simple combination of assets, such as a long position in a 10-year Treasury bond and a short position in a 2-year Treasury note.

- A fundamental factor, such as a portfolio of securities formed by using regression analysis or optimization to track an economic variable like inflation.
- A security attribute, such as a portfolio formed by ranking assets according to an observable attribute like the price-to-book value ratio.
- A statistical factor, such as a combination of securities that explains variation in returns and which is identified using Principal Components Analysis.

In all cases, factors are labels for portfolios of investable securities. These factor portfolios may appear to have strong diversification properties because they often have low or even negative correlations with each other. Meanwhile, asset classes are usually positively correlated with each other and often highly correlated. It, therefore, might seem that factors are better diversifiers than asset classes. Unfortunately, this reasoning is flawed. Factor-mimicking portfolios typically include short positions, which force their correlations to fall below those of asset classes. If we were to allow the same amount of shorting in structuring asset classes, we would observe equally low or negative correlations among asset classes.[1]

EQUIVALENCE OF ASSET CLASS AND FACTOR DIVERSIFICATION

We now know that the low correlations we observe among factors are an artifact of short positions in the portfolios constructed to replicate them. Therefore, why should we expect factors to offer greater diversification than asset classes? We should not. Instead, we should expect asset classes and factors to produce identical efficient frontiers and thus the same degree of diversification as long as three conditions prevail:

1. Assets define the opportunity set.
2. Both efficient frontiers are derived with the same constraints.
3. Both efficient frontiers measure expected return and risk in the same units.

This equality can be proved mathematically. (See, for example, Idzorek and Kowara, 2013.) It is also quite intuitive when one considers that we can express any combination of factors as a combination of the underlying assets that constitute the factors.

An empirical example may help to illustrate this point. Suppose we identify principal components from the covariance matrix of the asset classes we introduced in Chapter 2. (See Chapter 25 for an explanation of Principal Components Analysis.) These principal components are uncorrelated to each other, are equal in number to the original asset class universe, and span the same opportunity set as the asset classes. We can express any portfolio that is formed from the asset classes as a combination of these factors. Figure 8.1 plots efficient frontiers constructed from asset classes and principal components.

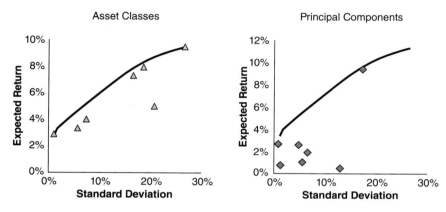

FIGURE 8.1   Asset class and principal component efficient frontiers.

The average asset class correlation is 0.23, and four of the asset class correlations are above 0.60. The principal components by construction are uncorrelated. We have translated our investment universe from one set (asset classes) to another set (factors), but we have not at all changed the opportunity set. For any chosen set of investment constraints, the efficient frontiers associated with the asset class universe and the factor universe are identical. To see why this must be so, note that any portfolio built from factors can also be built from the asset classes, so whatever allocation is optimal for the asset classes must be optimal for the factors, and vice versa.[2] Although this logic is straightforward, investors are often confused because, as we mentioned previously, many factors include short positions in the asset classes. Table 8.1 shows the portfolio weights corresponding to each statistical factor, scaled so that their absolute values sum to 1.

The bottom line is that forming an optimal portfolio from principal components is no different than forming an optimal portfolio directly from asset classes, if we allow the same amount of short positions. Moreover, if we were to build a long-only portfolio from factors, we would need to combine the factors such that we offset their short positions with long positions in other factors, which would result in a long-only asset class portfolio.

TABLE 8.1   Principal Components

Asset Classes	Principal Components (sum of absolute value of weights equals 1)						
	1 (%)	2 (%)	3 (%)	4 (%)	5 (%)	6 (%)	7 (%)
US Equities	19.7	−12.4	26.8	36.9	−16.6	1.5	−0.2
Foreign Developed Market Equities	24.3	−4.6	28.4	−37.0	3.1	0.6	0.1
Emerging Market Equities	38.8	−13.4	−32.3	1.6	2.7	1.6	−0.4
Treasury Bonds	0.1	−2.2	5.0	7.8	33.5	48.8	−9.9
US Corporate Bonds	3.1	−3.3	6.6	10.9	42.2	−38.5	6.0
Commodities	13.9	64.0	1.0	5.6	0.9	0.3	−0.4
Cash Equivalents	0.1	0.2	0.0	0.3	0.9	8.6	83.1
Expected Return	9.5	0.5	2.0	1.1	2.6	0.8	2.7
Standard Deviation	17.3	13.0	6.6	5.5	4.8	1.3	0.8
Percentage of Variation Explained	60.7	20.4	9.0	5.6	4.0	0.2	0.1

Now let us turn to the second fallacy about factors – the notion that factors are more effective than assets in reducing noise.

NOISE REDUCTION

Investors must choose whether to allocate across granular asset universes, such as individual securities, or across consolidated asset universes, which consist of pre-combined groups of securities such as asset classes or factors. A more granular approach always produces a more efficient frontier "in-sample," because granular data contain more information and offer a broader opportunity set. However, as we move out of sample, aggregated information becomes more reliable than granular information, because errors in our estimates of the return and risk of individual securities tend to cancel each other out when we aggregate the securities into groups. It does not necessarily follow, though, that grouping securities into factors reduces noise more effectively than grouping them into asset classes. We need to think carefully about why one approach might be superior to another. Let us first consider asset classes.

Asset class characteristics are easy to observe, and they change very slowly. For example, it is plain to see whether a security is a stock or a bond, and whether it is domestic or foreign. The industry in which a firm operates is also easy to observe. Moreover, these characteristics are persistent. Asset classes are also capitalization weighted; thus, when security prices change, their weights within the asset classes change proportionately. The composition of an asset class is, therefore, stable.

Now let us consider factors. A security's factor attributes, such as its price-to-book value ratio, change significantly through time. Other attributes, such as a security's sensitivity to inflation, also change through time. Moreover, a security's sensitivity to an economic variable is not directly observable. We must infer it by using regression analysis, the result of which is imprecise. Therefore, the process of mapping securities onto factors introduces incremental noise of its own, which we call mapping error. The securities that tracked a factor best historically may be different from those that best track it in the future. Asset classes based on stable and observable characteristics do not have mapping error, but factor groupings do. Given these considerations, it seems reasonable to expect asset classes to be less noisy than factors. But we need not rely on reason alone. We can empirically test how well each grouping scheme reduces noise.

Table 8.2 shows the instability of means and covariances associated with industry and factor groupings of the same underlying universe of securities.[3] It reveals that these groupings are exposed to essentially the same degree of instability arising from independent-sample error, interval error, and small-sample error. Errors in means are measured by the average standard deviation, whereas errors in covariances are measured as a modified root-mean-squared error. (See Chapter 19 for a detailed description of this measure.)

TABLE 8.2 Instability of Industry, Size, Value, and Momentum Portfolios

	Return Instability* (average) (%)	Covariance Instability** (average)
10 Industry Portfolios	20.9	0.39
10 Size Portfolios	24.9	0.39
10 Value Portfolios	22.3	0.41
10 Momentum Portfolios	22.9	0.38

* Measured as standard deviation of returns.
** Modified root-mean-squared error.

It is important to note that these measures do not include mapping error, which would undoubtedly increase the instability of the size, value, and momentum portfolios beyond the instability of the industry portfolios. Of course, one could argue that with sufficient trading it is possible to avoid mapping error because the attributes are observable at each point in time, but frequent updating would drive up trading costs. Therefore, investors either achieve less noise reduction by grouping securities into factors as opposed to industries, or they achieve the same noise reduction with factors but at a greater cost.

THE BOTTOM LINE

We have shown that factors do not offer better diversification than assets. We have also shown that they do not reduce noise more effectively than assets. However, factors are useful for other reasons. For example, analyzing a portfolio's factor exposures could help investors to understand and manage risk more effectively. Also, some factors carry risk premiums that could help investors to enhance returns. And some investors can add value because they are skilled at predicting factor behavior. But we should weigh these potential benefits of factor investing against the incremental noise and trading costs associated with factor replication.

For the reasons outlined above, some investors may wish to condition their portfolios to align with specific factors of interest such as value, inflation, or growth. What are these investors to do? Rather than attempting to replicate factors directly, we recommend instead that investors employ multi-goal optimization to construct asset class portfolios that are conditioned to track a desired factor profile. We present a detailed treatment of this approach, including a case study, in Chapter 16.

RELATED TOPICS

- Chapter 1 defines the characteristics of an asset class, including those that distinguish asset classes from factors.
- Chapter 16 shows how to track a desired set of factor exposures while continuing to invest in asset classes, thereby unifying asset allocation and factor investing.
- Chapter 19 shows how to form portfolios that account for covariance instability.

REFERENCES

Cocoma, P., Czasonis, M., Kritzman, M., and Turkington, D. 2017. "Facts about Factors," *Journal of Portfolio Management*, Vol. 43, No. 5.

Idzorek, T. and Kowara, M. 2013. "Factor-Based Asset Allocation vs. Asset-Class-Based Asset Allocation," *Financial Analysts Journal*, Vol. 69, No. 3 (May/June).

NOTES

1. For details, see Cocoma, Czasonis, Kritzman, and Turkington (2017).
2. This fact always holds for principal components. Factors defined in other ways may or may not span the entire opportunity set presented by the underlying asset classes.
3. This analysis is based on data from Kenneth French's website, spanning January 1927 through December 2015.

CHAPTER 9

1/N

FALLACY: EQUALLY WEIGHTED PORTFOLIOS ARE SUPERIOR TO OPTIMIZED PORTFOLIOS

Optimized portfolios are designed to maximize expected return for a chosen level of risk by accounting for differences in expected returns, standard deviations, and correlations. Yet it has been argued that equally weighted portfolios outperform optimized portfolios out of sample. The "1/N" approach to investing assigns asset weights based purely on the number of asset classes, N, and ignores all other information. Those who favor this naïve allocation method believe that estimation error is so insurmountable that incorporating any views about expected return and risk damages portfolios more than it helps them.

Should we really conclude that expectations about return, risk, and correlation, derived from some combination of theory and data, are useless for portfolio construction? We argue not. The notion that 1/N is superior to optimization is based on tests that blindly extrapolate small-sample historical means as estimates of expected return. It is this naïve approach to estimating expected return and not the process of optimization that is flawed. Thoughtful practitioners know not to rely on recent return outcomes as expected returns. Successful portfolio optimization does not require perfect estimates of return and risk – merely estimates that are plausible. If we use reasonable intuition along with long samples of historical data to estimate optimization inputs, optimization regularly outperforms 1/N out of sample.

THE CASE FOR 1/N

The case for 1/N is appealing. It is simple. It avoids concentrated positions. It always outperforms the worst-performing asset class. And it always allocates some amount to the best-performing asset class.

One of the most influential studies supporting 1/N is by DeMiguel, Garlappi, and Uppal (2009). They performed out-of-sample backtests on seven different data sets and used 14 different methods to estimate inputs, including

Bayesian shrinkage for managing estimation error. They found that, on average, 1/N portfolios generated Sharpe ratios 50% higher than optimized portfolios.

SETTING THE RECORD STRAIGHT

We argue that the perceived failure of optimization arises from overreliance on short return samples to estimate expected returns. For example, DeMiguel, Garlappi, and Uppal used rolling 60- and 120-month return samples to estimate expected returns. These estimates are prone to small-sample error, and in many cases are utterly implausible. For example, what should we expect about the future return of the equity market if it experienced a significant downturn over the past five years? Should we expect another five-year loss contrary to capital market theory and long-term evidence? Most informed investors would expect the future return of the equity market to bear some positive relationship to its riskiness and not to its recent performance. In fact, those who believe in long-term valuation cycles might believe that equity prices are more likely to rise following a downturn. In any event, most thoughtful investors rely on information beyond short-term historical returns to form expectations about the future.

As an analogy, think of optimization as a sophisticated navigation system. 1/N is the navigational equivalent of wandering aimlessly in search of our destination, ignoring not only the GPS instructions but also any posted road signs. We argue that it is better to use the GPS; we just need to specify the correct destination. If our goal is to drive to the beach on Saturday but we mistakenly instruct the GPS to take us to the office, we should not fault the GPS for directing us to the office. But those who favor 1/N think of optimization this way.

EMPIRICAL EVIDENCE IN DEFENSE OF OPTIMIZATION

In a 2010 article, Kritzman, Page, and Turkington conducted backtests to compare optimization to 1/N. They tested a wide range of applications, including allocation across broad asset classes, equity industries, factors, individual stocks, commodities, hedge fund styles, and actively managed funds. In each case, they constructed long-only portfolios with weights that sum to 1 but were otherwise unconstrained. They used three different methods to estimate expected returns, each of which is simple yet avoids the drawbacks of relying on short-sample means. The first method assumes constant expected returns across assets, which yields the minimum-variance portfolio. The second method derives expected returns from risk premiums spanning multiple decades prior to the start of the backtest. The third method estimates expected returns from long historical samples to reflect all monthly return data available up to that point in time. They calculated covariance matrices as sample covariances from rolling 5-, 10-, and 20-year windows, as well as from all available historical data.[1]

In total, Kritzman, Page, and Turkington evaluated more than 50,000 optimized portfolios. As a measure of overall performance, they reported average Sharpe ratios for each category of tests. They evaluated asset allocation in the context of asset/liability management with an investable universe of US equity, foreign equity, US government bonds, US corporate bonds, real estate investment trusts (REITs), commodities, and cash equivalents. Their test period spanned 1978 to 2008 with portfolios reoptimized yearly and held until the following year. In their analysis of asset allocation, the capitalization-weighted market portfolio and the 1/N portfolio delivered similar Sharpe ratios of around 0.7. The minimum-variance and long-term risk premium approaches fared better, with Sharpe ratios above 1.0. To prove a point, the authors also tested a set of completely contrived yet plausible expected returns (which we happen to know were chosen by one of the coauthors while on vacation at the beach and communicated by phone to the office), which resulted in an even higher Sharpe ratio. Though less directly related to the asset allocation focus of this book, the tests for industry and factor allocation using data beginning in 1926 supported the same conclusions, as did out-of-sample tests on commodities (since 1971), active funds (since 1987), hedge fund styles (since 1996), and individual US stocks (since 1998). In these experiments, the authors intentionally used simple models to demonstrate the efficacy of optimization. One could easily make a stronger case for optimization by building portfolios in line with best practices.

PRACTICAL PROBLEMS WITH 1/N

Although 1/N is provocative in its simplicity and appealing when simplistically evaluated, it is difficult to defend for additional reasons beyond the fact that it does not work. First, equal weighting is not sensitive to return and risk estimates; instead, it is entirely dependent on the choice of the asset class universe. Each asset class is assigned equal importance regardless of how many there are. Splitting an asset class into two subcomponents would, in effect, nearly double that asset class's allocation. The 1/N approach essentially transfers the risk of input estimation error to the risk of selecting the right asset classes.

Second, the 1/N heuristic offers investors only one portfolio irrespective of their attitude toward risk. The efficient frontier allows investors the choice of a wide variety of portfolios, each with different combinations of expected return and risk.

Third, equal weighting ignores the capacity of each asset class as well as a variety of other considerations, beyond expected return and risk, that might favor one asset class over another.

BROKEN CLOCK

As the adage goes, even a broken clock is right twice a day. It is possible, given certain conditions, that mean-variance analysis will direct investors toward an equally weighted portfolio. We reverse-engineer the optimization process to determine what equal weighting implies for expected returns and covariances. In the absence of constraints, the optimal portfolio is given by the following expression, where Σ is the covariance matrix and μ is a vector of expected returns (see Chapter 25 for details):

$$w^* = \frac{1}{\lambda}\Sigma^{-1}\mu \qquad (9.1)$$

For any level of risk aversion, the optimal weights are proportionately identical, so for convenience we ignore this multiple and express this relationship as a proportionality:

$$w^* \propto \Sigma^{-1}\mu \qquad (9.2)$$

Equation 9.2 reveals that for the optimal allocation to equal 1/N, the expected returns, μ, must be proportional to the sum of the rows of the covariance matrix:

$$\mu \propto \Sigma 1 \qquad (9.3)$$

It is worth noting that the Capital Asset Pricing Model (CAPM) implies that expected returns are proportional to the systematic risk of each asset class, estimated as its regression beta (or in proportionality terms, its covariance) with the market portfolio, w_m:

$$\mu \propto \Sigma w_m \qquad (9.4)$$

To the extent that market capitalization weights differ from equal weights, 1/N and CAPM imply different expected returns. Ultimately, these relationships show that it is possible, though not necessarily likely, that optimal weights will equal 1/N. To justify 1/N in terms of optimality, one needs to believe that prices are adequately efficient to reflect their covariances with other assets accurately and yet at the same time do not converge to the CAPM market portfolio equilibrium.

THE BOTTOM LINE

The bottom line is that 1/N makes sense only for investors who believe they have no insight whatsoever about differences in the expected returns and risk of asset classes. We encourage investors who have access to historical data and who are capable of sound judgment to apply optimization to identify the portfolio that best suits their investment goals.

RELATED TOPICS

- Chapter 2 describes the foundation of mean-variance analysis in detail.
- Chapter 7 corrects the misperception that optimizers are hypersensitive to small errors in return and risk inputs.
- Chapter 13 offers enhanced techniques for forecasting asset class expected returns, standard deviations, and correlations.

REFERENCES

DeMiguel, V., Garlappi, L., and Uppal, R. 2009. "Optimal versus Naïve Diversification: How Inefficient Is the 1/N Portfolio Strategy?" *Review of Financial Studies*, Vol. 22, No. 5 (May).

Kritzman, M., Page, S., and Turkington, D. 2010. "In Defense of Optimization: The Fallacy of 1/N," *Financial Analysts Journal*, Vol. 66, No. 2 (March/April).

NOTE

1. We used monthly data to calculate covariances, with the exception of commodities, hedge fund styles, and actively managed funds, for which we used daily data. In each case, we multiplied the covariance matrix by the frequency of the data to convert it to annual units.

CHAPTER 10

Policy Portfolios

FALLACY: POLICY PORTFOLIOS MATTER

Investors often articulate a set of portfolio weights called a "policy port-folio." It is intended to reflect one's unique circumstances and preferences, such as the desired balance between expected return and risk. It is intended to provide a stable reference point, a portfolio that reliably satisfies the investor's needs. However, fixed-weight portfolios have wildly unstable risk; thus, they fail to satisfy investor preferences through time. What investors crave is stability in performance. Allocation weights are just a means to that end. Instead of a rigid policy portfolio, we argue it is better to have a flexible portfolio policy.

RISK INSTABILITY

The purpose of investing is to grow wealth, but competitive markets do not offer free lunches; they conspire to ensure that higher expected return comes at the expense of higher risk. Investors must therefore balance two compet-ing objectives: the desire to grow wealth and the desire to avoid loss.

It is important to understand this trade-off and to strike the right bal-ance. It does not make sense, however, to express the solution to this trade-off as a set of "policy portfolio" weights, because risk is not constant through time. A static allocation cannot reflect an essential feature of investor pref-erences when the properties of the underlying assets are always changing. Figure 10.1 highlights the severity of this problem. It shows rolling three-year standard deviations of monthly returns for the conservative, moder-ate, and aggressive portfolios we introduced in Chapter 2. We divide each three-year observation by the median of the corresponding portfolio over the entire sample. All three portfolios suffer nearly the same amount of risk

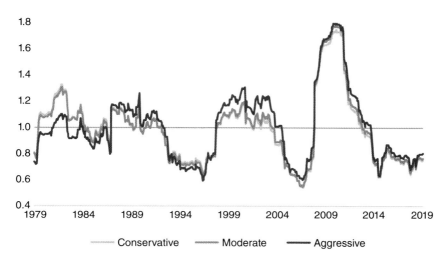

FIGURE 10.1 The instability of risk.

instability in relation to their long-run level of risk. Realized volatility varies from 40% below the median to more than 70% above the median.

WHAT INVESTORS WANT

Most investors do not derive satisfaction from their portfolio's asset class weights. The feature of a portfolio that truly matters is its distribution of return outcomes. When we fill our car with gas (or electricity, as the case may be), it is not for love of gasoline (or of electric charge) but because there is somewhere we need to go. Likewise, portfolio weights serve no purpose other than to deliver a desirable return distribution.

RESPONDING TO RISK REGIMES

One way to implement a flexible portfolio policy is to adjust exposure in response to shifting risk conditions. Let us illustrate this concept using an extremely simple rule: allocate each month to whichever portfolio – conservative, moderate, or aggressive – had an annualized volatility closest to 8% in the preceding 12 months. The strategy holds riskier allocations when recent risk conditions have been benign, and it pivots to safer allocations when risk rises. If recent volatility levels tend to persist, we should expect this flexible policy to achieve a more stable risk profile.

TABLE 10.1   Characteristics of realized three-year volatilities

	Policy Portfolios			Flexible Portfolio Policy
	Conservative	Moderate	Aggressive	
Max-Min Spread/Median	1.21	1.24	1.22	0.75
75-25th Percentile Spread/ Median	0.34	0.34	0.37	0.18

Table 10.1 summarizes the distribution of three-year volatility for the fixed-weight portfolios and the flexible portfolio policy from 1979 to 2019. The spread between the highest and lowest three-year volatility and the spread between the 75th and 25th percentiles (both shown relative to the median) are substantially smaller for the flexible dynamic strategy.

Figure 10.2 shows the dynamic strategy's three-year rolling risk over time as a multiple of its median value compared to the same measure for the fixed-weight moderate portfolio. In this example, there are six clear episodes in which the moderate portfolio experiences greater divergence from its typical level of risk as compared to the flexible approach.

Of course, there are many other ways to implement a flexible portfolio policy. The illustration we have presented above is notably simplistic. Kritzman (2013) offers a more realistic example whereby indicators of fragility pertaining to both the portfolio and the broader market are used to anticipate shifts in future volatility. He shows that the disparity in risk, defined as the largest minus smallest volatilities that occur in three-year windows, falls

FIGURE 10.2   Risk variation over time.

from 11% to around 5%. Moreover, the predictive nature of those signals also anticipates the average returns of risky assets, which makes the rotational strategy even more compelling. In Chapter 22, we discuss additional techniques for implementing dynamic strategies, including regime-switching models. Investors may also opt to reallocate according to their qualitative judgment, provided they keep expected return and risk within the bounds of the policy. The benefits of adjusting allocations must, of course, survive the added burden of transaction costs. Our goal in this chapter is not to prescribe a specific flexible policy, but rather to highlight the inherent limitations of overly rigid allocations.

THE BOTTOM LINE

It is better to have a flexible portfolio policy with a stable risk profile than a rigid policy portfolio with an unstable risk profile. The distribution of returns is what truly matters; portfolio weights are just a means to that end. There is nothing intrinsically valuable about weights because the properties of the assets to which they pertain are always changing.

RELATED TOPICS

- Chapter 19 shows how to measure the instability of asset covariances and build fixed-weight portfolios with more stable risk profiles.
- Chapter 22 applies regime-switching models to dynamically adjust portfolio weights.

REFERENCE

Kritzman, M. 2013. "Risk Disparity," *The Journal of Portfolio Management*, Vol. 40, No. 1 (Fall).

CHAPTER 11

The Private Equity Leverage Myth

FALLACY: PRIVATE EQUITY VOLATILITY SCALES WITH ITS LEVERAGE

The global private equity market has expanded rapidly in recent years as investors have sought to participate in the high returns that the asset class has delivered historically. Assets under management rose from $2.4 trillion in 2010 to an estimated $6.5 trillion in 2020.[1] Yet, investors who employ mean-variance analysis to form portfolios still struggle to identify the optimal allocation to private equity because they are unsure how to estimate its volatility.

It is widely understood that the observed standard deviation of private equity is artificially low due to the positive autocorrelation of its quarterly returns.[2] When returns are positively autocorrelated over shorter intervals, deviations accumulate more quickly than when returns are independent from one period to the next. As a result, the standard deviation over longer intervals is higher than what we would estimate by extrapolating the shorter-interval standard deviation.[3] Put differently, volatility no longer scales with the square root of time in the presence of autocorrelation. This positive autocorrelation arises in privately held assets due to the way they are priced. Prices of listed securities are available continually when markets are in session, whereas secondary private asset transactions occur infrequently, if ever.[4] Private equity investors therefore resort to quarterly appraisals to value their funds based on discounted cash flow analysis as well as recent transactions involving comparable companies. The backward-looking nature of these appraisals introduces autocorrelation, which artificially smooths private equity returns and dampens their apparent volatility. In Chapter 17, we show how investors can de-smooth private equity returns using a first-order autoregressive model. This approach yields higher and more realistic estimates for private equity volatility than do its raw quarterly returns.

Nonetheless, recognizing that it may be unreliable for a variety of reasons, some investors ignore the observed volatility of private equity entirely.[5] They instead attempt to estimate private equity volatility by applying a leverage multiple to the volatility of public equity.[6] Proponents of this approach argue that the underlying public companies are similar and that the two asset classes differ predominantly in their capital structure: private equity typically employs greater leverage. Leveraged buyout funds are so named because they often purchase companies, finance the purchases with leverage, take the companies private, restructure them, and then take them public again. However, this approach yields standard deviation estimates for private equity that are much higher than its observed standard deviation, even after it is de-smoothed. In fact, volatility estimates derived from de-smoothed returns suggest that the volatility of private equity is similar to that of public equity. How is this possible, given that private equity is significantly more leveraged? This puzzle is the focus of this chapter.

THE PRIVATE EQUITY LEVERAGE PUZZLE

In theory, the volatility of an equity stake in a company should scale directly with leverage absent other effects, as shown in Equation 11.1:

$$\sigma_E = L\sigma_A \qquad (11.1)$$

In Equation 11.1, σ_E equals equity volatility, L equals leverage (assets/equity), and σ_A equals asset volatility. Asset volatility reflects the volatility of the firm's underlying, fundamental business absent any leverage. In the case of a real estate holding company, it would depend in part on the volatility of property values and rents. In the case of an airline, it would depend in part on the spread between ticket revenues and fuel costs. All things being equal, we would expect an additional unit of leverage to increase equity volatility by one unit regardless of the sector or business model.

Axelson, Jenkinson, Stromberg, and Weisbach (2013) show that buyout firms have approximately two times more leverage than their public counterparts. Therefore, given Equation 11.1 and assuming similar asset volatility between the two groups, we would expect buyout equity's volatility to be approximately two times that of public equity's volatility. This is not what we observe empirically.

In joint research with our colleague Megan Czasonis, we undertook a range of experiments to model the relationship between leverage and volatility, which we summarize in this chapter.[7] Table 11.1 compares public and private equity volatility over the period December 1996 through September 2018.

TABLE 11.1 Expected and Actual Volatility of Private Equity (December 1996–September 2018, Annualized)

		Expected		Actual	
	Public Equity (%)	Private Equity (%)	Ratio	Private Equity (%)	Ratio
Quarterly	16.3	32.6	2.00	9.9	0.61
Annual	17.8	35.5	2.00	15.4	0.87
Triennial	17.6	35.2	2.00	17.0	0.97

We use the S&P 500 Index to represent public equity and the buyout segment of the State Street Private Equity Index to represent private equity. We measure the volatility of quarterly total returns for the S&P 500 and quarterly Internal Rate of Return (IRR) for private equity.[8] To account for the smoothing effect appraisals have on private equity valuations, we also measure the volatility of overlapping annual and triennial returns.[9] The first column reports public equity's volatility, the second set of columns shows the expected volatility of private equity assuming it is twice that of public equity (given that it has two times more leverage), and the third set of columns reports private equity's actual volatility.

The results presented in Table 11.1 are counterintuitive because they do not reveal the expected relationship between volatility and leverage. The volatility of private equity increases significantly over longer measurement intervals due to the autocorrelation of its returns. But even at a triennial frequency (an interval length long enough to capture much of the impact of autocorrelation in quarterly returns), we observe that private equity volatility is lower than public equity volatility when we would expect it to be twice as large.[10] We need not assume a leverage multiple of 2.0 to arrive at this puzzling conclusion. Even if we were to assume a leverage multiple of 1.1, we would still expect private equity volatility to exceed public equity volatility. But it does not.

LEVERAGE AND VOLATILITY IN THE PUBLIC EQUITY MARKET

To solve this puzzle, we seek first to establish the relationship between leverage and volatility in the public markets. We can then port this conceptual framework to the private markets, where the underlying companies are similar but funds are more opaque. To do this, we compile data for S&P 500 constituents from March 2001 through October 2018. Each month during this period we

1. sort stocks into quartiles according to their borrowing cost[11] (a proxy for the fundamental risk of their underlying businesses, irrespective of the degree of leverage),

2. sort stocks into quartiles according to their leverage (asset-to-equity ratio) within each fundamental risk quartile, and
3. record the monthly returns of these 16 portfolios over the full sample.

This experiment enables us to evaluate the impact of leverage while controlling for differences in fundamental risk across firms. Specifically, within each fundamental risk quartile, we compare the volatility of the portfolio of firms with the highest leverage to the volatility of the portfolio of firms with the lowest leverage. These ratios are reported in Figure 11.1 (light gray bars). For comparison, we also show the ratio of leverage for the same portfolios (dark gray bars). For example, on average, within the universe of firms with the lowest fundamental risk (quartile 1), the most levered firms have twice as much leverage as the least levered firms and the volatility of their returns is 30% greater (or 1.3 times as much).

If leverage functioned as expected based on Equation 11.1, the volatility ratios should be of similar magnitude to the leverage ratios. However, for every quartile of fundamental risk, they are about half of what we would expect. Moreover, the rightmost bars report results for portfolios that ignore fundamental risk (they are single-sort portfolios formed on leverage alone). If borrowing costs were an effective proxy for fundamental risk, we would expect a stronger relationship between leverage and volatility for the double-sort portfolios than for the single-sort portfolios. Again, this is not the case.

We extend this analysis in three ways to test the robustness of this conclusion: we introduce additional controls for fundamental risk, we perform cross-sectional and time series panel regressions with a range of controls, and we examine anecdotal evidence from specific companies.

FIGURE 11.1 High leverage portfolios versus low leverage portfolios (control variable: borrowing costs).

Controlling for Fundamental Risk

We extend the experiment described above to include additional control variables, including both the level and volatility of free cash flows associated with the underlying firms. All else being equal, companies with higher and more stable cash flows relative to their book value are inherently less risky. Still, we find that the volatility ratio of highly levered firms to firms with low leverage does not come close to matching the ratio of their leverage. The conditional leverage ratios (akin to those presented in Figure 11.1) ranged between 2.1 and 2.2, whereas the conditional volatility ratios ranged between 0.9 and 1.1. These results do not reveal the expected relationship between leverage and volatility.

Regressions with Additional Controls

We also perform panel regressions to determine whether differences in volatility correspond to differences in leverage. We run two variants of the regression: one that captures the time series relationship between equity volatility and leverage and another that captures the cross-sectional relationship. The first regression tells us whether changes in a firm's leverage are associated with subsequent changes in the same firm's volatility in future periods. The second regression tells us whether, during the same period, firms with higher leverage tend to have higher volatility than firms with lower leverage. In the time series regression, we control for differences in leverage across firms, and in the cross-sectional regression, we control for differences in leverage from one year to the next. We also perform variants of each regression to control for various effects including to

- control for the overall degree of leverage in the market from one year to the next,
- exclude financial and utility companies, recognizing that their capital structure may differ systematically from other sectors, and
- exclude the global financial crisis period of 2008–2009, given that extraordinary events during this period could distort results.

For the cross-sectional regression, we run variants to

- exclude financial and utility companies, for the same reason described above,
- control for borrowing costs, at the firm level,
- control for the level of cash flows at the firm level, and
- control for the volatility of cash flows at the firm level.

The last three variants of the regression are designed to control for the underlying volatility of a company's assets. The leverage coefficient in our regressions, which we would expect based on theory to be equal to 1.0, is close to zero. It ranges from −0.08 to 0.10. In only one regression calibration could we reject the null hypothesis that the leverage coefficient equals zero. When we control the cross-sectional regression for the volatility of cash flows at the firm level, we found that the leverage coefficient was statistically significant at the 95% level; but it was in the wrong direction! It was equal to −0.08. Given this evidence of the lack of association between leverage and volatility in the public equity market, it is unsurprising that private equity volatility shows no correspondence to leverage either.

Anecdotal Evidence

We next searched for anecdotal evidence to shed light on the lack of correspondence between leverage and volatility. We studied two companies that underwent extreme changes in leverage during a point in their history. These examples, shown in Figure 11.2, illustrate that volatility can be highly time-varying even during periods when leverage is relatively stable:

- The volatility of Motorola stock varied widely between 1991 and 2013, reaching a high of 70% during the global financial crisis and a low of approximately 20% in recent years. Yet its leverage hardly changed at all during this period. Furthermore, when the company tripled its leverage between 2015 and 2018, there was no apparent impact on its volatility.
- There does not appear to be any discernible relationship between the leverage and volatility of Clorox, either. For example, the firm has gradually reduced its leverage since 2011 only to see its share price volatility rise.

These examples reveal why a time series regression cannot detect a relationship. Even surrounding dramatic changes in the leverage of both firms, we do not observe commensurate changes in volatility. In fact, these two companies both increased their leverage following steep declines in volatility. The degree of leverage appears to be an endogenous, firm-specific decision; it stands to reason that low-risk companies incur more leverage, all else being equal, precisely because their lower credit risk enables them to do so.

FIGURE 11.2   Leverage and volatility: Motorola and Clorox.

THE BOTTOM LINE

The observed volatility of private equity is unrealistically low compared to the volatility of public equity. Investors have recognized that this apparent low volatility arises from the fact that valuations are based on appraisals that are anchored to prior period valuations. This practice has the effect of smoothing returns. Investors can offset this effect by estimating volatility from rolling longer-interval returns such as annual or triennial returns. With this adjustment, private equity volatility is like public equity volatility. Of course, it will differ by sub-categories within private equity.

Be that as it may, many investors believe that private equity volatility should be much higher than public equity volatility because private equity is much more highly levered than public equity. Theoretically, volatility should scale directly with leverage. However, it turns out that private equity volatility, adjusted for smoothing, is approximately equal to public equity volatility despite its much greater leverage, which presents a puzzle. To address this puzzle, we resorted to analyzing the relationship between leverage and volatility in the public market, where data is easier to come by. Using sorts as well as time series and cross-sectional regressions, we were unable to detect any relationship between leverage and volatility that conforms even remotely to the theoretical relationship of leverage and volatility. To put it bluntly, our results were robustly insignificant.

Next we sought to understand why we could not uncover a statistical relationship between leverage and private equity. First, we reviewed the time series properties of leverage and volatility for two companies. We discovered that leverage is often stable for long periods, whereas volatility is highly time varying. This is the proximate cause of why we cannot detect a time series relationship. In practice, companies have several sources of implicit leverage, such as pension or insurance liabilities, which obscure the effect of explicit leverage. These experiments, combined with anecdotal evidence from specific companies, suggest to us that the relationship of leverage and volatility is hopelessly obscured by a variety of confounding effects. This complexity renders it difficult, if not impossible, to control systematically for these factors in public markets let alone in private markets where the required data is scarce.

We assert that the volatility we estimate from longer-interval private equity returns (to offset the effect of valuation smoothing) is the correct approximation of private equity volatility because it approximates the actual distribution of outcomes realized by private equity investors over longer horizons. When applied to the data, this approach yields the stubborn conclusion that private equity volatility is similar to public equity volatility despite its higher leverage. Why is this the case? It could be that buyout fund managers prefer to invest in companies whose underlying business activities are inherently less risky and can therefore bear higher leverage, which increases profits. Whatever the reason, our findings debunk the widespread misconception that private equity has higher volatility than public equity volatility as a result of its higher leverage.

RELATED TOPICS

- Chapter 5 discusses why it is beneficial to estimate risk from longer-interval returns.
- Chapter 17 shows how to account for the illiquidity of private assets in portfolio construction.

REFERENCES

Anson, M. 2013. "Risk Management and Risk Budgeting in Real Estate and Illiquid Asset Classes," *CFA Institute Conference Proceedings*, Vol. 23, No. 5.

Anson, M. 2016. Asset Allocation with Private Equity, " *The Journal of Investment Consulting*, Vol. 17, No. 1.

Anson, M. 2017. "Measuring Liquidity Premiums for Illiquid Assets, " *The Journal of Alternative Investments*, Vol. 20, No. 2.

Axelson, U., Jenkinson, T., Stromberg, P., and Weisbach, M. 2013. "Borrow Cheap and Buy High? The Determinants of Leverage and Pricing in Buyouts," *Journal of Finance*, Vol. 68, No. 6 (December).

Czasonis, M., Kinlaw, W., Kritzman, M., and Turkington, D. 2021. "Private Equity and the Leverage Myth," *The Journal of Alternative Investments*, Vol. 23, No. 3 (Winter).

Czasonis, M., Kritzman, M. and Turkington, D. 2019. "Private Equity Valuations and Public Equity Performance," *The Journal of Alternative Investments*, Vol. 22, No. 1 (Summer).

NOTES

1. For details, see "Private Markets 2020: A New Decade for Private Markets," McKinsey & Company, 2020.
2. For example, Anson (2013, 2016, 2017) finds that the serial correlation in private equity returns extends back three to four quarters.
3. The opposite is true when autocorrelation is negative; in this case, the standard deviation over longer intervals is lower than what we would expect. For more on this effect, as well as its causes and consequences, see Chapter 5.
4. In some cases, private equity investments are traded on a secondary market. However, these trades occur infrequently or, in most cases, not at all. They are therefore not a reliable source of information for price discovery.
5. For example, Czasonis, Kritzman, and Turkington (2019) find evidence that private equity managers produce positively biased valuations that appear to be rationalized by information that should not be relevant.
6. For examples, refer to the literature review in Czasonis, Kinlaw, Kritzman, and Turkington (2021).
7. For a comprehensive description of our experiments and results, see Czasonis, Kinlaw, Kritzman, and Turkington (2021).
8. The State Street Private Equity Index captures the pooled Internal Rate of Return (IRR) each quarter for 3,097 private equity funds in which State Street clients are limited partners. The IRR calculation incorporates quarterly net asset values (NAVs) for each fund as well as daily net cash flows that occurred throughout the quarter. The index captures a total commitment size of $3.1 trillion as of September 30, 2019.

9. Measuring volatility from longer-interval returns has the same effect as de-smoothing because multi-period returns capture the effects of serial correlation in shorter-interval returns. Longer-interval returns have the advantage that they represent an actual investment outcome, and they do not require a model to estimate.
10. Other studies, such as Anson (2016), find that de-smoothed private equity returns have higher volatility than public equities. Estimates vary based on the source of private equity data and the specific de-smoothing methodology. We therefore base our conclusions on the volatility of longer-interval private equity returns that we discuss later in the chapter.
11. Czasonis, Kinlaw, Kritzman, and Turkington (2021) proxy borrowing costs with Worldscope item 08356, "Interest Rate-Estimated Average," which is computed as interest expense divided by the sum of short-term debt, current long-term debt, and long-term debt. We exclude observations with zero borrowing costs, negative borrowing costs, and those that reside in the 5% right tail of the distribution. All data are from the Worldscope database obtained via Datastream.

CHAPTER 12

Necessary Conditions for Mean-Variance Analysis

THE CHALLENGE

Mean-variance analysis is much more robust than commonly understood. For a given time horizon or assuming returns are expressed in continuous units, if returns are elliptically distributed and investor utility is upward sloping and concave, mean-variance analysis delivers the same result as maximizing expected utility. And even if returns are not elliptically distributed, mean-variance analysis yields the true utility-maximizing portfolio as long as utility is a quadratic function of wealth. (See Chapters 2 and 25 for more detail about elliptical distributions.)

But what if returns are not elliptical and utility is not quadratic? In this case, mean-variance analysis must be viewed as an approximation rather than an equality. But in almost all cases it is an exceptionally good approximation. Elliptical distributions are very good approximations of empirical return distributions. (For example, they allow for excess kurtosis.) Moreover, we can approximate many plausible utility functions as a quadratic function. Levy and Markowitz (1979), for example, used Taylor series to approximate a variety of power utility functions, thereby demonstrating the broad applicability of mean-variance analysis. Markowitz and Blay (2014) offer further discussion on the broad applicability of mean-variance analysis for a range of practical circumstances.

There are, however, plausible situations in which mean-variance analysis is not suitable. Specifically, if investors have preferences that are not well described by mean and variance and returns do not conform to an elliptical distribution, we must resort to an alternative portfolio formation process. Returns are not elliptically distributed if they are skewed or if, within the return sample, there are disparate subsamples that display significantly different correlations. Elliptical distributions do not capture these features. Investors who allocate across asset classes with these features, and who have a sharp aversion to losses that exceed a threshold, may be better served with a portfolio solution other than the mean-variance optimal portfolio.

DEPARTURES FROM ELLIPTICAL DISTRIBUTIONS

The notion of an elliptical distribution is straightforward to understand. Let us begin by considering a single asset class whose returns are normally distributed. The distribution looks like a bell-shaped curve centered on the mean of the returns. It is symmetric because the probability of a specific return depends only on how far the return is from the mean, regardless of whether the deviation is positive or negative. Now, consider two asset classes whose returns are jointly normally distributed. Imagine a scatter plot of their returns. If we were to draw a set of ellipses all centered on the average of the return pairs, and if the returns were evenly distributed along the boundaries of the ellipses, implying that each observation located on a boundary has an equal probability of occurrence, the distribution would be elliptical. It follows that the shape of the ellipses is completely determined by the covariance matrix. If the assets are uncorrelated and have equal variances, the scatter plot will be approximately circular. If one asset has greater variance than the other, the scatter plot will resemble an ellipse. And if the assets are correlated, the ellipses will be tilted to reflect co-movement. The multivariate normal distribution assigns a probability density to each ellipse. By changing these densities, we create an infinite variety of non-normal, but elliptically symmetric distributions, including those with fat tails to represent an increased likelihood of extreme events. With more than two assets, the ellipses become ellipsoids, but the concept remains the same.

It should be clear from this description that elliptical distributions do not allow asymmetry. They are convenient to study because any portfolio comprising elliptically distributed assets will also follow an elliptical distribution whose returns can be described solely by mean and variance. However, as we next discuss, return distributions are not always symmetric.

Skewness

Skewness is a statistical measure that captures asymmetry in a single-variable distribution. It is known as the third moment of a distribution (after normalizing), and it is based on deviations of returns from the mean that are each raised to the third power, averaged, and normalized for ease of interpretation. Unlike a symmetric distribution, which has a skewness of zero, a skewed distribution has disproportionately more large returns on one side of the mean than on the other. The payout of an out-of-the-money

TABLE 12.1   Skewness over Increasing Return Intervals

	Monthly	Annual	5-Year
US Equities	−0.54	−0.37	0.34
Foreign Developed Market Equities	−0.44	0.50	1.77
Emerging Market Equities	−0.52	0.04	1.05
Treasury Bonds	0.50	0.95	1.24
US Corporate Bonds	0.41	1.03	1.53
Commodities	−0.24	−0.22	0.64
Cash Equivalents	0.60	0.48	0.54

put option, for example, is clearly negatively skewed, with a high probability of small gains from collecting the option premium, and a low probability of a massive loss if the underlying asset falls below the strike price. Entire markets may behave the same way in which gains are incremental and losses are precipitous, or, if we are lucky, the reverse.

More generally, all asset returns become more positively skewed as they compound over time, and the longer the horizon, the greater the effect. Table 12.1 shows the skewness of returns measured over different intervals for the asset classes we introduced in Chapter 2.

Asset-Specific Tail Distributions

Ellipticality allows for symmetric fat tails, but the shape of the tails must be uniform across asset classes. Kurtosis, which is the fourth moment of a distribution (after normalizing), is used to measure the thickness of the tails of a distribution. Kurtosis is calculated in a similar fashion to skewness, except that return deviations are raised to the power four rather than three. Table 12.2 shows kurtosis, in excess of the normal distribution's kurtosis of 3, for all asset classes in our sample universe. If we believe these differences are meaningful, such that corporate bonds truly do entail greater risk of extreme returns than equities, for example, we may wish to account for these features in portfolio construction. In Chapter 19, we show how estimation error gives rise to excess kurtosis in a stability-adjusted return distribution. We find that the risk of some asset classes is less stable than that of others, leading to asymmetric kurtosis across asset classes, which results in a nonelliptical return distribution.

Figure 12.1 plots the skewness and excess kurtosis for each asset class pair for an annual horizon. The combination of these two measures provides a useful summary of a return distribution's non-normality. We apply a

TABLE 12.2 Excess Kurtosis over Increasing Return Intervals

	Monthly	Annual	5-Year
US Equities	2.05	0.69	−0.41
Foreign Developed Market Equities	1.10	1.59	2.65
Emerging Market Equities	1.54	−0.22	0.60
Treasury Bonds	3.10	1.31	1.58
US Corporate Bonds	5.96	2.57	2.90
Commodities	2.05	0.24	0.14
Cash Equivalents	0.28	−0.14	−0.53

FIGURE 12.1 Annual skewness, excess kurtosis, and statistical significance bands.

statistical test called the Jarque–Bera test to determine whether these departures from normality are significant, given the number of observations in the sample from which they are estimated.[1] The test statistic is a function of skewness squared and excess kurtosis squared, and the joint significance thresholds are, therefore, ellipses centered on the point (0,0), which corresponds to a normal distribution. The inner circle in Figure 12.1 is the 10% significance boundary, assuming our estimates come from a sample of 480

FIGURE 12.2 US and foreign equity returns (12-month horizon).

observations. However, even though we used 480 monthly observations, we computed rolling returns to represent an annual investment horizon; thus, it is more appropriate to characterize the number of independent data points as 40 (years). The outer circle is the boundary indicating 10% significance for a sample of 40 observations. Our data set shows that Treasury bonds, corporate bonds, and foreign equities are highly non-normal, due to a combination of positive skewness and positive excess kurtosis. US equities are negatively skewed and have positive excess kurtosis, but it is statistically plausible that this finding could arise due to noise, given our choice of data.

Nonlinear Asset Dependencies

The true relationships between assets may not be as straightforward as correlation coefficients suggest. Correlations only capture linear dependencies between variables. They do not describe the behavior of asset classes that provide diversification on the upside but tend to move in concert on the downside, for example. Figure 12.2 shows that US and foreign equities have interacted asymmetrically during our 40-year sample, and not in a good way. (For more on correlation asymmetry, see Chapter 6.)

DEPARTURES FROM QUADRATIC UTILITY

Most plausible utility functions are upward sloping, which implies a preference for more wealth rather than less, and they are concave, which implies that investors are risk averse. Power utility functions fit this description.

Quadratic functions (functions that depend only on mean and variance) are often quite good at approximating these types of utility functions, especially if we limit our attention to returns within a range that is reasonably likely to occur. Nevertheless, some investors have more complex utility functions that defy quadratic approximation. Perhaps the most relevant example, in our view, is a kinked utility function that represents sharp dissatisfaction with returns below some specified level. S-shaped utility, which stems from behavioral finance, is another alternative to power utility. Because it has an inflection point, it likewise cannot be described solely by mean and variance.

Kinked Utility Function

Suppose we accept the notion that we are more averse to losses than we are appreciative of gains. The next question we should ask ourselves is: To what extent do we dislike a loss compared to an equal-size gain? Or, put differently, how sharply curved is our utility as a function of a prospective change in wealth? If our asymmetric preference between a gain and a loss of the same size remains constant regardless of our starting wealth, we would display what is known as constant absolute risk aversion. If, on the other hand, our asymmetric preferences scale with our starting wealth, such that we are willing to risk the same proportion of our wealth as it grows, our utility function is described as constant relative risk aversion. A utility function that equals the logarithm of investor wealth and its generalization, power utility, conform to this principle. As their names imply, these types of utility functions assume that some aspects of our preferences are constant for all levels of wealth. But it is quite conceivable that many investors face sharp discontinuities in utility at certain levels of wealth. For example, a pension fund may be able to tolerate a decrease in its funding status up to a certain level, unpleasant as that may be, yet a decrease beyond that level could trigger increases in contributions from the plan sponsor. Those who must periodically refinance debt may need to maintain asset values above strict levels. And, in everyday life, there are those whose partners pledged loyalty through thick and thin, but when faced with a large loss, they sadly discover that their partners exaggerated. We describe these threshold-dependent preferences with a kinked utility function, as shown in Figure 12.3.

S-Shaped Utility Function

Behavioral economists suggest that people are risk averse when confronted with gains and risk seeking when they face losses. When asked to choose between a certain payout of $1,000 and a risky gamble that has an 80%

FIGURE 12.3 Kinked utility function.

FIGURE 12.4 S-shaped utility function.

chance of paying $250 and a 20% chance of paying $4,000, most respondents prefer the certain outcome. However, most people feel very differently about the opposite proposition, in which one must choose between a guaranteed loss and an uncertain one. In this case, people typically prefer a risky gamble that has an 80% chance of a $250 loss and a 20% chance of a $4,000 loss to a certain loss of $1,000. An S-shaped utility function, as shown in Figure 12.4, reflects these highly asymmetric preferences with a concave utility curve for gains and a convex curve for losses. (See Chapter 25 for additional details.)

FULL-SCALE OPTIMIZATION

For situations in which we believe returns are not elliptically distributed and investors have preferences that defy approximation by mean and variance, we must resort to an optimization process called full-scale optimization.[2] This approach is conceptually straightforward but computationally intensive. We search across all permissible sets of portfolio weights and select whichever combination produces the highest expected utility. Let us illustrate this process by maximizing a kinked utility function given annual returns for US stocks and Treasury bonds from 2006 through 2015. The first portfolio we consider, chosen arbitrarily for illustration, is 75% stocks and 25% bonds. As shown in Table 12.3, we compute the utility of the returns for each of the 10 years in our sample, and average them to obtain expected utility. This portfolio's utility suffers from the 2008 drop in equity values, which is penalized heavily by strong aversion to losses below −10%.

Figure 12.5 shows how expected utility changes with the stock and bond mix, and Table 12.4 shows expected utility for the utility-maximizing solution of 45% stocks and 55% bonds.

This example relies exclusively on past returns as a guide to the future, but full-scale optimization is much more flexible. If we have views that differ from the historical means of the asset classes, we add a constant to each return, thereby adjusting the mean to reflect our views. And if our views about the standard deviation differ from the historical values, we multiply the returns by a constant to force them to conform to our views. These

TABLE 12.3 Expected Utility for 75/25 Percent Stock/Bond Portfolio

	Stock Return (%)	Bond Return (%)	Stock Weight (%)	Bond Weight (%)	Portfolio Return (%)	Utility
2006	15.8	3.1	75	25	12.6	0.1188
2007	5.5	9.0	75	25	6.4	0.0618
2008	−37.0	13.7	75	25	−24.3	−1.7100
2009	26.5	−3.6	75	25	19.0	0.1736
2010	15.1	5.9	75	25	12.8	0.1201
2011	2.1	9.8	75	25	4.0	0.0396
2012	16.0	2.0	75	25	12.5	0.1178
2013	32.4	−2.7	75	25	23.6	0.2119
2014	13.7	5.1	75	25	11.5	0.1091
2015	1.4	0.8	75	25	1.2	0.0124

Expected Utility = −0.0745

FIGURE 12.5 Expected utility for different allocations to stocks (5% increments).

TABLE 12.4 Expected Utility for 45/55 Percent Stock/Bond Portfolio

	Stock Return (%)	Bond Return (%)	Stock Weight (%)	Bond Weight (%)	Portfolio Return (%)	Utility
2006	15.8	3.1	45	55	8.8	0.0844
2007	5.5	9.0	45	55	7.4	0.0717
2008	−37.0	13.7	45	55	−9.1	−0.0953
2009	26.5	−3.6	45	55	9.9	0.0948
2010	15.1	5.9	45	55	10.0	0.0954
2011	2.1	9.8	45	55	6.3	0.0615
2012	16.0	2.0	45	55	8.3	0.0797
2013	32.4	−2.7	45	55	13.1	0.1228
2014	13.7	5.1	45	55	8.9	0.0856
2015	1.4	0.8	45	55	1.1	0.0108

Expected Utility = 0.0611

adjustments preserve the higher moments – beyond mean and variance – and the asset class correlations, which is the key advantage of full-scale optimization.

THE CURSE OF DIMENSIONALITY

Although full-scale optimization is extremely flexible, it is computationally challenging. In our simple example, we only needed to consider 21 possible portfolios. But the problem's complexity grows very quickly as we add

TABLE 12.5   The Curse of Dimensionality

Number of Assets	Weight Increment (%)	Number of Possible Portfolios*
2	5	21
7	5	230,230
7	2.5	9,366,819
14	5	573,166,440
14	2.5	841,392,966,470
28	5	9,762,479,679,106
28	2.5	4,105,075,349,580,980,000
28	1.25	15,738,530,963,776,300,000,000,000

*The last two rows are approximations due to computer rounding error of multiplying and dividing very large numbers.

asset classes, extend the sample size, and refine the granularity of the search. Indeed, part of the beauty and practicality of mean-variance analysis is its tractability, even for large universes. Of course, computational power is far greater today than it was in 1952 when Markowitz introduced mean-variance analysis. We can evaluate hundreds of thousands of portfolios in a matter of seconds. This is enough to measure the utility of the 230,230 possible long-only portfolios of seven asset classes in increments of 5%, as we do in our upcoming example. As shown in Table 12.5, if the number of asset classes is doubled to 14, there are more than 573 million portfolios to consider. If we further double the number of asset classes to 28, and refine the search granularity to 1.25%, the number of possible portfolios explodes to more than 15 trillion-trillion, as shown in Table 8.5.[3] To put this final number in perspective, if we could evaluate the utility of 100,000 portfolios per second, it would take 360 times the age of the universe (estimated to be 13.82 billion years) to evaluate every portfolio. This phenomenon is known as the curse of dimensionality.

Not every portfolio is equally likely to be the solution, though. We can turn to efficient search algorithms to help find the optimal portfolio more efficiently than conducting an exhaustive search. There are many fast search techniques. One technique that is particularly effective is called a genetic search, which is inspired by evolutionary biology. This method starts with an "initial population" of weight vectors. Next, it introduces random mutations and combinations of existing vectors to form the next "generation," and proceeds by "mating" the most promising (highest utility) offspring until a dominant solution is found. As with most search algorithms applied to complex problems, it is possible that the algorithm will become trapped in a local maximum and will fail to converge to the globally optimal solution. Using an expansive initial population mitigates this risk, however.

We are limited in how we use full-scale optimization, but these limitations are more restrictive for security selection than for asset allocation. Moreover, in many applications, a less granular search proceeding in increments of 5% or 10% is sufficiently specific to provide useful insight.

APPLYING FULL-SCALE OPTIMIZATION

We now apply full-scale optimization to the asset classes introduced in Chapter 2, and we compare the result of this approach to the more traditional solution generated by mean-variance analysis. We backfill missing data from 1976 to 1988 for emerging market equities in order to hold the measurement period constant for our comparison. We define the set of possible returns as all overlapping 12-month returns. We shift the historical returns so that their means match the expected returns from our base case example, but we preserve the full details of the distribution of each asset class around its mean. We assume the investor has kinked utility. To the right of the kink we assume power utility with a risk aversion parameter of 5. To the left of the kink we impose an additional penalty of –5 for each unit of annual loss below –5%. Finally, we limit our search to portfolios that replicate the same expected returns as the conservative, moderate, and aggressive portfolios identified previously. We search for the optimal weights in increments of 5%.

Table 12.6 shows the full-scale optimal portfolios alongside the mean-variance optimal portfolios. We should first note that the standard deviations reported for the mean-variance optimal portfolios differ from what we showed in Chapter 2. The difference arises because we use overlapping 12-month returns to compute the standard deviations, whereas we measured the standard deviations from monthly returns and multiplied by the square root of 12 to annualize them in Chapter 2. The use of 12-month returns captures mean-reversion and trending in monthly returns, a topic we discuss further in Chapter 5. Setting this issue aside for now, let us compare the performance of each full-scale optimal allocation to its mean-variance counterpart. Note that the conservative portfolio derived from full-scale optimization has a higher standard deviation than the mean-variance portfolio. This outcome reflects the fact that mean-variance analysis does not distinguish between upside and downside deviations. The full-scale solution's higher standard deviation reflects a preference for upside deviations. Overall, full-scale optimization succeeds in reducing excess kurtosis and eliminating, or at least mitigating, negative skewness. Its goal, given the kinked utility function, is to avoid large losses. The 1% value at risk shows a worst-case scenario that is not as bad as it is for the mean-variance solutions. It is interesting to note

TABLE 12.6 Full-Scale and Mean-Variance Allocations and Characteristics

	Conservative		Moderate		Aggressive	
	Full Scale	Mean Variance	Full Scale	Mean Variance	Full Scale	Mean Variance
US Equities	15.0%	15.9%	25.0%	25.5%	40.0%	36.8%
Foreign Developed Market Equities	0.0%	14.5%	5.0%	23.2%	0.0%	34.5%
Emerging Market Equities	15.0%	5.6%	25.0%	9.1%	40.0%	15.8%
Treasury Bonds	45.0%	15.5%	25.0%	14.3%	5.0%	0.0%
US Corporate Bonds	20.0%	11.4%	20.0%	22.0%	15.0%	8.9%
Commodities	0.0%	4.0%	0.0%	5.9%	0.0%	4.0%
Cash Equivalents	5.0%	33.2%	0.0%	0.0%	0.0%	0.0%
Expected Return	6.0%	6.0%	7.5%	7.5%	9.0%	9.0%
Standard Deviation	7.9%	7.6%	11.7%	11.7%	16.1%	16.3%
Skewness	0.70	−0.05	0.10	−0.09	−0.15	−0.24
Excess Kurtosis	1.19	1.65	0.78	1.66	0.66	1.28
Probability of Loss < −5%	3.4%	6.0%	12.6%	11.9%	17.9%	16.8%
1% Value at Risk	−13.4%	−18.5%	−26.6%	−30.0%	−39.7%	−43.0%

that the full-scale portfolios often have a greater probability of experiencing a loss that is worse than −5%. This result may seem surprising because we set our kink at −5% precisely to avoid such losses. Full-scale optimization is willing to accept a slight breach of this threshold in exchange for avoiding larger shortfalls which our kinked utility function deems to be much more painful. If we were committed to avoiding losses beyond the threshold at all costs, we could try imposing a steeper slope to the left of the kink, setting the kink threshold higher to provide a buffer, or adding a discontinuous jump to lower utility at the −5% threshold. When all is said and done, the objective is to engineer a portfolio that best matches our description of utility.

THE BOTTOM LINE

For a given time horizon or assuming returns are expressed in continuous units, if an investor's expected utility is quadratic or returns are elliptically distributed, mean-variance analysis yields the optimal portfolio. And if we can reasonably approximate expected utility with mean and variance, or if returns are elliptically distributed, mean-variance analysis will deliver a close approximation to the true utility-maximizing portfolio. If, however, we cannot approximate expected utility with just mean and variance and returns are not elliptically distributed, then we might be better off using full-scale optimization to identify the utility-maximizing portfolio. This would be the case for investors whose utility changes abruptly at a specific threshold, and who invest in asset classes with nonzero skewness, asymmetric correlations, or wide variation in kurtosis across asset classes. Though computationally intensive, full-scale optimization is suitable for asset allocation in which the number of asset classes is relatively small. It finds portfolios with the same expected return as a mean-variance analysis, yet delivers a risk profile that is tailored to each investor's unique preferences.

RELATED TOPICS

- Chapter 2 introduces the fundamentals of mean-variance analysis.
- Chapter 6 demonstrates how correlation asymmetry violates the assumption of elliptical asset returns distributions.
- Chapter 19 applies full-scale optimization to form portfolios with more stable risk profiles.

REFERENCES

Cremers, J.-H., Kritzman, M., and Page, S. 2005. "Optimal Hedge Fund Allocations," *Journal of Portfolio Management*, Vol. 31, No. 3 (Spring).

Jarque, C. and Bera, A. 1980. "Efficient Tests for Normality, Homoscedasticity and Serial Independence of Regression Residuals," *Economics Letters*, Vol. 6, No. 3.

Levy, H. and Markowitz, H. 1979. "Approximating Expected Utility by a Function of Mean and Variance," *American Economic Review* (June).

Markowitz, H. and Blay, K. 2014. *The Theory and Practice of Rational Investing: Risk-Return Analysis, Volume 1*. New York: McGraw-Hill.

NOTES

1. The Jarque–Bera test statistic is equal to $JB = \dfrac{N}{6} * \left(skewness^2 + \dfrac{excess\ kurtosis^2}{4} \right)$,

   and it follows a chi-squared distribution with 2 degrees of freedom. See Jarque and Bera (1980) for further details.

2. See Cremers, Kritzman, and Page (2005) for more on full-scale optimization.

3. To calculate the number of possible portfolios, think of each increment of weight as an item. Suppose we have 80 identical items representing 1.25% weight increments. We need to determine all the ways we can insert 27 dividers to form 28 groups, each of which represents a weight. We must now consider all permutations of 107 total items, which is 107 factorial, or $107! = 107*106*105*...*3*2*1$. We do not care about the ordering of the 80 items because they are identical, so we should divide by all the possible orderings of 80 items which is 80 factorial. Likewise, we should also divide by 27 factorial because the dividers are all equivalent to each other. In general, if we have k weight increments and N assets, the number of possible portfolios is $\dfrac{(k+N-1)!}{k!(N-1)!}$ which is sometimes called $k + N - 1$ choose $N - 1$.

CHAPTER 13

Forecasting

THE CHALLENGE

Mean-variance analysis requires investors to specify views for expected returns, standard deviations, and correlations. These properties of assets vary over time. Long-run averages are poor forecasts because they fail to capture this time variation. On the other hand, extrapolating from a short sample of recent history is ineffective because it introduces noise and assumes a level of persistence that does not occur reliably (see Chapter 19 on estimation error, and Chapter 9 on the fallacy of 1/N). As an alternative, investors may use additional data such as economic variables to project expected returns from the current values of those variables and their historical relationships to asset returns. However, this approach does not guarantee success because additional variables contribute noise along with information. The investor's challenge is to maximize the information content and minimize the noise, thereby generating the most effective predictions. In this chapter, we reinterpret linear regression to reveal the predictive information that comes from each historical observation in our sample, and we extend it to focus on a subset of the most relevant historical observations, which can significantly improve the quality of the forecasts. This procedure, which was introduced by Czasonis, Kritzman, and Turkington (2020), is called partial sample regression.

CONVENTIONAL LINEAR REGRESSION

Financial analysts face the challenge of mapping predictive variables onto the assets they want to forecast. The goal is to identify relationships from history that are likely to apply in the future. Let us begin by reviewing one of the most common forecasting techniques: linear regression. It assumes that the variable we are trying to predict, y_t, is a linear function of a set of predictive variables, x_t (a row vector), plus an error term, ε_t:

$$y_t = x_t \beta + \varepsilon_t \tag{13.1}$$

The simplicity of the linear model is attractive. Compared to a more complex model, it is less likely to overfit the data and identify spurious relationships. To find the vector of coefficients, β (a column vector), we solve for the values that minimize the sum of squared prediction errors between the model's forecasts, $\tilde{y}_t = x_t \beta$, and the actual values of the dependent variable:

$$\hat{\beta} = \min_{\beta} \left(\sum_{t=1}^{T} (y_t - \tilde{y}_t)^2 \right) \tag{13.2}$$

This method is called Ordinary Least Squares (OLS). It is quite like the portfolio optimization method we describe in Chapter 2, where we minimize risk as the sum of squared deviations of portfolio returns from their average. The solution to the linear regression problem is shown in matrix notation as follows:

$$\hat{\beta} = \left(X'X \right)^{-1} X'Y \tag{13.3}$$

$\hat{\beta}$ is the best linear unbiased estimate of the variable coefficients, which means they extract information from the data set as efficiently as possible, given their intended goal. To arrive at a forecast of the dependent variable, we multiply each variable in the x_t vector by its estimated coefficient in $\hat{\beta}$ and compute the sum, which in matrix notation is

$$\hat{y}_t = x_t \beta \tag{13.4}$$

Linear regression is a statistically robust process that performs well in many applications, but it has two important shortcomings. First, its traditional interpretation in terms of the relative importance of each variable does not match the way people intuitively extrapolate from past events, so it can be hard to reconcile model outputs with our judgment. Second, it does not capture nonlinear or conditional relationships between variables.

Next, we present a solution to these shortcomings. We show that by reinterpreting regression predictions as a weighted sum across observations – rather than a weighted sum across variable values – we align intuition with the way we naturally extrapolate from events. This insight leads to a new set of models called partial sample regressions, whereby omitting less relevant observations can substantially improve the quality of our forecasts.

REGRESSION REVISITED

Let us now approach the prediction challenge from a different perspective. Imagine we are given a set of historical observations for predictive variables, X (a matrix of stacked time observations), and a prediction target, y, and we are asked to generate a forecast for y_{t+1} in the future based on current values for x_t. How might we proceed?

One intuitive approach is to begin by measuring the similarity of each historical observation x_i, to today, x_t. We define multivariate similarity as the opposite (negative) of the Mahalanobis distance between the two points. It is also multiplied by 1/2 to compensate for the fact that x_i and x_t are compared twice by the multiplications in the formula. The Mahalanobis distance (as described in Chapter 25) represents the distance between two vectors as a function of the normalized distances between the respective elements of the vectors as well as the degree to which co-movement across variables is unusual. The larger the distance, the less similar two observations are, and vice versa.

$$similarity(x_i, x_t) = -\frac{1}{2}(x_i - x_t)\Omega^{-1}(x_i - x_t)' \qquad (13.5)$$

Here, Ω^{-1} is the inverse of the covariance matrix of the variables in X. (Note that we use Σ to denote the covariance matrix in other chapters, but we use the symbol Ω in this chapter to avoid confusion with summation operators in the formulas that follow.) All else being equal, similarity is higher when the values in x_i and x_t are closer to each other, and when the deviations in values align with common patterns for the variables. For example, if economic growth and inflation are positively correlated, a deviation of both variables in the same direction would not increase the distance by much, but a deviation in the opposite direction would. It is reasonable to think that in the next period, y might behave the same way it has behaved following similar periods in history. This is certainly more intuitive than predicting that y will behave as it has behaved following the most different periods in history.

What if there are two historical events that are equally like today, but different from each other? Suppose that one such observation is closer to the long-run mean than x_t, whereas the other is farther from the mean. Which of these observations contains better information for predicting y_{t+1}? The answer is that we should rely more on the unusual observation and less on the typical one, because the unusual observation likely contains more event-driven information, whereas the typical observation more likely reflects noise.

Following this intuition, we measure the informativeness of each observation as its Mahalanobis distance from the long-run average of X. We scale it by 1/2 as we did for similarity.

$$informativeness(x_i) = \frac{1}{2}(x_i - \bar{x})\Omega^{-1}(x_i - \bar{x})' \quad (13.6)$$

Together, similarity and informativeness tell us the relevance of each historical observation. Similarity compares each observation to the one we are using to forecast, whereas informativeness compares each observation to the average across the entire data set:

$$relevance(x_i) = similarity(x_i, x_t) + informativeness(x_i) \quad (13.7)$$

To build intuition for the measure of relevance, let us consider some examples. If a historical observation "A" is identical to x_t, the distance between them is zero, so A's similarity is as high as possible (similarity becomes less and less negative as distance falls). Therefore, A's relevance score equals its informativeness. All other observations must have a lower (more negative) similarity to x_t. If observation B is as informative as A but less similar to x_t, it has lower relevance for our forecast. The historical y value corresponding to B may help our prediction, but we should put less weight on it than A. An observation with low similarity, low informativeness, or both, could have a relevance of zero. We would ignore the y value that corresponds to this observation.

What does it mean if relevance is negative?[1] This is often the case. It occurs for historical observations that are informative in their own right, but also very different from x_t. For example, if x_t reflects robust economic growth, historical data from a severe recession probably has negative relevance. We might assume that such points are so different from x_t that we should predict the opposite of the y values that correspond to them. Amazingly, it turns out that if we multiply each historical value of y by that period's relevance and average the results, we end up with precisely the linear regression forecast. The following equations demonstrate this equivalence. For notational convenience and without loss of generality, we assume that all X and y variables are shifted to have means of zero.

$$relevance(x_i) = -\frac{1}{2}(x_i - x_t)\Omega^{-1}(x_i - x_t)' + \frac{1}{2}x_i\Omega^{-1}x_i' \quad (13.8)$$

$$relevance(x_i) = x_t\Omega^{-1}x_i' - \frac{1}{2}x_t\Omega^{-1}x_t' \tag{13.9}$$

$$\hat{y}_t = \frac{1}{N-1}\sum_{i=1}^{N} relevance(x_i)y_i \tag{13.10}$$

$$\hat{y}_t = \frac{1}{N-1}\sum_{i=1}^{N}\left(x_t\Omega^{-1}x_i' - \frac{1}{2}x_t\Omega^{-1}x_t'\right)y_i \tag{13.11}$$

$$\hat{y}_t = \frac{1}{N-1}\sum_{i=1}^{N}x_t\Omega^{-1}x_i'y_i - \frac{1}{2}x_t\Omega^{-1}x_t'\bar{y} \tag{13.12}$$

$$\Omega = \frac{1}{N-1}X'X \tag{13.13}$$

$$\Omega^{-1} = N-1(X'X)^{-1} \tag{13.14}$$

Because the average of y_i is zero:

$$\hat{y}_t = \sum_{i=1}^{N}x_t(X'X)^{-1}x_i'y_i \tag{13.15}$$

$$\hat{y}_t = x_t(X'X)^{-1}X'Y \tag{13.16}$$

$$\hat{y}_t = x_t\beta \tag{13.17}$$

In Equation 13.17, beta is the vector of coefficients from a traditional linear regression. Table 13.1 shows this equivalence for a simplified example with only one independent variable and samples for X and y that have means of zero. It is straightforward to expand to multiple variables and nonzero means, $\bar{y} = \frac{1}{N}\sum_{i=1}^{N}y_i$, using the following formula:

$$\hat{y}_t = \bar{y} + \frac{1}{N-1}\sum_{i=1}^{N} relevance(x_i)(y_i - \bar{y}) \tag{13.18}$$

TABLE 13.1 Equivalence of Prediction from Linear Regression and Relevance-Weighted Dependent Variable

	Traditional calculation		Relevance-weighted calculation			
Observation	X (%)	Y (%)	Similarity (to X = 10%)	Informativeness	Relevance	Scaled Y values (%)
1	−15	−10	−6.25	2.25	−4.00	20
2	−5	−20	−2.25	0.25	−2.00	20
3	0	10	−1.00	0.00	−1.00	−5
4	5	0	−0.25	0.25	0.00	0
5	15	20	−0.25	2.25	2.00	20
Slope:		1.1			Average:	11%
Prediction for X = 10%		11%				

In summary, we presume that more similar observations are more relevant, and that more informative observations are more relevant, all else being equal. We combine these two scores and apply the result as a "weight" to each historical observation of the dependent variable we wish to forecast. Summing across all observations produces the same forecast as linear regression. Viewed this way, it is interesting to note that to predict different y variables we need only replace the dependent variable observations while retaining the same historical relevance scores.

How Many Anecdotes Do We Need?

It is often said that the plural of "anecdote" is "data." Our observation-based perspective of regression analysis illustrates this point. If we include only the single most relevant observation, our forecast is that whatever happened at that time will reoccur. This forecast comes from the most relevant possible data, but it is noisy because it extrapolates from a single event. If instead we include every observation, our forecast aggregates across the full extent of available data. This forecast is statistically robust, but it may reflect noise from less-relevant observations. Most notably, it assumes that what happened during the most dissimilar historical periods will reoccur but in the opposite direction. For these bets to work, we need perfect symmetry. This is the essence of "linearity" in a linear model. It is not necessarily intuitive and may provide a poor description of the real world. For example, does it make more sense to predict health outcomes for a young, athletic woman from a data sample of her peers, or by predicting the opposite of what happens to old men with sedentary lifestyles?

We might decide to disregard data that are sufficiently irrelevant. The good news is that building a model with this sophistication is not difficult. All we need to do is censor the least relevant observations and form predictions from the remaining observations. This approach is called partial sample regression.

PARTIAL SAMPLE REGRESSION

In partial sample regression, we average over a subset of n observations, rather than the full data set N. With this change, we must generalize our previous formula for relevance-weighted observations in two ways. The final prediction formula is

$$\hat{y}_t = \bar{y} + \frac{1}{n-1} \sum_{relevant\ i's}^{n} relevance(x_i)(y_i - \bar{y}) \qquad (13.19)$$

In Equation 13.19, the mean is also computed on the relevant subsample $\bar{y} = \frac{1}{n} \sum_{relevant\ i's}^{n} y_i$. This formula converges to two intuitive edge cases. If we include all N observations, the estimate is equal to that of a standard linear regression. If we include only a single data point x_i that is precisely equal to x_t, the prediction equals y_i for that observation.

Comparison to Other Approaches

Partial sample regression may be viewed as an application of "kernel regression," which extrapolates from near-neighbors of each observation, but it includes two essential distinguishing features. First, using the Mahalanobis distance to assess similarity is not an arbitrary choice, but is motivated by the rigor of OLS linear regression. Second, we consider informativeness in addition to similarity.

Partial sample regression is also distinct from other common variants of linear regression. For example, we cannot simply perform a new linear regression on the filtered subsample of data. The new regression would implicitly compute new relevance scores that systematically underestimate true relevance and therefore bias the results, because it is not aware that we already restricted attention to a subset of highly relevant observations. Partial sample regression is also quite different from weighted least squares. Weighted least squares applies weights to observations before evaluating their covariances, whereas partial sample regression filters the observations after the covariance matrix has already been computed.

Of course, there are endless possibilities for complex models to capture the complex relationships of assets and predictive variables. The relative simplicity of partial sample regression, combined with its ability to detect conditional relationships, is its main advantage.

Predicting Returns of Factors and Asset Classes

Partial sample regression is a general approach that may be used to forecast anything. It provides statistical rigor along with intuitive appeal. Whether or not its forecasts are more reliable than those from other models is an empirical question. In practice, we find that it often performs better than traditional linear regression. In this section, we illustrate its value for predicting the returns of asset classes and factors from economic variables. (In Chapter 14, we apply it to forecasting the correlation between stocks and bonds.)

We use the following US economic data, each of which is computed as a year-over-year percentage change for a sequence of three consecutive years, as our X variables, in order to measure the relevance of the historical observations:

- Industrial production
- Inflation

As Y variables, we consider the following asset classes and factor premiums (the five factors proposed by Fama and French [2015] plus the traditional stock momentum factor) for the US market:

- Equities minus cash
- Government bonds minus cash
- Corporate bonds minus government bonds
- Commodities minus cash
- Small minus large stocks
- Value minus growth stocks
- High minus low profitability stocks
- High minus low investment stocks
- Positive minus negative momentum stocks

For a given prediction, we compute the relevance of each historical observation and identify the top 25%. First, let us consider a prediction that one might make as of mid-2020, using available observations for 2018 and 2019 and hypothesizing values for the full year of 2020. Specifically, let us assume that industrial production over these three years is 2.0%, 1.8%, and –6.0%, and that inflation is 1.9%, 2.3%, and 1.0%. Figure 13.1 shows the relevance of each historical three-year path together with the equity risk premium that prevailed in the following year.

Partial sample regression amounts to weighting the dependent variable observations in Figure 13.2 by their relevance and averaging them. In this example, the forecast for the equity risk premium conditional on the economic path we specified is 10.9%.

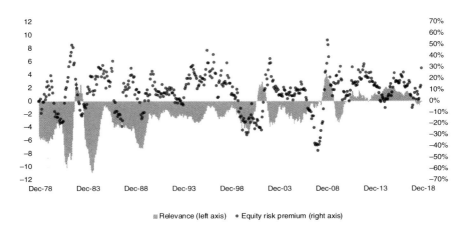

FIGURE 13.1 Relevance and dependent variable values for a sample input.

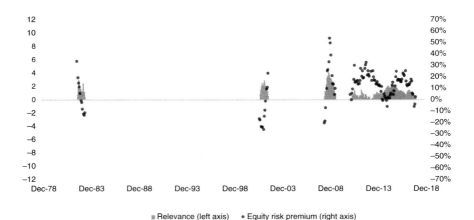

FIGURE 13.2 The most relevant observations.

FIGURE 13.3 Prediction efficacy for partial sample regression versus traditional linear regression (correlation of predicted and realized values).

Next, we repeat this prediction process for each historical observation in our data set, and for each asset class and factor premium. We then evaluate the correlation between predictions and actual occurrences of the dependent variable. Figure 13.3 shows that the correlation between predicted and realized values increases substantially in every case.

THE BOTTOM LINE

Investors may wish to adjust their portfolios as conditions change. An effective process requires accurate forecasts for expected returns, standard deviations, and correlations. Although some investors may choose to rely on qualitative judgment, others may prefer to use historical data as a guide. Naïve extrapolation of previous returns does not usually work well. Instead, investors can relate asset performance to a set of predictive variables. The analytical process becomes more intuitive when we reinterpret linear regression as a relevance-weighted average over historical observations. With this approach, it is often possible to improve forecasts by simply eliminating a portion of the less-relevant information.

RELATED TOPICS

- Chapter 9 discusses the importance of using reasonable expected returns as inputs to portfolio optimization.
- Chapter 14 applies partial sample regression to forecast the correlation between stocks and bonds.

REFERENCES

Czasonis, M., Kritzman, M., and Turkington, D. 2020. "Addition by Subtraction: A Better Way to Predict Factor Returns (and Everything Else)," *The Journal of Portfolio Management*, Vol. 46, No. 8 (September).

Fama, E. F. and French, K. R. 2015. "A Five Factor Asset Pricing Model," *Journal of Financial Economics*, Vol. 116, No. 1 (April).

NOTE

1. To be precise, interpreting the sign of an observation's relevance requires that we center relevance around zero by subtracting its average value (which will be negative), or equivalently that we augment the definition of relevance with the addition of the informativeness of x_t. Adding any constant to all of the relevance terms has no effect on the prediction because it amounts to a constant times the sum of deviations of Y, which is zero.

CHAPTER 14

The Stock–Bond Correlation

THE CHALLENGE

The stock–bond correlation is a critical consideration for constructing optimal portfolios and for assessing a portfolio's exposure to loss. For these purposes, investors should be less concerned about how stocks and bonds co-move from month to month and more concerned about how they co-move over the duration of their investment horizon. Most investors predict the correlation of longer-interval stock and bond returns by extrapolating the historical correlation of shorter-interval returns. This approach assumes that the stock–bond correlation is invariant to the return interval used to estimate it. This assumption only holds if the autocorrelations of stocks and bonds and their lagged cross-correlation are zero at all lags, which is hardly the case. Alternatively, investors may choose to estimate the correlation of longer-interval returns by computing it directly from independent or overlapping longer-interval observations, but this approach assumes that the correlation estimated from a long history is relatively constant across shorter subsamples, which also is contrary to evidence.

This chapter describes several innovations introduced by Czasonis, Kritzman, and Turkington (2020) for estimating longer-interval stock–bond correlations. We first show how to measure co-movement of stocks and bonds over multi-year horizons by taking into consideration how the stock and bond returns drift during this horizon. We then identify fundamental predictors of the long-horizon stock–bond correlation. We also show how to consider the path of economic variables, along with single observations, to forecast the stock–bond correlation. And we apply a technique called partial sample regression, which we introduced in Chapter 13, to filter out less relevant observations from our sample. We introduce these innovations to our forecasting model incrementally to generate the most reliable prediction of the stock–bond correlation.

SINGLE-PERIOD CORRELATION

To illustrate our approach, we focus on the correlation of five-year returns. We use the S&P 500 Index to estimate stock returns and the Bloomberg Barclays US Treasury Index to estimate bond returns.

The conventional approach to forecasting the correlation of five-year stock and bond returns is to extrapolate the correlation of monthly returns from a recent historical sample. This approach assumes that correlations are invariant to the return interval used to estimate them. However, this invariance would be true only if the returns of stocks and bonds were each serially independent at all lags and if their lagged cross-correlations were also zero at all lags. Chapter 5 describes this issue in detail.

Alternatively, we might consider calculating the correlation of independent or overlapping five-year returns from a long history of returns, but this approach assumes that the stock–bond correlation is relatively constant across shorter subsamples.

Therefore, the first order of business is to develop an approximation of the correlation of five-year stock and bond returns that captures the extent to which these returns move synchronously or drift apart during each five-year period.

Equation 14.1 captures the co-movement of the cumulative return of stocks and bonds for a chosen five-year period considering the average co-movement of stocks and bonds over the full sample of five-year returns:

$$single\ period\ correlation_{s,b} = \frac{\left(\dfrac{r_s - \mu_s}{\sigma_s}\right)\left(\dfrac{r_b - \mu_b}{\sigma_b}\right)}{\dfrac{1}{2}\left(\left(\dfrac{r_s - \mu_s}{\sigma_s}\right)^2 + \left(\dfrac{r_b - \mu_b}{\sigma_b}\right)^2\right)} \qquad (14.1)$$

In Equation 14.1, r_s and r_b equal the five-year cumulative returns of stocks and bonds, respectively; μ_s and μ_b equal the long-run arithmetic average returns of stocks and bonds, respectively; and σ_s and σ_b equal the standard deviations of the five-year stock and bond returns, respectively.

We refer to this measure as a single-period correlation, because it measures the co-movement of the cumulative returns of stocks and bonds for a single five-year period rather than the average correlation of five-year returns over the full sample. Each single-period correlation will differ from the long-run average correlation based on the period-specific co-movement of stocks and bonds.

For example, as shown in Figure 14.1, if the z-scores of stocks and bonds are identical for the period, the single-period correlation will equal 1.

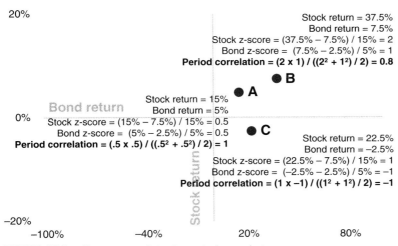

FIGURE 14.1 Illustration of single-period correlation.

If they are exactly opposite, the single-period correlation will equal −1. If they have the same sign but different magnitudes, the single-period correlation will lie between 0 and 1. And if they have different signs and different magnitudes, the single-period correlation will lie between −1 and 0. It is important to note that even though this measure relies on means and correlations estimated from the full sample of all five-year periods, it informs us about the co-movement of stocks and bonds for a single five-year period.

(Note: The average returns of stocks and bonds are 7.5% and 2.5%, respectively. The standard deviations of stocks and bonds are 15% and 5%, respectively.)

The single-period correlation is related to the correlation of a time series of stock and bond returns, which is called the Pearson correlation, in a precise mathematical way. It equals a weighted average of the single-period correlations throughout the sample, where the weights equal the informativeness of each period's returns:

$$Correlation(s, b) = \frac{1}{N} \sum_{t=1}^{N} \left(informativeness_t \times single\ period\ correlation_t \right) \quad (14.2)$$

In Equation 14.2, N equals the number of return periods in the sample, and $informativeness_t$ and $single\ period\ correlation_t$ are based on stock and bond returns ending at time t. In this context, informativeness is defined as the average of the squared z-scores of stock returns and bond returns for a given period. The calculation acknowledges that patterns of co-movement among variables are more meaningful when their magnitudes are large, as those observations are more likely to reflect events as opposed to noise. Later in this chapter, we will refer to the concept of informativeness again, but in the broader context of linear regression with independent variables.[1]

If, in Equation 14.2, we rewrite *informativeness* as the average squared z-score of stock and bond returns and substitute Equation 14.1 for *single-period correlation*, the correlation then becomes

$Correlation(s, b) =$

$$\frac{1}{N}\sum_{t=1}^{N}\left(\frac{1}{2}\left(\left(\frac{r_{s,t} - \mu_s}{\sigma_s} \right)^2 + \left(\frac{r_{b,t} - \mu_b}{\sigma_b} \right)^2 \right) \times \frac{\left(\frac{r_{s,t} - \mu_s}{\sigma_s} \right)\left(\frac{r_{b,t} - \mu_b}{\sigma_b} \right)}{\frac{1}{2}\left(\left(\frac{r_{s,t} - \mu_s}{\sigma_s} \right)^2 + \left(\frac{r_{b,t} - \mu_b}{\sigma_b} \right)^2 \right)} \right)$$

(14.3)

This expression simplifies to the average product of stock and bond z-scores over the full sample, which is equivalent to the full-sample covariance of stock and bond returns divided by the product of their full-sample standard deviations, the formula commonly used to measure a time series correlation:

$$Correlation(s,b) = \frac{1}{N}\sum_{t=1}^{N}\left(\left(\frac{r_{s,t} - \mu_s}{\sigma_s} \right)\left(\frac{r_{b,t} - \mu_b}{\sigma_b} \right) \right) = \frac{Cov(s,b)}{\sigma_s\sigma_b} \quad (14.4)$$

At this point, we believe we have made our case that the single-period correlation is a better representation of the correlation of five-year returns than the correlation of monthly returns because it captures the drift of stock and bond returns, whereas the correlation of monthly correlations does not. And we believe it is better than the correlation of either independent blocks of five-year returns or overlapping five-year returns because it recognizes that the stock–bond correlation varies through time, whereas the full-sample correlation does not.

We now move on to the fundamental predictors of the stock–bond correlation.

FUNDAMENTAL PREDICTORS OF THE STOCK–BOND CORRELATION

We use the following fundamental factors to predict the correlation of five-year stock and bond returns.

Fundamental Factors

- Economic growth (year-over-year percentage change in industrial production)
- Inflation (year-over-year percentage change in the Consumer Price Index, seasonally adjusted)
- Relative yield of stocks and bonds (earnings yield/10-year Treasury rate)
- Relative volatility of stock and bond yield (defined as the 5-year trailing volatility of the earnings yield/the 5-year trailing volatility of the 10-year Treasury rate)

We selected economic growth and inflation because they are key drivers of stock and bond returns, respectively, and the interplay between them may impact the stock–bond correlation. For example, a positive demand shock will increase both growth and inflation, which is likely to induce a divergence in stock and bond performance. By contrast, a supply-side shock, such as the 1970s oil crisis, may lead to higher inflation but lower growth, which is likely to push stock and bond prices in the same direction. We also selected the relative level and volatility of stock and bond yields because they likely affect investor demand for stocks versus bonds. For example, when stock and bond yields are similar, both assets are similarly attractive, implying a positive stock–bond correlation. However, when stock yields are meaningfully higher or riskier than bond yields, we might expect a negative stock–bond correlation.

MODEL SPECIFICATION

We define our variable of interest as the subsequent five-year single-period correlation because, as we discussed, we believe that investors care more about how stocks and bonds co-move throughout the course of their investment horizon than how they co-move from month to month. We test five models to predict the subsequent five-year single-period correlation. In all cases, we use data starting in January 1926 to forecast the single-period five-year correlation beginning in January 1930 through December 2018, and we update the predictions annually.

Prior to running the regression-based models (Models 2 through 5, below), we transform the dependent variable to prevent the models from predicting a correlation that violates the bounds of negative and positive one. First, we shift and re-scale the single-period correlation so that it ranges from zero to one:

$$SPC^*(s,b) = \frac{1 + single\ period\ correlation(s,b)}{2} \qquad (14.5)$$

Here, $SPC^*(s,b)$ is the shifted and re-scaled single-period correlation ranging from zero to one. Then, we apply the probit transformation so that it is unbound and consistent with the assumption of a normal distribution:

$$y = probit \ (SPC^*(s,b)) = \Phi^{-1}(SPC^*(s,b)) \tag{14.6}$$

In Equation 14.6, y is the probit of the shifted and re-scaled correlation, $SPC^*(s,b)$, estimated as the inverse of the cumulative distribution function of the standard normal distribution with probability $SPC^*(s,b)$.

After running the regressions, we transform the resulting predictions back so that they are correlations ranging from negative to positive one:

$$\hat{Y} = 2\Phi(\hat{y}) - 1 \tag{14.7}$$

In Equation 14.7, $\hat{y}$ is the predicted single-period correlation ranging from negative to positive one, $\hat{y}$ is the predicted probit of the shifted and re-scaled correlation, and Φ denotes the cumulative distribution function of the standard normal distribution.

Model 1: Naïve Extrapolation of Trailing Correlation

This model simply extrapolates the correlation of monthly stock and bond returns from the prior five-year period to predict the single-period correlation for the next five-year period. Not only is this approach the simplest way to model the stock–bond correlation, it is by far the most commonly used approach.

Model 2: Regression on Trailing Correlation

In this model, we regress the five-year single-period correlation on the correlation of monthly stock and bond returns from the prior five-year period. This approach differs from naïve extrapolation in that the intercept and slope will differ from 0 and 1, respectively, which is implied by naïve extrapolation.

Model 3: Regression on Fundamental Factors

In this model, we regress the five-year single-period correlation on four fundamental factors: industrial production, inflation, relative yield of stocks and bonds, and relative volatility of stock and bond yields, as we defined these variables earlier. The predictors are measured as of the end of the period prior to the estimation of the single-period correlation.

Model 4: Regression on Fundamental Factors Filtered for Relevance

In this model, we use the same predictors we used in Model 3, but we filter the historical observations for their relevance, based on a technique called partial sample regression, which we describe thoroughly in Chapter 13.

Partial sample regression relies on a mathematical equivalence. The prediction from linear regression is a function of the weighted average of the past values of the dependent variable in which the weights are the relevance of the past observations for the independent variables.

Relevance within this context has a precise meaning. It is the sum of the statistical similarity of the past observations to the current values for the independent variables, which is the negative of their Mahalanobis distances, and the informativeness of the past observations, which equals their Mahalanobis distances from the average values of the independent variables.

In other words, prior periods that are like the current period but are different from the historical average are more relevant than those that are not.

Once we determine the relevance of the past observations, we isolate the 25% most relevant observations and take their relevance-weighted average to come up with our prediction for the stock–bond correlation.

Model 5: Regression on the Path of Fundamental Factors Filtered for Relevance

In this model, we redefine industrial production and inflation as paths. Instead of including just the prior periods' values for industrial production and inflation, we include values for the prior five periods, along with the prior period values for the relative stock and bond yield and the relative volatility of the stock and bond yield. Therefore, the five-year single-period correlation in period $t + 1$ is regressed on industrial production and inflation for periods t, $t - 1$, $t - 2$, $t - 3$, and $t - 4$, and relative stock and bond yield and relative volatility of the stock and bond yield in period t. Moreover, we filter the historical observations for their relevance, as we did for Model 4.

MODEL RESULTS

Figure 14.2 shows the correlation of the model predictions and the actual subsequent single-period correlations of five-year returns.

Figure 14.2 reveals some interesting insights. First, the most common approach to forecasting the stock–bond correlation, which is to

FIGURE 14.2 Correlation of model predictions and actual correlations.

extrapolate the correlation of monthly returns, is tied for being the least reliable approach. It is tied with regressing the five-year single-period correlation on the correlation of monthly stock and bond returns from the prior five-year period. Fitting the observations shifts the intercept and slope away from 0 and 1, respectively, but it does not improve the explanatory power. The introduction of fundamental variables to predict the stock–bond correlation significantly improves explanatory power, but the largest improvement comes from filtering the historical observations for their relevance. And there is further benefit to replacing single observations for industrial production and inflation with paths.

Next we evaluate these models by applying a nonparametric procedure, called the Henriksson–Merton test, to determine how well these models anticipate whether the subsequent level of the stock–bond correlation would be positive or negative.[2] Specifically, we calculate the percentage of times each model predicted the subsequent correlation would be positive when it was positive and the percentage of times each model predicted the subsequent correlation would be negative when it was negative. We also test to determine how well these models predict whether the change in the subsequent correlation would be positive or negative. These percentages would sum to 2 if a model perfectly predicted the sign of the stock–bond correlation level or change. If a model could not determine if the subsequent level or change in correlation would be positive or negative, these percentages would sum to 1. Any value between 1 and 2 would be indicative of some degree of predictive power. A value below 1 would indicate that a model was worse than random, or more forgivingly, a reverse indicator. Table 14.1 shows the Henriksson–Merton scores for the five models we tested.

TABLE 14.1   Henriksson–Merton Scores: Positive Versus Negative

Prediction Models	Level		Change	
	Statistic	P-value	Statistic	P-value
Trailing correlation of monthly returns, extrapolated	1.06	0.29	1.13	0.19
Trailing correlation of monthly returns, fitted	1.20	0.06	1.13	0.19
Fundamental variables	1.25	0.04	1.18	0.12
Fundamental variables, filtered for relevance	1.27	0.01	1.18	0.12
Fundamental variables, paths and filtered for relevance	1.29	0.00	1.41	0.01

Table 14.1 reveals that the innovations described earlier are, on balance, beneficial to forecasting the subsequent sign of both the level and change in the stock–bond correlation. In combination, they provide the most reliable forecasts.

THE BOTTOM LINE

Investors rely on the stock–bond correlation to construct optimal portfolios and to assess risk. For many, if not most, applications, investors care less about how stocks and bonds co-move month to month than about their co-movement over the duration of their investment horizon. The most common approach to estimating the longer-term correlation of stocks and bonds is to extrapolate the correlation of monthly returns over a prior period. This approach is decidedly unreliable. We introduced the notion of a single-period correlation to address the problem that the autocorrelations and lagged cross-correlations of stock and bond returns are nonzero, and that longer-horizon correlations are not stationary. We then identified several fundamental variables to predict the longer-horizon stock–bond correlation. We included paths as well as single observations in our regressions, and we filtered historical observations for their statistical relevance. We found that these innovations significantly improved the reliability of our forecast of the stock–bond correlation.

RELATED TOPICS

- Chapter 13 introduces partial sample regression, which we apply to forecast the stock–bond correlation.

REFERENCES

Chow, G., Jacquier, E., Kritzman, M., and Lowry, K. 1999. "Optimal Portfolios in Good Times and Bad," *Financial Analysts Journal*, Vol. 55, No. 3 (May/June).

Czasonis, M., Kritzman, M., and Turkington, D. 2020. "Addition by Subtraction: A Better Way to Predict Factor Returns – And Everything Else," *The Journal of Portfolio Management*, Vol. 46, No. 8 (September).

Czasonis, M., Kritzman, M., and Turkington, D. 2021. "The Stock-Bond Correlation," *The Journal of Portfolio Management*, Vol. 47, No. 3 (February).

Henriksson, R. and Merton, R. 1981. "On Market Timing and Investment Performance. II Statistical Procedures for Evaluating Forecasting Skills," *Journal of Business*, Vol. 54, No. 4.

Kinlaw, W., Kritzman, M., and Turkington, D. 2014. "The Divergence of High- and Low-Frequency Estimation: Causes and Consequences," *The Journal of Portfolio Management*, Special 40th Anniversary Issue.

NOTES

1. In linear regression, informativeness takes into account the correlations of the independent variables with each other, as these effects are distinct from the dependent variable, which is the object of the analysis. In the context of estimating the Pearson correlation, informativeness takes into account only the magnitude of individual variables because the correlation itself is the object of the analysis. For more on partial sample regression, see Czasonis, Kritzman, and Turkington (2021); for more on the Mahalanobis distance and its application to financial turbulence, see Chow, Jacquier, Kritzman, and Lowry (1999); for more on the divergence of high- and low-frequency correlations, see Kinlaw, Kritzman, and Turkington (2014).

2. This nonparametric procedure was introduced by Henriksson and Merton (1981).

CHAPTER 15

Constraints

THE CHALLENGE

Investors who deploy optimization to form portfolios often intervene in the optimization process by constraining the allocation to certain asset classes. Constraints, however, reduce a portfolio's efficiency. We show how to produce more efficient portfolios without imposing constraints. And at the same time, we address the concerns that induce investors to impose constraints in the first place.

WRONG AND ALONE

Why do investors constrain their portfolios knowing that these constraints will produce a suboptimal result given their views about expected return and risk? The argument typically put forth is that investors lack sufficient conviction in their views. We disagree. Consider the following thought experiment. Imagine you know for certain the long-term future means, standard deviations, and correlations of the asset classes that you use to form your portfolio. Your conviction is, therefore, absolute. Nevertheless, it is likely that you will still be reluctant to allocate your portfolio in a way that is notably different from the norm, because within short subperiods the asset class returns most likely will diverge substantially from their long-term means, both positively and negatively, merely as a function of their standard deviations. You may well be able to tolerate subperiods of poor performance if most other investors experience similar poor performance, but you would likely be much less comfortable if you were the only investor to experience poor performance. Investors take comfort in the company of others when they perform poorly. We argue that investors constrain their portfolios, not because they lack conviction in their views but rather, because they are averse to being wrong and alone – wrong because

145

TABLE 15.1   Potential Absolute and Relative Performance Outcomes

Relative Returns	Absolute Returns	
	Favorable	Unfavorable
Favorable	1. Great	2. Tolerable
Unfavorable	3. Tolerable	4. Very Unpleasant

they perform poorly during a particular subperiod, and alone because they are the only one to perform poorly at that time. Table 15.1 illustrates the potential outcomes when investors care simultaneously about absolute and relative performance.

If we accept that investors care not only about how they perform in an absolute sense but also about how their performance compares to that of other investors, there are four possible outcomes. An investor could achieve favorable absolute returns and at the same time outperform his or her peers, which would be great as represented by Quadrant 1. Alternatively, an investor might outperform the competition but fall short of an absolute target (Quadrant 2). Or an investor might generate a high absolute return but underperform the competition (Quadrant 3). Quadrants 2 and 3 would probably be tolerable because the investor would produce superior performance along at least one dimension. However, it would likely be very unpleasant if an investor generated an unfavorable absolute result and at the same time performed poorly relative to other investors (Quadrant 4). It is the fear of this outcome that induces investors to constrain their portfolios toward a "normal" asset mix.

MEAN-VARIANCE-TRACKING ERROR OPTIMIZATION

Although the imposition of constraints reduces the odds of being wrong and alone, it does so inefficiently because investors choose constraints arbitrarily.

Recall from Chapter 2 that we identify portfolios along the efficient frontier by maximizing expected utility as shown in Equation 15.1:

$$E(U) = \mu_p - \lambda_{RA}\sigma_p^2 \qquad (15.1)$$

In Equation (15.1), $E(U)$ equals expected utility, μ_p equals portfolio expected return, λ_{RA} equals risk-aversion, and σ_p equals portfolio standard deviation.

When investors impose constraints on the optimization process, they are employing an ad hoc procedure for addressing their aversion to tracking error (being alone). Tracking error is a measure of relative risk. Just as the standard deviation measures dispersion around an average return, tracking error also measures dispersion, but instead around the average relative return between a portfolio and its benchmark. Imagine subtracting a sequence of benchmark returns from a sequence of portfolio returns covering the same period. The standard deviation of these differences is what we call tracking error.

If we care only about relative performance, we could define our returns net of a benchmark and optimize in dimensions of expected relative return and tracking error. This approach would address our concern about deviating from the norm, assuming our benchmark represents normal investment choices. However, we would fail to address any concern we might have about absolute results. Given that investors likely care about both absolute and relative performance, we should expand expected utility to encompass both dimensions of risk, as shown in Equation (15.2):[1]

$$E(U) = \mu_p - \lambda_{RA}\sigma_p^2 - \lambda_{TEA}\xi_p^2 \qquad (15.2)$$

Here, λ_{TEA} equals tracking error aversion, and ξ_p equals portfolio tracking error. We can express this multirisk expected utility formula as a function of the portfolio weight vector, noting that tracking error is the standard deviation of relative returns against the benchmark portfolio, w_B:

$$E(U) = w'\mu - \lambda_{RA}w'\Sigma w - \lambda_{TEA}(w - w_B)'\Sigma(w - w_B) \qquad (15.3)$$

Note that the objective function does not include a term for the expected relative return. There is no need to distinguish between the expected absolute return and the expected relative return because they differ only by the expected return of the benchmark, which is a constant value independent of the portfolio weights. By maximizing expected absolute return, we are effectively maximizing the expected relative return. However, standard deviation and tracking error are not linearly related; thus, we must include both risk terms.

Efficient Surface

This measure of investor satisfaction simultaneously addresses concerns about absolute and relative performance. Instead of producing an efficient frontier in two dimensions, though, this optimization process produces an efficient surface in three dimensions: expected return, standard deviation, and tracking error, as displayed in Figure 15.1.

The efficient surface is bounded on the upper left by the traditional mean-variance (MV) efficient frontier, which includes efficient portfolios in

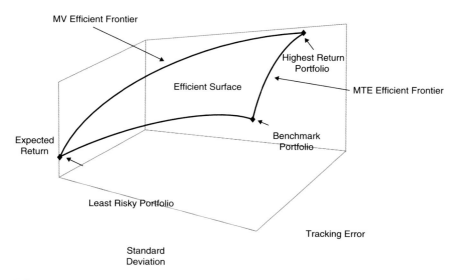

FIGURE 15.1   Efficient surface.

dimensions of expected return and standard deviation. The right boundary of the efficient surface is the mean-tracking error (MTE) efficient frontier. It comprises portfolios that offer the highest expected return for varying levels of tracking error. The efficient surface is bounded on the bottom by combinations of the least risky portfolio and the benchmark portfolio. The lower-left corner of the efficient surface is the least risky portfolio in terms of standard deviation. The upper-right corner of the efficient surface is a portfolio that is allocated entirely to the asset class with the highest expected return. The lower-right corner of the efficient surface is the benchmark port-folio, which has no tracking error.

All of the portfolios that lie on this surface are efficient in three dimen-sions. It does not follow, however, that a three-dimensional efficient portfo-lio is efficient in any two dimensions. Only the maximum expected return portfolio is efficient in all three dimensions. Consider, for example, the least risky portfolio. Although it is on both the MV efficient frontier and the efficient surface, if it were plotted in dimensions of just expected return and tracking error, it would appear very inefficient compared to a bench-mark that includes high-expected-return assets such as stocks and long-term bonds. This portfolio has a low expected return compared to the benchmark and yet a high degree of tracking error.

We should expect this approach to optimization to deliver results that are superior to constrained MV optimization in the following sense. For a given combination of expected return and standard deviation, it should produce a portfolio with less tracking error. Or for a given combination of expected return and tracking error, it should identify a portfolio with a lower standard deviation. Or finally, for a given combination of standard deviation and tracking error, it should deliver a portfolio with a higher expected return than that from constrained MV analysis. Most of the portfolios identified by constrained MV analysis would lie beneath the efficient surface. In fact, the only way in which mean-variance-tracking error optimization would fail to improve upon a constrained MV analysis is if the investor knew in advance what constraints were optimal. But, of course, this knowledge could only come from a mean-variance-tracking error optimization.

Iso-Expected Return Curve

Some investors may be more concerned about absolute performance, whereas others may care more about relative performance. We can construct an iso-expected return curve to assist investors in addressing this trade-off. An iso-expected return curve plots portfolios that all have the same expected return in dimensions of standard deviation and tracking error, as shown in Figure 15.2.

Investors who worry more about absolute performance will prefer portfolios to the left on the iso-expected return curve, whereas those who are more concerned with tracking error will prefer portfolios farther to the right

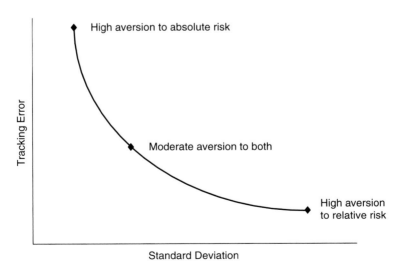

FIGURE 15.2 Iso-expected return curve.

on the curve. There is a unique iso-expected return curve for every level of expected return.

THE BOTTOM LINE

The bottom line is that constrained mean-variance optimization is inefficient because it determines arbitrarily the maximum or minimum allocation to various asset classes. Investors resort to constraints because they are fearful of performing poorly while deviating from the norm. Investors can address this issue more efficiently by identifying a benchmark that represents a "normal asset allocation" and expanding their objective function to include terms for aversion to tracking error.

REFERENCE

Chow, G. 1995. "Portfolio Selection Based on Return, Risk, and Relative Performance," *Financial Analysts Journal*, Vol. 51, No. 2 (March/April).

NOTE

1. For further details about this approach, see Chow (1995).

CHAPTER 16

Asset Allocation Versus Factor Investing

THE CHALLENGE

Many investors think of a portfolio as a composition of factor exposures, yet the vehicles available for investment are financial securities or aggregations of them such as asset classes. Moreover, investment in a collection of securities that is designed to mimic factor behavior introduces mapping error, which increases portfolio risk. This chapter shows how to construct portfolios of asset classes that at the same time reflect an investor's preferences for specific factor exposures.

Investors typically construct portfolios from asset classes because asset classes are easy to observe and directly investable. Factors, by contrast, are not always readily observable, nor are they directly investable. Investors must identify combinations of assets that best track the behavior of factors. And because the mapping functions between assets and factors change through time, investors who choose to allocate to factors are exposed to an additional source of uncertainty beyond the uncertainty of the factor performance.

Nevertheless, some investors prefer to allocate to factors because they believe asset classes are defined arbitrarily and do not capture the fundamental determinants of performance as directly as factors do. Also, some factors carry risk premiums that are not available from asset classes.

In this chapter, we show that investors can have it both ways. We propose that investors use asset classes as the building blocks for forming portfolios, but combine them in a way that balances the portfolio's expected return and risk with the investor's factor preferences.

PORTFOLIO CONSTRUCTION

Markowitz Objective Function

The conventional approach to constructing portfolios is to maximize expected utility, which is defined in Equation 16.1.[1] This methodology is thoroughly described in Chapter 2.

$$E(U) = \mu_p - \lambda_{RA}\sigma_p^2 \qquad (16.1)$$

In Equation 16.1, $E(U)$ equals expected utility, μ_p equals portfolio expected return, λ_{RA} equals risk aversion, and σ_p^2 equals portfolio variance. We proceed by estimating the expected returns for the asset classes as well as the covariances between every pair of asset classes. We then solve for the asset class weights that maximize expected utility for a given level of risk aversion. This approach ignores any preferences we may have regarding factor exposures.

Augmented Objective Function

In order to take factor preferences into account, we augment Equation 16.1 to include a term for a preferred factor profile along with an additional term that captures our aversion to deviating from this factor profile, as shown in Equation 16.2:

$$E(U) = \mu_p - \lambda_{RA}\sigma_p^2 - \lambda_{DFP}\xi_{FP}^2 \qquad (16.2)$$

Here, λ_{DFP} equals aversion to deviations from the factor profile, and ξ_{FP} equals deviations from the factor profile, which we define as the tracking error of a given portfolio to the factor profile. These factors could be macroeconomic variables such as economic growth or they could be company attributes such as leverage.

A desired factor profile may consist of exposures to multiple factors, each of which is measured in different units. For variables measuring quantities that compound over time, such as economic growth, it may be preferable to record their changes in value as logarithms. We may also wish to rescale the changes (or log changes) in variables so that they have similar volatilities. Then, we can obtain historical observations for a composite factor profile by taking a weighted average of the observations for each individual factor, where the weights reflect our preference for exposure to each individual factor.

For example, if we wish to build a portfolio that is relatively resilient to stagflation, in which the economy experiences stagnant growth coupled with high inflation, we would assign a negative weight to economic growth, meaning that the portfolio would be constructed to perform well when economic growth declines, and a positive weight to inflation, meaning that the portfolio would be constructed to perform well when inflation increases, to the extent possible given the additional goals of increasing expected return and lowering portfolio volatility across all economic scenarios.

Macroeconomic Variables Versus Market Variables

When we introduce a factor profile comprising macroeconomic variables we must deal with an additional complexity. Macroeconomic variables have relatively stable values compared to asset classes. This is because macroeconomic variables are not traded. The prices investors assign to tradable assets reflect their expectations about the level and uncertainty of future income. Macroeconomic variables reflect realized economic activity, or in the case of consensus estimates, expectations about the mean value of the macroeconomic variable. These values do not incorporate information about the uncertainty of the future value of the variable, as do asset prices. Consequently, the covariances between asset classes and macroeconomic variables are relatively small, just as the covariances between high-risk and low-risk asset classes are small. Therefore, in order to build a portfolio that is reasonably sensitive to a comparatively stable factor profile, we need to rescale the factor changes by multiplying them by a constant greater than 1. Otherwise, minimizing tracking error to something that is relatively stable is the same as minimizing total volatility.

Finally, we create a time series of the weighted factor changes, which constitutes our factor profile. We then calculate its standard deviation and its correlations with the asset classes that we will use to form our factor-sensitive optimized portfolio. We next illustrate this process.

CASE STUDY

As we alluded to in our discussion thus far, there are five steps to building a factor-sensitive optimal portfolio:

1. Identify factors to which we seek exposure, either positive or negative.
2. Create factor time series by recording changes in the factor values measured in log units and rescaling them to render the portfolio reasonably sensitive to changes in factor values.
3. Define a factor profile by calculating a weighted average of rescaled factor changes in accordance with our factor preferences.

4. Estimate the expected returns, standard deviations, and correlations of the asset classes as well as the standard deviation of the factor profile and its correlations with the asset classes.
5. Solve for a factor-sensitive optimal portfolio by maximizing an expanded objective function that incorporates both aversion to absolute risk and aversion to deviations from the factor profile.

Suppose, for example, that we wish to allocate our portfolio across the seven asset classes we introduced in Chapter 2 and that we are concerned that the economy will enter a period of stagflation. We therefore create a factor profile that reflects a −33% exposure to growth in US industrial production and a +100% exposure to US CPI inflation. We select these values because the standard deviation of the inflation factor is approximately one third that of the growth factor. With this factor profile, we would expect our portfolio to vary inversely with economic growth and positively with changes in inflation, to the extent allowed by our choice of asset classes and the aversion we specify to deviating from the factor profile. Table 16.1 shows the expected returns, standard deviations, and correlations of the asset classes as well as the standard deviation of the factor profile and its correlations with the asset classes. We estimated the asset class expected returns based on the equilibrium approach described in Chapter 2 using annual returns from January 1988 through December 2019. We select this period because data for emerging market equities are not available prior to 1988, and we are therefore unable to estimate its correlation with the factor profile until that date. We use annual returns to correct for the autocorrelation in the monthly industrial production and inflation data, which would distort our estimates. We use these same annual returns to estimate the standard deviations and correlations of the asset classes. We estimate the standard deviation and correlations of the factor profile based on a weighted average of rescaled log changes in industrial production and consumer prices using a scaling coefficient of 10.

Next, we use Equation 16.2, together with the inputs in Table 16.1, to form three optimal portfolios: one that ignores our factor preferences, one that assumes that our aversion to deviating from the factor profile equals 0.5, and one that assumes our aversion to deviating from the factor profile equals 0.75. In each case, we constrain the expected return of the portfolio to equal 7.5%, corresponding to the return of our moderate portfolio. These portfolios, along with their expected returns and standard deviations, are shown in Table 16.2.

If we are indifferent to our portfolio's sensitivity to stagflation (aversion = 0) and assuming our risk aversion coefficient equals 1, the optimal

TABLE 16.1　Return and Risk Assumptions for Asset Classes and Factors

Asset Classes	Expected Return (%)	Standard Deviation (%)	Correlations							
			a	b	c	d	e	f	g	h
a US Equities	8.9	17.0								
b Foreign Developed Equities	9.9	19.8	0.81							
c Emerging Market Equities	12.3	30.3	0.59	0.78						
d Treasury Bonds	3.3	5.4	−0.16	−0.36	−0.25					
e US Corporate Bonds	4.5	5.8	0.40	0.22	0.33	0.59				
f Commodities	8.2	26.0	0.28	0.37	0.47	−0.04	0.21			
g Cash Equivalents	3.6	2.4	0.13	−0.03	0.07	0.48	0.25	0.32		
h Growth	n/a	38.2	0.52	0.49	0.31	−0.19	0.02	0.41	0.12	
i Inflation	n/a	12.1	0.15	0.16	0.38	0.19	0.26	0.73	0.65	0.22

TABLE 16.2   Factor-Sensitive Optimal Portfolios

	Aversion: 0 (%)	Aversion: 0.5 (%)	Aversion: 0.75 (%)
US Equities	24.6	20.7	19.5
Foreign Developed Equities	24.4	8.5	3.9
Emerging Market Equities	7.2	17.2	20.1
Treasury Bonds	17.2	12.4	11.0
US Corporate Bonds	20.4	29.6	32.3
Commodities	6.2	11.6	13.2
Cash Equivalents	0.0	0.0	0.0
Expected Return	7.5	7.5	7.5
Standard Deviation	11.3	11.7	11.9

portfolio favors US equities, foreign developed equities, and US Treasury and corporate bonds. If we are moderately concerned with stagflation (aversion = 0.5), the optimal portfolio reallocates from equities to bonds and commodities. If we are substantially concerned with stagflation, the magnitude of these shifts increases even further.

These changes are intuitive. Table 16.1 reveals that bonds, which offer investors safe harbor during recessions, have the lowest correlations with the growth factor. Commodities, which are often seen as an inflation hedge, have the highest correlation with the inflation factor. We also observe that the factor-sensitive portfolios have a preference for emerging market equities over foreign developed equities. Why is this the case? Among the equity asset classes, emerging market equities have the highest correlation with both inflation and commodities as well as the lowest correlation with growth. Some emerging economies are heavily weighted toward commodity and natural resource production. These markets may decouple with US equities during periods when inflation and commodity prices are rising and growth (as measured by US industrial production) is weak.

The reason we are willing to accept the higher standard deviation of the factor-sensitive portfolios, relative to the unconditional portfolio, is because we expect their conditional performance to be better should economic growth stagnate and inflation rise. Table 16.3 supports this reasoning. It shows the performance of these three portfolios during episodes of concomitant stagnant economic growth and rising inflation. We define stagflation periods as years between 1988 and 2019 that fall within the top quartile of our factor profile (high inflation, low growth) and non-stagflation periods as the complementary sample.

TABLE 16.3 Conditional Average Annual Returns of Factor-Sensitive Optimal Portfolios (1988–2019)

	Aversion: 0 (%)	Aversion: 0.5 (%)	Aversion: 1.0 (%)
Stagflation Years	2.7	4.9	5.6
Non-Stagflation Years	8.7	8.2	8.1

We observe that the factor-sensitive portfolios perform significantly better during years characterized by stagflation. But this conditional outperformance comes at the cost of lower average performance during non-stagflation years.

THE BOTTOM LINE

Investors typically construct portfolios from asset classes because asset classes are readily observable and directly investable. But some investors prefer to allocate to factors because they believe asset classes are defined arbitrarily and do not capture the fundamental determinants of performance as directly as factors do. Also, some factors carry risk premiums that are not available from asset classes. We describe how investors can have it both ways by continuing to invest in asset classes but in a way that conforms to an investor's preference for a chosen factor profile.

We showed how to construct a factor profile from rescaled log changes in macroeconomic variables. We then showed how to augment the classic Markowitz objective function to include a term for aversion to deviating from a factor profile. We illustrated this integrated approach with a case study that showed how the composition and performance of the optimal portfolios change as we vary our degree of aversion to deviations from the factor profiles. We produced in-sample results showing that factor-sensitive portfolios performed better during regimes when the factors behave in accordance with our expectations, compared both to their performance during the full sample and relative to the unconditioned portfolio during the factor-conditioned subsample.

Finally, we wish to emphasize that this methodology for integrating asset allocation and factor investing is very general. Although we illustrated it with a simple example based on seven broad asset classes and two macroeconomic factors, it can be applied to a variety of settings, such as the construction of portfolios that are sensitive to security attributes such as value and leverage, or the construction of portfolios that are sensitive to unavailable asset classes.

RELATED TOPICS

- Chapter 8 outlines the differences between assets and factors, including the important distinction that assets are directly investable, whereas factors are not.
- Chapter 15 employs multi-goal optimization in a similar fashion to this chapter, but with the goal of tracking a benchmark portfolio as opposed to a factor profile.

REFERENCES

Bergeron, A., Kritzman, M., and Sivitzky, G. 2018. "Asset Allocation and Factor Investing: An Integrated Approach," *The Journal of Portfolio Management*, Vol. 44, No. 4 (Quantitative Special Issue).

Chow, G. 1995. "Portfolio Selection Based on Return, Risk, and Relative Performance," *Financial Analysts Journal*, Vol. 51, No. 2 (March/April).

Markowitz, H. 1952. "Portfolio Selection," *Journal of Finance*, Vol. 7, No. 1 (March).

NOTES

1. The approach was introduced by Harry Markowitz, in his classic article "Portfolio Selection." See Markowitz (1952).
2. This framework is similar to the approach introduced by Chow (1995) that we described in Chapter 15 for dealing with aversion to tracking error. For more on its application to integrate factor investing and asset allocation, see Bergeron, Kritzman, and Sivitzky (2018).

CHAPTER 17

Illiquidity

THE CHALLENGE

One of the most vexing challenges of asset allocation is determining how to treat illiquid asset classes. For the most part, investors have employed arbitrary techniques to address this issue. For example, some investors impose a direct constraint on the allocation to illiquid asset classes. Others assign a liquidity score to asset classes and optimize subject to a constraint that this score meet a certain threshold. It has also been proposed that liquidity be added as the third dimension in the optimization process.[1] These approaches require investors to relate liquidity to expected return and risk in an arbitrary fashion. We describe an alternative technique that translates illiquidity directly into units of expected return and risk, so that investors need not address this trade-off arbitrarily.

SHADOW ASSETS AND LIABILITIES

We begin by considering the many ways in which investors use liquidity. For example, investors depend on liquidity to meet capital demands. They rely on liquidity to rebalance their portfolios. To the extent investors are skillful at tactical asset allocation, they depend on liquidity to profit from this skill. Investors require liquidity to exploit new opportunities or to exit from strategies they no longer expect to add value. And they require liquidity to respond to shifts in their risk tolerance. These considerations reveal that liquidity has value beyond the need to meet demands for cash. Therefore, investors bear an illiquidity cost to the extent they are unable to trade any portion of their portfolios.

Our approach for unifying illiquidity with expected return and risk is to create shadow assets and liabilities whose expected return and risk reflect the manner in which investors deploy liquidity. Shadow assets and liabilities do not require additional capital beyond what is already contained in the portfolio. Instead, we treat them as overlays just as we treat forward contracts for currency hedging.

If investors deploy liquidity to improve the expected utility of a portfolio, we attach a shadow asset to the liquid asset classes in the portfolio, because these asset classes enable investors to improve the portfolio. We think of activities that are intended to improve a portfolio as "playing offense."

Consider tactical asset allocation. Some investors choose to allocate funds to an external manager, who then engages in tactical asset allocation. In this situation, we would consider the expected return and risk[2] of this allocation to comprise the expected return and risk associated with the default or average allocation of the strategy (the beta component) as well as the expected return and risk associated with the active deviations of the strategy (the alpha component).

Other investors engage in tactical asset allocation through internal management by shifting the allocation across some of the liquid asset classes within the portfolio. Strategic asset allocation typically accounts for the expected return and risk of the liquid asset classes assuming they are held constant, but ignores the incremental return and risk associated with tactical deviations from the constant weights. We argue that investors should attach a shadow asset to the liquid asset classes in the portfolio to account for the incremental return and risk expected from the internally executed tactical shifts. This approach is consistent with the way in which external managers who engage in tactical asset allocation are treated in the asset allocation process.

Investors also use liquidity to preserve the expected utility of a portfolio. We think of these activities as "playing defense." Consider rebalancing a portfolio. Investors construct portfolios they believe are optimal, given their views and attitudes about expected return and risk. Once the portfolio is established, however, prices change and the portfolio's weights drift away from the optimal weights, thus rendering the portfolio suboptimal. To the extent that the portfolio includes illiquid asset classes, it may not be possible to rebalance to the optimal weights, in which case the portfolio will remain suboptimal. We should, therefore, attach a shadow liability to those asset classes in the portfolio that cannot be moved, because they limit the extent to which an investor is able to restore the optimal weights.

Conceptually, our approach to illiquidity is straightforward. We attach a shadow asset to the liquid asset classes of a portfolio to account for the way liquidity is deployed to improve its expected utility. And we add a shadow liability to the illiquid asset classes in a portfolio to account for the extent to which illiquidity prevents investors from preserving the portfolio's expected utility. The challenge is to measure the expected return and risk of these shadow allocations, which we discuss next.

EXPECTED RETURN AND RISK OF SHADOW ALLOCATIONS

Investors typically estimate the expected return and risk of explicit asset classes from some combination of historical data and theoretical asset pricing models. Unfortunately, there is no data for shadow allocations, nor are there any theories on which to rely. We must, therefore, resort to simulation or backtests to estimate the expected return and risk of shadow allocations. We focus on three common uses of liquidity: tactical asset allocation, portfolio rebalancing, and cash demands.

Tactical Asset Allocation

It is becoming more common for investors to manage the asset mix of their portfolios dynamically, either in response to their expectations about the relative performance of asset classes or to maintain a particular risk profile. As we discussed in Chapter 3, Samuelson (1998) presented a compelling rationale for tactically managing the asset mix of a portfolio, arguing that markets are microefficient and macroinefficient.

Be that as it may, many investors engage in tactical asset allocation; therefore, we must estimate the expected return and risk of this activity if we are to introduce this activity as a shadow asset. If the investor relies on objective and quantifiable trading rules, we simply backtest these rules to estimate their expected return, standard deviation, and correlation. If, instead, the investor relies on a subjective and nonquantifiable process, we are left to estimate the risk and return properties of this activity subjectively. Once we estimate the expected return and risk of the tactical asset allocation shadow asset, we include it in the optimization menu and set its weight equal to the sum of the weights of the liquid asset classes that are being tactically managed. Of course, we must adjust for the extent to which investors employ leverage or derivatives to execute the tactical shifts when setting the weight of the shadow asset.

Portfolio Rebalancing

As we mentioned earlier, price changes cause the actual asset mix of a portfolio to drift away from its target weights, thus rendering the portfolio suboptimal. Some investors rely on heuristic rebalancing rules to rebalance their portfolios. For example, some investors rebalance quarterly or at some other frequency, whereas others rebalance when asset class weights have drifted a certain distance from their target weights. Other investors apply a more rigorous method to determine the optimal rebalancing schedule. They compare the cost of rebalancing with the cost of suboptimality and employ a variation of dynamic programming to determine the optimal rebalancing schedule. We discuss this approach to rebalancing in Chapter 21. In any event, an investor must periodically rebalance a portfolio to preserve its optimality. Because rebalancing is intended to preserve the optimality of a portfolio rather than enhance it, we attach a shadow liability to the illiquid asset classes within the portfolio that prevent an investor from fully restoring the optimal weights. Because we attach a shadow liability to the illiquid asset classes that cannot be rebalanced, we estimate the expected cost of not rebalancing rather than the expected return of rebalancing. In the optimization process, we treat this cost as a negative expected return. We must resort to simulation to estimate the expected cost of not rebalancing. Moreover, we estimate this cost as a certainty equivalent, which means we do not need to estimate the uncertainty of the cost. Chapter 25 discusses certainty equivalents in detail, and we also describe them in Chapter 4.

Based on our assumptions for the expected returns, standard deviations, and correlations of the portfolio's asset classes, we apply Monte Carlo simulation to generate many paths for the value of the portfolio over a given horizon at a specified frequency. We conduct this simulation under two scenarios: one in which we do not rebalance the portfolio and one in which we rebalance the portfolio at the chosen frequency assuming a particular transaction cost.

These simulations produce two distributions for the portfolio's value at the end of the horizon. We convert each distribution into a certainty equivalent and subtract the certainty equivalent of the rebalancing simulation from the certainty equivalent of the simulation without rebalancing. This value, which will be negative, is the cost we assign to the shadow liability. We constrain the weight of this shadow liability to equal the sum of the weights of the illiquid asset classes.

Cash Demands

Investors periodically need to raise cash in order to meet demands for capital. Pension funds, for example, need to make benefit payments. Many endowment funds and foundations invest in private equity and real estate funds, which demand cash periodically as investment opportunities emerge. Private investors occasionally may need to replace lost income to meet their consumption requirements. If the cash flows into a portfolio are insufficient to satisfy these payments, the investor will need to liquidate some of the assets. These liquidations can drive a portfolio away from its optimal mix and, to the extent that a portfolio is allocated to illiquid asset classes, the investors may not be able to restore full optimality. Just as is the case with rebalancing, we measure this cost in certainty equivalent units and attach it to the illiquid asset classes as a shadow liability.

In rare instances, investors may not be able to liquidate enough of their portfolio to meet all cash demands, in which case the investor may need to borrow funds. In these circumstances, we attach another shadow liability to the illiquid asset classes to reflect the cost and uncertainty of borrowing.

OTHER CONSIDERATIONS

Before we illustrate our approach to incorporating illiquidity into the asset allocation process, we must address several complications: the effect of performance fees on risk and expected return, the valuation of illiquid assets, and the distinction between partial and absolute illiquidity.

Performance Fees

Performance fees cause the observed standard deviation of illiquid asset classes to understate their risk, because performance fees reduce upside returns but not downside returns. We correct for this bias by reverse-engineering the fee calculation to derive a volatility measure that correctly captures downside deviations.[3]

Moreover, performance fees overstate the expected return of a group of funds, because a fund collects a performance fee when it outperforms but does not reimburse the investor when it underperforms. Consider, for example, a fund that charges a 2% base fee and a performance fee of 20%. A fund that delivers a 10% return in excess of the benchmark on a $100 million portfolio collects a $2 million base fee and a $1.6 million performance fee for a total fee of $3.6 million. The investor's return net of fees, therefore, is 6.4%. Now suppose an investor hires two funds, each of which charges a base fee of 2% and a performance fee of 20%. Assume that both these funds have an expected return of 10 percent over the benchmark. The investor might expect an aggregate net return from these two funds of 6.4%. However, if one fund produces an excess return of 30% and the other fund delivers an excess return of –10%, the investor pays an aggregate fee of $4.8 million, and the net return to the investor is 5.2% instead of 6.4%. Therefore, if the illiquid asset classes comprise funds that charge performance fees, we should adjust their risk and return to account for the effect of performance fees.

Valuation

Fair-value pricing dampens the observed standard deviation of many illiquid asset classes such as infrastructure, private equity, and real estate, because underlying asset valuations are assessed in a way that anchors them to prior-period values. We therefore need to de-smooth their returns to eliminate this bias. We do so by specifying an autoregressive model of returns.[4] Then we invert it to derive a de-smoothed series of returns. We estimate standard deviations and correlations from this de-smoothed return series.

Absolute Versus Partial Illiquidity

Thus far, we have implicitly treated illiquidity and liquidity as binary features. We should instead distinguish between absolute illiquidity and partial illiquidity. Absolute illiquidity pertains to asset classes that cannot be traded for a specified period of time by contractual agreement or asset classes that are prohibitively expensive to trade within a certain time frame. These are the asset classes to which we attach shadow liabilities.

The asset classes that we describe as liquid asset classes are not perfectly liquid because they are costly to trade or may require significant time to trade. We therefore adjust their expected returns by the cost of trading or by the extent to which trading delays reduce the benefit of trading. We nevertheless attach shadow assets to these partially illiquid asset classes because ultimately they are tradable, which must confer at least some benefit.

CASE STUDY

We now illustrate this process by introducing US real estate to the moderate portfolio from Chapter 2. Our objective is to determine how the optimal allocation to real estate changes when we account for its illiquidity. We use the NCREIF Property Index to measure the standard deviation of real estate and its correlations with the other asset classes.[5] Table 17.1 shows the expected returns, standard deviations, and correlations of our liquid asset classes augmented with estimates for real estate.[6]

We derive the real estate standard deviation and correlations using the "raw" NCREIF returns; we do not yet adjust for performance fees or valuation smoothing. Real estate has characteristics of both equity (because the principal is invested in real estate equity) and fixed income (because it provides a relatively stable yield). Therefore, most investors expect real estate to offer an expected return that is higher than fixed income but lower than equities. For this illustration, we choose a value of 6%. It would be

TABLE 17.1 Expected Returns, Standard Deviations, and Correlations (Unadjusted)

	Expected Return (%)	Standard Deviation (%)				Correlations			
			a	b	c	d	e	f	g
a US Equities	8.8	16.6	1.00						
b Foreign Developed Market Equities	9.5	18.6	0.66	1.00					
c Emerging Market Equities	11.4	26.6	0.63	0.68	1.00				
d Treasury Bonds	4.1	5.7	0.10	0.03	-0.02	1.00			
e US Corporate Bonds	4.9	7.3	0.31	0.24	0.22	0.86	1.00		
f Commodities	6.2	20.6	0.16	0.29	0.27	-0.07	0.02	1.00	
g Real Estate	6.0	4.3	0.07	0.10	-0.07	-0.09	-0.18	0.15	1.00

straightforward for an investor with a different view to change this assumption and update these results.

Table 17.1 suggests that real estate is a highly attractive asset class. It has the lowest standard deviation and the lowest average correlation with the other asset classes. It offers the highest return-to-risk ratio by far; this would be true even if its expected return were only 4%, equal to that of Treasury bonds. Table 17.2 shows the optimal allocation excluding real estate (which is the moderate portfolio from Chapter 2) as well as the optimal portfolio including real estate, based on the assumptions in Table 17.1. When we include real estate, we constrain the portfolio to have the same expected return as the moderate portfolio (7.5%), so that the two allocations are comparable.

Table 17.2 confirms the ostensible attraction of real estate; nearly two-thirds of the portfolio is allocated to it. Few, if any, experienced investors, however, would find this portfolio acceptable. A closer inspection reveals that real estate is riskier than its 4.3% standard deviation suggests. The NCREIF index declined by nearly 24%, more than five times its standard deviation, during the global financial crisis (Q3 2008 through Q4 2009). This drawdown is especially surprising given that it was included in the sample from which we estimated the 4.3% standard deviation.

To derive more reasonable allocations, we must first adjust our standard deviation and correlation estimates to correct the bias introduced by performance fees and valuation smoothing. As we mentioned earlier, performance fees reduce upside volatility but not downside volatility. The standard deviation does not distinguish between upside and downside volatility. The formula for this adjustment is presented in the Appendix to this chapter. Specifically, we assume that the real estate portfolio is managed by a single fund and that this fund charges a base fee of 2% annually and a performance

TABLE 17.2 Optimal Allocations Including and Excluding Real Estate (Unadjusted)

Asset Classes	Excluding Real Estate (%)	Including Real Estate (%)
US Equities	25.5	8.2
Foreign Developed Market Equities	23.2	11.3
Emerging Market Equities	9.1	16.3
Treasury Bonds	14.3	0.0
US Corporate Bonds	22.0	0.0
Commodities	5.9	0.0
Real Estate	n/a	64.3

fee equal to 20% of returns that exceed a 2% hurdle rate. After this adjustment, the standard deviation of real estate rises from 4.3% to 4.9%.

Next, we adjust for the downward bias that fair-value pricing imposes on the standard deviation of real estate returns. This bias arises from the way in which appraisers value individual properties. Specifically, they compile a sample of comparable properties that have sold recently and use this sample to estimate fair value. To improve precision, the appraiser must look further back in time to identify more comparable observations. This creates a smoothing effect, akin to a moving average, which reduces the standard deviation of returns. Implicit in this process is an inherent trade-off between precision and timeliness. A large sample results in a valuation estimate that is more precise but stale, whereas a small sample results in a valuation estimate that is timely but less precise.

However appraisers choose to manage this trade-off, it is an empirical fact that real estate returns are highly smoothed. The first-order autocorrelation of the quarterly returns in our sample is 78%. To de-smooth the returns, we invert a first-order autoregressive model as we described in the previous section. We show the detail of this adjustment in the Appendix to this chapter. After this adjustment, the standard deviation of real estate rises threefold, from 4.9% to 15.0%. This estimate is much more realistic. For example, it renders more probable the 24% loss that US real estate experienced during the global financial crisis. This adjustment also increases slightly the correlation between real estate and equity asset classes and decreases slightly the correlation between real estate and fixed income asset classes. These adjusted estimates are shown in Table 17.3.

Next, we show how to identify optimal allocations that account for liquidity. We begin by estimating the return and standard deviation arising from three uses of liquidity: tactical asset allocation, portfolio rebalancing, and funding cash demands.

Tactical Asset Allocation

Based on past performance, we assume that the investor's tactical asset allocation program will produce an excess return of 40 basis points and a tracking error of 80 basis points per year, resulting in an information ratio of 0.50 after costs. If there were no track record, an investor could also derive these estimates by backtesting a tactical asset allocation strategy. Tactical asset allocation is a proactive use of liquidity; it serves to improve the expected utility of the portfolio. We therefore attach these return and standard deviation values as a shadow asset to the liquid asset classes within the portfolio.

TABLE 17.3 Expected Returns, Standard Deviations, and Correlations (Adjusted for Performance Fees and Valuation Smoothing)

	Expected Return (%)	Standard Deviation (%)	Correlations								
			a	b	c	d	e	f	g	h	i
a US Equities	8.8	16.6	1.00								
b Foreign Developed Market Equities	9.5	18.6	0.66	1.00							
c Emerging Market Equities	11.4	26.6	0.63	0.68	1.00						
d Treasury Bonds	4.1	5.7	0.10	0.03	-0.02	1.00					
e US Corporate Bonds	4.9	7.3	0.31	0.24	0.22	0.86	1.00				
f Commodities	6.2	20.6	0.16	0.29	0.27	-0.07	0.02	1.00			
g Real Estate	6.0	15.0	0.14	0.13	0.01	-0.19	-0.12	0.12	1.00		

Rebalancing

To estimate the benefit that rebalancing brings to the portfolio, we simulate 10,000 five-year paths given the assumptions presented in Table 17.1. Along each path, we record the performance of two portfolios: one that we rebalance at the end of each year and one that we never rebalance. When we rebalance the first portfolio, we deduct transaction costs which we assume to equal 20 basis points for all asset classes. We then compute the difference between the two portfolios' certainty equivalents based on their end-of-horizon return distributions. This difference, which represents the suboptimality cost that arises from asset weight drift, is equal to 16 basis points yearly. We use certainty equivalents to reflect the fact that any drift in weights is undesirable; portfolios with higher expected returns will have too much risk, whereas those with lower risk will have too little expected return. There is no risk associated with a certainty equivalent, so we assume that the standard deviation associated with this benefit is zero. Rebalancing is a defensive use of liquidity; it preserves the utility of the portfolio. We therefore attach this value to the illiquid component of the portfolio (in this case, real estate) as a shadow liability.

Cash Demands

We employ simulation to estimate the benefit that comes from an investor's ability to meet cash demands. Specifically, we assume the following:

- Cash demands arise randomly in sizes equal to 1%, 2%, or 3% of portfolio value with probabilities of 10%, 10%, and 5%, respectively. We therefore assume that, in any given quarter, there is a 25% (10 + 10 + 5) chance that a cash demand will arise and a 75% chance that there will be no cash demand.
- To meet cash demands, the investor sells US equities, foreign developed market equities, and Treasury bonds in amounts proportional to their allocations.
- When cumulative cash demands along any particular path exceed 10% of the starting portfolio value, the investor ceases to deplete liquid assets and begins borrowing at an annualized rate of 5% to meet further cash demands.
- We do not allow cash demands along any particular path to exceed 20% of the starting portfolio value.

Of course, the actual values for these assumptions vary significantly from one investor to the next. A major advantage of this approach is that we can customize the simulation to account for the unique circumstances of any given investor. Some investors may calibrate the simulation to include cash inflows that can help to offset cash demands.

We measure two distinct costs associated with these simulations: borrowing cost and suboptimality cost. Borrowing cost is straightforward: it is the average annual interest incurred along each path expressed as a percentage of the illiquid assets. Suboptimality cost is the incremental suboptimality that arises when we tap liquid assets to fund cash demands, which distorts the portfolio's allocation. To measure suboptimality cost, we first compute the certainty equivalent of a scenario in which we never rebalance, and we tap a subset of liquid assets (or borrow) to meet cash demands, as described above. We then compute the certainty equivalent of a scenario in which we rebalance annually, and we withdraw funds from all asset classes, proportionally, to meet cash demands. The difference between these two certainty equivalents represents the suboptimality costs attributable to cash demands. It is incremental to the suboptimality cost associated with rebalancing, which is driven purely by the immobility of illiquid asset classes.

The ability to meet cash demands without borrowing or distorting portfolio weights is a defensive use of liquidity; it preserves the utility of the portfolio. We therefore attach these values to real estate as a shadow liability. Exposure to illiquid assets is more costly to investors who have high cash demands than to investors who have low cash demands, all else being equal.

Table 17.4 shows the expected return and standard deviation of the shadow asset and liability as well as their components.

TABLE 17.4 Expected Return and Standard Deviation of Shadow Asset and Liability

	Return (basis points)	Standard Deviation (basis points)	Attached to
Shadow Asset			
Tactical Asset Allocation	40	80	Liquid Assets
Total Shadow Asset	40	80	Liquid Assets
Shadow Liability			
Suboptimality Cost from Weight Changes	16	0	Illiquid Assets
Suboptimality Cost from Cash Demands	18	0	Illiquid Assets
Borrowing Cost from Cash Demands	17	10	Illiquid Assets
Total Shadow Liability	51	10	Illiquid Assets

To identify the optimal allocation that accounts for liquidity, we must attach the shadow asset and liability to the appropriate explicit assets in the portfolio. Table 17.5 combines the expected returns, standard deviations, and correlations for the liquid assets and real estate from Table 17.3 with the expected return and standard deviation for the shadow asset and liability.

In this example, we assume that the shadow asset and liability are uncorrelated with the explicit assets. We could relax this assumption. For example, if the performance of the tactical asset allocation strategy were negatively correlated with broad equity market performance, we could assume a negative correlation between the shadow asset and the equity asset classes. This would result in a higher optimal allocation to liquid assets because the deployment of liquidity would introduce beneficial diversification to the underlying portfolio.

To compute optimal allocations with the shadow asset and liability, we must impose two additional constraints on the mean-variance analysis:

1. We constrain the allocation to the shadow asset to equal to the sum of allocation to the liquid asset classes.
2. We constrain the allocation to the shadow liability to equal the allocation to real estate.

We also continue to constrain the expected return of the portfolio to equal 7.5% in order to isolate the impact of the adjustments for performance fees, valuation smoothing, and liquidity on the optimal allocations. Table 17.6 shows this sequence of optimal allocations. In this example, we assume that real estate is fully illiquid and the other asset classes are perfectly liquid. In practice, we could account for partial illiquidity by adjusting their expected returns to account for transaction costs.

The first two columns of Table 17.6 are repeated from Table 17.1 to facilitate comparison. The third column shows the optimal allocation that accounts for the fee and de-smoothing adjustments to real estate, but not for liquidity. Collectively, these two adjustments result in a dramatic, two-thirds reduction in the real estate allocation. The last column shows the optimal allocation in which we have adjusted for illiquidity by including the shadow asset and liability. The 13.0% allocation to the shadow liability is equal to the 13.0% allocation to real estate. The 87.0% allocation to the shadow asset is equal to the total allocation to liquid assets. Overall, the allocation to real estate falls from 64.3% with no adjustments to 13.0% when adjusted for fees, smoothing, and liquidity. This impact is presented graphically in Figure 17.1. We suspect that the allocation represented in the final column of Table 17.6 would strike most investors as reasonable.

TABLE 17.5 Expected Returns, Standard Deviations, and Correlations (Adjusted for Performance Fees and Valuation Smoothing) and Including Shadow Asset and Liability

	Expected Return (%)	Standard Deviation (%)	Correlations								
			a	b	c	d	e	f	g	h	i
a US Equities	8.8	16.6	1.00								
b Foreign Developed Market Equities	9.5	18.6	0.66	1.00							
c Emerging Market Equities	11.4	26.6	0.63	0.68	1.00						
d Treasury Bonds	4.1	5.7	0.10	0.03	-0.02	1.00					
e US Corporate Bonds	4.9	7.3	0.31	0.24	0.22	0.86	1.00				
f Commodities	6.2	20.6	0.16	0.29	0.27	-0.07	0.02	1.00			
g Real Estate	6.0	15.0	0.14	0.13	0.01	-0.19	-0.12	0.12	1.00		
h Shadow Asset	0.4	0.8	0.00	0.00	0.00	0.00	0.00	0.00	0.00	1.00	
i Shadow Liability	-0.5	0.1	0.00	0.00	0.00	0.00	0.00	0.00	0.00	0.00	1.00

TABLE 17.6 Optimal Allocations Accounting for Performance Fees, Valuation Smoothing, and Liquidity

Asset Classes	Excluding Real Estate	No Adjustments	Adjusted for Fees and Smoothing	Adjusted for Fees, Smoothing, and Liquidity
US Equities	25.5	8.2	18.5	19.6
Foreign Developed Market Equities	23.2	11.3	18.7	18.8
Emerging Market Equities	9.1	16.3	11.6	9.7
Treasury Bonds	14.3	0.0	0.1	15.4
US Corporate Bonds	22.0	0.0	26.2	19.5
Commodities	5.9	0.0	2.2	3.9
Real Estate	0.0	64.3	22.8	13.0
Shadow Asset	n/a	n/a	n/a	87.0
Shadow Liability	n/a	n/a	n/a	13.0
Expected Return	7.5	7.5	7.5	7.5
Standard Deviation	10.8	7.5*	10.2	9.6

* The standard deviation of this portfolio is artificially low because it is based on real estate returns that have not been adjusted for performance fees or valuation smoothing.

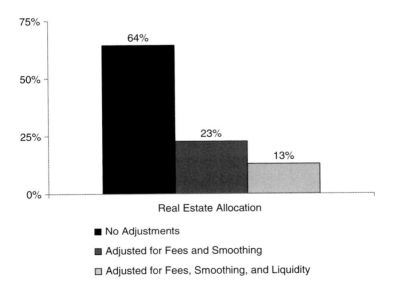

FIGURE 17.1 Optimal allocation to real estate with and without adjustments.

In this example, we have assumed that the investor has only three uses for liquidity. In practice, investors are likely to derive other benefits from liquidity (and costs from illiquidity) as well. We can expand this simulation framework to account for a wide array of liquidity benefits and illiquidity costs. We have also assumed that there is only one illiquid asset class: real estate. We could easily expand this framework to incorporate other illiquid asset classes such as private equity and infrastructure, each of which may have different degrees of illiquidity.

THE BOTTOM LINE

Most investors recognize there are costs associated with holding illiquid assets, but they have struggled to account for them explicitly when constructing portfolios. We propose that investors identify the specific benefits they derive from liquidity as well as the costs they incur from illiquidity. We introduce a simulation framework to estimate the return and standard deviation associated with these benefits and costs. We then determine whether liquidity is used offensively to improve a portfolio or defensively to preserve the quality of a portfolio. In the former case, we attach a shadow asset to the liquid portion of the portfolio, and in the latter case, we attach a shadow liability to the illiquid portion of the portfolio. These shadow allocations enable us to account for liquidity when we estimate the optimal allocation to illiquid asset classes. But we must first adjust for the biases that performance fees and appraisal-based valuations introduce to illiquid assets.

This approach explicitly accounts for the impact of liquidity on a portfolio in units of expected return and risk, thereby enabling investors to compare liquid and illiquid asset classes within a single unified framework. It also highlights several important features of liquidity:

- Liquidity can be used offensively as well as defensively. Therefore, even long-horizon investors with positive cash flows incur opportunity costs to the extent any fraction of their portfolio is illiquid.
- The optimal exposure to illiquid assets is specific to each investor. The illiquidity premium that is priced into illiquid asset classes reflects the average investor's liquidity needs. To the extent an investor's liquidity needs differ from the average, the investor must take this into account. Failing to do so is akin to ignoring investor-specific taxes or liabilities; it will almost certainly produce a suboptimal result.
- Liquidity explicitly affects a portfolio's expected return and risk. It need not be treated as a distinct feature of a portfolio nor measured in arbitrary units.

RELATED TOPICS

- Chapter 11 discusses the challenge of properly estimating the volatility of private equity.
- Chapter 21 shows how to devise an optimal rebalancing strategy (for suitably liquid assets) and, like this chapter, uses certainty equivalents to quantify the suboptimality cost of one prospective return distribution compared to another.

APPENDIX

Performance Fee Adjustment

For a single fund that charges a base fee and a performance fee on an annual basis, Equation 17.A1 computes the net return r_n, where r_g is the gross return, p is the performance fee, and b is the base fee. We reverse this formula to solve for the gross return, as shown in Equation 17.A2. The standard deviation of gross returns is not influenced by the dampening effect of performance fees, which truncates the upside of the return distribution but not the downside:

$$r_n = r_g - b - \max(0, p(r_g - b)) \tag{17.A1}$$

$$r_g = \begin{cases} r_n + b & for \ r_n < 0 \\ \dfrac{r_n}{1-p} + b & for \ r_n \geq 0 \end{cases} \tag{17.A2}$$

In practice, performance fees may be subject to additional hurdle rates (beyond the base fee) and are often accrued on a monthly basis throughout the year. It is straightforward to measure the impact of performance fees in these contexts using simulation.

De-smoothing Adjustment

To de-smooth a return series, we employ a simple first-order autoregressive model as shown by Equation 17.A3. This equation assumes that the return in a period, r_t, is a linear function of the return in the previous period plus an intercept and an error term:

$$r_t = A_0 + A_1 r_{t-1} + \varepsilon \tag{17.A3}$$

A_1 is the autoregressive coefficient, A_0 is the intercept term, and ε is the error term. To estimate the de-smoothed return in period t, we first subtract the smoothed component of the return in period t, which is explained by the return in period $t-1$. We then divide this residual by $(1-A_1)$ to "gross up" the de-smoothed component to account for the portion of the return that we removed. This calculation is given by Equation 17.A4:

$$r_t' = \frac{r_t - A_1 r_{t-1}}{1 - A_1} \tag{17.A4}$$

where r_t' is the de-smoothed return.

REFERENCES

Kinlaw, W., Kritzman, M., and Turkington, D. 2013. "Liquidity and Portfolio Choice: A Unified Approach," *Journal of Portfolio Management*, Vol. 39, No. 2 (Winter).

Lo, A., Petrov, C. and Wierzbicki, M. 2003. "It's 11pm – Do You Know Where Your Liquidity Is? The Mean-Variance Liquidity Frontier," *Journal of Investment Management*, Vol. 1, No. 1 (First Quarter).

Samuelson, P. A. 1998. "Summing Up on Business Cycles: Opening Address," in *Beyond Shocks: What Causes Business Cycles*, edited by J. C. Fuhrer and S. Schuh. Boston: Federal Reserve Bank of Boston.

NOTES

1. See, for example, Lo, Petrov, and Wierzbicki (2003).
2. When we speak of risk in this context, we assume that correlations are accounted for.
3. Refer to the Appendix for details on the performance fee adjustment.
4. Refer to the Appendix for details on the de-smoothing algorithm.
5. The NCREIF Property Index is a quarterly index tracking the performance of core institutional property markets in the United States. For details, see www .ncreif.org.
6. Whereas historical returns for the liquid asset classes are available monthly from January 1976 (with the exception of emerging markets equities, as discussed in Chapter 2), historical returns for the NCREIF index are available quarterly from Q1 1978. Therefore, we perform Maximum Likelihood Estimation to derive standard deviation and correlation estimates for real estate and augment our base case assumptions with these estimates. For additional applications of this methodology, see Kinlaw, Kritzman, and Turkington (2013).

CHAPTER 18

Currency Risk

THE CHALLENGE

Most investors recognize that it is possible to reduce the risk of a global portfolio by hedging some portion of its foreign currency exposure, but they face the challenge of determining which currencies to hedge, how much to hedge, and what instruments to use. Some investors choose not to hedge at all. In this chapter, we evaluate the prevailing arguments for and against currency hedging. We show how to derive a range of linear and nonlinear hedging strategies, and we evaluate their impact on expected portfolio performance. Finally, we review the economic rationale that explains why the risk-minimizing currency-hedging policy varies across currencies and home countries.

WHY HEDGE?

Investors who chose not to hedge foreign currency exposure typically rationalize their decision by making one or both of the following assertions:

- In the long run, currencies revert to the mean, and their returns wash out. We have a long investment horizon. So why bother?
- Currencies introduce diversification to the portfolio. We want to retain this diversification rather than hedge it away.

There is ample evidence to contradict the first assertion. For example, the British pound declined from USD 4.96 in 1850 to approximately USD 1.30 in September 2016. As we write this chapter, in the wake of the UK's historic "Brexit" vote to leave the European Union, we do not know any investors who are forecasting that the pound will revert to its mid-nineteenth-century levels. Moreover, there is compelling evidence to suggest that currency hedging reduces risk even over much shorter horizons. Schmittmann (2010) evaluates the benefits of hedging diversified equity and fixed-income portfolios over the period from 1975 through 2009. For investors based in the United States, Germany, Japan, and the United Kingdom, he finds that hedging currency exposure reduces portfolio risk significantly for periods of up to five years.

Even if exchange rates do revert to the mean over the long run, it does not necessarily follow that hedging is inappropriate. To survive in the long run, investors must endure whatever losses they suffer along the way. Few investment boards meet only once, at the end of the investment horizon; most are interested keenly in interim performance. In many cases, as we soon demonstrate, investors significantly reduce their exposure to within-horizon losses by hedging currency exposure. Indeed, if we accept that we cannot predict the direction of currency moves, there seems to be little reason not to hedge away all of the risk that currencies introduce.

What about the diversification argument? Investors often overestimate the diversification benefits of currencies, because they mistakenly focus on the correlation between the returns of a particular foreign currency, denominated in the investor's home currency, and the returns of a foreign asset, denominated in its local currency. This correlation is often quite low. However, it does not properly measure the diversification that the foreign currency introduces to the portfolio. The relevant correlation is that between the foreign currency and the foreign asset, both denominated in the investor's home currency. This correlation is always higher, because a component of the foreign asset's return comes directly from the need to translate investment value back to one's home currency at an uncertain future exchange rate. Consider an example from Chen, Kritzman, and Turkington (2015). The correlation between UK equities (as measured by the returns of the MSCI U.K. Index denominated in British pounds) and the dollar-pound exchange rate was 9% over the period from March 1993 through March 2013. However, when both the currency and the equity index were denominated in US dollars, the correlation was +48%.

WHY NOT HEDGE EVERYTHING?

These counterarguments may tempt some investors to hedge all of their currency exposure, particularly if they believe that currency returns will be zero in the long run. Indeed, from a return perspective, currency hedging is a zero-sum game: a forward contract that generates a positive return for one investor generates a negative return for another.[1] But hedging 100% of a portfolio's currency exposure is rarely the risk-minimizing solution. Consider a straightforward scenario with one foreign asset and one currency forward contract. The variance of the hedged portfolio is given by the familiar two-asset variance equation:

$$\sigma_p^2 = w_a^2 \sigma_a^2 + w_c^2 \sigma_c^2 + 2w_a \sigma_a w_c \sigma_c \rho_{a,c} \qquad (18.1)$$

Here, σ_p^2 is the variance of the hedged portfolio, w_a is the asset weight, w_c is the forward contract weight, $\rho_{a,c}$ is the correlation between the asset and the forward contract, and σ_a^2 and σ_c^2 are the variances of the asset and the forward contract, respectively. If we assume that the asset weight is 100%, then Equation 18.1 collapses to

$$\sigma_p^2 = \sigma_a^2 + w_c^2 \sigma_c^2 + 2\sigma_a w_c \sigma_c \rho_{a,c} \qquad (18.2)$$

To identify the forward contract weight that minimizes the variance of the portfolio, we take the derivative of Equation 18.2 with respect to w_c. This derivative is shown in Equation 18.3:

$$\frac{d\sigma_p^2}{dw_c} = 2w_c \sigma_c^2 + 2\sigma_a \sigma_c \rho_{a,c} \qquad (18.3)$$

To calculate the minimum-variance hedge ratio, we set this derivative equal to zero and solve for w_c. This gives us Equation 18.4, which equals the regression beta of the asset with respect to the forward contract, as a negative value:

$$w_c = -\frac{\sigma_a}{\sigma_c} \rho_{a,c} = -\beta \qquad (18.4)$$

This relationship is intuitive:

- A higher correlation between the asset and the currency indicates that the currency introduces more risk and less diversification, all else being equal, and results in a higher minimum-variance hedge ratio.
- A higher standard deviation of the currency relative to the asset indicates that we require less notional exposure to the currency to hedge the same amount of risk.

Therefore, higher currency volatility (relative to asset volatility) results in a lower minimum-variance hedge ratio, all else being equal.

To illustrate this concept, consider the following example. Suppose that a fixed-income portfolio with a 5% standard deviation is exposed to a currency with a 6% standard deviation and that the correlation between the portfolio and the currency is 0.60. Equation 18.4 shows that the

FIGURE 18.1   Minimum-variance hedge ratio.

minimum-variance hedge ratio equals $0.05 / 0.06 \times 0.60$ or 50 percent.[2] Figure 18.1 shows the standard deviation of the portfolio as a function of the percentage of the portfolio that is hedged. It is apparent from that the minimum-variance hedge ratio is 50%.

It is also apparent from Figure 18.1 that a hedge ratio of 100% does not minimize portfolio risk, given our assumptions about standard deviation and correlation. In fact, in this example, the fully hedged portfolio has the same standard deviation as the unhedged portfolio! When computing the minimum-variance hedge ratio, it is common practice to constrain the solution to lie between 0% and 100% of the exposure to the currency. A hedge ratio that is lower than 0% increases currency exposure. A hedge ratio above 100% reduces currency exposure beyond the portfolio's explicit currency exposure. We examine the notion of overhedging later in this chapter.

There are two other approaches to hedging that deserve consideration: the minimum-regret hedge ratio and the universal hedge ratio. Some investors advocate hedging 50% of currency exposure, regardless of the correlations and standard deviations. Proponents of this approach argue that it minimizes the potential for an investor to experience regret should either the 0% or the 100% hedge ratio produce the highest return ex-post. We take issue with this approach for three reasons. First, it implies that investors suffer a reduction in utility when the hedging strategy underperforms but do not enjoy an increase in utility when it outperforms. Sophisticated investors maximize their expected utility given the full distribution of potential outcomes, including gains as well as losses. Second, the most prominent empirical study in support of the minimum-regret approach is based on a flawed assumption. Gardner and Wuilloud (1995) conducted backtests to compare mean-variance optimal hedge ratios to a constant 50% hedge ratio.

However, they constructed the optimal hedge ratios using historical currency returns as expected returns. (Recall our critique of this assumption in Chapter 9.) Because currency returns vary widely over short horizons, this approach results in extreme hedge positions. A more reasonable approach, which is common in practice, is to assume 0% expected returns for currencies and identify the hedge ratios that minimize portfolio risk. Finally, should investors wish to control the risk that their hedging policy underperforms an alternative hedging policy, they can employ multirisk optimization to do so explicitly. (See Chapter 15 for details.) Kinlaw and Kritzman (2009) show how mean-variance-tracking error optimization simultaneously minimizes portfolio risk and the likelihood that the hedging policy will underperform the unhedged portfolio.[3]

The universal hedge ratio was proposed by Black (1989). He showed that, given certain assumptions, all investors should hedge the same proportion of their currency exposure. In particular, he assumed that all investors have the same risk tolerance, wealth, and portfolio composition. However, as noted by Adler and Prasad (1992), these assumptions do not hold in the real world; hence, the universal hedge ratio is likely to be suboptimal for most investors.

LINEAR HEDGING STRATEGIES

The minimum-variance hedge ratio is an example of a linear hedging strategy; the return of the hedged portfolio is a linear function of the hedged currencies' returns. Linear hedging neutralizes not only the potential losses from currencies but also the gains. In the next section, we examine nonlinear hedging strategies, which preserve the upside that potential currencies bring to the portfolio while also protecting against losses. Table 18.1 summarizes six linear hedging strategies that we evaluate in this chapter and the upper bound constraints associated with each. The lower bound for all these hedging strategies is 0% because we do not want to take positions that increase currency exposure.

Currency-specific hedging is an extension of minimum-variance hedging, but it is more efficient because it is less constrained. It identifies an individual hedge ratio for each currency rather than a uniform hedge ratio across all currencies. The investor therefore retains some exposure to currencies that offer relatively more diversification than volatility and hedges exposure to those that have the opposite properties. To identify the currency-specific hedge ratios that minimize variance, we employ the same conceptual framework that we use to derive the minimum-variance hedge ratio. However, the problem is more complex because we must solve for a vector of hedge ratios rather than a single hedge ratio. There are many more parameters to

TABLE 18.1   Linear Hedging Strategies and Their Constraints

Linear Hedging Strategies	Asset Weight Constraints	Currency-Hedging Constraints
Unhedged	Fixed	Each hedge position = 0
Full Hedging	Fixed	Each hedge position = Portfolio exposure to each currency
Currency-Specific Hedging	Fixed	Each hedge position ≤ Portfolio exposure to each currency
Allow Cross-Hedging	Fixed	Total hedge positions ≤ Portfolio's total currency exposure
Allow Overhedging	Fixed	Total hedge positions ≤ 100%
Allow Asset Reallocation	Variable	Total hedge positions ≤ 100%

estimate: the standard deviation of each asset class, the standard deviation of each currency, the correlations between the asset classes and the currencies, and the correlations between the currencies. We solve this problem with mean-variance analysis. Specifically, we maximize expected utility as a function of a vector of weights, as shown in Equation 18.5:

$$EU(w) = w'\mu - \lambda w'\Sigma w \qquad (18.5)$$

Here, w is a column vector of N asset and currency weights, μ is a row vector of expected returns, and Σ is the covariance matrix. The parameter λ reflects the investor's risk aversion. Because we assume that asset class weights are constrained at fixed values and expected currency returns are zero, λ falls out of the equation along with the term $w'\mu$.[4]

Cross-hedging and overhedging are extensions of currency-specific hedging. To allow cross-hedging, we constrain the total amount of hedging such that it is less than or equal to the total amount of foreign currency exposure. This strategy is less constrained than currency-specific hedging because it may cross-hedge one currency with another. One advantage of this approach is that it can hedge currencies that are more expensive to trade using correlated, proxy currencies that are less expensive to trade.

In the case of overhedging, we allow the total amount of hedging to exceed the amount of foreign currency exposure in the portfolio. This strategy, which hedges implicit as well as explicit currency exposure, caps total hedge positions at 100% of portfolio value.

Finally, we consider an approach in which we identify the optimal asset mix and the hedge positions simultaneously rather than sequentially.[5] This approach lifts the constraint, imposed by all the previous strategies, that we identify the currency hedge positions given a fixed set of asset class weights.

To illustrate these strategies, we now apply them to our aggressive base case portfolio from Chapter 2. We choose the aggressive portfolio because it has the most foreign exposure. Figure 18.2 shows the portfolio's exposure

FIGURE 18.2 Currency exposure as a percentage of portfolio value.

to each currency. To reduce complexity, we focus only on the 10 currency exposures that are greater than 1% of the total portfolio's value.[6]

Table 18.2 shows expected returns, standard deviations, and correlations for the portfolio as well as the currencies to which it is exposed. Currency dynamics evolve over time as the global political and economic landscape changes. For example, the European Monetary Union introduced the euro in 1999, and the Indian government removed its peg on the rupee in 1991. To capture dynamics that are relevant to the current environment, we derive the parameters in Table 18.2 from monthly returns from the period starting in January 2006 and ending in December 2015.

Table 18.3 shows the fixed asset class weights as well as the currency-hedging positions for each of the six strategies presented in Table 18.1. It also shows the standard deviation of each portfolio and its within-horizon value at risk.

Table 18.3 offers a variety of useful insights:

- The fully hedged portfolio has a lower standard deviation than the unhedged portfolio, but not as low as the other hedging strategies, which are less constrained.

- The currency-specific hedge positions do not reduce standard deviation significantly relative to the fully hedged portfolio. Currency exposures do not introduce meaningful diversification benefits to the portfolio, so the optimal solution is to hedge almost all the exposure. The sole exception is the Japanese yen, which is not hedged. Table 18.2 reveals that the yen diversifies global equity exposure; it is the only currency that is negatively correlated with the three equity asset classes in the portfolio.

- The cross-hedging solution uses the Australian dollar and, to a lesser extent, the South African rand to hedge all the portfolio's currency exposure. Again, Table 18.2 reveals the proximate cause for this selection. The Australian dollar has the highest correlation with foreign developed market equities and emerging market equities of any currency; it therefore offers the most effective hedge.

- The final hedging strategy identifies the risk-minimizing hedging policy and the optimal asset mix simultaneously. To facilitate comparison, we constrain this solution to have the same expected return as the other portfolios. Also, to ensure that the asset mix is palatable, we control for tracking error relative to the overhedged portfolio.[7] Despite these constraints, this solution offers the largest reduction in standard deviation. This is because it lifts a much more impactful constraint: the requirement that the risk-minimizing currency positions be computed conditioned on a fixed asset mix. In theory, the simultaneous approach always dominates the sequential approach.[8] This is true because the ability to hedge the asset classes in advance changes their risk and diversification

TABLE 18.2 Expected Returns, Standard Deviations, and Correlations for Assets and Currencies

	Expected Return (%)	Standard Deviation (%)	Correlations															
			a	b	c	d	e	f	g	h	i	j	k	l	m	n	o	p
a US Equities	8.8	16.3	1															
b Foreign Developed Market Equities	9.5	19.4	0.90	1														
c Emerging Market Equities	11.4	25.3	0.79	0.90	1													
d Treasury Bonds	4.1	4.3	-0.30	-0.26	-0.22	1												
e US Corporate Bonds	4.9	5.7	0.33	.45	0.45	0.48	1											
f Commodities	6.2	22.3	0.50	0.60	0.63	-0.30	0.14	1										
g EUR	0.0	10.9	0.49	0.66	0.60	0.02	0.30	0.57	1									
h JPY	0.0	9.5	-0.26	-0.17	-0.15	0.48	0.20	-0.07	0.12	1								
i GBP	0.0	9.0	0.44	0.60	0.56	-0.27	0.19	0.64	0.60	-0.04	1							
j CHF	0.0	12.0	0.27	0.48	0.47	0.16	0.34	0.42	0.74	0.30	0.43	1						
k CAD	0.0	10.2	0.66	0.73	0.76	-0.26	0.29	0.64	0.57	-0.07	0.61	0.35	1					
l KRW	0.0	12.7	0.62	0.69	0.73	-0.04	0.42	0.40	0.62	0.09	0.41	0.60	0.53	1				
m AUD	0.0	14.6	0.62	0.77	0.82	-0.04	0.47	0.67	0.74	0.03	0.62	0.61	0.74	0.70	1			
n TWD	0.0	5.2	0.51	0.62	0.69	-0.05	0.26	0.54	0.58	0.20	0.47	0.60	0.52	0.68	0.66	1		
o INR	0.0	8.8	0.51	0.62	0.65	-0.05	0.42	0.31	0.49	0.01	0.40	0.46	0.49	0.52	0.61	0.47	1	
p ZAR	0.0	14.6	0.60	0.71	0.77	-0.10	0.39	0.46	0.53	-0.10	0.45	0.47	0.58	0.60	0.73	0.54	0.54	1

TABLE 18.3 Risk-Minimizing Hedge Ratios (%)

	No Hedging	Full Hedging	Currency-Specific Hedging	Cross-Hedging	Overhedging	Asset Class Reallocation
Hedgeable Foreign Exposure as Percentage of Portfolio	38.1	38.1	38.1	38.1	100.0	100.0
Total Hedge Positions as Percentage of Portfolio	0.0	38.1	30.6	38.1	100.0	100.0
Asset weights						
US Equities	36.8	36.8	36.8	36.8	36.8	33.1
Foreign Developed Market Equities	34.5	34.5	34.5	34.5	34.5	31.3
Emerging Market Equities	15.8	15.8	15.8	15.8	15.8	22.0
Treasury Bonds	0.0	0.0	0.0	0.0	0.0	10.1
US Corporate Bonds	8.9	8.9	8.9	8.9	8.9	1.4
Commodities	4.0	4.0	4.0	4.0	4.0	2.1
Cash Equivalents						
Hedging Positions	Exposure	Weight	Weight	Weight	Weight	Weight
EUR	9.8	-9.8	-9.8	0.0	0.0	0.0
JPY	7.5	-7.5	0.0	0.0	0.0	0.0
GBP	6.2	-6.2	-6.2	0.0	0.0	0.0
CHF	3.0	-3.0	-3.0	0.0	0.0	0.0
CAD	2.6	-2.6	-2.6	0.0	-27.0	-25.5
KRW	2.5	-2.5	-2.5	0.0	-21.1	-21.6
AUD	2.2	-2.2	-2.2	-31.2	-28.8	-28.7
TWD	1.9	-1.9	-1.9	0.0	0.0	0.0
INR	1.4	-1.4	-1.4	0.0	0.0	-0.2
ZAR	1.1	-1.1	-1.1	-6.8	-23.1	-24.0
Portfolio						
Expected Return	9.0	9.0	9.0	9.0	9.0	9.0
Standard Deviation	16.7	14.9	14.8	12.9	9.1	8.7
Within-Horizon Value at Risk*	30.0	26.3	25.9	21.9	13.7	12.7

* Within-horizon value at risk is for a three-year horizon with a 95% confidence level expressed as a percentage of portfolio value.

properties and, hence, their relative weights in an optimal portfolio. For example, in this illustration, the simultaneous solution holds more of the riskiest asset class (emerging market equities) because it is able to offset this risk by hedging highly correlated currencies that are bound together by global growth and commodity prices, such as the Australian dollar and the South African rand. In practice, the simultaneous approach may be impractical. To the extent investors have greater conviction in their estimates of return and risk for asset classes than for currencies, it makes sense to identify the optimal asset mix first.

NONLINEAR HEDGING STRATEGIES

We now evaluate currency-hedging strategies that employ options. These strategies are classified as nonlinear because the return of the hedged portfolio is a nonlinear function of the hedged currency returns, owing to the asymmetry of option payouts. The primary benefit of options compared to forward contracts is that they preserve the potential for the investor to participate in upside currency returns while hedging the downside. Of course, investors must pay a premium for this upside potential.

To begin, we consider a straightforward approach in which the investor holds a portfolio of put options: one for each of the 10 major currency exposures in the portfolio. We assume that these options expire every three months, at which time the investor purchases a new set of options. We also assume that the options are at the money and that we purchase enough options to hedge a notional amount equal to the portfolio's explicit exposure to each currency.

To evaluate the performance of the options strategy, we employ Monte Carlo simulation. We choose to simulate rather than backtest the option strategy because a backtest represents only a single pass through history whereas simulation enables us to evaluate a wide range of outcomes in which options expire both in and out of the money. We calibrate these simulations so that the currencies and asset classes have the same expected returns, standard deviations, and correlations, as in the linear hedging analysis.

1. We construct three-year quarterly return paths for asset classes and currencies based on the expected returns, standard deviations, and correlations shown in Table 18.2.
2. We calculate and record the following values for each quarter:
   a. The price of an at-the-money option on each currency at the beginning of the quarter.[9]
   b. The payoff of each option at the end of the quarter.

    c. The total return of each option over the quarter, as a percentage of the notional exposure to each currency.

3. We combine the option returns with the returns of the unhedged portfolio to evaluate their impact on its returns along the path.

4. We repeat this process 10,000 times to generate a large sample of paths.

Table 18.4 shows that the investor pays an average quarterly premium of 0.93% to protect the portfolio from currency depreciation. On average, this premium is offset by the payoff at the end of each quarter, which has an average value of 0.92%. Because the options are at the money, and we are holding 10 of them, the portfolio of options generates a payoff 93% of the time. During quarters when the portfolio has a negative return, the average payoff on the option portfolio is even higher, 1.49%. When the foreign asset classes in the portfolio are down, the average payoff and probability of a positive payoff are higher again. However, the incremental change is slight due to the high correlation between the domestic and foreign components of the portfolio.

Figure 18.3 shows the impact of the unhedged, linear, and nonlinear hedging strategies on the distribution of currency returns within the portfolio. The asymmetric payoff associated with the put options is visible in the truncated left tail.

In this analysis, we set the notional exposure to each option equal to the explicit notional exposure to the underlying currency. This is the nonlinear equivalent of full hedging. In practice, as is the case with linear hedging, it may be optimal to hedge more or less than this amount of a currency exposure. It may also be optimal to combine linear and nonlinear hedging instruments. To identify optimal hedging strategies that account for these complexities, we employ full-scale optimization as opposed to mean-variance analysis.[10] Full-scale optimization accounts for the non-normality

TABLE 18.4 Hedging Performance with Individual Quarterly Put Options (%)

	Across all Periods	When Portfolio Is Down	When Foreign Assets Are Down
Mean Option Premium as Percentage of Portfolio	0.93	0.93	0.93
Mean Option Payoff as Percentage of Portfolio	0.92	1.49	1.50
Probability of Payoff > 0	93.39	99.76	99.86

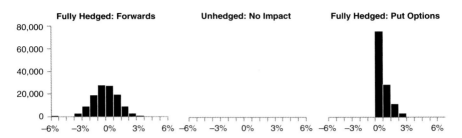

FIGURE 18.3 Impact of hedging strategies on distribution of portfolio currency returns (quarterly).

of option returns and enables us to specify a variety of utility functions. We assume that investors wish to protect against currency losses while retaining upside potential; thus, we perform full-scale optimization using the kinked utility function given in Equation 18.6. (See Chapter 12 for more details about full-scale optimization.)

$$U_{kinked}(R) = \begin{cases} \dfrac{1}{1-\theta}(1+R)^{1-\theta} - 1, & \text{for } r \geq k \\ \dfrac{1}{1-\theta}((1+R)^{1-\theta} - 1) - \omega(k - R), & \text{for } r < k \end{cases} \qquad (18.6)$$

The term $U_{kinked}(R)$ is expected utility, R is the return of the portfolio, k is the location of the kink, θ is the curvature, and ω is the slope. With this utility function, investor satisfaction drops precipitously when returns fall below the kink. (See Chapter 12 for a depiction of a kinked utility function.)

When we perform full-scale optimization, we allow for positions in each option and forward contract to vary between 0% and 100%, but we constrain the total positions to be no more than 100%. We set the curvature, θ, and slope, ω, equal to 5, and k equal to 0 to reflect aversion to loss. The results of the full-scale optimization are shown in Table 18.5.[11] In addition to the optimal forward and option positions, Table 18.5 shows the following values for unhedged, optimal linear, and optimal nonlinear (full-scale) hedging strategies:

- Probability of experiencing a quarterly loss
- Average size of quarterly losses
- Within-horizon value at risk for a one-year period with 95% confidence

TABLE 18.5   Full-Scale Optimal Hedging Results with Forwards and Options (%)

	Unhedged	Linear Optimal (Overhedging)	Full-Scale Optimal with 0% Threshold
Unhedged Portfolio	100.0	100.0	100.0
Forward Positions			
EUR	0.0	0.0	0.0
JPY	0.0	0.0	0.0
GBP	0.0	0.0	0.0
CHF	0.0	0.0	0.0
CAD	0.0	−27.0	−34.3
KRW	0.0	−21.1	−28.8
AUD	0.0	−28.8	−11.9
TWD	0.0	0.0	0.0
INR	0.0	0.0	0.0
ZAR	0.0	−23.1	−25.0
Put Option Positions			
EUR	0.0	0.0	0.0
JPY	0.0	0.0	0.0
GBP	0.0	0.0	29.9
CHF	0.0	0.0	0.0
CAD	0.0	0.0	10.2
KRW	0.0	0.0	0.0
AUD	0.0	0.0	0.0
TWD	0.0	0.0	9.9
INR	0.0	0.0	33.9
ZAR	0.0	0.0	0.0
Probability of Return < 0%	42%	35%	35%
Average Return < 0%	−6.7	−3.1	−2.8
Within-Horizon Value at Risk*	−23.5	−10.3	−9.5

*Within-horizon VaR is for a one-year horizon with a 95% confidence level and quarterly monitoring.

The optimal linear solution, which is the overhedging strategy repeated from Table 18.3, reduces the probability and average magnitude of losses relative to the unhedged portfolio. However, the full-scale solution, which accounts for the non-normality of option returns as well as the investor's preference for upside versus downside returns, shows additional improvement in these metrics. It is notable from these results that the nonlinear solution uses options to hedge the British pound, Taiwanese dollar, and

Indian rupee, which are left unhedged in the linear solution. Evidently, hedging these exposures with forward contracts does not reduce the portfolio's standard deviation, but hedging them with put options reduces the likelihood and magnitude of losses.

Investors may also wish to consider the following nonlinear hedging strategies. We can also measure their benefits and costs with simulation.

- Basket option – This strategy purchases a single option to hedge the portfolio's collective currency exposure. A basket option is cheaper than a portfolio of put options, because diversification among the currencies reduces the volatility of the basket. However, it also reduces the average payout.
- Foreign asset contingent option – This strategy purchases a basket option that pays off only when two outcomes occur simultaneously: a loss in the foreign asset component of the portfolio and a loss in the collective currency basket. In other words, this option provides protection only in periods when both currencies and foreign assets are down. This strategy may appeal to an investor who is able to tolerate adverse currency outcomes when they are offset by gains in the underlying assets. Because it offers less protection overall, this strategy is less expensive than a basket option.
- Total portfolio contingent option – This strategy is equivalent to the one described above; however, the first contingency is linked to the entire portfolio rather than to the foreign asset component.

THE BOTTOM LINE

We have shown that the optimal hedging strategy rarely, if ever, hedges all currencies in the same proportion. This result is driven by the empirical fact that some currencies are more correlated with assets than others. Likewise, investors in certain countries should hedge more than investors in other countries. Some may wonder whether these results are based on economic intuition or merely statistical anomalies that are unlikely to persist in the future. We argue that correlations differ for sound economic reasons. Each currency is inexorably linked to its underlying economy and varies with the unique set of macroeconomic factors that influence that economy. For example, the Swiss franc is often viewed as a safe-haven currency that investors buy during market crises. As a result, it tends to be less correlated with global equity markets, particularly during turbulent periods. Therefore, most investors should not hedge the Swiss franc because it introduces favorable diversification to their portfolio. Swiss investors, on the other hand, may want to hedge more than investors in other countries because foreign currencies, denominated in Swiss francs, tend to have higher correlations with global equity markets.

This intuition may sound plausible, but to formulate a hedging policy, we must have confidence that these relationships will persist. This chapter presents in-sample results. That is, we compute the hedge ratios and evaluate their performance using the same sample of returns (or simulated returns drawn from the same distribution). In practice, realized results differ from expectations and the performance of these strategies will depend on the persistence of the inputs from one period to the next. Kinlaw and Kritzman (2009) present an extensive empirical study of both equity and multi-asset class portfolios. They conclude that currency standard deviations and correlations are reasonably persistent through time. The economic rationale described above, combined with the empirical persistence of these relationships, should give investors some degree of comfort that history serves as a reasonable guide to the future behavior of currencies.

RELATED TOPICS

- Chapter 2 introduces mean-variance analysis, which we use in this chapter to optimize currency hedge ratios.
- Chapter 12 introduces full-scale optimization, which we use in this chapter to optimize positions to currency options that have highly non-normal distributions.

REFERENCES

Adler, M. and Prasad, B. 1992. "On Universal Currency Hedges," *Journal of Financial and Quantitative Analysis*, Vol. 27, No. 1.

Black, F. 1989. "Universal Hedging: Optimizing Currency Risk and Reward in International Equity Portfolios," *Financial Analysts Journal*, (July/August).

Chen, W., Kritzman, M., and Turkington, D. 2015. "Alternative Currency Hedging Strategies with Known Covariances," *Journal of Investment Management*, Vol. 13, No. 2 (Second Quarter).

Chow, G. 1995. "Portfolio Selection Based on Return, Risk, and Relative Performance," *Financial Analysts Journal*, Vol. 51, No. 2 (January/February).

Cremers, J., Kritzman, M. and Page, S. 2005. "Optimal Hedge Fund Allocations," *Journal of Portfolio Management*, Vol. 31, No. 3 (Spring).

Gardner, G. and Wuilloud, T. 1995. "Currency Risk in International Portfolios: How Satisfying Is Optimal Hedging?" *Journal of Portfolio Management*, Vol. 21, No. 3 (Spring).

Garman, M. and Kohlhagen, S. 1983. "Foreign Currency Option Values," *Journal of International Money and Finance*, Vol. 2, No. 3 (December).

Jorian, P. 1994. "Mean Variance Analysis of Currency Overlays," *Financial Analysts Journal*, Vol. 50, No. 3 (May/June).

Kinlaw, W. and Kritzman, M. 2009. "Optimal Currency Hedging in and out of Sample," *Journal of Asset Management*, Vol. 10, No. 1 (April).

Schmittmann, J. M. 2010. "Currency Hedging for International Portfolios," *IMF Working Paper* (June).

Siegel, J. 1975. "Risk, Interest Rates, and the Forward Exchange," *Quarterly Journal of Economics*, February 1975.

NOTES

1. Currency hedging is not a zero-sum game from a risk perspective because it is possible for both forward contract counterparties to reduce their risk by hedging. Also, Siegel's paradox shows currency returns to be nonzero collectively for investors on both sides of an exchange rate change. For example, if the dollar increases from 1 to 1.2 versus the euro, the euro only declines to 0.83 (1/1.2 = 0.83). Thus, the net percentage change across the two currencies is positive 3% (0.2 − 0.17 = 0.03). See Siegel (1975).

2. When an investor hedges a positive exposure to a currency, the hedge position is negative. Therefore, we refer to hedge ratios as positive values even though the associated position is negative (short).

3. Mean-variance tracking error optimization was introduced by Chow (1995).

4. In some cases, investors may wish to account for the transaction cost associated with hedging each currency. In these instances, costs should be included as negative values in the expected returns vector μ, and the λ parameter represents the units of cost the investor is willing to pay to reduce standard deviation by one unit.

5. This hedging strategy is like the one proposed by Jorian (1994).

6. We exclude the RMB from our analysis due to trading restrictions in this currency.

7. Specifically, we employ mean-variance-tracking error optimization to identify this portfolio. We use a tracking error aversion parameter of 5 and an absolute risk aversion parameter of 1. See Chow (1995) for details.

8. The opportunity set for the simultaneous solution includes all possible combinations of asset and currency weights, including the sequential solution. So it is possible that the two solutions could be equivalent but the sequential approach cannot outperform the simultaneous approach ex ante.

9. We value the options using the Garman-Kohlhagen model. We assume that the volatility of each currency is equal to its full-sample standard deviation from

the period 2006 through 2015. We also assume that the domestic and foreign interest rates are equal to their average values from this period. See Garman and Kohlhagen (1983) for details.

10. For more details, see Cremers, Kritzman, and Page (2005).

11. To reduce the computation time, we perform the full-scale optimization on the first 1,000 of the 10,000 three-year paths from our Monte Carlo simulation. This represents a total of 12,000 quarters, or 300 years of simulated returns.

CHAPTER 19

Estimation Error

THE CHALLENGE

The goal of asset allocation is to choose a portfolio to hold for some future period. In Chapter 2 we assumed, implicitly, that we know the true expected returns and covariances of the asset classes. In practice, we must estimate these values based on imperfect information. The inputs to optimization are subject to error, and therefore, so are the optimal portfolio weights. Some investors believe that estimation error is so severe as to render optimization a hopeless exercise. We disagree with this extreme view, as we discussed in Chapters 7 and 9. Here are some reasons to remain calm:

- Grouping securities into asset classes that are internally homogeneous and externally heterogeneous reduces noise. We need only estimate the properties of a handful of asset classes, as opposed to hundreds or thousands of underlying securities for which we may lack both information and intuition. (See Chapters 1 and 8.)
- If two asset classes are close substitutes for one another, errors in their expected returns lead to large errors in the optimal weights, but these misallocations across highly similar asset classes have little impact on the portfolio's return and risk, if the portfolio weights are reasonably constrained. If, on the other hand, asset classes are very different from each other, errors in their expected returns do not affect the optimal weights very much. (See Chapter 7.)
- Most of the arguments against optimization rely on unrealistic extrapolation of historical mean returns as estimates of expected returns. When we use common sense, alongside empirical evidence, to estimate expected returns, optimization outperforms naïve equal weighting out-of-sample. (See Chapter 9.)

Nevertheless, we should acknowledge that our predictions of return and risk are subject to error, and we should do as much as possible to construct portfolios that deliver value in the face of estimation error. The traditional approach to addressing this challenge is to make portfolios less sensitive to errors. We advocate a different approach. We argue that the risk characteristics of some asset classes are more stable than those of others. Therefore, we should structure portfolios that emphasize asset classes with more stable risk characteristics and rely less on asset classes with less stable risk characteristics. By doing so, we hope to create portfolios that have more reliable risk profiles out-of-sample.

TRADITIONAL APPROACHES TO ESTIMATION ERROR

Before we discuss this new approach to managing estimation error, called stability-adjusted optimization, let us review the conventional approaches to dealing with estimation error.

Bayesian Shrinkage

The most extreme approach to estimation error is simply to avoid estimation altogether and build an equally weighted portfolio. In Chapter 9, we do our best to discourage this approach.

Bayesian shrinkage is a related but somewhat gentler approach to controlling estimation error. In the early eighteenth century, the British statistician and philosopher Thomas Bayes introduced a statistical procedure for combining prior beliefs with observed data to form expectations about the future. Bayes' theorem defines the "posterior" probability as the probability that a parameter will take on a specified value given the fact that we observe a sample of data. The posterior probability is equal to our "prior" belief about the probability that the parameter will take on that value, multiplied by the likelihood of observing the data given that we hold that prior belief.

Suppose, for example, that we want to forecast the standard deviation of a particular asset class. As our prior belief, we might presume that the true standard deviation lies within the range of 10% to 20% and is most likely to equal 15%. If we must choose a specific forecast, we should choose 15%. Now suppose that we obtain data for this asset class showing that its standard deviation ranged from 5% to 15% but most frequently equaled 10%. What should we now conclude is the best estimate for its standard deviation? Our prior belief suggests that 15% is very likely, but the data suggest that this value is not likely. Conversely, the data alone imply that 10% is the most likely value, but this contradicts our original belief. Taken together, the most likely value for its standard deviation is 12.5%. If we had shown much higher conviction in our prior belief, assuming, for instance, that the true value fell in a narrow range of 14% to 16%, then the posterior forecast in this example would be closer to 14.4%.

We should think of Bayesian shrinkage as updating a prior belief after observing data. Alternatively, we can think of it as reducing reliance on noisy data by compressing the data-driven estimates toward some basic belief. One such belief is that all assets are indistinguishable from one another, which means they all have equal expected returns, standard deviations, and correlations. In this case, the 1/N portfolio is optimal. Bayesian shrinkage is a compromise between a purely data-driven approach and one that is completely agnostic. Compared to purely data-driven estimates, those based on Bayesian shrinkage are more like each other, and they tend to produce less concentrated portfolios. However, they are likely to produce biased estimates and may overlook important differences across asset classes.

Resampling

Michaud and Michaud (2008) propose a technique called resampling. Rather than computing a single efficient frontier from a given set of data, this procedure calls for repeatedly drawing random small samples from within the data, generating a new efficient frontier for each sample, and then averaging the portfolio weights for a particular risk level on the efficient frontiers. Portfolios on the resampled frontier are less likely to contain "corner solutions," in which optimal weights equal the prespecified – and quite likely arbitrary – lower or upper allocation limits set for each asset class. If we impose a long-only constraint whereby 0% is the lowest allowable weight, resampled portfolios will probably have fewer 0% weights, because it takes only one random sample with a nonzero allocation to pull the average above zero. Proponents of resampling view this as a desirable result, because it leads to less concentrated allocations, like Bayesian shrinkage. However, we should note that the least stable asset classes are the ones most likely to experience an increase in their allocations away from zero. This result occurs because resampled inputs that are extremely favorable receive large allocations, whereas those that are extremely unfavorable are constrained to a minimum weight of 0%. Unstable asset classes have larger extremes, thus pulling the average weight higher. We should, therefore, question whether this bias resulting from the asymmetric effect of constraints is good. If we remove weight constraints, this bias will disappear, but we know from first principles that the resampled frontier will then converge to the original mean-variance efficient frontier (for additional discussion of this point, see Scherer, 2002).

Robust Optimization

Robust optimization considers a wide set of expected returns and risk, and selects the portfolio that suffers the least in the most adverse scenario. This approach is sometimes called "minimax" optimization; it aims to minimize the maximum loss. The approach we next describe, called stability-adjusted optimization, is like robust optimization in that we seek to identify a portfolio that is resilient to estimation error. But stability-adjusted optimization is different. Whereas robust optimization focuses on only the worst outcome, stability-adjusted optimization considers the entire distribution of outcomes.

STABILITY-ADJUSTED OPTIMIZATION

Bayesian shrinkage and resampling produce portfolios that are less sensitive to estimation error by obscuring it. Stability-adjusted optimization, by contrast, highlights estimation error and uses this information as a distinct component of risk in the portfolio formation process. It effectively renders a portfolio more sensitive to estimation error, but in a good way. It increases a portfolio's reliance on covariances with less error and reduces its reliance on covariances with greater error. In order to describe this approach, which we confess is rather complicated, we begin by introducing a taxonomy of estimation error.

Types of Estimation Error

Mean-variance analysis requires estimates of expected return and covariance, and both are subject to errors. However, we do not address errors in expected returns for two reasons. First, the degree of difficulty in forecasting the mean return of an asset class over some future period is highly related to the standard deviation of its returns. Volatile asset classes have more dispersion in realized returns, and their historical data is plagued by greater noise, reducing confidence in data-derived estimates. Conveniently, standard deviation is already a core component of mean-variance analysis. All else being equal, mean-variance analysis favors asset classes with less potential for errors in means. We simply increase the risk aversion parameter to penalize assets with unstable returns.[1] Second, it is hard to generalize about errors in expected returns because investors estimate them in many ways. The best expected return forecasts are likely to incorporate judgment and depend on diverse sources of information. For these reasons, we focus on covariances, which are commonly extrapolated from history.

Covariances are subject to several sources of estimation error. (We use the term *covariances* to refer to the entire covariance matrix across a collection of assets. Each diagonal variance represents the covariance of an asset with itself.) Investors face small-sample error because realized covariances typically pertain to a period that is shorter than the return sample from which they are estimated. Investors also face independent-sample error because future covariances are independent of past covariances. And they face interval error because covariances estimated from short-interval returns, such as monthly returns, do not accurately describe how asset classes covary over the longer intervals, which is what concerns investors. And, if they use factors, investors also face mapping error because the collection of assets that will best track a factor in the future differ from those that tracked the factor most reliably in the past. These four sources of error are all distinct from one another, and they can be measured in common units. Figure 19.1 presents a visual description of these four sources of estimation error and summarizes how they are measured from historical returns. Next, we discuss each source of estimation error in detail, following the framework presented in Cocoma, Czasonis, Kritzman, and Turkington (2017).

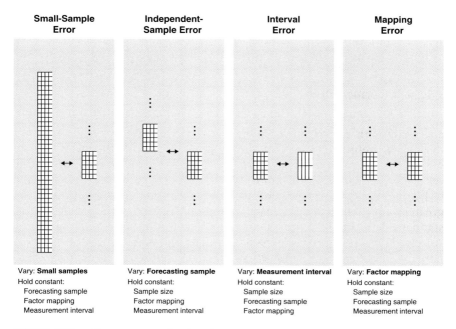

FIGURE 19.1 Components of estimation error.

Small-Sample Error

Small-sample error arises because the covariances that concern investors pertain to an investment horizon that is typically much shorter than the return history they use to estimate them. To isolate the impact of small-sample error, we compare estimates from one long sample to those of all the subsamples within the long sample, holding everything else constant. To summarize the degree of error for a pair of assets, A and B, we use a variant of a statistic called the root-mean-squared-error. We compare each small-sample estimate to the large-sample estimate, square these differences, take the average, and then compute the square root of this result. Before we perform this calculation, though, we must address three nuances.

First, we modify the covariances by essentially taking their square root. If we were to evaluate individual errors in units of squared deviations (variances or covariances), we would substantially exaggerate the outliers. Therefore, whereas the covariance between two assets is the product of their correlation ρ_{AB} and their individual volatilities σ_A and σ_B,

$$Covariance(A, B) = \rho_{AB}\sigma_A\sigma_B \qquad (19.1)$$

we define the modified covariances as follows, which in the case of a single asset is equivalent to its standard deviation:

$$Modified\ Covariance(A, B) = \rho_{AB}\sqrt{\sigma_A\sigma_B} \qquad (19.2)$$

Second, in order to compare covariances across assets, we must express errors in common units. We therefore divide by a normalization factor, which is the square root of the product of asset class standard deviations. For a single asset class, the normalization factor is equivalent to its standard deviation:

$$Normalization\ Factor(A, B) = \sqrt{\sigma_A\sigma_B} \qquad (19.3)$$

Third, we evaluate errors for all overlapping subsamples within our longer sample. If we were to use nonoverlapping subsamples, we would have very few observations, and the results would depend on our choice of the starting and end dates of the first subsample. It is, therefore, possible that we would not observe important behavior if it were spread across two subsamples and obscured by the other observations in each subsample. The use of overlapping subsamples mitigates this issue. Using overlapping subsamples does not introduce a bias; however, we should note that the results are less reliable than they would be had we used the same number of independent subsamples.

Based on the adjustments described above, we compute small-sample error as follows:

Small Sample Error = SSE(A,B)

$$= \sqrt{\frac{1}{K} \Sigma_{j=1}^{K} \left(\frac{\rho_{AB,m,j} \sqrt{\sigma_{A,m,j}\sigma_{B,m,j}} - \rho_{AB,m} \sqrt{\sigma_{A,m}\sigma_{B,m}}}{\sqrt{\sigma_{A,m}\sigma_{B,m}}} \right)^2} \qquad (19.4)$$

The subscript j refers to estimates from each of K overlapping subsamples of a chosen size (60 months, for example), and the subscript m refers to the use of monthly estimates. The periodicity is monthly in this calculation, but we vary it later when we measure interval error. Monthly data are usually appropriate for asset allocation, but these equations apply to any frequency of returns. For the diagonal entries in the covariance matrix, we restate this formula as shown in Equation 19.5. It is merely a special case of the more general expression for covariances, but we show it here because it reinforces the logic of the methodology.

$$SSE(A,A) = \sqrt{\frac{1}{K} \Sigma_{j=1}^{K} \left(\frac{\sigma_{A,m,j} - \sigma_{A,m}}{\sigma_{A,m}} \right)^2} \qquad (19.5)$$

Independent-Sample Error

Investors face independent-sample error because future realizations are independent of historical estimates. To isolate independent-sample error, we hold constant the size of each return window and compute errors across all contiguous subsample pairs. The first subsample, denoted by subscript $\widehat{m},j$, provides an estimate of covariance, which is then compared to the covariance that occurs in the immediately following subsample of the same size, denoted by subscript m,j. We proceed in this fashion for every pair of contiguous subsamples. We normalize each error by the full-sample normalization factor, as before. For clean attribution of errors, we also subtract the impact of small-sample error, because it is embedded in the calculation of independent-sample error. Therefore, the formula for independent-sample error is

Independent Sample Error = ISE(A,B)

$$= \sqrt{\frac{1}{K} \Sigma_{j=1}^{K} \left(\frac{\rho_{AB,m,j} \sqrt{\sigma_{A,m,j}\sigma_{B,m,j}} - \rho_{AB,\widehat{m},j} \sqrt{\sigma_{A,\widehat{m},j}\sigma_{B,\widehat{m},j}}}{\sqrt{\sigma_{A,m}\sigma_{B,m}}} \right)^2 - SSE(A,B)^2}$$

$$(19.6)$$

As before, we provide the simplified formula for single-asset-class variances, for illustration:

$$ISE(A,A) = \sqrt{\frac{1}{K}\Sigma_{j=1}^{K}\left(\frac{\sigma_{A,m,j} - \sigma_{A,\hat{m},j}}{\sigma_{A,m}}\right)^2 - SSE(A,A)^2} \qquad (19.7)$$

We should note that it is possible, though somewhat unusual, for the first term under the square root sign to exceed small-sample error. This situation may occur, for instance, if errors are large but strongly clustered into regimes and therefore well predicted by recent historical samples. In that case, we could assign a value of zero to independent-sample error, as it cannot be negative. Alternatively, we could measure independent-sample error and small-sample error simultaneously using the first term under the square root sign in Equation 19.7, and forgo any further attribution of the error to independent- or small-sample error. Again, this issue does not occur often and is of small consequence.

Interval Error

Investors face interval error because risk can vary significantly depending on whether it is estimated from high- or low-frequency observations. It is commonly assumed that the standard deviation scales with the square root of time, and that correlations are invariant to the return interval used to measure them. These two common assumptions are, of course, approximations of reality. Unfortunately, the quality of the approximation is often very bad. For more on this issue, and its implications for portfolio construction, risk estimation, and performance measurement, see Chapter 5.

As one example, Figure 19.2 shows monthly US and emerging market equity log returns from January 1988 (when the emerging market data is first available) through December 2015. The monthly returns of these two asset classes are 68% correlated. Figure 19.3 shows, strikingly, that the correlation of five-year returns for these two asset classes, over the exact same time period, falls to –4%. In this example, we use cumulative log returns to remove the impact of compounding. (See Chapter 25 for more information about log returns.)

Interval error does not pertain to estimates from one sample versus another. Instead, it reflects the fact that the same return sample yields conflicting risk estimates for different measurement intervals. Interval error exists whenever returns exhibit serial dependence. Let x represent the logarithm of one plus the returns of an asset, X, and let σ_x represent the standard

FIGURE 19.2 Monthly returns of US and emerging market equities.

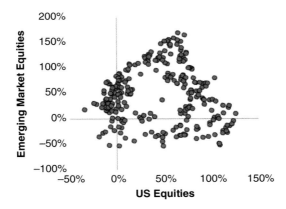

FIGURE 19.3 Five-year returns of US and emerging market equities.

deviation of x over some specified periodicity, such as monthly. The standard deviation of longer-interval returns spanning q periods is given by

$$\sigma(x_t + \ldots + x_{t+q-1}) = \sigma_x \sqrt{q + 2\sum_{j=1}^{q-1}(q-j)\rho_{x_t,x_{t+j}}} \qquad (19.8)$$

The term $\rho_{x_t,x_{t+j}}$ is the autocorrelation of x with its j-th lag. If all auto-correlations equal zero, then the standard deviation scales precisely with the square root of time. However, if any of the autocorrelations are nonzero, this assumption gives an incorrect estimate of longer-horizon risk. We derive a similar relationship for the correlation between two assets X and Y, in terms of their log returns x and y:

$$\rho\left(x_t + \ldots + x_{t+q-1}, y_t + \ldots + y_{t+q-1}\right)$$
$$= \frac{q\rho_{x_t,y_t} + \sum_{j=1}^{q-1}(q-j)(\rho_{x_{t+j},x_t} + \rho_{x_t,y_{t+j}})}{\sqrt{q + 2\sum_{j=1}^{q-1}(q-j)\rho_{x_t,x_{t+j}}}\sqrt{q + 2\sum_{j=1}^{q-1}(q-j)\rho_{y_t,y_{t+j}}}} \tag{19.9}$$

Long-interval correlations depend on lagged cross-correlations, ρ_{x_{t+j},x_t} and $\rho_{x_t,y_{t+j}}$, in addition to the autocorrelations of both return series. If all lagged correlations in this expression are set equal to zero, it simplifies to the contemporaneous correlation ρ_{x_t,y_t}, which would then apply to any horizon.

To compute interval error in practice, we directly estimate covariances using overlapping longer interval returns such as annual returns, convert the results to monthly periodicity, and subtract covariances estimated from monthly data in the same subsample. We normalize by the same denominator as before.

$$Interval\ Error = IE(A,B)$$
$$= \sqrt{\frac{1}{K}\sum_{j=1}^{K}\left(\frac{\rho_{AB,ann,j}\sqrt{\sigma_{A,ann,j}\sigma_{B,ann,j}}/12 - \rho_{AB,m,j}\sqrt{\sigma_{A,m,j}\sigma_{B,m,j}}}{\sqrt{\sigma_{A,m}\sigma_{B,m}}}\right)^2} \tag{19.10}$$

$$IE(A,A) = \sqrt{\frac{1}{K}\sum_{j=1}^{K}\left(\frac{\sigma_{A,ann,j}/\sqrt{12} - \sigma_{A,m,j}}{\sigma_{A,m}}\right)^2} \tag{19.11}$$

Mapping Error

Factors are subject to mapping error, but assets are not. Because assets define the investment opportunity set (see Chapter 8), factors must be mapped onto assets to be investable. The weights that best track a factor in the future are not known in advance. They must be estimated, which introduces error. To quantify mapping error, we focus on one subsample at a time, denoted by subscript j. We first derive factor-mimicking portfolios using this subsample and compute their covariances in that same sample. We then subtract the covariances of the factor-mimicking portfolios whose weights are constructed from the immediately preceding independent subsample, but which are evaluated using the returns in subsample j. We use the subscript $\hat{A}\hat{B}$ to refer to factor-mimicking portfolios built from the prior return subsample. We once again normalize each error and calculate mapping error as

$$Mapping\ Error = ME(A,B)$$

$$= \sqrt{\frac{1}{K}\sum_{j=1}^{K}\left(\frac{\rho_{AB,m,j}\sqrt{\sigma_{A,m,j}\sigma_{B,m,j}} - \rho_{\hat{A}\hat{B},m,j}\sqrt{\sigma_{\hat{A},m,j}\sigma_{\hat{B},m,j}}}{\sqrt{\sigma_{A,m}\sigma_{B,m}}}\right)^2} \qquad (19.12)$$

$$ME(A,A) = \sqrt{\frac{1}{K}\sum_{j=1}^{K}\left(\frac{\sigma_{A,m,j} - \sigma_{\hat{A},m,j}}{\sigma_{A,m}}\right)^2} \qquad (19.13)$$

Composite Instability

By construction, these four components of estimation error are mutually independent, which means we can combine them into a composite instability score by summing the squared value of each error and taking the square root of the sum. It is helpful to think about each individual error as the "standard deviation" of the error attributable to that source. As we add more sources of errors, the composite instability score increases, but by less than the sum of the errors. The composite instability score implicitly accounts for the fact that errors diversify each other.

$$Composite\ Instability\ Score(A,B)$$

$$= \sqrt{SSE(A,B)^2 + ISE(A,B)^2 + IE(A,B)^2 + ME(A,B)^2} \qquad (19.14)$$

Equation 19.15 summarizes errors across the entire covariance matrix:

$$Total\ Covariance\ Error = \sqrt{\frac{1}{N^2}\sum_{A=1}^{N}\sum_{B=1}^{N}E(A,B)^2} \qquad (19.15)$$

$E(A,B)$ could be any of the four errors or the composite instability score. By averaging across all elements in the covariance matrix, we capture the relative importance of standard deviations and correlations. An error in one of N standard deviations matters more than an error in one of $N(N-1)/2$ correlations. The total covariance error calculation naturally overweights standard deviations because errors in the volatility of an asset are reflected throughout the row and column of that asset in the matrix. Collectively, errors in correlations are also important. These errors are reflected in every element of the matrix except the diagonal.

Empirical Analysis of Asset Class Errors

Table 19.1 shows the errors corresponding to the six major asset classes we introduced in Chapter 2. (We exclude cash equivalents because their volatility is small to begin with.) These calculations apply the above formulas to monthly returns from January 1976 through December 2015. We set the small-sample window equal to 60 months, and the interval-error window equal to 12 months. The bottom row in Table 19.1 shows the total error averaged across each element in the six-by-six covariance matrix. We see that interval error contributes the most to covariance instability, on average, whereas independent-sample error contributes the least. Recall that it is the sum of squared errors of each type of error, not the sum of raw values that equals composite instability.

Composite instability and its components differ across asset classes. The remainder of the table shows errors in standard deviations for each asset class. Consider commodities, for example. Its small-sample error of 0.25 tells us that, for a randomly chosen 60-month period, its standard deviation is likely to be 25% higher or 25% lower than its standard deviation estimated from the full 40-year sample. Its relatively low independent-sample error implies that trailing 60-month standard deviations are better predictors of future standard deviations for commodities than other asset classes. Lastly, it has more interval error than other asset classes, which means that its standard deviation tends to differ quite a lot when computed from monthly returns as opposed to annual returns.

TABLE 19.1 Risk Instability Across Asset Classes (in Standardized Units)

Errors in Standard Deviation	Small-Sample Error	Independent-Sample Error	Interval Error	Composite Instability
US Equities	0.19	0.28	0.27	0.43
Foreign Developed Market Equities	0.17	0.21	0.29	0.40
Emerging Market Equities	0.15	0.21	0.25	0.36
Treasury Bonds	0.17	0.13	0.22	0.31
US Corporate Bonds	0.26	0.25	0.16	0.39
Commodities	0.25	0.12	0.30	0.40
Total Covariance Matrix Error	0.23	0.15	0.29	0.41

It is important to remember that these results pertain to monthly data, a five-year investment horizon, and differences between monthly and annual measurement intervals. We chose this calibration to accord with common practice for asset allocation, but we could just as easily have run this analysis with different assumptions. If so, we should expect somewhat different results. Ultimately, the calibration of these metrics should match – or at least approximate – the way an investor estimates risk and evaluates it out-of-sample.

BUILDING A STABILITY-ADJUSTED RETURN DISTRIBUTION

Table 19.1 shows that estimation error may vary quite substantially across asset classes. We now apply a method introduced by Kritzman and Turkington (2016) to construct better-behaved portfolios based on this information about the relative stability of covariances. Rather than assume future returns come from a multivariate normal distribution with a given covariance matrix, we model the distribution of asset class returns as a composite of many different normal distributions, each of which has its own covariance structure. As we discuss in more detail shortly, this composite return distribution is not normal, nor is it likely to be elliptical. (See Chapter 12 for a discussion of ellipticality.)

We begin by estimating covariance matrices for every overlapping subsample of a chosen size (such as five years) drawn from a large historical return sample, based on the return interval that interests us. For each subsample, we also estimate a covariance matrix from its complement in the large sample based on shorter-interval returns such as monthly returns. We calculate matrices of covariance errors by subtracting each complementary-sample covariance matrix from its corresponding small-sample covariance matrix. In contrast to the previous section, in which we computed each source of error separately, these error matrices account for all three components of estimation error simultaneously. (We do not include mapping error because we assume we are investing in asset classes, which are directly investable.) They reflect small-sample error because the subsamples Σ_{si} are smaller than complementary samples Σ_{ci}. They reflect independent-sample error because the subsamples are independent of their complements in the large sample. And they reflect interval error because the subsamples and their complements use different return intervals to compute covariances.

Next, we add each of the error matrices to a baseline covariance matrix, such as the full-sample covariance.[2] We now have a collection of many covariance matrices which represents risk in the presence of estimation error. Then, holding expected returns constant, we use Monte Carlo simulation to draw many – say, 1,000 – random returns from the multivariate normal distribution corresponding to each error-adjusted covariance matrix. We combine all simulated returns to form the stability-adjusted distribution. We use this distribution as we would any other to form a portfolio. We have effectively internalized within this composite distribution the estimation error that prevailed throughout a wide range of regimes in our historical sample. Figure 19.4 presents a visualization of this procedure.

Even though we constructed the stability-adjusted return distribution from normal distributions, it is distinctly non-normal. Why is this so? It is true that the sum of normally distributed variables is normally distributed. And according to the central limit theorem, it is also true that the sum of many independent random variables that are not themselves normally distributed converge to a normal distribution. These forces create a strong pull toward normality when variables are summed. However, we are not summing random variables when we build the stability-adjusted return distribution. Rather, we are mixing distributions drawn from different assumptions into one composite distribution. We do so for hundreds of subsample covariance matrices.

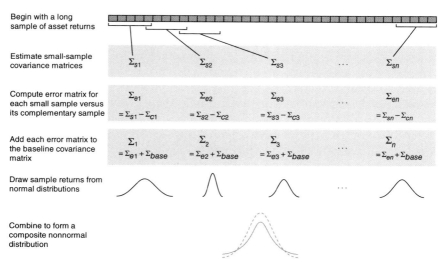

FIGURE 19.4 Constructing the stability-adjusted return distribution.

It is easy to visualize why the result is non-normal if we imagine combining just two subsamples, one with a low standard deviation that leads to a high concentration of observations close to the mean in the composite distribution and the other with higher standard deviations that has more outlying observations in the composite distribution. Figure 19.5 reveals that the composite distribution is non-normal: it has positive excess kurtosis.[3]

Now consider a hypothetical multivariate mixture of two asset classes with 0% means, with equal variances, and which are positively (+0.8) correlated half of the time and negatively (–0.8) correlated the other half of the time. This combination, shown in Figure 19.6, displays a complex

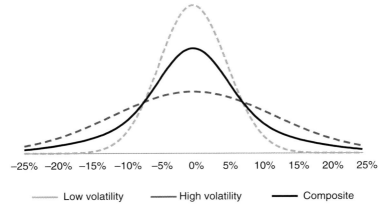

FIGURE 19.5 Mixture of two normal distributions.

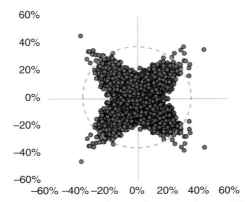

FIGURE 19.6 Multivariate mixture of asset classes with unstable correlation.

interaction between asset classes. It defies description by the average correlation of zero, which would imply that the returns would be spread evenly along the boundary of any concentric circle centered on the average of the observations.

The stability-adjusted distribution will always be symmetric, but it will never be normal. And it will be elliptical only if correlations are reasonably stable through time and all asset classes have the same amount of instability in their standard deviations. This situation never occurs in practice, so we can safely assume that the distribution is not elliptical. This finding has important implications for portfolio construction.

DETERMINING THE OPTIMAL ALLOCATION

In Chapter 12, we explained that for a given time horizon or assuming returns are expressed in continuous units, mean-variance analysis is identical to maximizing expected utility if returns are elliptically distributed or if utility is quadratic. We can rule out ellipticality for the stability-adjusted return distribution, so our choice between mean-variance analysis and full-scale optimization hinges on the utility function. (See Chapter 12 for a description of full-scale optimization.) Mean and variance are good descriptors of upward-sloping concave utility functions, such as the log-wealth utility function. In these situations, we estimate the covariance matrix from the stability-adjusted return sample and apply mean-variance analysis to identify the optimal portfolio.

However, some investors face thresholds and therefore have preferences that are better represented by a kinked utility function that displays sharp aversion to losses below a given threshold. In this case it may be preferable to apply full-scale optimization to the stability-adjusted return sample to account for the nuances in its distribution. We compare both approaches in our empirical analysis.

EMPIRICAL ANALYSIS

We test stability-adjusted optimization using the 40-year return history for the seven asset classes we used in our base case example in Chapter 2. In this analysis, we focus exclusively on the moderate portfolio from our base case, which targets an expected return of 7.5%. We select overlapping sub-samples of 60 months and use annual returns to compute the long-interval covariances. We evaluate the portfolios based on returns that are completely independent of the returns used to build them by following the procedure described below:

1. We select the first five-year subsample from the full sample and set it aside.
2. We then build a stability-adjusted return sample using the remaining data in the original sample.
3. Next, we use this complementary sample to build six portfolios: a portfolio that ignores errors, one that applies Bayesian shrinkage,[4] and one formed from the stability-adjusted return sample, all using full-scale optimization, and then again using mean-variance analysis.
4. We repeat steps 1 through 3 for all 36 testing samples, which are overlapping periods ending in December.
5. Using a variety of metrics, we evaluate each portfolio in the subsample that was held out of the complementary sample used to form it.

Table 19.2 presents the results of this experiment based on full-scale optimization. As in Chapter 12, we assume a kinked utility function with a

TABLE 19.2 Full-Scale Optimization

Average Optimal Weights	Ignoring Errors (%)	Bayesian Shrinkage (%)	Stability Adjusted (%)
US Equities	25.0	20.1	33.3
Foreign Developed Market Equities	19.6	18.9	16.7
Emerging Market Equities	13.6	17.2	11.8
Treasury Bonds	20.1	13.9	27.9
US Corporate Bonds	15.6	15.3	7.9
Commodities	3.8	5.7	1.4
Cash Equivalents	2.4	8.9	1.0
10 Percentile Worst Outcome Across Testing Samples			
12-Month Volatility	16.9	16.9	15.8
12-Month Value at Risk (10% significance)	−24.1	−23.9	−22.9
12-Month Value at Risk (5% significance)	−28.5	−28.3	−25.2
Worst 12-Month Return	−32.7%	−32.5%	−29.3%

baseline of power utility with a risk aversion parameter of 5, and an added penalty of 5 units of utility per unit of loss below –5% per year. In each optimization, we allow the weights of each asset class to vary from 0% to 50% in 5% increments, and we draw 500 random observations from each individual training covariance matrix to form the stability-adjusted return distribution. On average, the stability-adjusted portfolios favor US equities and Treasury bonds compared to the other approaches, and they tend to invest less in corporate bonds, commodities, and cash equivalents. Even though Bayesian shrinkage allocates the portfolio more evenly across asset classes than error-blind optimization, it produces no meaningful benefit. The stability-adjusted portfolios fare slightly better, truncating the rare, but extreme, losses by up to 3.3 percentage points. The relatively modest size of this benefit occurs because there is limited opportunity to improve stability with a static asset mix.

Next, we show results for mean-variance analysis. The leftmost panel of results in Table 19.3 shows results for optimization disallowing short positions in the asset classes, as was the case for the full-scale optimization example. The strong similarity of these results to those of full-scale optimization should give us comfort. Even in the presence of kinked utility and nonelliptical distributions, mean-variance analysis yields a compelling approximation.

The rightmost panel of Table 19.3 shows the results when we allow portfolios to take short positions or leverage in each asset class down to –100% or up to 200% of total wealth, respectively. As we might expect, optimizing by ignoring estimation error performs poorly when we allow short positions and leverage. Though not apparent from the average weights, this approach sometimes takes large long and short positions based on the assumption that these positions hedge each other's risk. Unfortunately, they may fail to do so out-of-sample, thereby exposing the portfolio to large losses. The Bayesian approach largely avoids this trap and produces consistent performance. Interestingly, the stability-adjusted portfolios perform better, on average, with less onerous constraints. In short, the impact of errors becomes more important when there are fewer constraints, because constraints act as natural protection against very large, yet misguided, allocations.

Figure 19.7 summarizes the benefits of stability-adjusted optimization in the three settings we tested.

TABLE 19.3 Mean-Variance Approach to Stability Optimization

	Long Only			Long-Short		
Average Optimal Weights	Ignoring Errors (%)	Bayesian Shrinkage (%)	Stability Adjusted (%)	Ignoring Errors (%)	Bayesian Shrinkage (%)	Stability Adjusted (%)
US Equities	24.7	21.2	32.5	24.6	21.2	33.4
Foreign Developed Market Equities	19.4	18.8	18.0	19.3	18.8	20.2
Emerging Market Equities	14.1	16.7	10.9	13.8	16.7	13.0
Treasury Bonds	22.4	13.7	24.6	30.7	13.7	56.7
US Corporate Bonds	13.9	14.8	12.3	12.2	14.8	–13.1
Commodities	3.6	5.9	1.3	4.0	5.9	–5.4
Cash Equivalents	1.9	9.0	0.3	–4.7	9.0	–4.8
10 Percentile Worst Outcome Across Testing Samples						
12-Month Volatility	17.1	17.1	15.8	18.7	17.1	16.1
12-Month Value at Risk (10% significance)	–25.3	–24.9	–23.5	–29.9	–24.9	–21.8
12-Month Value at Risk (5% significance)	–29.7	–28.9	–25.9	–34.6	–28.9	–23.9
Worst 12-Month Return	–33.0	–32.6	–30.1	–35.7	–32.6	–28.2

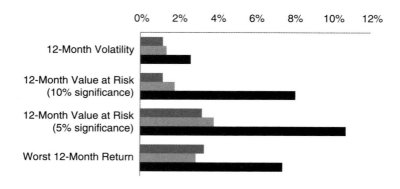

FIGURE 19.7 Stability adjustment improvement to optimization that ignores errors (10% worst outcomes).

THE BOTTOM LINE

We argue that estimation error does not at all invalidate optimization. Nevertheless, we should not ignore it. Traditional approaches to managing estimation error, such as Bayesian shrinkage and resampling, reduce a portfolio's sensitivity to estimation error. We recommend an alternative approach to addressing estimation error called stability-adjusted optimization. This approach measures the vulnerability of covariances to estimation error and internalizes this information in a new stability-adjusted return sample. This approach assumes implicitly that the relative stability of covariances is persistent. This makes intuitive sense. Correlations that are large in absolute value most likely reflect enduring structural relationships. Those that are small in absolute value more likely reflect noise and therefore shift more regularly through time. Thus, covariances that reflect large absolute correlations should be more stable than those that reflect low absolute correlations.

Whatever the reason, we offer empirical evidence that stability-adjusted portfolios are less vulnerable to extremely adverse outcomes than portfolios that ignore estimation error or those that rely on Bayesian shrinkage. Nevertheless, to the extent that estimation error is evidence of shifting regimes, a dynamic approach to asset allocation may offer a better solution than a portfolio of fixed weights. We explore this issue in Chapters 10 and 22.

RELATED TOPICS

- Chapter 5 explores interval error in detail.
- Chapter 8 discusses mapping error in the context of factor investing.
- Chapter 12 introduces full-scale optimization, which we apply in this chapter.
- Chapters 10 and 22 illustrate the benefits of dynamic allocation for achieving more stable risk profiles.

REFERENCES

Cocoma, P., Czasonis, M., Kritzman, M., and Turkington, D. 2017. "Facts about Factors." *Journal of Portfolio Management*, Vol. 43, No. 5 (Special QES Issue).

Kritzman, M. and Turkington, D. 2016. "Stability-Adjusted Portfolios," *Journal of Portfolio Management*, Vol. 42, No. 5 (QES Special Issue).

Michaud, R. O. and Michaud, R. O. 2008. *Efficient Asset Management: A Practical Guide to Stock Portfolio Optimization and Asset Allocation, Second Edition.* New York: Oxford University Press, Inc.

Scherer, B. 2002. "Portfolio Resampling: Review and Critique," *Financial Analysts Journal*, Vol. 58, No. 6 (November/December).

NOTES

1. It is possible that expected return forecasts will be biased, and other methods for reducing their susceptibility to error may be warranted.
2. We typically also recenter each error covariance matrix by subtracting the element-by-element median covariance matrix, prior to adding the baseline matrix. This correction ensures that we are not shifting the average covariances away from the baseline matrix, but just adding instability around them. Finally, if some of the resulting covariance matrices are not invertible, we apply a standard correction using Principal Components Analysis to render them positive-definite (see Chapter 25 for more details).
3. This simplified example pertains to a mixture of two distributions. The same effect holds for mixtures of larger (finite) numbers of distributions. Excess kurtosis also arises in the limit as the number of distributions we combine grows arbitrarily large. The mixture of an infinite, continuous set of normal distributions will, in fact, converge to the familiar Student's t-distribution if the set of variances that describes the multitude of normal curves follows an inverse gamma

distribution. The inverse gamma distribution is a reasonable assumption, which, like variance, does not permit negative values. This theoretical relationship is useful because the Student's t-distribution is well known to have fatter tails than the normal distribution.

4. We shrink the standard deviations by blending them equally with their cross-sectional mean, and we do the same for the correlations.

CHAPTER 20

Leverage Versus Concentration

THE CHALLENGE

Theory shows that it is preferable to apply leverage to a less risky portfolio than to concentrate a portfolio in riskier assets for the purpose of raising expected return. This theoretical result, however, relies upon assumptions that may be only partially valid, if at all. In this chapter, we relax the assumptions that produce this theoretical result to match real-world conditions, and we re-examine the efficacy of leverage and concentration. We find that what is theoretically indisputable does not always hold empirically when we introduce more plausible assumptions.

LEVERAGE IN THEORY

The notion that investors are better served by applying leverage to a less risky portfolio rather than concentrating a portfolio in riskier assets in order to raise expected return has an impressive theoretical lineage. As we discussed in Chapter 2, Markowitz (1952) introduced portfolio theory, which shows how to combine risky assets into efficient portfolios that yield the highest expected return for a given level of risk. He called a continuum of such portfolios the efficient frontier. Tobin (1958) showed that the investment process can be separated into two distinct steps: the construction of an efficient portfolio as described by Markowitz, and the decision to combine this efficient portfolio with a risk-free investment. This two-step process is called the separation theorem. Tobin showed that there is a unique portfolio along the efficient frontier, which when combined with lending or borrowing at the risk-free interest rate dominates all other portfolios along the efficient frontier. This is the tangency portfolio, denoted as M in Figure 20.1. The curved line represents the efficient frontier, whereas the straight line emanating from the vertical axis at the risk-free rate depicts the efficient

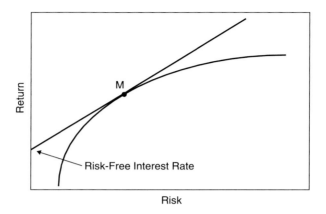

FIGURE 20.1   Efficient frontier with borrowing and lending.

frontier with borrowing or lending. It is called the capital market line. The segment of the capital market line between the vertical axis and its tangency point with the efficient frontier represents a combination of lending and portfolio M. That segment of the capital market line that continues beyond portfolio M represents a combination of portfolio M and borrowing at the risk-free rate, which is to say, leverage.

Sharpe (1964) extended Markowitz's and Tobin's insights to develop a theory of market equilibrium under conditions of risk, which he called the Capital Asset Pricing Model. Sharpe showed that portfolio M is the market portfolio comprising all investable assets in proportion to their total value, assuming all investors have identical expectations for returns, standard deviations, and correlations. In equilibrium, the market portfolio offers the maximum achievable diversification. It follows that investors who seek returns above or below the expected return of the market portfolio prefer points along the capital market line as opposed to the efficient frontier, because these combinations of the market portfolio and borrowing or lending offer less risk than portfolios along the efficient frontier. Or, for investors who target a given level of risk, it follows that leveraging lower-risk asset classes increases expected returns more than concentrating a portfolio in riskier asset classes.

Each building block of this elegant result rests on certain assumptions, which may be convenient, but often fail to conform to real-world conditions. Portfolio theory, for example, assumes either that returns are elliptically distributed or that investor preferences are well approximated by mean and variance. It also assumes implicitly that investors can estimate expected returns, standard deviations, and correlations reasonably well.

The separation theorem assumes that investors can borrow or lend an unlimited amount of funds at the risk-free rate without being required to meet margin calls or to post collateral. And the Capital Asset Pricing Model assumes that investors have the same expectations for returns, standard deviations, and correlations. We relax these assumptions individually, and then collectively, to match real-world conditions.

We first assume that investor preferences may be better described by a kinked utility function than a smooth concave function, and we combine this assumption with empirical distributions that are not elliptically distributed.

Next, we acknowledge that investors make errors when they estimate expected returns, standard deviations, and correlations. We consider three types of estimation error: independent-sample error, interval error, and small-sample error. Independent-sample error refers to the discrepancy between historical mean returns, standard deviations, and correlations and future realizations of these values. Interval error refers to the discrepancy between standard deviations and correlations estimated from high-frequency observations, such as monthly returns, and longer-horizon extrapolations of these values, such as annual and multi-year standard deviations and correlations. To the extent that lagged correlations are nonzero, standard deviations do not scale with the square root of time, and correlations differ depending on the return interval used to estimate them. Small-sample error addresses the fact that investors typically use large samples of historical returns to determine the expected returns, standard deviations, and correlations of smaller samples. (See Chapter 19 for more details about estimation error.)

Next, we relax the assumption that investors can borrow at the risk-free rate by adding a premium to this rate. We could extend this analysis to account for collateral, margin calls, and the opportunity cost of deploying capital to collateralize borrowing instead of deploying it in more productive ways. For simplicity, we do not account for these complexities in this chapter.

Finally, we allow for heterogeneous expectations of returns, standard deviations, and correlations by assuming certain investors are skilled at forecasting future returns.

LEVERAGE IN PRACTICE

The aggressive portfolio we derived in Chapter 2 has an expected return of 9%. Suppose this return is not sufficient for our needs. What if we require a 10% expected return? One way to achieve this outcome is to concentrate the portfolio in asset classes with higher expected returns. This optimal

TABLE 20.1 Leverage Versus Concentration in Theory

	Optimal Concentrated Portfolio Weights	Optimal Levered Portfolio Weights
US Equities	25.2%	43.7%
Foreign Developed Market Equities	39.2%	39.7%
Emerging Market Equities	35.6%	15.6%
Treasury Bonds	0.0%	39.2%
US Corporate Bonds	0.0%	31.5%
Commodities	0.0%	10.7%
Borrowing	0.0%	−80.4%
Sum of Weights	100.0%	100.0%
Expected Return	10.0%	10.4%
Standard Deviation	18.6%	18.6%
Sharpe Ratio	0.35	0.37
Excess Return of Levered Portfolio		0.37%

portfolio, which is close to the right end of the efficient frontier, is shown in the first column of Table 20.1. Another way to increase expected return is to lever the portfolio. The second column of Table 20.1 shows the optimal levered portfolio that has the same risk as the concentrated portfolio. The expected return of the levered portfolio minus the expected return of the concentrated portfolio equals 0.37%. Given our assumptions, we would expect the levered portfolio to outperform the concentrated portfolio by 0.37% per year.

Because we have employed mean-variance analysis to identify these portfolios, the results presume that asset class returns are elliptically distributed or that investor preferences are well approximated by mean and variance. Neither assumption is literally true. We relax these assumptions in two distinct ways. First, we estimate the semi-standard deviation of the concentrated and levered portfolios from Table 20.1 given a nonelliptical distribution. The semi-standard deviation is simply the standard deviation calculated using the subsample of returns for each asset class that fall below the full-sample mean.[1] We also calculate the Sortino ratio, which is equivalent to the Sharpe ratio but with the semi-standard deviation as the denominator. Second, we calculate the expected utility of each portfolio based on a kinked utility function and convert these expected utilities into their certainty equivalent values.[2] These results are shown in Table 20.2.

TABLE 20.2   Leverage Versus Concentration with Nonelliptical Returns and Kinked Utility

	Optimal Concentrated Portfolio	Optimal Levered Portfolio
Expected Return	10.0%	10.4%
Standard Deviation	18.6%	18.6%
Sharpe Ratio	0.35	0.37
Semi-Standard Deviation	19.5%	19.3%
Sortino Ratio	33.3%	35.5%
Implied Return at 18.6% Semi-Standard Deviation	9.7%	10.1%
Excess Return of Levered Portfolio		0.42%
Kinked Utility (Levered – Concentrated)*		2.4
Certainty Equivalent (Levered – Concentrated)		0.38%

* This table shows the average utility of each portfolio over our sample period. We derive kinked utility assuming a kink at –5%, curvature of 5, and annual periodicity.

Although the levered and concentrated portfolios have the same standard deviation by design, they have different semi-standard deviations. Therefore, to make the returns comparable, we must adjust them based on their semi-standard deviation. To do this, we simply multiply the Sortino ratio of each portfolio by the standard deviation of 18.6% and add the risk-free rate of 3.5%. This calculation tells us the return we should expect from each portfolio assuming they have the same semi-standard deviation. Interestingly, the levered portfolio outperforms the concentrated portfolio by 0.42%. When we relax these assumptions, we find that the levered portfolio is expected to outperform the concentrated portfolio by an even greater margin. This result is counterintuitive in the sense that most investors might expect leverage to amplify, rather than reduce, the impact of non-normal distributions and asymmetric preferences. A closer inspection of the asset class semivariances provides insight into this result.

Table 20.3 reveals that equities and commodities have semi-standard deviations that exceed their standard deviations, whereas fixed-income asset classes have semi-standard deviations that are lower than their standard deviations. Because the levered portfolio is allocated 60% to fixed income, whereas the concentrated portfolio is allocated entirely to equities, the former

TABLE 20.3   Asset Class Semi-Standard Deviations

	Semi-Standard Deviation (%)	Standard Deviation (%)	Semi Minus Full (%)
US Equities	17.4	16.6	0.9
Foreign Developed Market Equities	19.5	18.6	0.9
Emerging Market Equities	28.0	26.6	1.4
Treasury Bonds	5.3	5.7	−0.4
US Corporate Bonds	7.0	7.3	−0.3
Commodities	21.4	20.6	0.8
Cash Equivalents	1.0	1.1	−0.1

has a lower semi-standard deviation than the latter. In this specific example, the normality assumption leads us to underestimate the outperformance of leverage relative to concentration.

The bottom two rows of Table 20.2 compare the levered and concentrated portfolios through the lens of a kinked utility function. We see from these results that the levered portfolio offers higher kinked utility than the concentrated portfolio, which is consistent with our analysis of semi-standard deviation. Although both portfolios experience returns below the kink approximately 20% of the time, the average loss below the kink is larger for the concentrated portfolio. We convert these average expected utilities into certainty equivalents by reversing the expected utility function (which expresses expected utility in terms of return) to solve for the return as a function of expected utility. We find that the levered portfolio has a certainty equivalent that is 0.38% higher than the concentrated portfolio.

Next, we drop the assumption that investors can estimate returns and covariances reliably and that the standard deviation scales with the square root of time (as was done in Chapter 19):

1. We partition our returns data into a testing subsample (the first 60 months in the sample) and a training subsample (the remaining 420 months in the sample).
2. We estimate the asset class covariances from the training subsample by annualizing monthly values.
3. We construct a concentrated portfolio with an expected return of 10%. For the expected return of each asset class, we use the full-sample expected returns from Chapter 2. This introduces estimation error because the returns realized in each testing subsample differ, often

significantly, from the full-sample values. For the expected covariance matrix, we use the annualized covariance matrix from the training subsample.

4. We construct a levered portfolio with the same expected standard deviation as the concentrated portfolio, based on the same return and covariance assumptions.
5. We record the realized return and standard deviation of the concentrated and levered portfolios based on the outcomes in the testing subsample. We use rolling one-year returns from the testing subsample to estimate covariances.
6. We roll the testing subsample forward one year, and repeat these steps until we have results for 36 testing samples. For each iteration, the training subsample includes all months in the full sample that are before and after the testing sample.

The results from this experiment, which we show in Table 20.4, account for independent-sample error, interval error, and small-sample error. In this table, the realized returns, standard deviations, and Sharpe ratios are averages across the 36 training subsamples. Because we average each measure individually, the reported return, standard deviation, and Sharpe ratio are not internally consistent. Therefore, to compare the levered and concentrated portfolios on a risk-equivalent basis, we multiply their average Sharpe ratios by their standard deviation of 18.6%. We find that leverage underperforms concentration by 47 basis points in the presence of estimation error. The likely cause of this underperformance is the tendency of the levered portfolio to magnify errors because it is less constrained than the concentrated portfolio.

TABLE 20.4   Leverage Versus Concentration with Estimation Error

	Optimal Concentrated Portfolio	Optimal Levered Portfolio
Average Realized Return	11.0%	11.4%
Average Realized Standard Deviation	16.8%	18.2%
Average Sharpe Ratio	0.54	0.51
Implied Return at 18.6% Standard Deviation	13.5%	13.0%
Excess Return of Levered Portfolio		−0.47%

TABLE 20.5   Leverage Versus Concentration with Borrowing Costs

	Optimal Concentrated Portfolio	Optimal Levered Portfolio
Expected Return	10.0%	10.2%
Standard Deviation	18.6%	18.6%
Sharpe Ratio	0.35	0.36
Excess Return of Levered Portfolio		0.17%

Next, we return to our theoretical baseline and relax the assumption that the investor can borrow at the risk-free rate. Specifically, we increase the borrowing cost by 25 basis points per year, such that the investor borrows at a rate of 3.75% (0.25% plus the risk-free rate of 3.5%).

Table 20.5 reveals that borrowing costs reduce the outperformance of the levered portfolio from 37 basis points to 17 basis points. A more comprehensive analysis could incorporate the opportunity costs associated with collateral and margin requirements; however, we do not account for those complexities here.

Next, we lift all the previously mentioned assumptions at the same time. These results are shown in Table 20.6. When we account for the real-world complexities of kinked utility with nonelliptical distributions, estimation error, and higher borrowing costs, we find that the levered portfolio underperforms the concentrated portfolio by 0.83% on a risk-equivalent basis.

The final assumption that we relax is that investors have homogeneous expectations for returns, standard deviations, and correlations. To introduce forecasting skill to our simulations, we modify the expected returns in each

TABLE 20.6   Leverage Versus Concentration with Kinked Utility, Nonellipticality, Estimation Error, and Higher Borrowing Costs

	Optimal Concentrated Portfolio	Optimal Levered Portfolio
Average Realized Return	11.3%	11.1%
Average Realized Standard Deviation	17.2%	18.8%
Average Sortino Ratio	0.56	0.52
Implied Return at 18.6% Standard Deviation	10.5%	9.6%
Excess Return of Levered Portfolio		−0.8%

FIGURE 20.2 Outperformance of leverage versus concentration.

of the optimizations to incorporate information from the testing sample. Specifically, we compute a weighted average expected return with a 95% weight on the full-sample expected returns from Chapter 2 and a 5% weight on the period-specific average returns from the testing samples. Effectively, 5% of the expected returns is in sample. Even a small amount of information about future outcomes has a dramatic impact on performance. Figure 20.2 summarizes the impact of lifting each constraint we have discussed in this chapter. At the bottom, it shows the outperformance of leverage in the presence of skill. Leverage is more valuable to investors with skill because it enables them to increase their exposure to asset classes that they expect to outperform.

THE BOTTOM LINE

It is apparent from Figure 20.2 that the outperformance of leverage over concentration, although theoretically sensible, does not always survive real-world conditions. We relax the following constraints individually and then collectively:

- The assumption that returns are elliptically distributed and that investor preferences can be approximated by mean and variance, as well as the assumption that means and covariances can be estimated reliably.
- The assumption that investors can borrow at the risk-free rate.
- The assumption that investors have homogeneous expectations for returns and covariances of asset classes, and that no investors have forecasting skill.

For the same level of risk, we find that the expected outperformance of the levered portfolio falls from 37 basis points in theory to −83 basis points after accounting for asymmetric preferences with nonelliptical distributions, and realistic borrowing costs. However, if we assume skill in forecasting returns, leverage outperforms concentration by 163 basis points despite all these complexities.

The results we present in this chapter reflect a specific set of asset classes and assumptions, and do not hold universally. However, this framework could be customized easily to accommodate a wide range of assumptions and scenarios.

RELATED TOPICS

- Chapter 19 shows how to quantify estimation error and form portfolios with more stable return distributions.

REFERENCES

Markowitz, H. 1952. "Portfolio Selection," *Journal of Finance*, Vol. 7, No. 1 (March).

Sharpe, W. 1964. "A Theory of Market Equilibrium under Conditions of Risk," *Journal of Finance*, Vol. 19, No. 3 (September).

Tobin, J. 1958. "Liquidity Preference as Behavior Towards Risk," *Review of Economic Studies*, Vol. 25, No. 2 (February).

NOTES

1. The deviations should be calculated against the full-sample mean. This way, the semi-standard deviation collapses to the standard deviation if the return distribution is symmetric. We compute the semi-standard deviations for each asset class, and then combine them with full-sample correlations to arrive at a semi-covariance matrix. We cannot compute semi-correlations because they would not be comparable to full-sample correlations.
2. In Chapter 25, we define the kinked utility function more precisely.

CHAPTER 21

Rebalancing

THE CHALLENGE

In Chapter 2, we showed how to identify an efficient asset mix given assumptions about the expected returns, standard deviations, and correlations of asset classes. In Chapter 12, we introduced full-scale optimization as a method to construct efficient portfolios when the assumptions necessary for mean-variance analysis do not hold. And, in Chapters 15 and 16, we showed how investors can use multi-goal optimization to construct portfolios that are sensitive to a benchmark or factor profile. Regardless of which method investors use to form portfolios, the portfolios become suboptimal almost immediately after implementation. Why? Price changes are not proportional across asset classes, so the portfolio weights drift away from the optimal targets over time. If there were no transaction costs, investors could trade daily, or even more often, to maintain the optimal weights. In practice, investors face a trade-off: they must balance the transaction cost of restoring the optimal weights against the cost of remaining suboptimal.

Most investors employ simple heuristics to manage this trade-off. Some implement calendar-based rebalancing policies, in which they rebalance each month, quarter, or year. Others impose tolerance bands in which they rebalance when the exposure to any asset class drifts more than two percentage points from its target, for example. These approaches are better than not rebalancing at all. But they are arbitrary. Is total cost minimized by tolerance bands of one percentage point or two percentage points? Should equity asset classes have wider bands than fixed-income asset classes? Should investors rebalance in periods when there has been little drift?

We propose that investors implement a rebalancing policy that minimizes explicitly the sum of transaction costs and suboptimality costs, including the expected future costs associated with each decision, at each point in time. Rebalancing is a multiperiod problem: a decision to rebalance today, or not, has implications for expected suboptimality and transaction costs in the future.

Sun, Fan, Chen, Schouwenaars, and Albota (2006) and Kritzman, Myrgren, and Page (2008) showed how to use dynamic programming to develop a rebalancing road map. This approach gives the optimal rebalancing decision for every possible combination of portfolio weights that may arise at each decision point during the investment horizon. They showed that this approach outperforms calendar and tolerance band approaches by reducing both transaction costs and suboptimality costs. Unfortunately, their dynamic programming solution suffers from the curse of dimensionality; it is intractable for portfolios with more than a few asset classes.

Markowitz and van Dijk (2003) introduced a quadratic heuristic to rebalance portfolios to capture changes in expected returns of assets through time. Kritzman, Myrgren, and Page (2009) applied this approach, which they call the Markowitz-van Dijk (MvD) heuristic, to the rebalancing problem. They show that the MvD solution is remarkably close to the dynamic programming solution for small numbers of assets, and that it scales manageably to several hundred assets. In this chapter, we begin with a simple example that illustrates the dynamic programming approach to highlight the intertemporal nature of the rebalancing problem. Then we show how the MvD heuristic can be used to rebalance portfolios in practice.

THE DYNAMIC PROGRAMMING SOLUTION

Dynamic programming was introduced by Bellman (1952) and has since been employed in a wide range of disciplines including biology, computer science, economics, and natural language processing. It is a method for solving a complex, multistage problem by breaking it down into an array of subproblems. Dynamic programming is computationally efficient because it saves the solution to each subproblem so it does not need to solve that subproblem again. It is often used in multiperiod optimization problems in which decisions in one period depend on the distribution of possible outcomes in future periods. In this context, Smith (1997) showed how to use dynamic programming to find the most desirable spouse. His results were highly intuitive. He showed that the optimal approach is to marry only a highly desirable partner in the early years, but if one does not come along, to lower one's standards as time runs out and desperation sets in.

To show how dynamic programming is applied to solve the rebalancing problem, consider a simple world with only two asset classes – stocks and bonds – and three potential return outcomes, as shown in Table 21.1. Specifically, there is a 25% chance that stocks and bonds will return 26% and 1%, respectively, a 25% chance that they will return −11% and 10%, respectively, and a 50% chance that they will both return 8%. Finally, assume

TABLE 21.1 Return Distribution and Expected Log-Wealth Utility for a 60/40 Portfolio

Probability (%)	Expected Returns (%)		Log-Wealth Utility	Product
	Stocks	Bonds		
25	26	1	ln[(1 + .26) × 60% + (1 + .01) × 40%]	0.0371
50	8	8	ln[(1 + .08) × 60% + (1 + .08) × 40%]	0.0385
25	−11	10	ln[(1 − .11) × 60% + (1 + .10) × 40%]	−0.0066
Weighted average	7.75	6.75		0.0690

that it costs 5 basis points to trade stocks and 7 basis points to trade bonds. Given these assumptions, an investor with log-wealth utility will allocate 60% of the portfolio to stocks and 40% to bonds.[1] This portfolio offers the maximum expected utility of 0.0690.

Figure 21.1 shows all the potential paths that the asset mix could take over two periods. At the end of the first period, there is a 25% chance that the mix would be 65/35, a 50% chance it would remain at 60/40 if both assets return 8%, and a 25% chance it would be 55/45. At the end of the second period, there is an even wider array of potential asset mixes. In the extremes, there is a 6.25% (25% × 25%) chance that the mix would be 70/30 and a 6.25% chance that it would be 50/50. At each point in this tree, the investor faces a decision: rebalance the portfolio to the optimal mix and incur transaction costs or do not rebalance, remain suboptimal, and thereby incur suboptimality costs.

To implement dynamic programming, we start by working backward from the end of period 2. Let us first consider the portfolio resulting from two successive 26% stock returns, which is 70% stocks and 30% bonds. We determine the utility of this portfolio by substituting a 70/30 stock/bond portfolio for the 60/40 portfolio in Table 21.1, which yields expected utility of 0.0689%. The certainty equivalent of the optimal 60/40 portfolio equals 1.071436 (or $e^{0.068881}$), whereas the certainty equivalent of a 70/30 portfolio equals 1.071308 (or $e^{0.068881}$).[2] Hence, the cost of suboptimality for the 70/30 portfolio equals the difference between these values: 1.27 basis points. This value is shown as the suboptimality cost (indicated by SC) next to the 70/30 allocation at the end of period 2.

How does this suboptimality cost compare to the cost of rebalancing? The cost of restoring the optimal weights equals 1.20 basis points or (0.10 × 0.0005 + 0.10 × 0.0007), given that we need to trade 10% of the portfolio

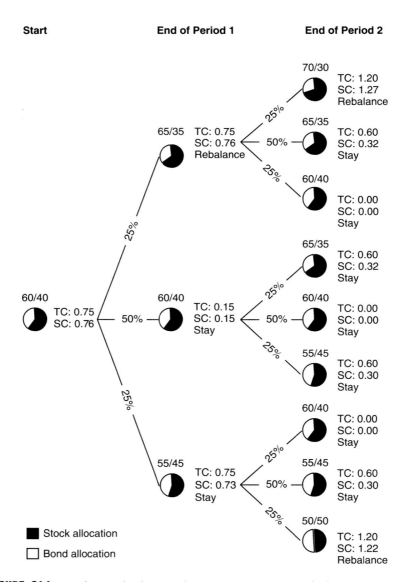

FIGURE 21.1 Trading and suboptimality costs over two periods (basis points).

out of stocks at a cost of 5 basis points and into bonds at a cost of 7 basis points. This value is shown as the transaction cost (indicated by TC) next to the 70/30 allocation at the end of period 2. Therefore, given a 70/30 stock/bond portfolio at the end of period 2, we would choose to rebalance to the optimal mix because the cost of rebalancing is less than the suboptimality cost. We perform the same calculations to determine the optimal decision for the eight other possible portfolios at the end of period 2.

Next we step back to the end of period 1. Now there are only three portfolios to consider, but each portfolio leads to three additional possible portfolios at the end of period 2. To identify the optimal decision at the end of period 1, we must therefore account not only for the cost of each choice in period 1, but also for the present value of each decision's expected future costs in period 2. Consider, for example, the 65/35 portfolio at the end of period 1. The costs associated with retaining this portfolio, rather than rebalancing it, are given by Equation 21.1:

$$
\begin{aligned}
C_1^{65/35} = 25\% \times \Big(\left| W_S^{70/30} - W_S^* \right| \times TC_S + \left| W_B^{70/30} - W_B^* \right| \times TC_B \Big) / (1+r) \\
+ 50\% \times \Big(CE^{60/40} - CE^{65/35} \Big) / (1+r) \\
+ CE^{60/40} - CE^{65/35}
\end{aligned}
\tag{21.1}
$$

$W_S^{70/30}$ is the stock weight in the 70/30 portfolio, W_S^* is the stock weight in the optimal portfolio (60%), TC_S is the transaction cost for stocks, $W_B^{70/30}$ is the bond weight in the 70/30 portfolio, W_B^* is the bond weight in the optimal portfolio (40%), TC_B is the transaction cost for bonds, r is the discount rate, $CE^{60/40}$ is the certainty equivalent of the 60/40 (optimal) portfolio, and $CE^{65/35}$ is the certainty equivalent of the 65/35 portfolio. We interpret this equation as follows:

- There is a 25% chance that this portfolio will lead to a 70/30 portfolio by the end of period 2. Given this outcome, we have just shown that it is optimal to rebalance to the 60/40 portfolio; hence we must account for this potential future rebalancing cost, discounted back to the current period. This is the first line of Equation 21.1.
- There is a 50% chance that the portfolio weights will remain at 65/35, in which case we have shown it is optimal to retain these weights; hence, we must account for the potential future suboptimality of this 65/35 portfolio, discounted back to the current period. This is the second line of the equation.
- Finally, there is a 25% chance that the portfolio will shift to a 60/40 portfolio at the end of period 2. In this case, there are neither suboptimality costs nor transaction costs to consider. Therefore, this outcome does not enter into the equation.
- In addition to these future costs, we must account for the fact that the 65/35 portfolio is suboptimal in the current period. This is the last line of the equation.

To determine the optimal choice for the 65/35 portfolio at the end of period 1, we compare the sum of these components from Equation 21.1 to the cost of rebalancing. The cost of rebalancing includes discounted future costs for the 60/40 portfolio. In this case, the rebalancing costs are lower than the suboptimality costs, so the optimal decision is to rebalance. We can repeat this entire exercise to determine the optimal choices given the other two portfolios at the end of period 1.

This illustration of dynamic programming highlights the intertemporal dependence of optimal rebalancing decisions. Unfortunately, as should be evident, this approach involves many calculations. And this was just a simple example. In practice, investors must rebalance many asset classes over extended periods, allowing for return distributions with far more than three outcomes. For a portfolio of 10 asset classes, there are 4.2 trillion possible portfolios and over 10,000 trillion trillion calculations to perform. Notwithstanding advances in computing power, it is computationally impossible to derive the optimal decisions for a 10-asset class portfolio based on a search across 1% intervals, even if we employ an army of industrious interns.[3] Dynamic programming suffers from the curse of dimensionality.

THE MVD HEURISTIC

Unlike dynamic programming, the MvD approach is manageable even for relatively large numbers of asset classes. Like the dynamic programming solution, it seeks to account for both current and future costs associated with the decision to rebalance or to remain suboptimal. To implement it, we first define a cost function associated with rebalancing from a current portfolio to a possible new portfolio. This cost function is given by Equation 21.2:

$$C_n = CE_o - CE_n + TC'|w_n - w_c| + d(w_n - w_0)'(w_n - w_0) \quad (21.2)$$

C_n is the cost of trading to a potential new portfolio. The terms CE_o and CE_n are the certainty equivalents of the optimal portfolio and the possible new portfolio, respectively. In practice, we calculate mean-variance utility rather than log-wealth utility. The difference between these two terms is the suboptimality cost of the possible new portfolio. The weights we choose could be suboptimal, intentionally, because we wish to consider rebalancing trades that may only partially restore optimal weights but incur fewer transaction costs. The vectors w_n and w_c are the weights of the possible new and current portfolios, respectively, and TC is a vector of transaction costs for each asset class. This term captures the transaction cost of trading from the current portfolio to the possible new portfolio. The vector w_0 represents the weights of the optimal portfolio, and d is a coefficient chosen to best approximate the true utility function. This last term is a quadratic function that approximates the discounted cost of future choices. We use Monte Carlo simulation to determine the value of d.[4] For a given set of current weights, w_c, we identify a set of possible new portfolio weights, w_n, that minimizes the cost function given by Equation 21.2.[5] The optimal rebalancing decision is to rebalance to these weights.

To demonstrate this approach, we return to the moderate portfolio that we defined in Chapter 2. We evaluate the performance of four distinct approaches to rebalancing for the moderate portfolio:

- No rebalancing. This strategy is the easiest to implement. We simply allow the portfolio to drift throughout the investment horizon.
- Calendar-based rebalancing. This strategy rebalances the portfolio back to the optimal targets on a fixed schedule, regardless of how much the weights have drifted. We consider monthly, quarterly, semiannual, and annual rebalancing schedules.
- Tolerance band rebalancing. This strategy rebalances the portfolio back to the optimal targets whenever any asset class weight breaches a predefined band around the optimal targets, regardless of how much time has elapsed since the last rebalance. We consider 1%, 3%, and 5% bands.
- Optimal MvD rebalancing. This strategy rebalances the portfolio each month to the weights that minimize the cost function given by Equation 21.2.

In practice, investors may consider other rebalancing strategies as well. For example, one approach is to use tolerance bands with varying sizes across asset classes. It is straightforward to evaluate any rebalancing strategy with this simulation framework.

Table 21.2 shows our transaction cost assumptions for each asset class. Investors who trade differently, or employ derivatives, may face a different set of transaction costs and should change these assumptions.

TABLE 21.2 Asset Class Transaction Costs

Asset Classes	Transaction Costs (basis points)
US Equities	20
Foreign Developed Market Equities	35
Emerging Market Equities	60
Treasury Bonds	5
US Corporate Bonds	50
Commodities	10
Cash Equivalents	3

TABLE 21.3 Performance of Rebalancing Strategies

Rebalancing Strategy	Average Trades per Year	Average Trade Size (%)	Annual Turnover (%)	Transaction Costs (bps)	Suboptimality Costs (bps)	Total Costs (bps)
Optimal	12	0.26	21.36	3.9	1.5	5.4
1% bands	5	0.6	18.4	5.8	0.5	6.3
3% bands	1	1.4	7.4	2.3	3.4	5.8
5% bands	0.3	2.2	4.3	1.4	5.5	6.9
Monthly	12	0.3	28.3	8.9	0.0	8.9
Quarterly	4	0.6	16.4	5.2	1.2	6.4
Semi-annually	2	0.8	11.6	3.7	1.8	5.5
Annually	1	1.2	8.3	2.6	3.1	5.7
No rebalance	0	0.0	0.0	0.0	17.0	17.0

To evaluate the performance of these strategies, we simulate 1,000 five-year paths using Monte Carlo simulation, given the return and risk assumptions specified in Chapter 2. We measure the average suboptimality cost and transaction cost incurred by each strategy, as well as the annual turnover, average trade size, and average number of trades per year. Table 21.3 shows the average performance of each rebalancing strategy.

The optimal rebalancing strategy offers the lowest overall cost of 5.4 basis points per year. As we should expect, the tolerance band rules incur more suboptimality costs and fewer transaction costs as the band size increases. The calendar-based rules incur more suboptimality costs and fewer transaction costs as the frequency of rebalancing decreases. If we never rebalance the portfolio, we incur very high suboptimality costs but no transaction costs. Figures 21.2 and 21.3 present graphically the trade-off between suboptimality and transaction costs.

In this example, we have assumed that all the asset classes are liquid and can be traded at reasonable cost. In some instances, the portfolio will include illiquid asset classes that cannot be rebalanced. In these cases, we would adapt our simulation framework to rebalance the liquid asset classes while allowing the illiquid asset classes to drift. This approach has the benefit of accounting for the correlations between liquid and illiquid asset classes. To see why this is important, consider a portfolio that includes an illiquid private equity asset class that is correlated with liquid public equities. If the portfolio is overweight in public equities and underweight in private equity, the suboptimality cost of this distortion may be low because the asset classes are close substitutes for one another. With this insight we are able to rebalance more selectively and avoid excessive trading costs.

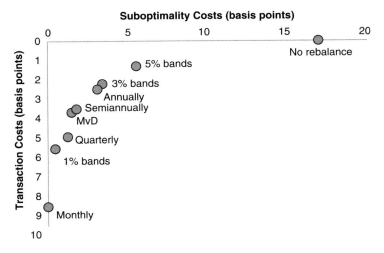

FIGURE 21.2 Rebalancing strategies: trade-off between transaction and suboptimality costs.

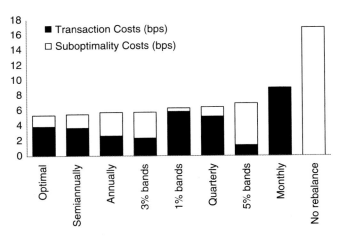

FIGURE 21.3 Rebalancing strategies: performance.

THE BOTTOM LINE

To develop an optimal rebalancing schedule, investors must evaluate the trade-off between the transaction costs of restoring a portfolio's weights to their optimal targets and the suboptimality cost of retaining the current weights. They should also account for the future costs associated with each decision. In this chapter, we present an optimal rebalancing methodology and show that it outperforms simpler rebalancing rules.

RELATED TOPICS

- Chapter 17 discusses rebalancing in the context of illiquid assets.

REFERENCES

Bellman, R. 1952. "On the Theory of Dynamic Programming," *Proceedings of the National Academy of Sciences*, Vol. 38, No. 8 (August).

Kritzman, M., Myrgren, S., and Page, S. 2008. "Rebalancing," *Economics and Portfolio Strategy*, (August).

Kritzman, M., Myrgren, S., and Page, S. 2009. "Optimal Rebalancing: A Scalable Solution," *Journal of Investment Management*, Vol. 7, No. 1 (First Quarter).

Markowitz, H. and van Dijk, E. L. 2003. "Single-Period Mean-Variance Analysis in a Changing World," *Financial Analysts Journal*, Vol. 59, No. 2 (March/April).

Smith, D. K. 1997. "Dynamic Programming: An Introduction," *Plus Magazine*, accessed at: plus.maths.org/content/dynamic-programming-introduction.

Sun, W., Fan, A., Chen, L-W., Schouwenaars, T., and Albota, M. 2006. "Optimal Rebalancing for Institutional Portfolios," *Journal of Portfolio Management*, Vol. 32, No. 2 (Winter).

NOTES

1. We use log-wealth utility in this example for simplicity. In practice, we assume mean-variance utility, which approximates log-wealth utility.
2. For more details on certainty equivalents, see Chapter 4 or the Appendix of Chapter 17.
3. For more details on the curse of dimensionality and optimal rebalancing, refer to Kritzman, Myrgren, and Page (2009).
4. We minimize cost at each decision point during the simulation. We continue to run simulations and change d until we find its best-performing value, which in this example is 0.30.
5. We could use a variety of optimization algorithms to minimize this cost function. We use the fmincon() function in Matlab.

CHAPTER **22**

Regime Shifts

THE CHALLENGE

Investors want to grow wealth and avoid large drawdowns along the way. But portfolios with higher expected returns also carry greater risk. Faced with this trade-off, investors choose portfolios that optimally balance their goal to grow wealth with their aversion to risk. This approach to portfolio selection implicitly assumes that risk is stable through time, which is far from true.

In Chapter 19, we showed that accounting for stability in portfolio construction helps to stabilize portfolio risk by reducing a portfolio's dependence on asset classes with unstable risk profiles. But even stability-adjusted portfolios experience large swings in standard deviations through time. As an alternative, we could engineer a portfolio to perform well in a given regime, with the hope that it holds its own when that regime does not come to pass. This strategy, like stability-adjusted optimization, selects a set of fixed weights, but it is constructed to perform well in a chosen regime that we fear the most or that we believe is most likely to occur. Unfortunately, this approach is also subject to large swings in portfolio risk. It is hard to stabilize the risk of a portfolio that has fixed weights. We discuss this issue in Chapter 10.

It may be preferable to allow our portfolio's asset mix to change through time. If we successfully predict future investment conditions, we should be able to outperform a static asset mix with tactical tilts. Of course, if our predictions are wrong, tactical trading may harm the portfolio more than it helps it. Furthermore, tactical strategies must add enough value to overcome the incremental trading costs they incur. This begs the question: are markets sufficiently macroinefficient to justify tactical asset allocation, or is this pursuit merely a fool's errand?

PREDICTABILITY OF RETURN AND RISK

Let us begin by distinguishing between the predictability of return and the predictability of risk. Predicting returns successfully is more valuable than predicting risk successfully, but it is also more difficult. According to the efficient markets hypothesis, asset returns follow a random walk. Assets cannot stray far from their fair value, the story goes, because arbitrageurs quickly buy undervalued assets and sell overvalued assets in pursuit of profits. Although this logic may apply only in a limited sense to small or illiquid markets where assets are expensive to trade, it should hold reasonably well for asset classes such as large capitalization stocks and government bonds. Yet even in highly liquid markets, some – notably Paul A. Samuelson – have argued that markets are macroinefficient because arbitrageurs lack sufficient capital, or risk appetite, to correct widespread mispricing across aggregations of thousands of securities the way they do for individual securities. Therefore, skilled investors might be able to predict asset class returns with some degree of reliability, though this is still a very challenging task.

Predicting risk is easier. The economic forces that affect long-run returns might not apply to the volatility of returns. Volatility – which we measure as the standard deviation of returns – arises from uncertainty about an asset's true value. In short, prices fluctuate when new information becomes available and investors react to it. Volatility depends on the significance of new information and the pace at which it arrives, and there are no fundamental laws governing how these processes should unfold. In other words, volatility lacks a clear equilibrium value. In fact, it is often the case that volatility clusters into regimes of high volatility and regimes of low volatility, which means it is partly predictable. This fact does not contradict the notion of an efficient market.

In this chapter, we investigate the use of regimes to manage risk, not to predict the direction of returns. We present two approaches to dealing with regime shifts. The first is regime-sensitive asset allocation, and the second is tactical asset allocation.

REGIME-SENSITIVE ALLOCATION

Figure 22.1 shows the monthly correlation between US equities and Treasury bonds for nonoverlapping five-year periods, as one example of the variability of risk. The gains and losses experienced by stocks and bonds generally aligned during the 1980s and 1990s, possibly due to their common sensitivity to interest rates and inflation. After that, their correlation turned sharply negative. Stocks and bonds became polarized as risky and safe, respectively, and they moved in opposite directions most of the time.

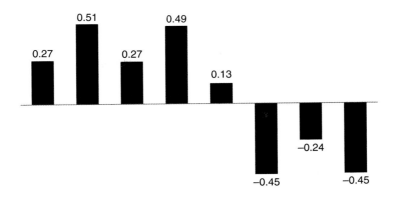

Five-Year Rolling Subsamples

FIGURE 22.1 Monthly correlation of US equities and Treasury bonds (five-year rolling subsamples).

Given the variability in the correlation of stocks and bonds, we might choose to define regimes based on macroeconomic variables such as inflation or interest rate policy. Alternatively, we could define regimes directly from the correlation between stocks and bonds. Both approaches are reasonable, but they consider the performance of only stocks and bonds. It might be better to define regimes in a way that captures the behavior of our entire investment universe. One way to do this is with a multivariate measure of financial turbulence.

Financial Turbulence

In Chapter 24, we show how to measure financial turbulence with a statistic called the Mahalanobis distance.[1] In a single number, financial turbulence characterizes the degree of unusualness in a cross section of asset class returns. It captures not only extreme price moves but also unusual correlations that affect a portfolio's diversification. The turbulence score for any given month t, equals

$$Turbulence_t = \frac{1}{N}(x_t - \mu)' \Sigma^{-1} (x_t - \mu) \qquad (22.1)$$

In Equation 22.1, x_t is a vector of monthly returns across asset classes, μ is a vector of average returns for each asset class over the full 40-year sample, and Σ^{-1} is the inverse of the covariance matrix computed from the 40-year sample. We multiply by $\frac{1}{N}$ so that the expected value of turbulence equals 1. The inverse covariance matrix puts the monthly returns in context, and this step is critically important. For example, stock prices may regularly move by 5 or 10% per month, but for bonds these returns would be extreme. Likewise, the divergence of two asset classes is surprising if they are positively correlated, but not if they are negatively correlated. The inverse covariance matrix embeds all the expected relationships across asset classes, based on the full sample of data.

We apply this formula to the six major asset classes in our empirical example (excluding cash equivalents): US equities, foreign developed market equities, emerging market equities, Treasury bonds, corporate bonds, and commodities. Figure 22.2 shows the historical monthly turbulence since 1976. It clearly spikes during well-known events such as the Black Monday stock market crash of 1987, the Russian debt default in 1998, and the global financial crisis in 2008. It also flags some less obvious periods of stress. These events carry important consequences for portfolio risk, even if they do not make newspaper headlines.

Portfolio Construction with Conditional Risk Estimates

Regime variables are informative if they describe differences in investment performance. Financial turbulence passes this test. Table 22.1 shows asset class standard deviations and correlations corresponding to the 10% most

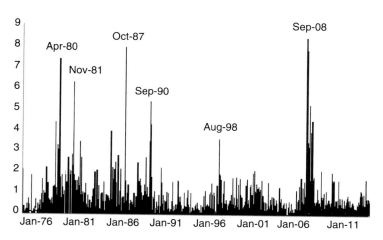

FIGURE 22.2   Financial turbulence.

TABLE 22.1 Risk Characteristics in Turbulent and Nonturbulent Regimes

	Standard Deviations (%)	Correlations				
		US Equities	Foreign Equities	EM Equities	Treasury Bonds	Corporate Bonds
Turbulent						
US Equities	27.4					
Foreign Developed Market Equities	29.6	0.74				
Emerging Market Equities	33.5	0.86	0.76			
Treasury Bonds	11.7	0.22	0.16	0.25		
US Corporate Bonds	16.3	0.44	0.39	0.49	0.84	
Commodities	27.6	0.29	0.27	0.31	−0.10	0.09
Nonturbulent						
US Equities	14.0					
Foreign Developed Market Equities	15.9	0.60				
Emerging Market Equities	23.6	0.51	0.61			
Treasury Bonds	4.7	0.06	−0.01	−0.09		
US Corporate Bonds	5.6	0.23	0.15	0.11	0.89	
Commodities	19.1	0.10	0.28	0.25	−0.04	−0.01
Difference						
US Equities	13.4					
Foreign Developed Market Equities	13.7	0.14				
Emerging Market Equities	9.9	0.34	0.15			
Treasury Bonds	7.0	0.16	0.17	0.33		
US Corporate Bonds	10.7	0.20	0.24	0.38	−0.05	
Commodities	8.5	0.19	−0.02	0.06	−0.05	0.10

turbulent months, which we call the turbulent sample, and the remaining 90% of months, which we call the nonturbulent sample.

Standard deviations are much higher during turbulent periods, as we should expect. Most of the correlations also increase when conditions are turbulent; hence, there is less potential for diversification. These conditions usually cause traditional portfolios to perform poorly. Should we optimize our portfolio for turbulent regimes, instead? We can, but we face the following trade-off. The more we engineer a portfolio to protect it from financial turbulence, the more we sacrifice optimality in nonturbulent periods. On the other hand, if we choose a portfolio that is optimized for nonturbulent times, we should brace for discomfort when turbulence occurs. Perhaps we should compromise, by tilting our portfolio toward asset classes that are more resilient to turbulence. Ideally, the portfolio will perform well when turbulence prevails without underperforming significantly during nonturbulent periods.

To implement this strategy, we optimize a portfolio based on a covariance matrix that blends covariances from both regimes. In our example, we use a simple average of the turbulent and nonturbulent covariance matrices. Because the turbulent sample represents only 10% of history, a 50% weight constitutes a substantial tilt toward the estimates that prevailed during turbulent regimes. Table 22.2 shows the moderate portfolio from Chapter 2 alongside a new portfolio based on the turbulence-conditioned covariance matrix. The allocations are meaningfully different, even though both portfolios target a 7.5% return and use the same expected return assumptions. The blended-covariance solution favors emerging market equities compared to US equities, and it substitutes cash equivalents for corporate bonds. The full-sample standard deviation increases from 10.8% to 11.5%, and the standard deviation in nonturbulent periods increases from 8.8% to 9.8%. However, the new portfolio reduces the standard deviation during turbulent regimes from 18.8% to 17.0%. This trade-off may or may not be worthwhile. The benefit this portfolio provides in turbulent regimes is modest. Moreover, we receive this benefit only 10% of the time, while we experience the cost of higher volatility 90% of the time. This result underscores the limitation of a static asset mix.

TABLE 22.2   Full-Sample and Regime-Conditioned Optimal Portfolios

Optimal Allocations	Full-Sample Covariances (%)	Blended Covariances (%)
US Equities	25.5	8.6
Foreign Developed Market Equities	23.2	21.0
Emerging Market Equities	9.1	26.0
Treasury Bonds	14.3	9.9
US Corporate Bonds	22.0	0.0
Commodities	5.9	6.4
Cash Equivalents	0.0	28.1
Expected Return	7.5	7.5
Full-Sample Standard Deviation	10.8	11.5
Nonturbulent Regime Standard Deviation	8.8	9.8
Turbulent Regime Standard Deviation	18.8	17.0

TACTICAL ASSET ALLOCATION

In contrast to portfolio rebalancing, which serves merely to restore the portfolio's optimal weights when price changes cause the asset class weights to drift away from their optimal targets, tactical asset allocation shifts a portfolio's composition proactively. To succeed, tactical asset allocation should add more value when it is correct than it subtracts when it is wrong. Or, it should be correct sufficiently often to compensate for its losses, on average. Overall, it must enhance expected utility compared to the static alternative, net of costs. To achieve this goal systematically, we need a predictive signal and a way to translate that signal into an investment decision.

Identifying a Predictive Signal

A good predictive signal is necessary, but not sufficient, to create a profitable tactical asset allocation strategy. Some investors might prefer to rely on their qualitative judgment, but we focus here on data-driven signals, in part because they are naturally more transparent and replicable. Let us continue with our analysis of turbulence. As we soon show, turbulence is predictive by virtue of its persistence.

There are, of course, other signals that might add value. Economic indicators such as growth and inflation might be valuable. Another indicator that has gained widespread traction in recent years is the absorption ratio, introduced by Kritzman, Li, Page, and Rigobon (2011). Like turbulence, it is derived statistically and based on asset prices. Whereas turbulence represents extreme dislocations in asset prices, the absorption ratio reveals whether the risk within an asset universe is highly concentrated or diffuse. When a small set of factors explains a large fraction of total risk, portfolios composed from those assets are vulnerable to large drawdowns because shocks tend to propagate quickly and broadly in such a setting. When risk is broadly distributed across many factors, negative shocks are more likely to have a localized and contained effect on portfolios. The absorption ratio is based on Principal Components Analysis (described in detail in Chapter 25). It equals the fraction of total variation in returns that is explained – or absorbed – by a subset of the most important statistical factors. Statistical factors are nothing more than sets of portfolio weights across a universe of assets, chosen in such a way that they are all uncorrelated and explain successively smaller fractions of total risk. Statistical factors do not have descriptive names, but they are convenient in that they always explain variation in the data as efficiently as possible.

We do not include empirical tests of economic indicators or the absorption ratio here, but the technique we are about to describe using financial turbulence applies as well to economic variables and the absorption ratio.

Detecting Regimes: Hidden Markov Models

We begin by defining a regime as a period in which an indicator, in this case financial turbulence, is above or below a threshold. We might devise a trading rule that positions a portfolio more defensively when turbulence is elevated and more aggressively when it is not. Even a simple rule like this might add value. However, simple thresholds have three important limitations. First, they fail to recognize persistence, which can lead to excessive trading. Second, by focusing only on the level of the indicator, this rule fails to account for shifts in its volatility, which may offer additional insight. Third, such a rule is sensitive to the choice of the threshold, which in many cases is an arbitrary choice.

Hidden Markov models offer a more sophisticated alternative. These models presume that the data we observe emanates from multiple regimes, each of which has a degree of persistence from one period to the next. For example, if we are in regime A this month, regime A might be more likely to prevail next month, as well. But there is also a chance that the regime will shift abruptly from A to B. The term *Markov* refers to the assumption that the underlying regime variable follows a Markov process in that next period's regime probability depends only on the regime we are in today. Unfortunately, we never know for certain which regime we are in, even with the benefit of hindsight. As their name suggests, the regimes in hidden Markov models are indeed hidden variables (sometimes called latent variables). We rely on a statistical method called Maximum Likelihood Estimation (MLE) to infer from the data which regime is most likely to explain each observation, given all the data that preceded and followed it. The solution is obtained by using a well-known and highly reliable search method called the Baum–Welch algorithm. (See the Appendix to this chapter for more detail.) By allowing for the presence of multiple regimes, we are better able to explain the complex behavior of many real-world variables. Recall from Chapter 19 that the composite mixture of two normal distributions does not yield another normal distribution, but a fat-tailed one.

Kritzman, Page, and Turkington (2012) use hidden Markov models to solve for the two normal distributions and regime transition probabilities that best explain historical data for US gross national product, US consumer price index, and market turbulence in US equities and currencies. In an intentionally contrived example in which data are drawn from known regimes that switch over time, the authors show that the true underlying behavior is much more likely to be recovered by a hidden Markov model than by a simple threshold. They also provide empirical evidence that economic data conforms to regimes. The authors demonstrate that relatively simple regime-switching strategies across risk premiums and asset classes outperform their static investment alternatives.

Let us explore a case study to make these concepts more tangible. We use financial turbulence as our regime indicator. The only parameters we need to specify are the number of regimes and the type of distribution we envision for our variable of interest in each regime. The model determines everything else. For this example, we ask the model to identify three distinct regimes that best explain historical turbulence.[2] It returns to us a transition matrix stating the probability of occurrence for each regime in the next period as a condition of the regime that prevails in the current period. The top panel of Table 22.3 shows the results of the model. We see that regime persistence, which comes from the diagonal entries of the transition matrix, is above 50% in all cases, which indicates predictive potential. We also see that it varies across regimes. The first regime, which happens to be the most

TABLE 22.3   Hidden Markov Model Fit and Conditional Asset Class Performance

	Calm	Moderate	Turbulent
Regime Persistence	92%	75%	67%
Turbulence Average	0.7	1.1	1.7
Turbulence Standard Deviation	0.2	0.3	0.6
Average Annual Return			
US Equities	15.0%	13.6%	−27.7%
Foreign Developed Market Equities	15.3%	5.7%	−12.0%
Emerging Market Equities	17.2%	21.7%	−26.0%
Treasury Bonds	5.9%	9.6%	12.3%
US Corporate Bonds	7.5%	10.2%	4.2%
Commodities	7.8%	7.8%	−17.1%
Cash Equivalents	3.9%	5.9%	7.4%
Standard Deviation			
US Equities	12.6%	20.2%	19.9%
Foreign Developed Market Equities	14.7%	19.6%	31.0%
Emerging Market Equities	21.3%	30.5%	32.5%
Treasury Bonds	4.2%	6.4%	12.1%
US Corporate Bonds	5.1%	7.8%	16.6%
Commodities	18.1%	21.3%	30.3%
Cash Equivalents	0.8%	1.1%	1.7%

persistent, has low average turbulence and low dispersion in outcomes. We label it "calm." We label the second regime "moderate" because it is characterized by a higher average return and a higher standard deviation. Finally, the third regime represents "turbulent" conditions. It is the least stable, yet still predictive. Keep in mind that we do not predetermine how the persistence, averages, and standard deviations align across regimes. The fact that regimes with worse investment conditions on average are also more uncertain and more fleeting is a feature of markets that turbulence and the hidden Markov model have jointly uncovered. If we tried to fit the same model on random data, it would either fail to find a solution or it would produce three indistinguishable regimes.

Now that we know more about the dynamics of turbulence, we link this information to asset class returns. The middle panel of Table 22.3 shows the average annualized return of our seven asset classes in each regime, and the bottom panel presents standard deviations. Again, recall that even with hindsight we do not know for certain which regime corresponds to each month in history. For this analysis, we simply assign the most likely regime to each month. Our findings are intuitive: calm periods are kind to investments, moderate periods have markedly elevated volatility despite sometimes-higher mean returns, and turbulent periods have very high risk and typically negative average returns. Figure 22.3 shows the probabilities associated with each regime through time.

Testing Out-of-Sample

To test the efficacy of our tactical asset allocation rule, we perform an out-of-sample backtest in which tactical decisions rely only on data available at each point in time. Our original turbulence calculation uses information spanning the entire 40-year sample, so we must recalculate it. Each month, we compute turbulence using the formula shown previously, but now we

FIGURE 22.3 Hidden Markov model regime probabilities.

FIGURE 22.4 Hidden Markov model regime probability forecasts (out-of-sample).

estimate means and covariances using the prior 60 months of returns. This process produces turbulence data starting in 1980. Next, we calibrate the hidden Markov model using historical data only. Starting in December 1990, we calibrate the model using the prior 10 years of turbulence, and we append new data each month to form a growing lookback window on which we recalibrate the model. Figure 22.4 shows the probability forecast of each regime per month, out-of-sample. Each month, the model supplies an updated probability that the current regime is calm, moderate or turbulent. Next, we forecast the probability that each regime will prevail next month by using the transition matrix to project the current regime probabilities forward one period. For example, the probability that regime A will prevail next month is equal to the probability that we are currently in regime A times the probability of remaining in regime A, plus the probability that we are currently in regime B times the probability of transitioning from B to A, plus the probability that we are currently in regime C times the probability of transitioning from C to A. The next-period probability of each regime, φ_{t+1}, is described succinctly by the product of the transition matrix of conditional regime probabilities and the current regime probabilities, φ_t:

$$\begin{bmatrix} P(\varphi_{t+1} = A) \\ P(\varphi_{t+1} = B) \\ P(\varphi_{t+1} = C) \end{bmatrix} = \begin{bmatrix} P(\varphi_{t+1} = A|\varphi_t = A) & P(\varphi_{t+1} = A|\varphi_t = B) & P(\varphi_{t+1} = A|\varphi_t = C) \\ P(\varphi_{t+1} = B|\varphi_t = A) & P(\varphi_{t+1} = B|\varphi_t = B) & P(\varphi_{t+1} = B|\varphi_t = C) \\ P(\varphi_{t+1} = C|\varphi_t = A) & P(\varphi_{t+1} = C|\varphi_t = B) & P(\varphi_{t+1} = C|\varphi_t = C) \end{bmatrix}$$

$$\times \begin{bmatrix} P(\varphi_t = A) \\ P(\varphi_t = B) \\ P(\varphi_t = C) \end{bmatrix} \tag{22.2}$$

Figure 22.4 shows the probability forecast of each forthcoming regime per month, out-of-sample.

There are many ways to specify portfolio weights using the regime signals in Figure 22.4. For illustration, we use the conservative, moderate, and aggressive portfolios from Chapter 2 and blend them in proportion to the regime probabilities at the end of each month. We then record the returns of each portfolio as well as the tactically blended portfolio over the following month. This rule depends on very few parameters, and it smoothly transitions the portfolio's composition among a conservative, moderate, and aggressive asset mix as regime probabilities shift. Table 22.4 and Figure 22.5 show that the tactical strategy produced the largest cumulative return, with a standard deviation substantially below that of the aggressive portfolio. It delivered a higher Sharpe ratio than the conservative portfolio at a return level 2.6% higher. We have little doubt that we could produce performance that is more compelling by devising more sophisticated strategies involving additional indicators, conditional return forecasts, and reoptimized conditional allocations. Also, though we have not adjusted our results for transaction costs, the amount of trading involved here is certainly reasonable and can be dialed up or down using trading thresholds, minimum holding periods, and other techniques.

TABLE 22.4   Backtest Performance

	Conservative	Moderate	Aggressive	Tactical
Annual Return	6.0%	7.6%	8.1%	8.6%
Annual Standard Deviation	6.0%	9.6%	13.8%	10.3%
Sharpe Ratio	0.54	0.50	0.38	0.57

FIGURE 22.5   Cumulative returns.

THE BOTTOM LINE

The fact that risk varies through time presents a challenge, but also an opportunity. We have proposed three methods for stabilizing portfolio risk. The first is stability-adjusted optimization, which we discussed in Chapter 19. It identifies portfolios that are less dependent on asset classes with relatively unstable risk profiles. The second method is to define a regime and to optimize for a portfolio that is more sensitive to the covariances that prevailed during that regime. Ideally, this regime-sensitive portfolio will perform well when the regime occurs, while holding its own the rest of the time. Both these approaches yield static portfolios that most likely will still experience wide swings in their volatility. The third method is to shift a portfolio's asset mix tactically based on regime indicators. By allowing weights to change in response to market conditions, tactical strategies are less constrained; therefore, they present greater flexibility than static portfolios. Although this additional flexibility may not always improve performance, we have provided encouraging evidence to suggest that some investors might profit from tactical trading, given the right insights and methods.

APPENDIX: BAUM–WELCH ALGORITHM

To fit a hidden Markov model to data, we select a characteristic to distinguish regimes, and we find the probability of transitioning from one regime to another, given our sample of historical values for the regime characteristic. Thankfully, the Baum–Welch algorithm turns this potentially laborious search into a computationally straightforward exercise. Its effectiveness stems from the use of both forward and backward search procedures, from which information is combined, refined, and recycled iteratively to get better and better estimates. A thorough discussion of the algorithm is beyond the scope of this book, but it is documented in detail by Baum, Petrle, Soules, and Weiss (1970) and others. Kritzman, Page, and Turkington (2012) offer an intuitive description with a simple example. Interested readers should refer to these other sources for mathematical details, but we provide some intuition below.

We implement the Baum–Welch algorithm by first guessing the probabilities of shifting from one regime to another, along with the mean and standard deviation of the regime characteristic for each regime. (In our case study, we used turbulence as the regime-defining characteristic.) These initial guesses are chosen arbitrarily. The algorithm then computes what are called "forward probabilities." For the first period, the algorithm evaluates the likelihood of each regime based on our initial guesses, together with that period's value for the regime characteristic and the distribution of the characteristic for each regime. For the next period, the algorithm evaluates the likelihood of each regime based on the new value of the characteristic and the same initial guesses, and accounting for the likelihood of each regime from the prior period. It iterates forward in this fashion until we have forward probabilities for every time period. We now have a time series for each regime that tells us how likely it is that we would observe that value for the regime characteristic given the distribution of the characteristic for each regime, based on everything that occurred previously. The algorithm captures the fact that some values for the regime characteristic are more likely to have come from one regime than another given their distributions. It also captures the fact that a regime is more likely if it is highly persistent and believed to have prevailed in the preceding months.

Next, the algorithm follows the same procedure in reverse, to generate backward probabilities. It then combines the forward probabilities and backward probabilities into "smoothed probabilities." These smoothed probabilities tell us the likelihood of each regime at each point in time, given what regimes were likely to have occurred before and after.

To summarize, the Baum–Welch algorithm applies forward and backward iteration to an initial set of assumptions to determine the relative likelihood of each regime at each point in time. The next step is the critical component that allows this algorithm to work. The algorithm uses the regime probabilities to form a new and better set of estimates for all the parameters. For example, it calculates the probability that each pair of successive observations of the regime characteristic comes from regime A "transitioning" to stay in regime A, divided by the probability of regime A overall. This produces a new and improved estimate of the first element in the transition matrix. Likewise, using information about which periods are most likely to be in regime A, the algorithm estimates the mean and standard deviation of the characteristic's distribution for regime A. These estimates also improve the original guesses. We then enter these new estimates into the algorithm and repeat the entire process. The estimates continually improve after each iteration, and they ultimately converge to a stable solution that best describes regime behavior in our sample of characteristic values. Technically speaking, the algorithm is only guaranteed to converge to a "local solution," but based on our experience, we find that it converges to stable and plausible parameters consistently.

RELATED TOPICS

- Chapter 10 illustrates the limitations of fixed-weight portfolios and the opportunities available from a more flexible, dynamic policy.
- Chapter 19 shows how to construct fixed-weight portfolios with more stable risk profiles compared to conventional approaches.

REFERENCES

Baum, L., Petrle, T., Soules, G., and Weiss, N. 1970. "A Maximization Technique Occurring in the Statistical Analysis of Probabilistic Functions of Markov Chains," *Annals of Mathematical Statistics*, Vol. 41, No. 1.

Chow, G., Jacquier, E., Kritzman, M., and Lowry, K. 1999. "Optimal Portfolios in Good Times and Bad," *Financial Analysts Journal*, Vol. 55, No. 3 (May/June).

Kritzman, M. and Li, Y. 2010. "Skulls, Financial Turbulence and Risk Management," *Financial Analysts Journal*, Vol. 66, No. 5 (September/October).

Kritzman, M., Li, Y., Page, S., and Rigobon, R. 2011. "Principal Components as a Measure of Systemic Risk," *Journal of Portfolio Management*, Vol. 37, No. 4 (Summer).

Kritzman, M., Lowry, K., and Van Royen, A.-S. 2001. "Risk, Regimes, and Overconfidence," *Journal of Derivatives*, Vol. 8, No. 3 (Spring).

Kritzman, M., Page, S., and Turkington, D. 2012. "Regime Shifts: Implications for Dynamic Strategies," *Financial Analysts Journal*, Vol. 68, No. 3 (May/June).

NOTES

1. Mahalanobis was an Indian statistician who first discovered the covariance-adjusted distance measure to group human skull samples into their most statistically likely cohorts. For more on the application of this measure to financial turbulence see Chow, Jacquier, Kritzman, and Lowry (1999), Kritzman and Li (2010), and Kritzman, Lowry, and Van Royen (2001).
2. Due to the inherent positive skewness of the distribution of turbulence values, we take their square roots before calibrating the hidden Markov model. In practice, this adjustment has a small impact on the result.

CHAPTER 23

Scenario Analysis

THE CHALLENGE

Scenario analysis requires investors to define prospective economic scenarios, assign probabilities to them, translate the scenarios into expected asset class returns, and identify the most suitable portfolio, given all these inputs. The main virtue of this process is that it is intuitive. Its main drawback is that the probabilities investors assign to the alternative scenarios are derived subjectively. These probabilities, therefore, are prone to biases and perhaps to the persuasion of the less informed. This chapter addresses this drawback by describing a scientific and empirical approach to determining the probabilities of prospective economic scenarios.

COMPARISON TO MEAN-VARIANCE ANALYSIS

Before we proceed, it may be useful to place scenario analysis within the context of mean-variance analysis. Both procedures are used to construct portfolios, but they are implemented quite differently, and they appeal to different types of investors. Nevertheless, they are conceptually similar.

Mean-variance analysis requires investors to specify the expected returns, standard deviations, and correlations of asset classes, and in turn it yields efficient portfolios, along with their expected returns and standard deviations. For a given time horizon or assuming returns are expressed in continuous units, if returns are approximately elliptically distributed,[1] then each portfolio's expected return and standard deviation account for all possible relevant scenarios[2] weighted by their likelihood of occurrence.

Nevertheless, many investors are uncomfortable with mean-variance analysis because it requires them to specify statistical features of asset classes, which they find unintuitive and difficult to estimate. As an alternative to mean-variance analysis, some investors prefer scenario analysis, in which they define potential economic scenarios that implicitly span the distribution of plausible outcomes. This approach captures risk more intuitively than mean-variance analysis. Rather than describe risk in terms of standard deviations and correlations, scenario analysis incorporates risk by the range of the scenarios that are put forth for consideration, along with their probabilities.

Although scenario analysis is more intuitive, this benefit comes at the expense of quantitative rigor because investors must rely on judgment to assign probabilities to the prospective scenarios. We show how to replace the subjective assignment of probabilities with an empirically driven scientific method based on a statistic called the Mahalanobis distance, which we apply in several other ways throughout this book. For example, in Chapter 13, we use this statistic to improve the forecast reliability of linear regression analysis. In Chapter 14, we apply it to forecast the stock–bond correlation. In Chapter 22, we use it to detect regime shifts. In Chapter 24, we apply it to stress testing portfolios. And in Chapter 25, we provide a technical review of the Mahalanobis distance.

THE MAHALANOBIS DISTANCE APPLIED TO SCENARIO ANALYSIS

The Mahalanobis distance was derived in the early 20th century by an Indian statistician, who used characteristics of the human skull to analyze similarity between various castes in India.[3] In the case of scenario analysis, we use the Mahalanobis distance to measure the statistical similarity of prospective economic scenarios to prevailing economic conditions.

Within this context, the Mahalanobis distance d is computed as follows:

$$d = (x - \gamma)' \Sigma^{-1} (x - \gamma) \tag{23.1}$$

In Equation 23.1, d equals the Mahalanobis distance, x equals the values of a set of economic variables used to characterize a prospective economic scenario, γ equals the prevailing values of the economic variables, and Σ is the historical covariance matrix of changes in values for those variables. For details on this approach, see Czasonis, Kritzman, Pamir, and Turkington (2020).

Persistence Versus Mean Reversion

Equation 23.1 measures the similarity of prospective economic scenarios to current economic conditions. This approach implicitly assumes that current economic conditions are likely to persist. However, there may be circumstances in which mean reversion is more likely than persistence. This could be the case when an economic trend has persisted for an unusually long period of time or when economic conditions have deviated far from their normal range. Mean reversion may also be a more reasonable prediction if we are forecasting scenarios far into the future. To reflect these circumstances, we replace deviations from current conditions, (x − γ), with deviations from normal conditions, (x − μ). More generally, investors may anchor probabilities to any chosen blend of current conditions and normal conditions, by introducing a variable, θ, which is a weighted average of current and normal conditions:

$$d = (x - \theta)' \Sigma^{-1} (x - \theta) \tag{23.2}$$

$$\theta = \omega\gamma + (1 - \omega)\mu \tag{23.3}$$

In Equations 23.2 and 23.3, ω is the weight applied to current conditions, and $(1 - \omega)$ is the weight applied to normal conditions. The covariance matrix, Σ, is estimated from the average of squared historical deviations. These historical deviations depend on the choice of θ. One may also use θ to express a view that economic conditions will tend toward a value other than the historical norm, for example, a set of conditions associated with good or bad stock market performance. Equation 23.4 shows the definition of the deviations we use to calculate the covariance matrix. Note that we use the economic conditions that occurred prior to each historical observation, x_{t-1}, rather than the current conditions, γ, which occur at the time we perform the analysis:

$$deviation_t = x_t - (\omega x_{t-1} + (1 - \omega)\mu) \tag{23.4}$$

Point in Time Versus Paths

How should we characterize the scenarios? Perhaps the most obvious approach would be to specify the values of key economic variables as of some future point in time. For example, if we are projecting scenarios one year ahead, we would describe alternative scenarios for the economy based on the most recently available values one year forward. Some of these values might be the most recent level of an indicator such as the slope of the yield curve, whereas others may be the most recently reported change in an indicator, such as the change in industrial production. With this point-in-time approach, we would specify the prospective scenarios as the point-in-time values of a group of economic variables.

However, we may want to consider not only where the economy might end up at some future date, but also the path it took to arrive there. In order to do so, we simply specify multiple values for each chosen economic variable, for both the prospective scenarios and for the anchor we use for computing the Mahalanobis distance. For example, we could specify three values for each variable, such as the early, middle, and late stages of alternative economic paths.

The point-in-time approach and the path approach are mathematically equivalent. They differ only in how nuanced we are in describing prospective scenarios. This idea is described more thoroughly in Kritzman, Li, Qiu, and Turkington (2021).

THE MAHALANOBIS DISTANCE AND PROBABILITY

The Mahalanobis distance is related to a scenario's probability of occurrence in the following sense. An observation with a high Mahalanobis distance will tend to occur less frequently than one with a low Mahalanobis distance. If the economic variables follow a multivariate normal distribution, the likelihood of a scenario decays as the Mahalanobis distance increases in accordance with an exponential function, which gives rise to the normal distribution. We measure the likelihood that we would observe a scenario as

$$likelihood \propto e^{-d/2} \qquad (23.5)$$

In Equation 23.5, d equals the Mahalanobis distance, e is the base of the exponential function, and $\propto$ denotes a proportionality relationship.[4]

It is important to note that we are not required to assume multivariate normality. For example, if we wish to assume fatter tails, we could replace d with d^j, where j is a value less than 1. This adjustment results in a slower decay and therefore assumes a greater relative likelihood of extreme outcomes.

We now have but one more step to derive the relative probabilities of the scenarios. Unlike mean-variance analysis, which implicitly subsumes all possible future scenarios, scenario analysis considers only a finite set of potential scenarios, which is hardly exhaustive. We therefore rescale the likelihoods so they sum to one. These rescaled values represent the relative probabilities of the scenarios.

To summarize, we determine the relative probabilities of prospective scenarios as follows:

1. We define a finite set of prospective economic scenarios as combinations of economic variables at a future point in time or as a multi-stage path.

2. We use Equation 23.2 to calculate the Mahalanobis distances of the prospective scenarios from the prevailing and normal values of the variables used to define the scenarios.
3. We use Equation 23.5 to convert each prospective scenario's Mahalanobis distance into a measure of relative likelihood.
4. We rescale the likelihoods to sum to one, which we interpret as probabilities.

One might be tempted to think that this process yields probabilities based on the historical prevalence of the projected scenarios. This is not the case. The probability of a prospective scenario is determined by its similarity to the anchor (for example, current or normal economic conditions) and by how the economic variables co-moved historically even if the scenario's defining values never actually occurred historically.

REVISING PROBABILITIES

Suppose the statistically derived scenario probabilities contradict our intuition about the likelihood of one of the scenarios. This could occur because one of the values we assigned to an economic variable is empirically implausible – in other words, we made a mistake. Or it could occur because we feel strongly that a scenario is more or less likely than history would suggest. In either event, it could be instructive to see what changes in the scenario specifications would be required to force the statistical probabilities to converge to our intuitive probabilities.

We cannot solve this problem analytically. Instead, we must resort to an iterative procedure to find the solution. We do so by taking the partial derivatives of the probability we are targeting with respect to the economic variables across all the scenarios and iteratively change the values of the economic variables by arbitrarily small amounts that are proportional to the direction and size of the partial derivatives. We repeat this process until the rescaled probability of the targeted scenario equals our desired value. After doing so, we should consider how the other scenario probabilities change to ensure that we are comfortable with all the new probabilities.

To determine these derivatives, we first compute the derivatives of the Mahalanobis distance, d_m, with respect to each of the vectors of economic conditions, x_m, for a given scenario, m, to arrive at the collective set of changes that will have the largest impact on the Mahalanobis distance for that scenario. The set of derivatives for each scenario is called the gradient:

$$\nabla d_m\left(x_m\right) = 2\Sigma^{-1}\left(x_m - \theta\right) \tag{23.6}$$

In Equation 23.6, ∇d_m is the gradient of the Mahalanobis distance as a function of its vector of inputs, Σ^{-1} is the inverse of the covariance matrix of historical deviations, and θ is the vector of economic variables used to represent the anchor. The gradient tells us the directions and proportions to adjust each element of x_m to have the greatest impact for a given scenario, m. We repeat this calculation for every scenario.

Equation 23.6 gives the sensitivity of the Mahalanobis distance to the economic variables, but this is only an intermediate step. Our goal is to determine the sensitivity of the rescaled probabilities to the economic variables. These probabilities are a function of the raw probabilities from Equation 23.5, which themselves are a function of the Mahalanobis distances from Equation 23.1. We therefore have a set of nested functions, which requires us to apply the chain rule of calculus to determine the ultimate derivatives of interest; that is, the derivatives of the rescaled probabilities with respect to the economic variables. The resulting sensitivity, in simplified form, is given by Equation 23.7:

$$\nabla p_{target}\left(x_m\right) = \left(p_{target} - \delta_{target}\left(m\right)\right) p_m \Sigma^{-1}\left(x_m - \theta\right) \tag{23.7}$$

In Equation 23.7, ∇p_{target} is the gradient of the probability of a chosen target scenario as a function of the vector of inputs for a chosen scenario m, p_{target} is the original probability of the target scenario, p_m is the original probability of scenario m, and the term $\delta_{target}\left(m\right)$ is equal to one if scenario m is the same as the scenario for which we are targeting a probability and it is equal to zero otherwise

We identify the scenario that has the largest directional derivative, and we adjust the vector of that scenario's economic conditions by a small increment in this direction. We proceed iteratively until the probability equals our desired target.

CASE STUDY

Let's consider three prospective scenarios in the context of the dramatic economic downturn in 2020 driven by the global COVID-19 pandemic.

- Scenario 1: Stable recovery
- Scenario 2: Volatility
- Scenario 3: Depression

And let us suppose that the economy has been on a path of steady, moderate growth. We use the following variables to characterize the recent path of the economy and these prospective scenarios:

- US Industrial Production (annual percent change)
- US Inflation (annual percent change)

Table 23.1 shows the values for these economic variables for the recent path of the economy (projecting a plausible 2020 value as of the time of writing at mid-year) along with the three prospective scenarios. We apply Equation 23.2 to calculate the Mahalanobis distance of each prospective scenario from the recent path, and Equation 23.6 to convert these distances into probabilities, and we convert these raw probabilities into relative probabilities, as shown.

Now suppose we disagree with the 4% probability associated with the Depression scenario. We believe its probability should be 10%. We apply Equations 23.6 and 23.7 to determine the smallest adjustments we need to make in order to arrive at a 10% probability for Depression. Table 23.2 shows the derivatives and the initial revisions that are required to move toward the 10% target probability for the Depression scenario.

After 30 iterations, we arrive at the fully revised values in Table 23.3 that comport with a 10% probability of occurrence for Scenario 2.

At this point, we should check to see that we are comfortable with the new values for the economic scenarios as well as the new probabilities for the other scenarios. Assuming we are satisfied, we proceed to the next step, which is to map these economic variables onto asset class returns.

TABLE 23.1   Current Path and Prospective Scenarios

				Prospective Paths		
Scenarios	Recent path[*]			Stable Recovery (%)	Volatility (%)	Depression (%)
Growth	2018	2.0%	2021	2.5	2.0	−5.0
Growth	2019	1.8%	2022	2.0	−3.0	−2.0
Growth	2020[*]	−6.0%	2023	3.0	3.0	0.0
Inflation	2018	1.9%	2021	2.0	2.0	1.0
Inflation	2019	2.3%	2022	2.0	1.0	0.0
Inflation	2020[*]	1.0%	2023	1.5	4.0	1.5
	Probability Estimate:			26.6	69.3	4.2

[*]*Projecting hypothetical values as of end of 2020, for illustration.*

TABLE 23.2 Initial Revisions

		Prospective Paths						
		Stable Recovery		Volatility		Depression		
		Derivatives	Revisions (%)	Derivatives	Revisions (%)	Derivatives	Revisions (%)	
Growth	2021	1.23	0.0008	-0.28	-0.0002	8.94	0.0058	
Growth	2022	2.36	0.0015	-1.60	-0.0010	7.85	0.0051	
Growth	2023	3.61	0.0023	4.87	0.0031	-0.43	-0.0003	
Inflation	2021	1.19	0.0008	0.70	0.0005	11.55	0.0075	
Inflation	2022	1.27	0.0008	3.91	0.0025	13.01	0.0084	
Inflation	2023	-0.38	-0.0002	11.35	0.0073	3.91	0.0025	

TABLE 23.3 Revised Scenario Probabilities

Scenarios		Prospective Paths		
		Stable Recovery (%)	Volatility (%)	Depression (%)
Growth	2021	2.51	2.00	–4.95
Growth	2022	2.02	–3.01	–1.95
Growth	2023	3.02	3.03	0.00
Inflation	2021	2.01	2.00	1.07
Inflation	2022	2.01	1.02	0.07
Inflation	2023	1.50	4.07	1.52
Probability Estimate:		29.0	61.0	10.0

MAPPING ECONOMIC VARIABLES ONTO ASSET CLASS RETURNS

Thus far, we have assigned probabilities to prospective economic scenarios that are defined as a set of values for selected economic variables. However, we do not invest in economic variables. We invest in asset classes. Therefore, we need to translate these projections of economic variables into expected returns for the asset classes we will use to construct our portfolios. To do so, we apply a novel prediction technique called partial sample regression. This technique is described thoroughly in Chapter 13, but it may be beneficial to summarize it here.

Partial sample regression is based on the notion that the prediction from a linear regression equation is mathematically equivalent to a weighted average of the past values of the dependent variable (the asset class returns) in which the weights are the relevance of the independent observations (the values for the economic variables). Relevance within this context has a precise meaning. It is the sum of the statistical similarity of the past observations to the current values for the independent variables, which is the negative of their Mahalanobis distances, and the informativeness of the past observations, which equals their Mahalanobis distances from the average values of the independent variables. All else being equal, past observations that are more like the current observations and more different from their historical averages are more relevant.

Partial sample regression is a two-step technique. We first regress the asset class returns on the values for the economic variables to determine the relevance of the observations for the independent variables. We then use the mathematical equivalence of the prediction from linear regression and the weighted average of the past values of the dependent variable to estimate each asset class's return based on a subset of the observations that is filtered for relevance.

Suppose we wish to consider alternative portfolios comprising US equities, Treasury bonds, and Treasury bills. By applying the partial sample regression technique to monthly data beginning December 1978 and ending December 2019, the estimated returns for each asset class and for each prospective scenario are given in Table 23.4.

Table 23.5 shows three portfolios we wish to consider, along with their expected returns, which we calculate as the product of the returns from Table 23.4 and the asset class weights.

These results reveal important trade-offs. In terms of cumulative returns, the aggressive portfolio is expected to perform the best in a stable recovery scenario, but the worst in other scenarios. Even though we do not explicitly consider each portfolio's standard deviation, we can implicitly take risk into account by the range of scenarios we put forth, along with the probabilities we assigned to them. However, this approach assumes that all investors have the same tolerance for risk, which, of course, is unlikely.

TABLE 23.4 Asset Class Returns

		Stable Recovery (%)	Volatility (%)	Depression (%)
US Equities	2021	8.8	−3.9	−17.4
	2022	10.9	−18.0	−4.2
	2023	11.9	12.6	17.4
Foreign Equities	2021	2.8	−2.7	−19.9
	2022	5.2	−20.3	−8.9
	2023	8.0	12.1	13.3
EM Equities	2021	3.7	5.0	−17.8
	2022	4.3	−20.5	4.7
	2023	7.5	30.8	23.8
Treasuries	2021	1.2	2.7	4.2
	2022	1.4	4.0	4.5
	2023	1.4	−2.1	2.4
Corporates	2021	2.3	−0.5	−0.5
	2022	3.1	−0.1	7.5
	2023	3.1	6.0	9.4
Commodities	2021	−1.6	14.6	−15.7
	2022	2.6	−39.7	−25.6
	2023	−7.9	5.2	8.6
Cash Equivalents	2021	−1.9	−2.0	−1.0
	2022	−1.9	−1.0	0.0
	2023	−1.5	−4.0	−1.5

TABLE 23.5 Portfolio Returns

		Stable Recovery (%)	Volatility (%)	Depression (%)
	2021	1.8	−1.1	−8.5
Conservative	2022	2.7	−10.3	−4.3
	2023	3.1	2.2	3.9
	Cumulative	**7.8**	**−9.4**	**−9.0**
	2021	3.8	−0.7	−12.6
Moderate	2022	5.4	−15.0	−5.0
	2023	5.8	7.6	9.2
	Cumulative	**15.8**	**−9.2**	**−9.4**
	2021	4.9	−1.7	−18.3
Aggressive	2022	6.8	−20.5	−7.3
	2023	8.1	11.9	12.5
	Cumulative	**21.2**	**−12.6**	**−14.8**

Most investors are risk averse, which means that they dislike a given size loss more than they like an equal size gain. These preferences are typically expressed by defining utility as a concave function of portfolio return. We may apply any utility preferences we wish to the forecasted distribution of portfolio returns across scenarios.

THE BOTTOM LINE

Scenario analysis requires investors to define prospective economic scenarios, assign probabilities to them, translate the scenarios into expected asset class returns, and identify the best portfolio, given all these inputs. The greatest challenge to scenario analysis is determining each scenario's relative probability. This chapter shows how to apply the Mahalanobis distance to determine these probabilities. Moreover, it shows how to modify the scenarios in order to render the empirically based probabilities consistent with one's views about their likelihood of occurrence. It then goes on to describe a novel technique called partial sample regression analysis, which is covered more thoroughly in Chapter 13, for mapping economic variables onto asset class expected returns. Finally, this chapter shows how to select the most suitable portfolio based either on the portfolios' expected returns or their expected utilities.

Although the procedures described in this chapter are complex to construct, they are simple to implement. Moreover, they establish a solid scientific foundation to support a popular but hitherto subjective approach for constructing and managing portfolios.

RELATED TOPICS

- Chapter 13 shows how to use partial sample regressions to forecast asset returns.
- Chapter 14 uses partial sample regression and paths of economic variables to forecast the stock–bond correlation.

REFERENCES

Czasonis, M., Kritzman, M., Pamir, B., and Turkington, D. 2020. "Enhanced Scenario Analysis," *The Journal of Portfolio Management,* Vol. 46, No. 4 (March).

Kritzman, M., Li, D., Qiu, T., and Turkington, D. 2021. "Portfolio Choice with Path Dependent Scenarios," *Financial Analysts Journal,* Vol. 77, No. 1 (First Quarter).

Mahalanobis, P. C. 1927. "Analysis of Race-Mixture in Bengal," *Journal of the Asiatic Society of Bengal*, Vol. 23, 301–333.

Mahalanobis, P. C. 1936. "On the Generalised Distance in Statistics," *Proceedings of the National Institute of Sciences of India*, Vol. 2, No. 1, 49–55.

NOTES

1. In two dimensions (two asset classes), an elliptical distribution is a distribution whose observations are evenly distributed along the boundaries of ellipses that are centered on the mean observation of the scatter plot. It therefore has no skewness, but it may have non-normal kurtosis. This concept extends to distributions with more than two dimensions, though it cannot be visualized beyond three dimensions. For a given time horizon or assuming returns are expressed in continuous units, mean-variance analysis assumes either that returns are elliptically distributed or that investor preferences are well approximated by mean and variance.
2. By "relevant" we mean combinations of asset class returns that are reasonably feasible given the assumed distribution.
3. See Mahalanobis (1927) and Mahalanobis (1936).
4. The probability density function for the multivariate normal distribution has a similar form, but includes a constant term that ensures the cumulative probability of all possible outcomes equals one. The scaling is irrelevant to our analysis because we are interested in the relative probabilities of a discrete set of scenarios which we rescale to sum to one.

CHAPTER 24

Stress Testing

THE CHALLENGE

G. H. Hardy, the legendary mathematician, once claimed that his greatest disappointment in life was learning that someone had discovered an application for one of his theorems. Although Hardy's disinterest in practical matters was a bit extreme, it sometimes seems that scholars view the real world as an uninteresting special case of their models. This disinterest in real-world complexity, unfortunately, often brings unpleasant consequences. In this chapter, we address two simplifications about risk that often lead investors to underestimate their portfolios' exposure to loss. First, investors typically measure risk as the probability of a given loss, or the amount that can be lost with a given probability, at the end of their investment horizon, ignoring what might occur along the way. Second, they base these risk estimates on return histories that fail to distinguish between calm environments, when losses are rare, and turbulent environments, when losses occur more commonly. In this chapter, we show how to estimate exposure to loss in a way that accounts for within-horizon losses as well as the regime-dependent nature of large drawdowns.

END-OF-HORIZON EXPOSURE TO LOSS

Probability of Loss

We measure the likelihood that a portfolio will experience a certain percentage loss at the end of a given horizon by computing the standardized difference between the percentage loss and the portfolio's expected return, and then converting this quantity to a probability by assuming returns are normally distributed. Unfortunately, asset class returns are not normally distributed. Returns tend to be lognormally distributed, because compounding causes positive cumulative returns to drift further above the mean than the distance negative cumulative returns drift below the mean.[1] (See Chapter 25 for more details about lognormality.) This means that logarithmic returns, also called continuous returns, are more likely to be described by a normal distribution. Therefore, in order to use the normal distribution to estimate probability of loss, we must express return and the standard deviation in continuous units, as shown in Equation 24.1. We provide the full mathematical procedure for converting returns from discrete to continuous units in Chapter 25.

$$Pr_{end} = N\left[\frac{\ln(1+L) - \mu_c T}{\sigma_c \sqrt{T}}\right] \qquad (24.1)$$

In Equation 24.1, Pr_{end} equals the probability of loss at the end of the horizon, $N[\ ]$ is the cumulative normal distribution function, ln is the natural logarithm, L equals the cumulative percentage loss in discrete units, μ_c equals the annualized expected return in continuous units, T equals the number of years in the investment horizon, and σ_c equals the annualized standard deviation of continuous returns.

Value at Risk

Value at risk gives us another way to measure a portfolio's exposure to loss. It is equal to a portfolio's initial wealth multiplied by a quantity equal to the expected return over a stated horizon minus the portfolio's standard deviation multiplied by the standard normal variable[2] associated with a chosen probability. Again, we express return and the standard deviation in continuous units. But we convert the continuous percentile return $(\mu_c T + \sigma_c \sqrt{T} N^{-1}[p_L])$ to a discrete return before multiplying it by initial wealth, as shown in Equation 24.2. As Equations 24.1 and 24.2 reveal, probability of loss and value at risk are flip sides of the same coin:

$$VaR = W \times \left(\exp\left(\mu_c T + \sigma_c \sqrt{T} N^{-1}[p_L]\right) - 1\right) \qquad (24.2)$$

Here, VaR equals value at risk, μ_c equals the annualized expected return in continuous units, T equals the number of years in the investor's horizon, $N^{-1}[p_L]$ is the inverse cumulative normal distribution function evaluated at a given probability level, σ_c equals the annualized standard deviation of continuous returns, and W equals initial wealth.

These formulas assume that we observe our portfolio only at the end of the investment horizon and disregard its values throughout the investment horizon. We argue that investors should and do perceive risk differently. They care about exposure to loss throughout their investment horizon and not just at its conclusion.

WITHIN-HORIZON EXPOSURE TO LOSS

Within-Horizon Probability of Loss

To account for losses that might occur prior to the conclusion of the investment horizon, we use a statistic called the first passage time probability, which gives the probability that a portfolio will depreciate to a particular value over some horizon if it is monitored continuously.[3] It is equal to

$$Pr_{within} = N\left[\frac{\ln(1+L) - \mu T}{\sigma\sqrt{T}}\right] + N\left[\frac{\ln(1+L) + \mu T}{\sigma\sqrt{T}}\right](1+L)^{\frac{2\mu}{\sigma^2}} \quad (24.3)$$

Here, Pr_{within} equals the probability of a within-horizon loss, and the other terms are defined as they were for the end-of-horizon probability of loss.

The first part of this equation, up to the second plus sign, gives the end-of-horizon probability of loss, as shown in Equation 24.1. It is augmented by another probability multiplied by a constant, and there are no circumstances in which this constant equals zero or is negative. Therefore, the probability of loss throughout an investment horizon must always exceed the probability of loss at the end of the horizon. Moreover, the within-horizon probability of loss rises as the investment horizon expands in contrast to the end-of-horizon probability of loss, which diminishes with time, as we discussed in Chapter 4.

Within-Horizon Value at Risk

We use the same first passage time equation to estimate within-horizon value at risk. Whereas value at risk measured conventionally gives the worst outcome at a chosen probability at the end of an investment horizon, within-horizon value at risk gives the worst outcome at a chosen probability from inception to any time throughout an investment horizon. It is not possible to solve for within-horizon value at risk analytically. We must resort to a numerical method. We set Equation 24.3 equal to the chosen confidence level and solve iteratively for L. Within-horizon value at risk equals L multiplied by initial wealth.

These two measures of the within-horizon exposure to loss bring us closer to the real world because they recognize that investors care about drawdowns that might occur throughout the investment horizon. But they ignore another real-world complexity, to which we now turn.

REGIMES

Thus far we have assumed implicitly that returns come from a single distribution. It is more likely that there are distinct risk regimes, each of which may be normally distributed but with a unique risk profile. For example, we might assume that returns fit into two regimes, a calm regime characterized by below-average volatility and stable correlations, and a turbulent regime characterized by above-average volatility and unstable correlations. The returns within a turbulent regime are likely to be event driven, whereas the returns within a quiet regime perhaps reflect the simple fact that prices are noisy.

We detect a turbulent regime by observing whether or not returns across a set of asset classes behave in an uncharacteristic fashion, given their historical pattern of behavior. One or more asset class returns, for example, may be unusually high or low, or two asset classes that are highly positively correlated may move in the opposite direction.

There is persuasive evidence showing that returns to risk are substantially lower when markets are turbulent than when they are calm. This is to be expected, because when markets are turbulent investors become fearful and retreat to safe asset classes, thus driving down the prices of risky asset classes. This phenomenon is documented in Table 24.1. For additional background and details, see Kritzman and Li (2010).

This description of turbulence is captured by a statistic known as the Mahalanobis distance, with which you should be familiar. It is used to determine the contrast in different sets of data. In the case of returns, it

TABLE 24.1 Conditional Annualized Returns to Risky Assets January 1976–December 2015

	10% Most Turbulent Months (%)	Other 90% (%)
US Equities	−5.5	13.7
Foreign Developed Market Equities	−10.0	13.1
Emerging Market Equities	−43.0	20.4
Commodities	−12.5	8.2

captures differences in magnitude and differences in interactions, which can be thought of, respectively, as volatility and correlation surprise:

$$Turbulence_t = \frac{1}{N}(x_t - \mu)' \Sigma^{-1} (x_t - \mu) \qquad (24.4)$$

In Equation 24.4, x_t equals a set of returns for a given period, μ equals the historical average of those returns, and Σ is the historical covariance matrix of those returns.

The term $(x_t - \mu)$ captures extreme price moves. By multiplying this term by the inverse of the covariance matrix, we capture the interaction of the returns, and we render the measure scale independent, as well. We multiply by $\frac{1}{N}$ so that the average turbulence score across the data set equals 1. We illustrate this concept with a scatter plot of US and foreign developed market equities shown in Figure 24.1.

Each dot represents the returns of US and foreign equities for a particular period, such as a day or a month. The center of the ellipse represents the average of the joint returns of US and foreign equities. The observations within the ellipse represent return combinations associated with calm periods, because the observations are not particularly unusual. The observations outside the ellipse are statistically unusual and therefore likely to characterize turbulent periods. Note that some returns just outside the narrow part of the ellipse are closer to the ellipse's center than some returns within the

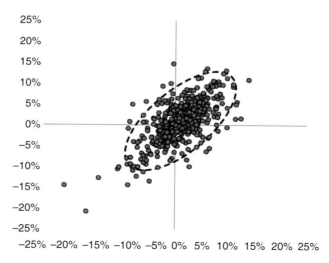

FIGURE 24.1   Scatter plot of US and foreign equities.

ellipse at either end. This illustrates the notion that some periods qualify as unusual not because one or more of the returns was unusually high or low, but instead because the returns moved in the opposite direction that period despite the fact that the asset classes are positively correlated, as evidenced by the positive slope of the scatter plot.

This measure of turbulence is scale independent in the following sense. Observations that lie on a given ellipse all have the same Mahalanobis distance from the center of the scatter plot, even though they have different Euclidean distances.

We suggest that investors measure probability of loss and value at risk not based on the entire sample of returns but, rather, on the returns that prevailed during the turbulent subsamples, when losses occur more commonly. This distinction is especially important if investors care about losses that might occur throughout their investment horizon, and not only at its conclusion.

Full-Sample Versus Regime-Dependent Exposure to Loss

Recall the moderate portfolio we derived in Chapter 2. It had an expected return of 7.5% and a standard deviation of 10.8%. Given a confidence level of 1% and based on a sample of returns beginning in January 1976 and ending in December 2006, without any knowledge of the pending global financial crisis, and using the conventional approach to estimating value at risk, we would have concluded that this portfolio had a 1% chance of losing as much as 14.2% of its initial value at the end of a five-year investment horizon.

If we had segregated the 20% most turbulent months from the same 30-year history leading up to the global financial crisis, and used this information to estimate exposure to loss throughout the investment horizon and not just at its conclusion, we would have instead concluded that this same portfolio had a 1% chance of losing as much as 45% of its starting value, as shown in the bottom right quadrant of Table 24.2. In fact, this portfolio lost 35.9% of its value during the global financial crisis.

TABLE 24.2 Value at Risk (1%)

	Full Sample (%)	Turbulent Regime (%)
End of horizon	−14.2	−38.6
Within horizon	−29.3	−45.0

TABLE 24.3   Probability of 35.9% or Greater Loss

	Full Sample (%)	Turbulent Regime (%)
End of horizon	0.0	1.4
Within horizon	0.0	4.7

Table 24.3 shows that, based on the conventional approach to estimating probability of loss, we would have concluded that such a loss had no reasonable chance of occurrence. But again, if we recognized that losses typically occur during turbulent periods, and we considered outcomes that might occur along the way, we would have estimated that this portfolio had nearly a 5% chance of experiencing such a large drawdown, as we show in Table 24.3.

THE BOTTOM LINE

Investors dramatically underestimate their portfolios' exposure to loss, because they focus on the distribution of returns at the end of the investment horizon and disregard losses that might occur along the way.

Moreover, investors base their estimates of exposure to loss on full-sample standard deviations, which obscures episodes of higher risk that prevail during turbulent periods. It is during these periods that losses are likely to occur. Complexity is inconvenient but not always unimportant.

RELATED TOPICS

- Chapter 4 discusses the fallacy of time diversification.
- Chapter 22 applies financial turbulence to identify and anticipate regime shifts.

REFERENCES

Karlin, S. and Taylor, H. 1975. *A First Course in Stochastic Processes (2nd ed.).* San Diego: Academic Press.

Kritzman, M. and Li, Y. 2010. "Skulls, Financial Turbulence and Risk Management," *Financial Analysts Journal,* Vol. 66, No. 5 (September/October).

Kritzman, M. and Rich, D. 2002. "The Mismeasurement of Risk," *Financial Analysts Journal,* Vol. 58, No. 3.

NOTES

1. For example, a positive 10% return will accumulate to 21% over two periods, whereas a −10% return will fall to 19% over two periods.
2. A standard normal variable is a normally distributed random variable with expected value 0 and variance 1.
3. The first passage probability is described in Karlin and Taylor (1975). Kritzman and Rich (2002) showed how investors could use it to estimate the within-horizon probability of loss and continuous value at risk.

CHAPTER 25

Statistical and Theoretical Concepts

This chapter provides a brief introduction to concepts in statistics and portfolio theory. We include a fair amount of math, but we do our best to avoid excessive complexity. Our intent is to establish a sufficient foundation for this book that is reasonably clear, but this review is by no means comprehensive. We therefore include references to other sources that provide a more thorough and technical treatment of these topics.

DISCRETE AND CONTINUOUS RETURNS

We define the discrete return R_t for an asset from time $t-1$ to t as the change in price over some period plus any income generated, all divided by the price at the beginning of the period:

$$R_t = \frac{P_t - P_{t-1} + I_t}{P_{t-1}} \tag{25.1}$$

Next, we denote the log return of the asset using a lowercase r_t:

$$r_t = \ln(1 + R_t) \tag{25.2}$$

Here, $\ln(x)$ is the natural logarithm function. The log return represents the continuous rate of return for the period. In other words, it is the instantaneous rate of return that, if compounded continuously, would match the asset's realized total return. The natural logarithm of x is simply the exponent to which the special number e, which is approximately equal to 2.71828, is raised to yield x. Therefore, the logarithm is the inverse of the exponential function, which we denote as exp(x), or equivalently e^x. To express the discrete return R_t, we reverse Equation 18.2, as follows:

$$R_t = \exp(r_t) - 1 \qquad (25.3)$$

Together, the exponential and logarithmic functions relate continuously compounded growth rates to returns that occur over discrete time intervals. Discrete time is observable and measurable, whereas continuous time is not. The returns we compute from data are in discrete units, but we often use continuous returns in analysis because they have important properties, which we discuss later.

ARITHMETIC AND GEOMETRIC AVERAGE RETURNS

The arithmetic average return for an asset (also called the mean return) is one of the most obvious and informative summary statistics. Suppose an asset is worth \$100 initially, appreciates to \$125 after one year, and falls back to \$100 after the second year. The discrete annual returns are +25% and –20%. The arithmetic average of the discrete returns is equal to the sum of the two returns divided by 2: $(0.25 + (-0.20)) \times \frac{1}{2} = 0.025 = 2.5\%$. More generally, for T time periods the arithmetic average is

$$\mu_{arithmetic} = \frac{1}{T} \sum_{t=1}^{T} R_t \qquad (25.4)$$

The 2.5% average return we calculated for our hypothetical asset presents a conundrum. It implies that the asset gained value on average, yet it was worth the same amount at the end of two periods as it was at the beginning. This apparent contradiction occurs because the arithmetic average of discrete returns ignores the effect of compounding. For this reason, the geometric average, which accounts for compounding, is more appropriate for summarizing past investment performance. In this example, the geometric average of discrete returns is equal to $[(1 + 0.25)(1 - 0.20)]^{1/2} - 1 = 0$, which agrees with the cumulative growth of the asset. For T time periods, the geometric return is given by

$$\mu_{geometric} = \sqrt[T]{\prod_{t=1}^{T}(1 + R_t)} - 1 \qquad (25.5)$$

We also arrive at the geometric average by converting the discrete returns to continuous returns, taking the arithmetic mean of the resulting continuous returns, and then converting the result back to a discrete return:

$$\exp\left(\ln([(1+0.25)(1-0.20)]^{1/2})\right)-1=0 \tag{25.6}$$

$$\exp\left((\ln(1+0.25)+\ln(1-0.20))\times\frac{1}{2}\right)-1=0 \tag{25.7}$$

Stated generally:

$$\mu_{geometric}=\exp\left(\frac{1}{T}\sum_{t=1}^{T}r_t\right)-1 \tag{25.8}$$

Given that the arithmetic average ignores that returns compound over multiple periods, why should we bother with it? It turns out that the arithmetic average has a very important advantage in a portfolio context. As we discuss in Chapter 2, the arithmetic average of a weighted sum of variables is equal to the sum of the arithmetic averages of the variables themselves. This relationship does not hold for the geometric average. In order to arrive at the average return of a portfolio from the averages of the assets within it, we must use arithmetic averages.

STANDARD DEVIATION

Average return tells us nothing about the variation in returns over time. To analyze risk, we must look at deviations from the average. The larger an asset's deviations from its average return – in either a positive or negative direction – the riskier it is. We use a statistic called the standard deviation, σ, to summarize the variability of an asset's returns, and we calculate it as the square root of the average of squared deviations from the mean:

$$\sigma=\sqrt{\frac{1}{T}\sum_{t=1}^{T}(R_t-\mu)^2} \tag{25.9}$$

We must square the deviations before we average them; otherwise, the average would equal zero. By taking the square root of the average squared deviations, we convert this measure back to the same units as the original returns. The standard deviation is a summary measure because the squared deviations are averaged together. As we will see later, there are nuances in the actual deviations that are not captured by the standard deviation.

The average of the squared deviations is called the variance. We often use the variance when we perform mathematical operations, but its square root, the standard deviation, is a more intuitive description of risk, and it has useful properties that we discuss later.

Equation 25.9 shows what is known as the population parameter for the standard deviation because it multiplies the sum of the deviations by $\frac{1}{T}$. It turns out that this estimate of the standard deviation is biased. It underestimates the true standard deviation because it implicitly assumes we know the true mean return for the asset, which we do not. We solve this problem by using $\frac{1}{T-1}$ instead. The resulting estimate is called the sample statistic. We use the sample statistic for the empirical analysis in this book, but we describe risk statistics in terms of the population parameters in this section of this chapter for convenience. The distinction is not very important in practice, especially when there are many observations.

CORRELATION

When two assets are combined, the standard deviation of the combination depends not only on each asset's standard deviation, but also on the degree to which the assets move together or in opposition. The correlation between two assets is a statistical measure of their co-movement. Correlations can be as low as -1, which indicates complete opposite movement, and as high as $+1$, which indicates they move in perfect unison. A correlation of 0 suggests that assets are uncorrelated with one another. Correlations are computed by multiplying each deviation for asset A with the deviation for asset B for the same period, averaging these products across all periods, and dividing the result by the product of the standard deviations of both variables to normalize the measure:

$$\rho_{A,B} = \frac{\frac{1}{T}\sum_{t=1}^{T}(R_{A,t} - \mu_A)(R_{B,t} - \mu_B)}{\sigma_A \sigma_B} \tag{25.10}$$

Correlation, therefore, captures the degree to which deviations align for two assets, on average. Just as there are aspects of risk that are not captured by the standard deviation, there are aspects of co-movement that are not captured by correlation. Nevertheless, correlations are very useful for summarizing the similarities or differences in the way asset returns interact.

COVARIANCE

The covariance between two assets equals their correlation multiplied by each of their standard deviations. It reflects the tendency of assets to move together as well as the average size of their movements. The covariance between two assets A and B over T periods is also equal to the numerator from Equation 25.10:

$$Cov(A, B) = \frac{1}{T-1}\sum_{t=1}^{T}(R_{A,t} - \mu_A)(R_{B,t} - \mu_B) = \rho_{A,B}\sigma_A\sigma_B \qquad (25.11)$$

Variance is a special case of covariance. It is the covariance of an asset with itself. A covariance matrix, which contains the variances of every asset and the covariances between every pair of assets, under many conditions, provides an excellent summary of risk for any universe of N assets. The covariance matrix, denoted in matrix notation as Σ, is an NxN matrix in which the element in the i-th row and j-th column contains the covariance between the i-th and j-th assets. Diagonal entries are variances. A covariance matrix is always symmetric because its entries for i, j and j, i are identical.

COVARIANCE INVERTIBILITY

Portfolio applications require covariance matrices to be invertible. Essentially, this means that it must be possible to derive a matrix called the covariance matrix inverse, which, when multiplied by the covariance matrix, returns an identity matrix with ones along its diagonal and zeros everywhere else. In very general terms, we can think of the covariance matrix as a measure of risk, and its inverse as a matrix that neutralizes that risk. The inverse covariance matrix is essential for portfolio optimization, as we discuss in Chapter 2.

For a covariance matrix to be invertible, it must be internally consistent. Imagine being presented with a blank 10-by-10 grid and asked to fill in values for a covariance matrix. The challenge might resemble a giant Sudoku problem in which prior choices constrain future possibilities. If asset A is highly correlated to asset B, and asset B is highly correlated to asset C, then asset A is very likely to be correlated to asset C. With a large web of cross-asset relationships, it is not hard to construct covariance matrices that imply impossible asset interactions.

Luckily, when we use enough returns to estimate a covariance matrix, it is guaranteed to be invertible. We have a problem only when we have more assets N in our universe than we have independent historical returns T on which to estimate the covariance matrix, or if we override empirical covariances with our views. To be invertible, a matrix must be positive-semi-definite, which means that any set of asset weights is guaranteed to produce a portfolio with non-negative variance. Negative variance cannot exist, so any covariance matrix that implies negative variance is flawed. We are more likely to encounter a problem when the number of assets is large, such as in security selection as opposed to asset allocation. But if the need arises, we can "correct" the covariance matrix using a technique that involves Principal Components Analysis.

Principal Components Analysis is a useful technique for many applications. It decomposes a covariance matrix into a matrix, V, composed of eigenvectors in each column, and a diagonal matrix of eigenvalues, D:

$$\Sigma = VDV' \qquad (25.12)$$

Eigenvectors are completely orthogonal to each other, and they span the entire set of asset returns. Though the elements in each eigenvector do not sum to one (their squared values sum to one), we interpret an eigenvector as a set of portfolio weights. The top eigenvector, also called the top principal component, is the portfolio with the highest possible variance. It explains more variation in the returns than any other vector. Its corresponding eigenvalue represents its variance. All subsequent eigenvectors are completely uncorrelated to those that came before, and they explain successively lower amounts of variation in the asset returns.

A matrix is positive-semi-definite if all of its eigenvalues are greater than or equal to zero. An eigenvalue equal to zero implies there is a combination of assets that yields zero risk, or, put differently, that there are two distinct portfolios with exactly opposite return behavior. The presence of redundant portfolio combinations may pose a challenge to portfolio construction, because there may not be a unique optimal portfolio. The existence of a negative eigenvalue is far more troubling, because it implies that we can create a portfolio with negative risk. Obviously, that is impossible. The covariance matrix is inconsistent and does not represent feasible relationships among assets.

To render a matrix positive-semi-definite, we replace offending eigenvalues with zeros and reconstruct the covariance matrix using this new assumption. To render it positive-definite, we substitute small positive values. Problematic eigenvalues tend to be small to begin with, so these adjustments have a relatively minor effect on the matrix. Nevertheless, we should approach these adjustments with care.

MAXIMUM LIKELIHOOD ESTIMATION

In practice, the amount of historical returns available for each asset class may differ. Non-equal history lengths present a choice. We could use the common sample and discard the extra returns for the asset classes with longer histories. Or we could restrict our investment universe to include only asset classes with long return histories, and thereby forego the potential benefits of including asset classes with shorter histories. A third, and perhaps more appealing option, is to make use of all available returns by using Maximum Likelihood Estimation (MLE).

We can use MLE for means as well as for covariances. The MLE method solves for the parameter that is most likely to have produced the observed returns. It is a general technique used throughout statistics, and it accommodates missing returns easily. We do not describe the implementation of MLE algorithms in detail, but the techniques are well documented elsewhere and are available in common statistical software packages.

Nevertheless, here is an intuitive description of MLE. Suppose we have an asset class with a long history of returns and one with a short history. The short history is common to both asset classes. Therefore, in order to estimate a covariance that pertains to both asset classes for the long history, we incorporate information about the interaction of the two asset classes during the short history that is common to both of them. We use this information, along with the returns of the asset class with the long history that preceded the short history, to arrive at a covariance that is statistically the most likely value. This approach produces estimates that are statistically consistent, and likely to be positive-semi-definite. We can also use the MLE estimates to "backfill" missing historical returns conditioned on the returns available at each point in time. Backfilling procedures are useful when we require a full empirical sample.[1]

MAPPING HIGH-FREQUENCY STATISTICS ONTO LOW-FREQUENCY STATISTICS

We have assumed so far that means and covariances pertain to the time interval over which historical returns are measured. However, we often use monthly returns to estimate the properties of annual returns, for example. It turns out that mapping statistics estimated from high-frequency observations onto low-frequency statistics is not a trivial exercise. Let us assume for now that returns are independent and identically distributed (IID) across time. In other words, they do not trend or mean-revert, and their distribution remains stable. We relax this important assumption in Chapters 5 and 19, but doing so is beyond the scope of our current discussion. Even for IID returns, though, something interesting happens when we consider the impact of compounding. As we measure compound returns over longer and longer periods, the distribution of returns changes shape. Compound returns cannot be less than −100%, but they can grow arbitrarily large. Overall, losses are compressed by compounding, and gains are amplified. The longer the time horizon, and the more volatile the assets, the more dramatic this downside compression and upside extension will be.

We solve this problem by converting statistics into their continuous counterparts (described earlier in this chapter), applying the time horizon adjustment to continuous returns, and translating the result back to discrete returns. It is indeed true that average return scales linearly with time for IID continuous returns. Likewise, standard deviations scale with the square root of time under these conditions.

Here is how we adjust for the time horizon. We begin with discrete high-frequency returns (monthly or daily, not milliseconds), and we convert them to continuous units using the following formulas:

$$\sigma_c = \sqrt{\ln\left(\frac{\sigma_d^2}{(1+\mu_d^2)}+1\right)} \tag{25.13}$$

$$\mu_c = \ln(1+\mu_d) - \frac{\sigma_c^2}{2} \tag{25.14}$$

Next, we multiply μ_c by the frequency we desire, such as 12 to convert from monthly to annual units, and we multiply σ_c by the square root of that frequency. These statistics now apply to the longer horizon, but they are still in continuous units. We convert them back to discrete units using the following formulas:

$$\mu_d = \exp(\mu_c + \sigma_c^2/2) - 1 \tag{25.15}$$

$$\sigma_d = \sqrt{\exp(2\mu_c + \sigma_c^2)(\exp(\sigma_c^2)-1)} \tag{25.16}$$

See Markowitz and Blay (2014) for more detail on these mechanics as well as other topics relevant to return distributions and utility.

PORTFOLIOS

Assume that we create a portfolio with weights w_i that sum to one across N assets and we rebalance the portfolio weights at the beginning of each period. The discrete return of portfolio p from year $t-1$ to t is a simple weighted average of the discrete returns for the assets:

$$R_{p,t} = \sum_{i=1}^{N} w_i R_{i,t} \tag{25.17}$$

Here R_i is the discrete return of asset i. The mean return for the portfolio is then

$$\mu_p = \sum_{i=1}^{N} w_i \mu_i \qquad (25.18)$$

This relationship holds because the expected value of a sum of variables is equal to the sum of the variables' expected value. We compute the variance of an N-asset portfolio as a sum across every pair of assets:

$$\sigma_p^2 = \sum_{i=1}^{N} \sum_{j=1}^{N} w_i w_j \sigma_i \sigma_j \rho_{ij} \qquad (25.19)$$

Matrix algebra offers more succinct notation for portfolio arithmetic. Throughout this book, we indicate vectors and matrices in formulas using bold font. We assume vectors to be column vectors unless stated otherwise. For a vector w of N weights across assets, a vector μ of their means, an NxN covariance matrix Σ, and using the symbol $'$ to denote the matrix transpose, we express the portfolio's mean and variance as

$$\mu_p = w'\mu \qquad (25.20)$$

$$\sigma_p^2 = w'\Sigma w \qquad (25.21)$$

PROBABILITY DISTRIBUTIONS

A probability distribution defines a random variable's possible values and how likely they are to occur. Discrete distributions (not to be confused with discrete returns) allow a fixed set of values and assign a probability between zero and one to each outcome such that the sum of the probabilities equals one. Specifically, we say that a random variable R_A takes on one of K values $R_A = a_k$ with probability $P(R_A = a_k) = p_{a_k}$:

$$\sum_{k=1}^{K} U(a_k) p_{a_k} = 1 \qquad (25.22)$$

It is often more useful to study variables that take on any of the infinite values in some range. In this case, the distribution is continuous and is defined as a probability density function (PDF). Strictly speaking, the probability that the variable takes on any value, such as 0.013425, is zero because point values are infinitely small and there are infinitely many of them. But we can easily calculate the probability that a variable will take on a value within a defined range using an integral to capture the area under the curve.

If R_A has a continuous probability distribution with PDF $f_{R_A}(x)$, its integral, which measures the area underneath its curve, equals one when summed across all possible values:

$$\int f_{R_A}(x)dx = 1 \qquad (25.23)$$

THE CENTRAL LIMIT THEOREM

The central limit theorem is a profound result in statistics. It states that the sum (or average) of many random variables is approximately normally distributed, as long as the underlying variables are IID and have finite variance. This result is powerful because the normal distribution is described entirely by its mean and variance, whereas the component distributions might be far more complicated. Given that many processes in nature, and in finance, involve outcomes that are aggregations of many other random events, we should expect to see many variables with distributions close to normal. And indeed we do.

THE NORMAL DISTRIBUTION

The normal (or Gaussian) distribution looks like a bell-shaped curve. It is centered around the mean with tails that decay symmetrically on both sides. The normal distribution has many attractive properties:

- It characterizes the sum of large numbers of other variables, regardless of their distribution, due to the central limit theorem.
- It is fully described by its mean and variance. Fitting a normal distribution to data requires estimating only two parameters.
- The sum of normally distributed variables is also normally distributed.

Whereas a single-variable normal distribution is described by its mean and variance, a multivariate normal distribution is described by its mean vector and covariance matrix.

HIGHER MOMENTS

The statistics of mean and variance are special cases of a more general way to describe distributions, known as moments. It is easier to conceptualize what are known as the "central" moments of a distribution. Each moment is, quite simply, the average of all deviations from the mean raised to a specified power. The first central moment is the (signed) average of each return minus the mean, which is always equal to zero. The second central moment is the variance, which we have already discussed at length in this chapter. Subsequent moments are often termed "higher moments," and they measure departures from normality. The third central moment measures asymmetry. It is often normalized by dividing by the standard deviation cubed, and is called skewness. If larger returns are disproportionately positive, the distribution will be positively skewed, and the opposite will be true for negative returns. The fourth central moment divided by standard deviation raised to the fourth power is called kurtosis, and it is often evaluated in relation to the kurtosis of a normal distribution. Distributions with larger kurtosis than a normal distribution (which has a kurtosis equal to 3) are said to be leptokurtic; they have larger probabilities of extreme positive and negative outcomes than a normal distribution. Those that have lower kurtosis than a normal distribution are platykurtic, with greater probability of moderate outcomes. We can proceed in this fashion indefinitely, computing higher and higher moments, but the first four are usually adequate to describe the salient features of asset returns.

THE LOGNORMAL DISTRIBUTION

The effect of compounding introduces skewness to returns. Consider, for example, a bet that either gains 1% or loses 1% with equal probability. If such a bet is taken once per month, the distribution of monthly returns will be symmetric. However, the compound return of two successive losses is −1.99%, whereas the equally likely return of successive gains is 2.01%. After five years, the spread widens to 81.67% for 60 gains and only −45.28% for 60 losses. In fact, the increase in wealth associated with any sequence of compound gains is larger than the decrease in wealth for an equal-size, but opposite, series of compound losses. The distribution of returns has positive skewness. The lognormal distribution is positively skewed and captures this behavior. If we assume an asset's instantaneous rate of growth is normally distributed, then its discrete returns are lognormally distributed.

ELLIPTICAL DISTRIBUTIONS

Elliptical distributions are defined by the fact that the returns that lie along a given ellipsoid must be equally likely. This implies that the PDF depends on x only through its covariance-adjusted distance from its mean. Therefore, if x is a column vector random variable, μ is a column vector representing the mean of x, and Σ is the covariance matrix for x, the density is proportional to some function of the covariance-adjusted distance:

$$f(x) \propto g[(x - \mu)'\Sigma^{-1}(x - \mu)] \tag{25.24}$$

Based on this definition, we can make the following observations:

1. Elliptical distributions are symmetric.
2. The multivariate normal distribution is an elliptical distribution.
3. Elliptical distributions can have "fatter tails" than a normal distribution. However, the shape of the tails must be consistent across assets.

THE MAHALANOBIS DISTANCE

The covariance-adjusted distance between two points was introduced by Prasanta Chandra Mahalanobis in 1936 as an extension to an earlier multivariate distance measure he proposed in 1927. His namesake measure, the Mahalanobis distance, is defined as follows:

$$d = (x - \mu)'\Sigma^{-1}(x - \mu) \tag{25.25}$$

In Equation 25.25, x and μ are column vectors of observations for a set of variables, and sigma is the covariance matrix of the variables. Sometimes, the measure is defined as the quantity in Equation 25.25 divided by N, or as its square root. Whether or not we apply these adjustments, the measure offers an equivalent ranking of distance for a collection of points (such as various choices of x) from a chosen anchor (such as μ).

In everyday life, we are all familiar with the Euclidean distance between two points, which we can easily determine with a ruler or tape measure. The Euclidean distance between two points is a fact, but it does not offer any context. For example, suppose my house is two miles from the center of my town. Do I live near the center or far away from it? The Mahalanobis distance provides this context based on the overall distribution of houses in the town. If most people live within one mile of a dense urban center, then it is fair to say I live far away. Alternatively, if the town is rural with a typical distance (a standard deviation) of five miles from the town center, it would be fair to say I live close by. Thus, the Mahalanobis distance reflects the typical amount of variation that occurs in the data. But it does not stop there; the correlations among variables also matter. Imagine that most people live near a main road that runs southwest to northeast. A two-mile drive down Main Street may feel like less distance than a two-mile dirt road excursion in the opposite direction. The Mahalanobis distance reflects the direction we must travel to get from one point to another, and whether such a pattern of movement occurs frequently or only rarely in the data.

The beauty of the Mahalanobis distance is that it summarizes so much important context in a single number. When applied to any data set, it inherently standardizes the observations so they are comparable. It is an exceptionally useful measure. For example:

- It defines the class of elliptical distributions (see previous section).
- It forms the basis of linear regression analysis. See Chapter 13.
- It is used to group observations, including human skulls, into categories by statistical similarity. See Mahalanobis (1927, 1936).
- It is used to detect statistical outliers and measure financial market turbulence. See Chapters 22 and 24 as well as Chow, Kritzman, Jacquier, and Lowry (1999) and Kritzman and Li (2010).
- It is used to diagnose a range of diseases and medical conditions including obstructive sleep apnea and breast cancer. See Su, Chen, Chen, Wang and Hsiao (2012) and Nasief, Rosando-Mendez, Zagzebshi, and Hall (2019). See also Su and Li (2002).
- It is used to detect anomalies in self-driving vehicles. See Lin, Kalastchi, and Kaminka (2010).
- It is used to assess probabilities in scenario analysis as well as in economic forecasting. See Chapter 23 as well as Czasonis, Kritzman, and Turkington (2020) and Kinlaw, Kritzman, and Turkington (2020).

PROBABILITY OF LOSS

Assume that a portfolio has a discrete expected return μ_d and standard deviation σ_d over some specified time period, and that we want to measure the probability that ending wealth will fall below $(1 + L)$. For long horizons, the impact of compounding could be substantial, so we should assume that the portfolio's discrete returns, R_t, follow a lognormal distribution. The loss threshold in continuous return units is $\ln(1 + L)$, and we compute the continuous counterparts for the portfolio's expected return and standard deviation using Equations 25.13 and 25.14. Because μ_c and σ_c describe a normal distribution in continuous units, we estimate the probability of loss by applying the cumulative normal distribution function $N[\ ]$ as follows:

$$Probability(R_t < L) = p_L = N\left[\frac{\ln(1 + L) - \mu_c}{\sigma_c}\right] \qquad (25.26)$$

For more on the likelihood of loss see Kritzman (2000, 2003).

VALUE AT RISK

Value at risk is the inverse of probability of loss. It represents the worst outcome we should expect with a given level of confidence. We derive value at risk by solving for L in the previous equation, where $N^{-1}[\ ]$ is the inverse cumulative normal distribution function:

$$L = \exp(\mu_c + \sigma_c N^{-1}[p_L]) - 1 \qquad (25.26)$$

UTILITY THEORY

A utility function $U(W)$ expresses the satisfaction an investor receives from any specified level of wealth W. A utility function may take many forms, but a plausible utility function for a rational investor meets at least two criteria:

1. It is upward sloping, which means that the investor prefers more wealth to less.
2. It is concave, which means that the investor's incremental utility from a gain is less than the investor's incremental disutility from an equal-size loss.

This second point implies aversion to risk. Investors with more dramatic curvature in utility are inclined to invest more cautiously, whereas those with a relatively flatter utility function are inclined to invest more aggressively. See Kritzman (2003) for more on utility theory.

SAMPLE UTILITY FUNCTIONS

For ease of interpretation, we express utility in terms of the discrete period's return $R_t = \frac{W_t}{W_{t-1}} - 1$, which is simply the percentage change in wealth. Let us first consider the class of "power utility" functions, which takes the following form:

$$U_{power}(R) = \frac{1}{1-\theta}\left(\frac{1}{(1+R)^{\theta-1}} - 1\right) \qquad (25.28)$$

A given return is raised to the power $1-\theta$, where $\theta \geq 0$ but $\theta \neq 1$. Larger values for θ imply greater risk aversion. Investors who are characterized by this class of utility functions are said to have "constant relative risk aversion." This means that they prefer to maintain the same exposure to risky assets regardless of their wealth. In the limit, as θ approaches 1, power utility becomes the commonly used "log-wealth" utility function:

$$U_{log}(R) = \ln(1 + R) \tag{25.29}$$

ALTERNATIVE UTILITY FUNCTIONS

Some investors are strongly averse to losses that breach a threshold because it may cause their circumstances to change abruptly. They are characterized by a "kinked" utility function (Figure 25.1) which is equal to power utility (or alternatively, log utility) plus an additional penalty of ω for each unit of loss below a threshold, k:

$$U_{kinked}(R) = \begin{cases} \dfrac{1}{1-\theta}((1+R)^{1-\theta} - 1), \ for \ R \geq k \\ \dfrac{1}{1-\theta}((1+R)^{1-\theta} - 1) - \omega(k - R), \ for \ R < k \end{cases} \tag{25.30}$$

Behavioral economists have found that even though most people exhibit risk aversion with respect to gains in wealth, many display risk-seeking behavior when they face losses. Instead of accepting a guaranteed loss of some amount, these people prefer to gamble between a smaller loss and a

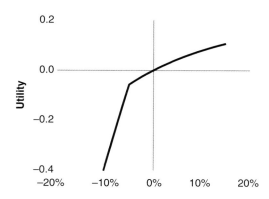

FIGURE 25.1 Kinked utility function.

FIGURE 25.2 S-shaped utility function.

larger loss in the hope that they can avoid some pain if they are lucky. An S-shaped utility curve (Figure 25.2) characterizes this preference.

$$U_{S-shaped}(R) = \begin{cases} -A(\theta - R)^{\gamma_1}, \ for \ R \leq \theta \\ +B(R - \theta)^{\gamma_2}, \ for \ R > \theta \end{cases} \tag{25.31}$$

While we believe that these utility functions describe a relevant cross section of investor preferences, they are by no means exhaustive. Many other utility functions have been proposed in the literature. We leave it to the reader to apply the concepts in this book to other specifications of investor utility.

EXPECTED UTILITY

We can use a utility function to describe an investor's relative preference among risky bets. For example, suppose that bet A offers a 50% chance of a 20% gain and a 50% chance of a 10% loss. Bet B offers a 50% chance of a 30% gain and a 50% chance of a 20% loss. Expected utility is the probability-weighted utility for each bet. Assuming log utility, the utility of each bet is

$$E[U_{log}(R_A)] = 0.5 \times \ln(1 + 0.20) + 0.5 \times \ln(1 - 0.10) = 0.03848 \tag{25.32}$$

$$E[U_{log}(R_B)] = 0.5 \times \ln(1 + 0.30) + 0.5 \times \ln(1 - 0.20) = 0.01961 \tag{25.33}$$

A log-wealth investor would prefer bet A in this example, given its higher expected utility.

CERTAINTY EQUIVALENTS

If we know an investor's expected utility for a risky bet, we can compute the size of a single risk-free return that yields identical utility. This quantity is called the "certainty equivalent." Given a utility function, an investor is indifferent to the uncertain outcome of the risky bet and the guaranteed certainty-equivalent return. Recalling our simple example, we use the exponential function, which is the inverse of the logarithm, to calculate the certainty equivalents for bets A and B:

$$CE_{log}(R_A) = \exp(0.03848) - 1 = 3.92\% \tag{25.34}$$

$$CE_{log}(R_B) = \exp(0.01961) - 1 = 1.98\% \tag{25.35}$$

MEAN-VARIANCE ANALYSIS FOR MORE THAN TWO ASSETS

For a universe of N assets, we express mean-variance expected utility as a function of a column vector of portfolio weights w, a column vector of expected returns μ, and an $N \times N$ covariance matrix Σ:

$$EU(w) = w'\mu - \frac{\lambda}{2} w'\Sigma w \tag{25.36}$$

To solve for the weights that maximize expected utility, we take its derivative with respect to the weight vector and set the derivative equal to zero:

$$0 = \frac{\partial EU(w)}{\partial w} = \mu - \lambda\Sigma w \tag{25.37}$$

Rearranging this expression, we find that the optimal weights are

$$w^* = \frac{1}{\lambda}\Sigma^{-1}\mu \tag{25.38}$$

These optimal weights are not subject to any constraints; they can be arbitrarily large positive or negative numbers and can sum to any amount. In this context, the investor's risk aversion changes the amount allocated to the optimal mix, but it does not change the relative allocation across assets.

Due to its mathematical simplicity, this unconstrained solution serves as a useful reference. These portfolios may require shorting and leverage, but they could be investible assuming we borrow to account for any funding shortfall (if the sum of the weights exceeds 100% of available capital) or invest excess proceeds at the risk-free rate (if the sum of the weights falls below 100% of available capital).

It is possible to derive analytical expressions for optimal weights subject to constraints (such as the analytical example presented in Chapter 7), but we will not delve into these mathematical solutions in detail. Many other books describe them thoroughly. Instead, we simply note that quadratic programming algorithms, which are easily accessible in popular software packages and programming languages, solve for mean-variance optimal weights in the presence of upper and lower bounds on each individual asset weight as well as equality and inequality constraints for sums of asset weights. (In Chapter 2, we review two specific methods of solving for optimal weights in the presence of constraints.)

EQUIVALENCE OF MEAN-VARIANCE ANALYSIS AND EXPECTED UTILITY MAXIMIZATION

For a given time horizon or assuming returns are expressed in continuous units, mean-variance analysis yields the same optimal portfolio as maximizing expected utility if either of two conditions holds:

1. Investor utility is a quadratic function.
2. Asset returns are elliptically distributed.

To understand the first point on an intuitive level, note that the quadratic utility function contains a linear term, which is a simple multiple of return, and a quadratic term, which is a multiple of return squared. Expected utility averages utility across a distribution of return outcomes, so it includes an average of the return and an average of the squared return. These two averages equal the mean and the variance, respectively, so we can completely describe utility in terms of a portfolio's mean and variance. If we restrict our attention to the portion of a quadratic utility curve in which utility is increasing, we know that the curve implies risk aversion; therefore, the portfolio that minimizes variance for a given level of return must also maximize expected utility (for some level of risk aversion).

Importantly, a portfolio composed of elliptical assets is itself elliptically distributed. The symmetry of the portfolio distribution is enough to guarantee that for any plausible utility function that is upward sloping and concave, we can obtain the expected utility-maximizing portfolio using mean-variance analysis. See Ingersoll (1987) for a detailed treatment of this topic.

With the facts described above, we may lay to rest some pervasive misunderstandings. In particular, the common claim that the validity of mean-variance analysis requires both normal distributions and quadratic utility is incorrect for many reasons. First, either of these conditions is irrelevant and unnecessary if the other is met. Second, non-normal distributions with fat tails do not invalidate mean-variance optimization as long as they are elliptical. And third, even if neither condition is met, the quadratic approximation is exceptionally good in most practical circumstances.

It is helpful to consider the validity of mean-variance optimization from multiple perspectives. Let us start by considering the perspective of an investor concerned with practicality and implementation. As stated earlier, it is true that if asset returns are non-elliptical and investor utility is not quadratic, then mean-variance analysis is not strictly equivalent to expected utility maximization. However, it usually provides a very good approximation to the true expected utility-maximizing result. It often requires extreme magnitudes of prospective portfolio returns (outside of historical experience) and exotic utility functions to erode the quality of this approximation. The quality of the approximation may be a matter of taste, and in some cases a matter of necessity. For further discussion of mean and variance approximations, see Samuelson (1970). In a 2016 interview conducted by Mark Kritzman,[2] Harry Markowitz provided important context on this point, as summarized in the following excerpts:

> *I justified mean-variance analysis as a practical way to approximately maximize expected utility. . . . Again, I never assumed quadratic utility. I never assumed Gaussian distributions. I assumed what was then – and still is now, to a great extent – the standard theory of rational decision making in the face of risk and uncertainty.*
> *Harry Markowitz (interview by Mark Kritzman)*

Now, let us consider the perspective of an investor who seeks a consistent theoretical motivation for optimal portfolio choice. From a theoretical standpoint, quadratic utility cannot apply in every conceivable circumstance because there will always be a point at which the curve changes from an upward slope to a downward one, implausibly suggesting that above some wealth level the investor begins to prefer less wealth to more.

Elliptical distributions pose theoretical problems too, in part because they unrealistically assign nonzero probabilities to negative asset prices. In addition, the reality that asset returns compound over time poses an essential challenge to the assumption of elliptical distributions. As we described earlier in this chapter, compounding creates skewed return distributions because successive gains are amplified while successive losses are compressed. A skewed distribution cannot be elliptical. Therefore, assets that are elliptically distributed for any chosen time interval (say, monthly) cannot be elliptically distributed over multiple intervals (say, yearly). Following this logic, the equivalence of mean-variance analysis to utility maximization cannot apply to multiple investment horizons at the same time.

In his 1969 paper,[3] Robert C. Merton reconciled this puzzle by demonstrating that under reasonable assumptions and when investors are able to trade continuously, mean-variance analysis applies to lognormal distributions, which are more realistic than normal distributions. In essence, casting mean-variance analysis in the context of continuous time finance removes the arbitrary choice of a time interval and allows the skewed nature of return compounding to coexist with the validity of mean-variance analysis. Merton (1975), for example, sets forth the principle of choosing the shortest feasible trading horizon as the most fundamental time interval to consider. This theory also shows that even with continuous trading, mean-variance analysis will not maximize utility if prices experience instantaneous jumps or gaps. Merton summarized the importance of these continuous-time insights, which also extend to asset pricing models such as the Capital Asset Pricing Model (CAPM) and Arbitrage Pricing Theory (APT) in a 2017 interview conducted by Mark Kritzman:[4]

> *I was able to reconcile the practical, intuitive, closed-form-solution optimal portfolio rules of the Markowitz-Tobin mean-variance theory with expected utility theory and a prototypical lognormal return distribution, which doesn't have the negative-price perversities that a normal one has.*
>
> *Robert C. Merton (interview by Mark Kritzman)*

MONTE CARLO SIMULATION

In some instances, simulation techniques are used to produce more reliable estimates of exposure to loss than the formulas we described earlier. For example, when lognormally distributed returns are combined in a portfolio, the portfolio itself does not have a lognormal distribution. The shape of the lognormal distribution varies across asset classes depending on the asset classes' expected growth rates and their volatility. Short positions cause an even more dramatic difference in volatility because their returns are negatively skewed due to compounding, whereas the returns to long positions are positively skewed. In these circumstances, we should simulate random normal return samples for the asset classes in continuous units, apply the effect of compounding, consolidate returns into a single portfolio, and compute risk metrics for the resulting portfolio distribution. We perform the following steps:

1. Draw one set of random returns from a multivariate normal distribution with a continuous mean and covariance equal to that of the asset classes.
2. Convert each continuous return to its discrete equivalent by raising e to the power of the continuous return and subtracting one.
3. Multiply the discrete asset class returns by the portfolio weights to compute the portfolio's return.
4. Repeat steps 1 through 3 to produce a sample of 1,000 portfolio returns.
5. Count the percentage of simulated returns that fall below a given threshold to estimate probability of loss, or sort returns according to their size and identify the return of the 50th most negative return (given a sample of 1,000) as the five percentile value at risk.

BOOTSTRAP SIMULATION

Bootstrap simulation is like Monte Carlo simulation, but the simulated observations are selected from an empirical distribution instead of a theoretical one like the lognormal distribution. For example, we could generate thousands of hypothetical one-year returns by repeatedly sampling a different collection of 12 months from history and combining them. In doing so, we preserve the empirical distribution of the asset classes, but we create many new multi-period samples on which to measure risk. This approach is particularly useful when modeling derivatives or highly skewed asset classes for which the choice of a theoretical distribution is not obvious. One disadvantage of bootstrapping is that it relies heavily on what happened in the past, which may or may not provide a reliable characterization of the future. Also, even though bootstrapping creates new synthetic samples, it still does not contain the full spectrum of possibilities in the way a theoretical distribution does.

REFERENCES

Chow, G., Jacquier, E., Kritzman, M., and Lowry, K. 1999. "Optimal Portfolios in Good Times and Bad," *Financial Analysts Journal*, Vol. 55, No. 3 (May/June).

Czasonis, M., Kritzman, M., and Turkington, D. 2020. "Addition by Subtraction: A Better Way to Forecast Factor Returns (And Everything Else)," *The Journal of Portfolio Management*, Vol. 46, No. 8 (September).

Ingersoll, J. Jr. 1987. *Theory of Financial Decision Making.* Lanham: Rowman & Littlefield Publishers.

Kinlaw, W., Kritzman, M., and Turkington, D. 2020. "A New Index of the Business Cycle." *Forthcoming in the Journal of Investment Management.*

Kritzman, M. 2000. *Puzzles of Finance: Six Practical Problems and Their Remarkable Solutions.* Hoboken, NJ: John Wiley & Sons, Inc.

Kritzman, M. 2003. *The Portable Financial Analyst: What Practitioners Need to Know.* Hoboken, NJ: John Wiley & Sons, Inc.

Kritzman, M. and Li, Y. 2010. "Skulls, Financial Turbulence, and Risk Management," *Financial Analysts Journal,* Vol. 66, No. 5 (September/October).

Kritzman, M. and Markowitz, H. 2017. "An Interview with Nobel Laureate Harry M. Markowitz," *Financial Analysts Journal,* Vol. 73, No. 4 (Fourth Quarter).

Kritzman, M. and Merton, R. C. 2018. "An Interview with Nobel Laureate Robert C. Merton," *Financial Analysts Journal,* Vol. 74, No. 1 (First Quarter).

Lin, R., Khalastchi, E., and Kaminka, G. 2010. "Detecting Anomalies in Unmanned Vehicles Using the Mahalanobis Distance," The Maverick Group, Computer Science Department, Bar-Ilan University, Ramat-Gan, Israel 52900.

Mahalanobis, P. C. 1927. "Analysis of Race-Mixture in Bengal," *Journal of the Asiatic Society of Bengal,* Vol. 23.

Mahalanobis, P. C. 1936. "On the Generalised Distance in Statistics," *Proceedings of the National Institute of Sciences of India,* Vol. 2, No. 1.

Markowitz, H. and Blay, K. 2014. *The Theory and Practice of Rational Investing: Risk-Return Analysis, Volume 1.* New York: McGraw-Hill.

Merton, R. C. 1969 "Lifetime Portfolio Selection under Uncertainty: The Continuous-Time Case," *Review of Economics and Statistics,* Vol. 51, No. 3 (August).

Merton, R. C. 1975. "Theory of Finance from the Perspective of Continuous Time," *Journal of Financial and Quantitative Analysis,* Vol. 10, No. 4 (November).

Nasief, H., Rosado-Mendez, I., Zagzebski, J., and Hall, T. 2019. "A Quantitative Ultrasound-Based Multi-Parameter Classifier for Breast Masses," *Ultrasound in Medicine & Biology,* Vol. 45, No. 7 (July).

Page, S. 2013. "How to Combine Long and Short Return Histories Efficiently," *Financial Analysts Journal,* Vol. 69, No. 1 (January/February).

Samuelson, P. A. 1970. "The Fundamental Approximation Theorem of Portfolio Analysis in Terms of Means, Variances and Higher Moments," *Review of Economic Studies,* Vol. 37, No. 4 (October).

Stambaugh, R. 1997. "Analyzing Investments Whose Histories Differ in Length," *Journal of Financial Economics,* Vol. 45, No. 3 (September).

Su, C. and Li, S. 2002. "A MD Based Classifier for Diagnosing Diseases," *Journal of Chinese Institute of Industrial Engineers,* Vol. 19, No. 5 (September).

Su, C., Chen, K., Chen, L., Wang, P., and Hsiao, Y. 2012. "Prediagnosis of Obstructive Sleep Apnea via Multiclass MTS," *Computational and Mathematical Methods in Medicine,* Vol. 2012.

NOTES

1. This approach to analyzing return samples with unequal history lengths was first proposed by Stambaugh (1997). Page (2013) also proposes an augmented approach in which residuals are sampled from within the short data set and used in the backfilling procedure to preserve higher moments of the distribution such as skewness and kurtosis.
2. See Kritzman and Markowitz (2017).
3. See Merton (1969).
4. See Kritzman and Merton (2018).

Glossary of Terms

The definitions in this glossary pertain to the context in which we use these words and terms in this book. They may have different meanings in other contexts.

1/N   A portfolio weighting strategy in which the asset classes within a portfolio are weighted equally. It has been argued that such a strategy performs better out-of-sample than optimized portfolios, but we argue to the contrary in Chapter 9. See also *Mean-variance analysis*.

Absolute illiquidity   A measure of illiquidity that applies to asset classes that cannot be traded for a specified period of time by contractual agreement or because they are prohibitively expensive to trade within that time frame. See also *Partial illiquidity*.

Absorption ratio   A measure of risk concentration that is equal to the fraction of the total variance of a set of asset returns explained or "absorbed" by a fixed number of eigenvectors. See also *Eigenvalues, Eigenvectors, Principal Components Analysis*, and *Risk concentration*.

Alpha   The risk-adjusted return of an asset or portfolio calculated as the asset's or portfolio's excess return net of the risk-free return less beta times the market's excess return net of the risk-free return. Alpha is more commonly construed as the difference between an actively managed portfolio's average return and the average return of a benchmark. See also *Beta* and *Capital Asset Pricing Model*.

Arithmetic average return   The sum of a series of discrete returns divided by the number of discrete returns in the series. The arithmetic average return is used as the expected return in mean-variance analysis instead of the geometric average return because, unlike the geometric average return, the arithmetic average return of a portfolio is equal to the weighted sum of the arithmetic averages of the asset classes within the portfolio. See also *Geometric average return* and *Mean return*.

Asset allocation   The process of allocating a portfolio across a group of asset classes. Investors typically employ mean-variance analysis to determine the optimal weights for a portfolio. See also *1/N, Asset class,* and *Tactical asset allocation*.

Asset allocation policy   See *Policy portfolio*.

Asset class   A stable aggregation of investable units that is internally homogeneous and externally heterogeneous, which, when added to a portfolio, raises its expected utility without benefit of selection skill, and which can be accessed cost-effectively in size. See also *Asset allocation, Expected utility, Externally heterogeneous,* and *Internally homogeneous.*

Autocorrelation   The association between values of a random variable and its prior values. First-degree autocorrelation measures the association of successive observations. Second-degree autocorrelation measures the association among every other observation. See also *Cross-correlation* and *Variance ratio.*

Autoregressive model   A regression model that relates values of random variables such as returns to their prior values. See also *Autocorrelation.*

Basket option   In currency hedging, a put option that protects a portfolio's collective currency exposure. A basket option is less expensive than a portfolio of put options because diversification across currencies reduces the volatility of the basket. However, it provides less protection than a portfolio of options because it pays off only if the currencies collectively breach the chosen strike price. See also *Put option.*

Baum-Welch algorithm   A search algorithm designed to find transition probabilities of a hidden Markov model. The algorithm works both forward and backward to determine the probabilities of transitions from one regime to another. See also *Hidden Markov model.*

Bayes theorem   A method for combining views with empirical observations. It defines the "posterior" probability as the probability that a variable will take on a specified value given the fact that we observe a sample of data. The posterior probability is equal to our "prior" belief about the probability that the parameter will take on that value, multiplied by the likelihood of observing the data given that we hold that prior belief.

Bayesian shrinkage   A procedure for mitigating the impact of estimation error when forming portfolios in which each estimate is blended with a prior view such as the cross-sectional mean or the estimate associated with the minimum-risk portfolio. See also *Estimation error.*

Beta   A measure of an asset's or portfolio's relative volatility with a reference portfolio, such as the market portfolio. It is estimated as the slope of a regression line relating an asset's or portfolio's excess return over the risk-free return to a reference portfolio's excess return over the risk-return. Within the context of the Capital asset pricing model, beta, when squared and multiplied by the market's variance, represents an asset's or portfolio's nondiversifiable risk. See also *Alpha, Capital asset pricing model,* and *Market portfolio.*

Bivariate distribution   A description of the linkage between each pair of potential returns and their probability of occurrence. See also *Normal distribution, Probability distribution,* and *Return distribution.*

Blended covariance   An estimate of covariance that is a blend of covariances from different regimes such as a calm regime and a turbulent regime. It is designed to address an investor's expectation of the relative likelihood of a particular regime or the investor's attitude toward a particular regime. See also *Financial turbulence.*

Bootstrap simulation A procedure by which new samples are generated from an original data set by randomly selecting observations with replacement from the original data. See also *Monte Carlo simulation.*

Call option An option that grants its owner the right but not the obligation to purchase an underlying asset at a previously agreed-upon price at or up to a specified future date (American) or only at a specified future date (European). See also *Put option.*

Capital Asset Pricing Model (CAPM) A theory of market equilibrium that partitions risk into two sources: that caused by changes in the market portfolio, which cannot be diversified away, and that caused by nonmarket factors, which can be diversified away. An asset's nondiversifiable risk is equal to its beta squared multiplied by the market portfolio's variance. The CAPM implies that investors should incur only nondiversifiable risk because they are not compensated for bearing diversifiable risk. The CAPM was developed simultaneously and independently by John Lintner, Jan Mossin, William Sharpe, and Jack Treynor. See also *Alpha*, *Beta*, and *Market portfolio.*

Capital call A demand for cash from a portfolio to fund benefit payments, investment opportunities associated with capital committed to private equity and real estate funds, or consumption needs. See also *Absolute illiquidity* and *Partial illiquidity.*

Capital market line In dimensions of expected return (vertical axis) and standard deviation (horizontal axis), a straight line emanating from the risk-free rate on the vertical axis and progressing with an upward slope to a point of tangency on the efficient frontier and beyond. The segment of the capital market line between the risk-free rate and the point of tangency represent combinations of the risk-free asset (lending) and the tangent portfolio. The segment of the capital market line beyond the point of tangency represents combinations of the tangency portfolio and borrowing at the risk-free rate. See also *Efficient frontier* and *Tangency portfolio.*

Central limit theorem The principle that the distribution of the sum or average of independent random variables, which are not necessarily individually normally distributed, will approach a normal distribution as the number of variables increases. See also *Normal distribution.*

Certainty equivalent A certain outcome that conveys the same amount of expected utility as the utility associated with a risky gamble. See also *Expected utility.*

Chain rule of calculus A formula for computing the derivative of a nested group of functions. If one variable is a function of another variable, which itself is a function of yet another variable, for example, we must use the chain rule of calculus to arrive at the derivative.

Chi-squared distribution   A distribution of the sum of the squares of a specified number of independent standard random normal variables. It is used to evaluate the significance of the difference between an empirically observed distribution and a theoretical distribution, for example. See also *Jarque-Bera test*.

Concave utility function   A description of investor preferences that assumes utility increases with wealth but at a diminishing rate, implying that investors derive a smaller increase in utility for a given increase in wealth than the disutility they suffer from a decrease in wealth of the same amount. See also *Expected utility, Kinked utility function, Log-wealth utility function, Power utility function, Quadratic utility function,* and *S-shaped utility function*.

Concentration   In asset allocation, the notion of increasing a portfolio's expected return by allocating the portfolio to a fewer number of asset classes with higher expected returns, instead of using leverage to increase expected return. See also *Asset allocation, Asset class,* and *Leverage*.

Constant absolute risk aversion   A measure of risk aversion which holds that investors prefer to maintain the same absolute amount of their wealth in risky assets irrespective of changes to their wealth. See also *Constant relative risk aversion, Log-wealth utility function,* and *Power utility function*.

Constant relative risk aversion   A measure of risk aversion which holds that investors prefer to maintain the same proportion of their wealth in risky assets as their wealth grows. See also *Constant absolute risk aversion, Log-wealth utility function,* and *Power utility function*.

Constraint   In asset allocation, a maximum or minimum limit on the allocation to a particular asset class or group of asset classes. See also *Asset allocation, Asset class, Mean-variance-tracking error optimization,* and *Wrong and alone*.

Contingent option   In currency hedging, a put option that pays off only if the currencies within the portfolio breach a chosen strike price and, at the same time, either the foreign component of the portfolio or the total portfolio also breaches a chosen strike price. See also *Put option*.

Continuous probability distribution   A probability distribution in which there are an infinite number of observations covering all possible values along a continuous scale. See also *Discrete probability distribution* and *Probability distribution*.

Continuous return   The rate of return that, if compounded continuously or instantaneously, would generate the corresponding discrete return. It is equal to the natural logarithm of the quantity 1 plus the discrete return. See also *Discrete return, e,* and *Natural logarithm*.

Continuously compounded growth rate   See *Continuous return*.

Correlation   A measure of the association between two variables. It ranges in value from 1 to –1. If one variable's values are higher than its average when another variable's values are higher than its average, for example, the correlation will be positive, somewhere between 0 and 1. Alternatively, if one variable's values are lower than its average when another variable's values are higher than its average, then the correlation will be negative. See also *Correlation asymmetry, Covariance, Exceedance correlation,* and *Single-period correlation.*

Correlation asymmetry The notion that the correlations of returns differ across subsamples that fall above or below a chosen threshold. Correlation asymmetry implies that investors should construct portfolios to account for correlations estimated from observations chosen from periods when a portfolio's main growth asset performs poorly. See also *Correlation* and *Exceedance correlation.*

Covariance A measure of the comovement of the returns of two assets that accounts for the magnitude of the moves. It is equal to the correlation between the two assets' returns times the first asset's standard deviation times the second asset's standard deviation. Combinations of assets that have low covariances are desirable because they offer greater diversification. See also *Correlation, Standard deviation,* and *Variance.*

Covariance matrix A matrix used in portfolio optimization, sometimes called a variance-covariance matrix, with an equal number of rows and columns, which contains the variances of a group of asset classes in the cells along the diagonal of the matrix and the covariances of the asset classes in the off-diagonal cells. See also *Covariance* and *Variance.*

Cross-correlation The association between the values of two random variables at various lags relative to each other. See also *Autocorrelation.*

Cross-hedging In currency hedging, the practice of using a forward contract on one currency to hedge a portfolio's exposure to another currency. See also *Overhedging.*

Cumulative probability distribution A probability distribution that measures, for example, the probability that a variable is less than or equal to a specified value. For a discrete distribution, the cumulative probability is calculated by summing the relative frequencies up to and including the value of interest. See also *Probability density function* and *Probability distribution.*

Cumulative return The rate of return that is equal to the product of the quantities 1 plus the discrete returns minus 1, or, equivalently, an asset's ending value divided by its beginning value minus 1, assuming reinvestment of income and controlling for contributions and disbursements. See also *Continuous return* and *Discrete return.*

Currency forward contract A contractual obligation between two parties to exchange a currency at a future date for a set price. The buyer of the forward contract agrees to pay the set price and take delivery of the currency on the agreed date, and is said to be long the forward contract. The seller of the forward contract agrees to deliver the currency at the set price on the agreed date, and is said to be short the forward contract. Usually these contracts are settled by a payment of cash rather than by an exchange of the currencies.

Data mining   The practice of searching for associations or patterns within a set of data using numerical search procedures rather than first hypothesizing an association or pattern and then testing for its presence.

Default asset mix   See *Policy portfolio.*

Density   With regard to a continuous probability distribution, the relative likelihood that a random variable takes on a given value. See also *Probability distribution.*

Dimensionality   In optimization, the number of distinct units, such as asset classes, factors, or securities, to be optimized. See also *Mean-variance analysis.*

Discrete probability distribution   A probability distribution that shows the percentage of observations falling within specified ranges, which collectively account for all of the observations. See also *Continuous probability distribution.*

Discrete return   The income produced by an asset during a specified period plus its change in price during that period, all divided by its price at the beginning of the period. Also called "periodic return." See also *Continuous return.*

Dynamic programming   A decision-making process that provides solutions to problems that involve multistage decisions in which the decisions made in prior periods affect the choices available in later periods. Dynamic programming is particularly suitable to portfolio rebalancing because whether we rebalance today influences what happens to our portfolio in the future. Dynamic programming was introduced by Richard Bellman in 1952, the same year that Markowitz published his landmark article on portfolio selection.

e   The base of the natural logarithm and the limit of the function $(1 + 1/n)^n$ as n goes to infinity. To five decimal places, it equals 2.71828. When *e* is raised to the power of a continuous return, it is equal to 1 plus the discrete return. See also *Continuous return, Discrete return,* and *Natural logarithm.*

Efficient frontier   A continuum of portfolios plotted in dimensions of expected return and standard deviation that offer the highest expected return for a given level of risk or the lowest risk for a given expected return. See also *Efficient surface, E-V maxim, Expected return, Mean-variance analysis,* and *Standard deviation.*

Efficient portfolio   A portfolio that resides on the efficient frontier. It has the highest expected return for its given level of risk. See also *Efficient frontier, E-V maxim,* and *Mean-variance analysis.*

Efficient surface   A representation of portfolios plotted in dimensions of expected return, standard deviation, and tracking error. It is bounded on the upper left by the traditional mean-variance efficient frontier, which comprises efficient portfolios in dimensions of expected return and standard deviation. The right boundary of the efficient surface is the mean-tracking error efficient frontier comprising portfolios that offer the highest expected return for varying levels of tracking error. The lower boundary of the efficient surface comprises combinations of the minimum-risk asset and the benchmark portfolio. See also *Efficient frontier* and *Tracking error.*

Eigenvalue   In Principal Components Analysis, the amount of variance associated with a given eigenvector. See also *Eigenvector* and *Principal Components Analysis*.

Eigenvector   In Principal Components Analysis, a linear combination of assets comprising both long and short positions that explains a fraction of the covariation in the assets' returns. See also *Eigenvalue* and *Principal Components Analysis*.

Elliptical distribution   In two dimensions (two asset classes), a distribution whose observations are evenly distributed along the boundaries of ellipses that are centered on the mean observation of the scatter plot. It therefore has no skewness, but it may have non-normal kurtosis. This concept extends to distributions with more than two dimensions, though it cannot be visualized beyond three. For a given time horizon or assuming returns are expressed in continuous units, mean-variance analysis assumes either that returns are elliptically distributed or that investor preferences are well approximated by mean and variance. See also *Kurtosis, Mean-variance analysis, Normal distribution, Skewness,* and *Symmetric distribution*.

End-of-horizon probability of loss   A measure of the likelihood that a portfolio will incur a particular percentage of loss as of the end of a specified investment horizon. See also *End-of-horizon value at risk, Within-horizon probability of loss,* and *Within-horizon value at risk*.

End-of-horizon value at risk   At a given probability the maximum loss or minimum gain that could occur at the end of a specified investment horizon. See also *End-of-horizon probability of loss, Within-horizon probability of loss,* and *Within-horizon value at risk*.

Equilibrium return   The asset class return that is expected to prevail when the asset classes within a market are fairly priced. It is equal to the risk-free return plus beta times the excess return of the market portfolio. It is often used as the default expected return in mean-variance analysis. See also *Capital Asset Pricing Model, Expected return,* and *Mean-variance analysis*.

Error maximization   The notion that mean-variance analysis, by construction, favors assets for which return is overestimated and risk is underestimated. This bias leads to two problems. First, the expected return of the optimized portfolio is overstated, while its risk is understated. Second, assets for which return is underestimated and risk is overestimated are underweighted in the optimized portfolio, whereas assets with opposite errors are overweighted. We argue in Chapter 7 that error maximization is not as problematic to asset allocation as some would have us believe. However, we discuss procedures for addressing estimation error in Chapter 19. See also *Estimation error* and *Mean-variance analysis*.

Estimation error   The difference between estimated values for expected returns, standard deviations, and correlations and the realizations of these values out-of-sample or, in the case of interval error, within the same sample but at different intervals. Estimation error can be partitioned into independent-sample error, interval error, mapping error, and small-sample error. See also *Error maximization, Independent-sample error, Interval error, Mapping error, Mean-variance analysis, Small-sample error, and Stability-adjusted optimization.*

Euclidean distance The ordinary straight-line distance between two points. In defining a turbulent risk regime, it is contrasted to the Mahalanobis distance, which is a measure of statistical unusualness. Observations with the same Mahalanobis distance may have different Euclidean distances.

E-V maxim The proposition by Harry Markowitz that investors choose portfolios that offer the highest expected return for a given level of variance. See also *Efficient frontier, Efficient portfolio,* and *Mean-variance analysis.*

Eventual acceptance property The notion that for a given finite number of bets there is a partial sum of them that is acceptable even though the bets are individually unacceptable. See also *Law of large numbers* and *Time diversification.*

Exceedance correlation The correlation of returns from subsamples that fall above or below a chosen threshold. See also *Correlation* and *Correlation asymmetry.*

Excess dispersion The fraction of an empirical distribution of longer-interval returns that falls outside the one standard deviation tails of the distribution that is implied by estimation from shorter-interval returns. It measures the extent to which extrapolation of volatility of shorter-interval returns mischaracterizes the volatility of longer-interval returns for the same return sample.

Excess return That part of return that exceeds the risk-free return. See also *Risk-free return.*

Exchange-traded fund (ETF) Modified unit trusts or mutual fund–type investment funds characterized by a dual trading process. Fund shares are created or redeemed through the deposit of securities to, or the delivery of securities from, the fund's portfolio. Secondary trading takes place on a stock exchange. The dual trading process permits the fund shares to trade very close to the net asset value at all times.

Expected return The average or probability weighted value of all possible returns. The process of compounding causes the expected return to exceed the median return. Thus, there is less than a 50% chance of exceeding the expected return. See also *Arithmetic average return, Geometric average return, Lognormal distribution,* and *Skewness.*

Expected utility The average or probability weighted utility or measure of satisfaction associated with all possible wealth levels. See also *Expected utility maximization* and *Utility function.*

Expected utility maximization The process of identifying the asset class weights within a portfolio that yield the highest possible expected utility. If investor utility is a quadratic function or returns are elliptically distributed, then for a given time horizon or assuming returns are expressed in continuous units, expected utility maximization is equivalent to mean-variance analysis. See also *Elliptical distribution, Full-scale optimization, Mean-variance analysis,* and *Quadratic function.*

Exponential function   A function that converts a continuous return to a discrete return by raising *e* to the power of the continuous return and subtracting 1. For example, 1.10 is the exponential of *e* raised to the power 0.0953. Thus, 10% is the discrete counterpart of the continuous return, 9.53%. See also *Continuous return, Discrete return, e,* and *Natural logarithm.*

Externally heterogeneous   A measure of the dissimilarity of an asset class from other asset classes or combinations of other asset classes within a portfolio. This attribute is a necessary but not sufficient condition for a group of assets to be considered an asset class. See also *Asset class* and *Internally homogeneous.*

Factor   An economic variable such as inflation or a group of securities with a particular attribute such as capitalization, or an eigenvector derived through Principal Components Analysis, that is believed to reflect a particular risk. See also *Eigenvector, Factor exposure, Factor-mimicking portfolio, Factor profile,* and *Fundamental factor.*

Factor exposure   The comovement of the returns of a portfolio or asset class with changes in the value of a factor, usually measured by regressing the portfolio or asset class returns on changes in the factor value. See also *Factor Factor-mimicking portfolio, Factor profile,* and *Fundamental factor.*

Factor-mimicking portfolio   A group of securities or asset classes that are selected and weighted to minimize tracking error between its returns and movements of a factor value. See also *Factor, Factor-mimicking portfolio, Factor profile,* and *Fundamental factor.*

Factor profile   A weighted average of the returns of a set of factors usually measured in log units. The squared deviations from a factor profile are incorporated into mean-variance optimization as an additional measure of risk. The objective function is structured to penalize deviations from the factor profile. This setup allows investors to allocate to assets, but in such a way that accounts for their factor preferences. See also *Factor, Factor exposure, Factor-mimicking portfolio, Fundamental factor,* and *Mean-variance optimization.*

Fair-value pricing   The practice of estimating the value of an asset for which market prices are unavailable. These valuations are usually positively autocorrelated because current valuations are usually anchored to prior valuations. The observed standard deviation of a series of returns estimated from fair values, therefore, is likely to understate the true risk of these assets.

Fat-tailed distribution   A probability distribution in which there are more extreme observations than would be expected under a normal distribution. Fat-tailed distributions are called leptokurtic. See also *Kurtosis, Leptokurtic distribution, Normal distribution,* and *Platykurtic distribution.*

Financial turbulence   A measure of the statistical unusualness of a cross section of returns during a particular period, taking into account extreme price movements, the convergence of uncorrelated assets, and the decoupling of correlated assets. It is measured as the Mahalanobis distance.

Firm fixed effect   In regression analysis, an effect that arises from an unobserved firm characteristic that is constant or non-random. One controls for firm fixed effects by introducing dummy variables into the regression equation. See also *Regression analysis.*

First passage time probability   A probability that measures the likelihood of a value penetrating a threshold at any time during a specified time horizon. See also *Within-horizon probability of loss* and *Within-horizon value at risk.*

Full-scale optimization   Given a utility function and sample of returns, an optimization technique that maximizes expected utility by repeatedly testing different asset mixes to determine the utility-maximizing portfolio. Full-scale optimization may be preferable to mean-variance analysis if the return sample is not elliptically distributed and the investor's utility function is not well approximated by mean and variance. See also *Elliptical distribution, Genetic search, Mean-variance analysis,* and *Skewness.*

Fundamental factor   An economic variable, such as inflation or industrial production, that is thought to explain differences in the returns and risk of assets. See also *Eigenvector, Factor, Factor exposure, Factor-mimicking portfolio, Factor profile,* and *Security attribute.*

Genetic search   A numerical search procedure inspired by evolutionary biology and used to implement full-scale optimization. This method starts with an "initial population" of weight vectors. Next, it introduces random mutations and combinations of existing vectors to form the next "generation," and proceeds by "mating" the most promising (highest utility) offspring until a dominant solution is found. See also *Full-scale optimization.*

Geometric average return   The average annual return that, when compounded forward, converts an initial value to an ending value. It is equal to the product of the quantities 1 plus the annual discrete returns, raised to the power 1 over the number of discrete returns, less 1. When based on historical returns, an initial value compounded forward at the geometric average return yields the median value. The natural logarithm of the quantity 1 plus the geometric average return equals the continuous return. Also called annualized return or constant rate of return. See also *Continuous return, Discrete return,* and *Expected return.*

Gradient   A vector of derivatives that measure the sensitivity of a variable of interest to small changes in a set of inputs. The size and sign of the derivatives indicate the magnitude and direction by which to change the inputs to iteratively converge toward a target value for the variable of interest.

Henriksson-Merton test   A nonparametric test of forecasting reliability. It produces a score equal to the sum of the percentage of times a forecast is correct when a variable is above a threshold and the percentage of times a forecast is correct when a variable is below a threshold. A score of 2 indicates perfect foresight. A score between 1 and 2 indicates some degree of foresight. A score of 1 equals no foresight. A score below 1 indicates foresight that is worse than random.

This test addresses situations in which a variable is above a threshold more than 50% of the time.

Hidden Markov model A model of the distribution of a variable, such as a financial indicator or asset return, that assumes the observed values come from multiple distributions that switch according to a hidden regime variable. Each regime has a degree of persistence from one period to the next. For example, if we are in regime A this month, regime A might be more likely to prevail next month, too. But there is also a chance that the regime will shift abruptly from A to B. The term *Markov* refers to the assumption that the underlying regime variable follows a Markov process in that next period's regime probability depends only on the regime we are in today. See also *Baum-Welch algorithm*.

Higher moment A central moment of a distribution beyond the first and second central moments that measures non-normality. A central moment is the average of all deviations from the mean raised to a specified power. The third central moment measures asymmetry and is called skewness, and the fourth central moment measures peakedness and is called kurtosis. See also *Kurtosis, Moment, Normal distribution*, and *Skewness*.

Identity matrix In matrix algebra, a square matrix with 1s in the diagonal elements and zeros in the off-diagonal elements. A matrix multiplied by its inverse will yield the identity matrix. See also *Inverse matrix, Invertible matrix,* and *Matrix algebra*.

Illiquidity The inability to trade an asset within a specified period of time without significantly and adversely affecting its price. See also *Absolute illiquidity, Illiquidity,* and *Partial illiquidity*.

Independent and identically distributed (IID) A condition in which successive draws from a population are independent of one another and generated from the same underlying distribution, implying that the parameters of an IID distribution are constant across all draws. See also *Random variable*.

Independent-sample error The differences in the average returns, standard deviations, and correlations of two nonoverlapping samples. See also *Estimation error, Interval error, Mapping error, Small-sample error,* and *Stability-adjusted optimization*.

Informativeness In partial sample regression, a component of relevance computed as the Mahalanobis distance of a set of observations for independent variables in a regression analysis from the average values of those variables. Observations that are more statistically distant from the means are said to be more informative than observations that are statistically closer to the means, because more distant observations are unusual and therefore more likely to be driven by events than by noise. See also *Mahalanobis distance, Multivariate similarity, Partial sample regression,* and *Relevance*.

Instantaneous rate of return See *Continuous return*.

Integral   A function that gives the area under the curve of the graph of another function. It is used to estimate a probability, given a continuous distribution of returns. See also *Probability distribution.*

Internally homogeneous   A measure of the similarity of the components within an asset class. This attribute is a necessary but not sufficient condition for a group of assets to be considered an asset class. See also *Asset class* and *Externally heterogeneous.*

Interval error   The differences in the standard deviations and correlations estimated from longer-interval returns and their values implied by estimating them from shorter-interval returns and converting them to longer-interval estimates. Standard deviations estimated from shorter-interval returns are typically converted to standard deviations of longer-interval returns by multiplying them by the square root of the number of shorter intervals within the longer interval, but this rule will give an incorrect answer if the returns have nonzero autocorrelations. Correlations are typically assumed to be invariant to the return interval used to calculate them, but this invariance will not hold if either of the return series has nonzero autocorrelations or if they have nonzero lagged cross-correlations. See also *Autocorrelation, Cross-correlation, Estimation error, Independent-sample error, Interval error, Mapping error,* and *Stability-adjusted optimization.*

Inverse gamma distribution   A continuous probability distribution that permits only positive values and is suitable to represent the distribution that contains an unknown variance. It can also be represented as a scaled inverse chi-squared distribution.

Inverse matrix   In matrix algebra, a matrix that is analogous to a reciprocal in simple algebra. A matrix multiplied by its inverse yields an identity matrix. An identity matrix includes 1s along its diagonal and 0s in all of the other elements. It is analogous to the number 1 in simple algebra, in that a matrix multiplied by an identity matrix yields itself. Multiplying a vector or matrix by the inverse of another matrix is analogous to multiplying a number by the reciprocal of another number; hence, the analogy with division. See also *Identity matrix, Invertible matrix,* and *Matrix algebra.*

Invertible matrix   In matrix algebra, a square matrix for which an inverse exists such that the inverse matrix times the original matrix times a vector gives back the same vector. In portfolio optimization, the covariance matrix is inverted to solve for the vector of optimal asset class weights. See also *Covariance matrix, Identity matrix, Inverse matrix,* and *Matrix algebra.*

Iso-expected return curve   In dimensions of standard deviation and tracking error, a curve comprising portfolios that all have the same expected return but different combinations of standard deviation and tracking error. See also *Mean-variance-tracking error optimization.*

Jarque–Bera test   A test used to determine whether departures from normality are significant, given the number of observations in the sample from which they are estimated. The test statistic is a function of skewness squared and excess kurtosis squared. See also *Chi-squared distribution*.

Kernel regression   A nonparametric technique for estimating conditional expectations in which the relation is nonlinear. See also *Partial sample regression*.

Kinked utility function   A utility function that is kinked because, for a small change in wealth at a particular threshold, utility changes abruptly rather than smoothly. See also *Constant relative risk aversion*, *Log-wealth utility function*, *S-shaped utility function*, and *Utility function*.

Kurtosis   A measure of a distribution's peakedness. It is computed by raising the deviations from the mean to the fourth power and taking the average of these values. It is usually represented as the ratio of this value to the standard deviation raised to the fourth power. A normal distribution has a kurtosis value equal to 3. See also *Higher moment, Normal distribution*, and *Skewness*.

Lagrange multiplier   In optimization, a variable introduced to facilitate a solution when there are constraints. It does not always lend itself to economic interpretation.

Law of large numbers   The principle that, as a sample becomes large, measures of its central tendency and dispersion become more accurate. See also *Central limit theorem, Eventual acceptance property,* and *Time diversification*.

Leptokurtic distribution   A distribution with a narrow peak and wide tails. Compared to a normal distribution, a larger proportion of the returns are located near the extremes rather than the mean of the distribution. It is also called a fat-tailed distribution. See also *Higher moment, Kurtosis, Normal distribution,* and *Platykurtic distribution*.

Leverage   In asset allocation, the notion of increasing a portfolio's expected return by borrowing and using the proceeds to increase investment in the tangency portfolio, as opposed to concentrating the portfolio in higher-expected-return asset classes in order to raise its expected return. See also *Asset allocation, Asset class,* and *Concentration*.

Linear hedging strategy   In currency hedging, a strategy that uses currency forward or futures contracts to offset the embedded currency exposure of a portfolio. This hedging strategy is called a linear hedging strategy because the portfolio's return is a linear function of the performance of the currencies to which the portfolio is exposed. See also *Nonlinear hedging strategy*.

Linear regression   A linear approach to modeling the relationship between a dependent variable and one or more explanatory variables or independent variables. See also *Ordinary least squares* and *Regression analysis*.

Logarithm   The power to which a base must be raised to yield a particular number. For example, the logarithm of 100 to the base 10 equals 2, because 10^2 equals 100. Prior to the advent of calculators, logarithms were convenient because, with an implement called a slide rule, one could multiply numbers by adding their logarithms. See also *e* and *Natural logarithm*.

Logarithmic return   See *Continuous return.*

Lognormal distribution   A distribution of returns that is positively skewed as a result of compounding. Compared to a normal distribution, which is symmetric, a lognormal distribution has a longer right tail than left tail and an average value that exceeds the median value. A lognormal distribution of discrete returns corresponds to a normal distribution of their continuous counterparts. See also *Normal distribution* and *Skewness.*

Log-wealth utility function   A concave utility function that assumes utility is equal to the logarithm of wealth. It is one of a family of utility functions that assume investors have constant relative risk aversion. For investors with a log-wealth utility function, as wealth increases, utility also increases but at a diminishing rate. See also *Constant relative risk aversion, Natural logarithm,* and *Utility function.*

Macroefficiency   The notion that aggregations of securities such as asset classes are priced efficiently. Paul A. Samuelson famously argued that investment markets are microefficient and macroinefficient. See also *Microefficiency* and *Samuelson dictum.*

Mahalanobis distance   A multivariate measure of difference. It was originally conceived of by the statistician Prasanta Chandra Mahalanobis to distinguish between the skulls of people belonging to different castes in India. It is applied to asset returns to distinguish turbulent periods from stable periods. See also *Financial turbulence, Informativeness, Multivariate similarity, Relevance,* and *Scenario analysis.*

Mapping error   In factor replication, the out-of-sample differences between the returns, standard deviations, and correlations of factor values and the returns, standard deviations, and correlations of the portfolio of securities designed to mimic their behavior. See also *Estimation error, Factor-mimicking portfolio, Independent-sample error, Interval error,* and *Small-sample error.*

Marginal utility   The change in expected utility given small changes in the weights of asset classes within a portfolio. It is computed as the derivative of expected utility with respect to an asset class weight. See also *Expected utility maximization.*

Market portfolio   In portfolio theory, the portfolio of all tradable securities held according to their relative capitalization. According to the Capital Asset Pricing Model, it is the tangency portfolio that joins the capital market line with the efficient frontier. In practice, it is usually approximated by a broad index of stocks and bonds. See also *Capital Asset Pricing Model, Capital market line, Efficient frontier,* and *Tangency portfolio.*

Markowitz-van Dijk heuristic   In portfolio rebalancing, an approximation of expected future costs resulting from rebalancing trades and suboptimal weights. It equals squared differences between the current portfolio weights and the optimal portfolio weights times a constant that is calibrated through simulation.

Matrix algebra   Algebraic operations performed on matrices to solve systems of linear equations. See also *Identity matrix, Inverse matrix, Invertible matrix, Matrix transpose,* and *Positive-semidefinite.*

Matrix transpose   In matrix algebra, for a given matrix, a new matrix whose rows are the columns of the original matrix. See also *Matrix algebra.*

Maximum Likelihood Estimation (MLE)   In asset allocation, a numerical procedure that gives the statistically most likely covariances of asset classes with short return histories compared to other asset classes under consideration. It is based on the returns that prevailed for the periods that are common to all asset classes, together with the returns of the asset classes with longer histories. See also *Covariance.*

Mean aversion   The tendency of an above-average return to be followed by another above-average return and a below-average return to be followed by another below-average return, resulting in a higher incidence of trends than would be expected from a random process. See also *Mean reversion* and *Random variable.*

Mean return   The arithmetic average return. See also *Arithmetic average return.*

Mean reversion   The tendency of an above-average return to be followed by a below-average return and a below-average return to be followed by an above-average return, resulting in a higher incidence of reversals than would be expected from a random process. See also *Mean aversion* and *Random variable.*

Mean-tracking error efficient frontier   A continuum of portfolios plotted in dimensions of expected return and tracking error that offers the highest expected return for a given level of tracking error or the lowest tracking error for a given expected return. See also *Efficient frontier, Efficient surface, E-V maxim, Expected return, Mean-variance analysis,* and *Standard deviation.*

Mean-variance analysis   An asset allocation process that identifies combinations of asset classes that offer the highest expected return for a given level of risk. See also *Efficient frontier, E-V maxim, Expected return, Standard deviation,* and *Variance.*

Mean-variance efficient frontier   See *Efficient frontier.*

Mean-variance optimization   See *Mean-variance analysis.*

Mean-variance-tracking error optimization   An asset allocation process that identifies portfolios that offer the highest expected return for a given combination of standard deviation and tracking error, or the lowest standard deviation for a given combination of expected return and tracking error, or the lowest tracking error for a given combination of expected return and standard deviation. It is suitable for investors who care about both absolute performance and relative performance. See also *Efficient surface* and *Mean-variance analysis.*

Microefficiency   The notion that individual securities are priced efficiently. Paul A. Samuelson famously argued that investment markets are microefficient and macroinefficient. See also *Macroefficiency* and *Samuelson dictum.*

Minimum-regret hedge ratio   A currency hedge ratio equal to 50% of a portfolio's currency exposure. It is argued that this hedge ratio minimizes regret should a strategy to hedge fully or not to hedge at all deliver the best performance. See also *Minimum-variance hedge ratio* and *Universal hedge ratio*.

Minimum-variance hedge ratio   The currency hedge ratio that is designed to minimize a portfolio's variance by explicitly accounting for the covariances among the currency forward contracts and between the currency forward contracts and the portfolio. See also *Minimum-regret hedge ratio* and *Universal hedge ratio*.

Moment   A measure of the shape of a distribution. It is the average of all observations (in the case of a raw moment) or all deviations from the mean (in the case of a central moment) raised to a specified power. The first raw moment is the mean. The second central moment is variance. The third and fourth central moments, after normalizing, are skewness and kurtosis, respectively. See also *Higher moment, Kurtosis, Normal distribution, Probability distribution, Skewness,* and *Variance.*

Monte Carlo simulation   A process used to simulate the performance of an investment strategy by randomly selecting returns from an underlying theoretical distribution such as a normal or lognormal distribution and subjecting the investment strategy to these randomly selected returns. See also *Bootstrap simulation, Lognormal distribution, Normal distribution,* and *Random variable.*

Multivariate distribution   The joint probability distribution of two or more random variables such as asset class returns. See also *Probability distribution.*

Multivariate similarity   A measure of the statistical similarity between past observations for the independent variables and the current observations for the independent variables. It is used to determine, in part, relevance in partial sample regressions and is calculated as the negative of the Mahalanobis distance between past observations of the independent variables and the current observations for the independent variables. See also *Informativeness, Mahalanobis distance, Partial sample regression,* and *Relevance.*

Natural logarithm   The power to which the value 2.71828 (*e*) must be raised to yield a particular number. Natural logarithms have a special property. The natural logarithm of the quantity 1 plus a discrete return equals the continuous return. For example, the natural logarithm of 1.10 equals 9.53%. If one invests $1.00 at a continuously compounded annual rate of 9.53% for one year, it would grow to $1.10 by the end of the year. See also *Continuous return, Discrete return, e,* and *Natural logarithm.*

Near neighbors   Observations within a sample that are closest or most similar to a given observation. See also *Multivariate similarity* and *Partial sample regression.*

Noise   The random variability around an expected value such as expected return.

Nonlinear hedging strategy   In currency hedging, a strategy that uses put options to protect a portfolio from the devaluation of currencies to which the portfolio is exposed. This hedging strategy is called a nonlinear hedging strategy because the portfolio's return is a nonlinear function of the performance of the currencies to which the portfolio is exposed. See also *Linear hedging strategy.*

Nonparametric procedure A procedure for statistical inference that does not depend on the use of a stylized function with parameters to describe the distribution of observations.

Non-stationarity The notion that the distribution of a variable is not stable across subsamples of a larger sample. If a variable is not stationary, deviations from the variable's average do not occur nonrandomly. This property prevents analysts from drawing reliable inferences about the full sample from subsamples. See also *Stationarity.*

Normal distribution A continuous probability distribution that often arises from the summation of a large number of random variables. It has the convenient property that its mean, median, and mode are all equal. Also, approximately 68% of its area falls within a range of the mean plus and minus one standard deviation, and approximately 95% of its area falls within a range of the mean plus and minus two standard deviations. See also *Central limit theorem* and *Lognormal distribution.*

Normative Within the context of asset allocation, behavior that describes what an investor should do rather than what an investor actually does. See also *Positive.*

Numerical method An iterative search process that is used to solve problems that cannot be solved analytically, which is to say, cannot be solved by using a formula.

Optimal portfolio A portfolio that maximizes an investor's expected utility, or, more prosaically, a portfolio that best balances an investor's desire to grow wealth with the investor's aversion to loss.

Ordinary least squares (OLS) A type of linear regression that estimates the dependent variable by minimizing the sum of the squares of the differences between the observed dependent variable in the given dataset and those predicted by the linear function. See also *Linear regression* and *Regression analysis.*

Overhedging In currency hedging, the practice of selling currency forward contracts in amounts that exceed the portfolio's exposure to the currencies either individually or collectively. See also *Cross-hedging.*

Overlay An investment or activity that does not require capital, such as a forward contract or a shadow allocation. See also *Shadow asset* and *Shadow liability.*

Panel regression A regression that is run simultaneously using cross-sectional data and time series data. See also *Regression analysis.*

Partial illiquidity A measure of illiquidity that applies to asset classes that are tradable without prohibitive delay or expense. See also *Absolute illiquidity.*

Partial sample regression A form of regression analysis in which the data set is filtered to censor observations for the independent variables that are not sufficiently relevant, in which relevance is defined as the sum of multivariate similarity and informativeness. The dependent variable is then predicted by taking a weighted average of the past observations for the dependent variable in which the weights are equal to their relevance. See also *Informativeness, Mahalanobis distance, Multivariate similarity, Regression analysis,* and *Relevance.*

Periodic return   See *Discrete return.*

Platykurtic distribution   A distribution with thin tails and a wider, flatter center. Relative to a normal distribution, more of its returns are clustered near the center of the distribution, and fewer lie in the extremes. See also *Higher moment, Kurtosis, Leptokurtic distribution,* and *Normal distribution.*

Playing defense   In asset allocation, activities that are intended to preserve the expected utility of a portfolio, such as portfolio rebalancing. See also *Playing offense.*

Playing offense   In asset allocation, activities that are intended to increase the expected utility of a portfolio beyond what would be expected by holding the composition of the portfolio constant, such as tactical asset allocation. See also *Playing defense.*

Policy portfolio   In the absence of views about the relative valuation of asset classes, the default portfolio an investor would hold. It is designed to balance an investor's desire to grow wealth with the investor's aversion to loss, and typically serves as the benchmark against which tactical asset allocation decisions are evaluated. See also *Asset allocation, Asset class, Mean-variance analysis, Security selection,* and *Tactical asset allocation.*

Portfolio theory   The science that describes how investors form efficient portfolios and choose the optimal portfolio. Portfolio theory was introduced in 1952 with the publication of *Portfolio Selection* by Harry Markowitz. See also *Efficient frontier, Efficient portfolio, E-V maxim, Expected utility maximization,* and *Mean-variance analysis.*

Positive   In asset allocation, behavior that describes what an investor actually does rather than what an investor should do. See also *Normative.*

Positive-semi-definite   A necessary and sufficient condition to preclude a matrix, A, from generating a negative number from the quadratic form $x'Ax$ for any possible vector x. In mean-variance analysis, it ensures the absence of negative variances. It is a necessary condition because, given the correlation between asset classes A and B, and between A and C, the correlation between B and C is restricted to a particular range of values. See also *Mean-variance analysis.*

Power utility function   A utility function in which utility is equal to wealth raised to a power less than 1. Investors whose preferences are defined by a power utility function have constant relative risk aversion. See also *Constant relative risk aversion, Expected utility, Log-wealth utility function,* and *Utility function.*

Preference free   An approach to valuation in which the value of an asset is invariant to investors' particular preferences with respect to risk. Instead, value is determined by the absence of arbitrage.

Principal component   See *Eigenvector.*

Principal Components Analysis (PCA) A statistical process that transforms a set of correlated variables into a new and comprehensive set of uncorrelated variables called eigenvectors or principal components. This transformation can be performed on a covariance matrix or a correlation matrix.

Private equity leverage puzzle The observation that the standard deviation of private equity, even after adjustment for the effects of performance fees and valuation smoothing, is not equal to the product of the ratio of its leverage to public equity leverage and the standard deviation of public equity.

Probability density function (PDF) A function that defines the probability distribution of a random variable. By integrating this function between two points, we identify the probability that the random variable will take on a value within the specified interval. See also *Probability distribution* and *Random variable*.

Probability distribution A description of the linkage between each potential outcome of a random variable, such as an asset class return, and its probability of occurrence. See also *Normal distribution*.

Probability of loss See *End-of-horizon probability of loss*.

Put option An option that grants its owner the right but not the obligation to sell an underlying asset at a previously agreed-upon price at or up to a specified future date (American) or only at a specified future date (European). See also *Call option*.

Quadratic function See *Quadratic utility function*.

Quadratic heuristic See *Markowitz-van Dijk heuristic*.

Quadratic utility function A function that equates expected utility to a portfolio's expected return minus a risk aversion coefficient times a portfolio's variance. It is an upward sloping concave function across a wide range of returns, but it eventually turns downward, implying perversely that investors prefer less return to more return beyond a certain return level. It is used to generate the efficient frontier in mean-variance analysis. Although investors do not technically have quadratic utility, it has been shown that mean and variance are sufficient for approximating power utility across a wide range of returns. See also *Constant relative risk aversion, Expected utility, Log-wealth utility function, Power utility function,* and *Utility function*.

Random variable A variable that takes on a value influenced by chance, such as the toss of a coin or next year's return on the stock market. See also *Random walk*.

Random walk A stochastic process in which future values of a random variable are unrelated to its current value. Variables that are believed to follow a random walk are said to be independent and identically distributed (IID). See also *Independent and identically distributed* and *Random variable*.

Regression analysis A statistical process for measuring the relationships between a dependent variable and one or more independent variables. See also *Alpha, Beta, Linear regression, Ordinary least squares,* and *Partial sample regression*.

Relevance In partial sample regression, a measure for censoring certain observations of the independent variables. It is equal to the sum of multivariate similarity and informativeness. See also *Informativeness, Mahalanobis distance, Multivariate similarity,* and *Partial sample regression.*

Return distribution A description of the linkage between each potential return and its probability of occurrence. See also *Normal distribution* and *Probability distribution.*

Risk aversion Technically, a preference for a certain prospect over an uncertain prospect of equal value. More generally, risk aversion equals an investor's dislike for uncertainty. See also *Risk aversion coefficient.*

Risk aversion coefficient In mean-variance analysis, a coefficient that multiplies portfolio risk to trade off the utility an investor receives from increases in expected return with the utility an investor loses from increases in portfolio variance. See also *Expected utility, Expected utility maximization, Mean-variance analysis,* and *Risk aversion.*

Risk concentration A market condition in which a large fraction of the variability of returns is driven by one or just a few factors or eigenvectors. It is measured by a statistic called the absorption ratio, which is the fraction of total variability of returns that is explained by the most important eigenvectors from a principal components analysis. See also *Absorption ratio, Eigenvector,* and *Principal components analysis.*

Risk parity An investment strategy in which the major components of a portfolio contribute equally to total portfolio risk, which occurs when the weight of each component is proportional to the inverse of its standard deviation. If all components have equal Sharpe ratios and correlations, a risk parity portfolio will deliver the highest Sharpe ratio. See also *Security market line, Sharpe ratio,* and *Standard deviation.*

Risk regime A period in which the return distribution of a set of asset classes differs significantly from the distribution of the entire sample. For example, it is common to partition return samples into calm risk regimes when returns, standard deviations, and correlations are similar to their historical averages, and turbulent regimes when returns, standard deviations, and correlations depart substantially from their historical averages. The Mahalanobis distance is often used to separate calm risk regimes from turbulent risk regimes. See also *Financial turbulence* and *Mahalanobis distance.*

Risk-free return The return available from an asset class that is assumed to be risk free, such as Treasury bills. Because Treasury bills do have some variability as well as reinvestment risk, they are not entirely risk free. Over longer investment horizons, and taking inflation into account, Treasury Inflation-Protected Securities (TIPS) are thought to be the least risky asset class. See also *Capital Asset Pricing Model.*

Riskless arbitrage The exchange of asset classes that have the same cash flows.

Robust optimization An optimization procedure that considers a wide set of expected returns and risk and selects the portfolio that suffers the least in the most adverse scenario. This approach is sometimes called "minimax" optimization; it aims to minimize the maximum loss.

Root-mean-squared error A summary of the degree of error present in a data sample. Errors are typically defined as differences between predictions and realizations. Squaring the errors ensures that they are all positive, taking their average (or mean) summarizes the extent of the errors, and taking the square root converts the result back to units of the original errors, as opposed to their squared values. If errors are defined relative to the mean of a given data set, the root-mean-squared error equals the standard deviation. We use root-mean-squared errors to quantify estimation error in Chapter 19.

Sample statistic A statistic, such as mean or standard deviation, that is estimated from a finite sample of returns, and therefore is vulnerable to estimation error. See also *Estimation error*.

Samuelson dictum The notion, proposed by Paul A. Samuelson, that investment markets are microefficient and macroinefficient. Samuelson argued that if an individual security is mispriced, a smart investor will notice and trade to exploit the mispricing, and by doing so will correct the mispricing. However, if an aggregation of securities such as an asset class is mispriced and a smart investor trades to exploit the asset class mispricing, the investor will not have the scale to revalue the entire asset class. It is typically revalued when an exogenous shock jolts a large number of investors to act in concert. Hence, microinefficiencies are fleeting and thus difficult to exploit, whereas macroinefficiencies tend to persist, thus allowing investors time to exploit them. See also *Macroefficiency* and *Microefficiency*.

Scenario analysis A portfolio selection process in which an investor defines prospective economic scenarios, assigns probabilities to them, translates the scenarios into expected asset class returns, and selects the portfolio with the highest expected return or expected utility, given all these inputs. Some sophisticated investors use the Mahalanobis distance to determine the relative likelihood of prospective scenarios. See also *Mahalanobis distance*.

Security attribute A feature such as capitalization or price/earnings multiple that distinguishes securities from one another. Securities with particular attributes are believed to carry risk premiums.

Security market line A line on a graph that depicts the relationship between beta on the horizontal axis and expected return on the vertical axis. If the Capital Asset Pricing Model holds, the security market line should have an intercept equal to the risk-free return and a slope of 1. Proponents of risk parity argue that the slope of the security market line is less than 1, thereby justifying overweighting low beta assets. See also *Beta, Capital Asset Pricing Model,* and *Risk parity*.

Security selection The activity of choosing individual securities within an asset class based on views about their relative valuation or other attributes that are believed to affect their performance, for the purpose of improving a portfolio's performance. See also *Tactical asset allocation.*

Semi-standard deviation The standard deviation calculated using only the subsample of returns that fall below the full-sample mean. See also *Standard deviation.*

Separation theorem The principle, put forth by James Tobin, that the investment process can be separated into two distinct steps: (1) the choice of a unique optimal portfolio along the efficient frontier and (2) the decision to combine this portfolio with a risk-free investment. See also *Capital Asset Pricing Model, Capital market line,* and *Efficient frontier.*

Shadow allocation See *Shadow asset* and *Shadow liability.*

Shadow asset An implicit allocation to an activity, defined in units of expected return and risk, that does not require capital and is expected to raise the expected utility of a portfolio, such as internally implemented tactical asset allocation. It is attached to the liquid asset classes within a portfolio that enable the activity. See also *Shadow liability.*

Shadow liability A penalty, defined in units of expected return and risk, that is attached to illiquid asset classes within a portfolio that prevent an investor from fully preserving the expected utility of a portfolio. For example, a shadow liability would be attached to illiquid asset classes that prevent an investor from rebalancing a portfolio to its optimal weights after price changes force the portfolio away from its optimal weights. See also *Shadow asset.*

Sharpe ratio An asset, asset class, or portfolio's expected return in excess of the risk-free return, all divided by its standard deviation. It is used to compare mutually independent investment alternatives. See also *Beta, Capital Asset Pricing Model,* and *Standard deviation.*

Similarity See *Multivariate similarity.*

Single-period correlation A measure of co-movement that captures the extent to which variables move synchronously or drift apart over a specified interval. It is intended to account for nonzero autocorrelation and cross-correlation of higher-frequency movement of the variables within the specified longer interval. It is also intended to address the time variation of correlations estimated from large samples of longer-interval observations. See also *Autocorrelation, Correlation, Cross-correlation, Divergence, Non-stationarity, Stationarity,* and *Z-score.*

Skewness The third central moment of a distribution. It measures the asymmetry of a distribution. A positively skewed distribution has a long right tail, and its mean exceeds its median, which in turn exceeds its mode. Both the mean and the median are located to the right of the peak, which represents the mode. Although there are more returns below the mean, they are of smaller magnitude than the fewer returns above the mean. The exact opposite properties hold for a negatively skewed distribution. Skewness is measured as the average of the cubed deviations from the mean. However, it is usually represented as the ratio of this value to the standard deviation cubed. A normal distribution has skewness equal to 0. See also *Higher moment, Kurtosis, Lognormal distribution,* and *Normal distribution.*

Small-sample error   The differences between the average returns, standard deviations, and correlations of a small subsample selected from within a large sample and the average returns, standard deviations, and correlations of the large sample. See also *Estimation error, Independent-sample error, Interval error, Mapping error,* and *Stability-adjusted optimization.*

Sortino ratio   An asset or portfolio's expected return in excess of the risk-free return, all divided by its semi-standard deviation. See also *Semi-standard deviation* and *sharpe ratio.*

S-shaped utility function   A utility function that assumes investors are risk seeking when they face losses and risk averse when they face gains. See also *Kinked utility function, Log-wealth utility function,* and *Power utility function.*

Stability-adjusted optimization   An asset allocation process that relies on a sample of returns that has been adjusted to account for the effect of estimation error on the shape of the return distribution. It treats the relative stability of covariances as a distinct component of risk. See also *Estimation error, Independent-sample error, Interval error,* and *Small-sample error.*

Stability-adjusted return distribution   See *Stability-adjusted optimization.*

Standard deviation   A measure of dispersion that is commonly used to measure an asset's riskiness. It is equal to the square root of the average of the squared deviations from the mean, and it is the square root of variance. Approximately 68% of the observations under a normal distribution fall within the mean plus and minus one standard deviation. See also *Normal distribution* and *Variance.*

Standard normal variable   The number of standard deviation units a particular value is away from the mean under a normal distribution. It is equal to the difference between the value of interest and the mean, divided by the standard deviation. A normal distribution converts a standardized variable into the corresponding area under a normal distribution by rescaling the distribution to have a mean of 0 and a standard deviation of 1. Also called normal deviate. See also *Normal distribution* and *Z-score.*

Stationarity   The notion that the distribution of a variable is stable across subsamples of a larger sample. It allows for individual observations to differ from the average value of the full sample but only randomly. This property allows analysts to draw stronger inferences about the full sample from subsamples than they would be able to if the variable was not stationary. See also *Nonstationarity.*

Statistical factor   See *Eigenvector.*

Symmetric distribution   A probability distribution that has no skewness. Unlike a normal distribution, it may have non-normal kurtosis. And, unlike an elliptical distribution, it allows for return pairs in a two-dimensional scatter plot to be unevenly distributed along the boundaries of ellipses that are centered on the mean observation of the scatter plot as long as they are distributed symmetrically. A symmetric distribution that is nonelliptical would apply to a return sample that comprises subsamples with substantially different correlations. See also *Elliptical distribution, Kurtosis, Normal distribution,* and *Skewness.*

Tactical asset allocation　　The activity of shifting a portfolio's asset class weights away from the policy portfolio based on views about the relative valuation of asset classes or changes in their risk, for the purpose of improving a portfolio's performance. See also *Asset allocation, Asset class,* and *Security selection.*

Tangency portfolio　　The portfolio located at the point of tangency of the capital market line with the efficient frontier. See also *Capital market line, Efficient frontier,* and *Separation theorem.*

Taylor series　　A polynomial function in which successive terms of x raised to a larger power are added to continually refine the approximation of any chosen function at a particular input value, based on the derivatives of that function at that value. This method was used by Levy and Markowitz to approximate power utility functions with mean and variance. See also *Power utility function.*

Time diversification　　The notion that above-average returns tend to offset below-average returns over long time horizons. It does not follow, however, that time reduces risk. Although the likelihood of a loss decreases with time for investments with positive expected returns, the potential magnitude of a loss increases with time. See also *Law of large numbers.*

Timing　　See *Tactical asset allocation.*

Tracking error　　A measure of dispersion that is commonly used to measure an asset class's relative risk. It is equal to the square root of the average of an asset class or portfolio's squared deviations from a benchmark's returns. See also *standard deviation.*

Tracking error aversion　　An investor's dislike for the uncertainty of a portfolio's returns relative to a benchmark's returns. See also *Risk aversion.*

Universal hedge ratio　　A single hedge ratio for all investors, proposed by Fischer Black, that applies to a portfolio's exposure to all currencies and is optimal if all investors have the same aversion to risk, the same portfolio composition, and the same wealth. See also *Minimum-regret hedge ratio* and *Minimum-variance hedge ratio.*

Utility function　　The relationship between varying levels of wealth and the happiness or satisfaction imparted by the different wealth levels. A commonly invoked utility function for financial analysis is the log-wealth utility function, which implies that utility increases at a decreasing rate as wealth increases. See also *Constant relative risk aversion, Kinked utility function, Log-wealth utility function, Power utility function, Quadratic utility function,* and *S-shaped utility function.*

Utility theory The axioms and principles that describe how investors relate wealth and changes in wealth to their perception of well-being. See also *Expected utility, Expected utility maximization*, and *Utility function*.

Value at risk See *End-of-horizon value at risk*.

Variance A measure of dispersion used to characterize an asset's riskiness. It is equal to the average of the squared deviations from the mean, and its square root is the standard deviation. See also *Standard deviation*.

Variance ratio A measure of serial dependence computed by dividing the variance of returns estimated from longer-interval returns by the variance of returns estimated from shorter-interval returns and then normalizing this value by dividing it by the ratio of the longer interval to the shorter interval. See also *Autocorrelation*.

Vector An array of variables such as returns.

Within-horizon probability of loss A measure of the likelihood that a portfolio will incur a particular percentage loss within a specified investment horizon, assuming the portfolio is monitored continuously throughout the horizon. It is estimated as a first passage time probability. See also *End-of-horizon probability of loss, End-of-horizon value at risk, First passage time probability*, and *Within-horizon value at risk*.

Within-horizon value at risk At a given probability, the maximum loss or minimum gain a portfolio could experience at any time throughout a specified investment horizon, assuming the portfolio is monitored continuously throughout the horizon. It is estimated numerically using a first passage time probability. See also *End-of-horizon probability of loss, End-of-horizon value at risk, First passage time probability*, and *Within-horizon probability of loss*.

Wrong and alone A situation in which an investor produces poor absolute performance and underperforms the benchmark at the same time. We argue that aversion to this dual failure compels investors to constrain their portfolios from deviating too far from the perceived norm.

Z-score A standardized measure of the difference of an observation from its mean, computed as the observation less the mean, divided by the standard deviation of the observations. See also *Single-period correlation* and *Standard normal variable*.

Index

Page numbers followed by *f* and *t* refer to figures and tables, respectively.